The Urban Villagers

The Urban Villagers

Group and Class in the Life of Italian - Americans

by Herbert J. Gans

FOREWORD BY Erich Lindemann, M.D.

Professor of Psychiatry, Harvard Medical School
Psychiatrist-in-Chief, Massachusetts General Hospital

The Free Press of Glencoe

To My Parents

FOREWORD

It may be surprising to the reader that this foreword is written by a psychiatrist. Let it be said right away that I believe the information contained in this volume to be a significant contribution to the problems of medicine and public health. The observations here recorded were made as part of a program of studies concerned with the hazards to health and emotional well-being involved in the forced relocation of families with different types of ethnic and cultural origin.

The problems of medical care—especially psychiatric care—and preventive services have been vastly complicated by our ignorance concerning basic attitudes and motivations of various types of people whom we are serving. The studies of Hollingshead and Redlich dealing with the different kinds of psychiatric treatment and with the different patterns of distribution of mental disease at different class levels have made it abundantly clear that the social structure including the habitat, aspirations, and adaptive resources of the people comprising an administrative district do make a great deal of difference for the discovery and care of mental disease.

Beyond this, many of the workers who are concerned with the positive aspects of mental health in terms of emotional well-being, satisfaction, achievement, and a productive life are hampered in social planning by ignorance and superstition concerning the most basic aspects of community life. Not only is information required about the family and kinship system and neighborhood organization, but also about basic value orientations as they affect men and women in their attitudes and aspirations for the development of the young, especially with respect to social controls and to the measure of permissible deviance. All these are much needed elements in a solid scientific foundation for health and social planning. The vivid image that this book creates concerning life in the West End of Boston and the hazards to health and emotional well-being at the time of the relocation experience presents a unique body of information. This then can be translated into the particular types of insight that are necessary for the different caretaking professions in church and school, in the hospital and public health services, in social agencies, and in the field of law enforcement.

The book has great significance for the medical profession—particularly for a large, teaching general hospital whose patients are generally comprised of members of low-income segments of the population. Its insights concerning their attitudes toward health and illness, perception of the doctor and medical care, and their inclination to seek help at times of crises from professional as well as family and neighborhood resources—all will be quite valuable for the future conduct of programs of medical services, and particularly for the plans of aftercare. In the field of mental disease, new drugs and more efficient treatment procedures in mental hospitals have already made it possible to reduce the "segregation" of the mentally ill into special facilities and to return them to family and community. Intelligent aftercare, however, would be impossible without the sort of intimate knowledge of family and community life and challenges that this book provides.

The material presented has been collected by a special technique, that of participant-observation. Thus, while many of the inferences, interpretations, and formulations are appealing and plausible, they lack the kind of solid quantitative demonstration that the human ecologist would like to see. In the case of the present volume, however, we are in the fortunate position of being able to look forward to more rigorous testing of many propositions gained from this study. This is so because it is part of a larger program which includes interview and focused observation studies to determine more precise patterns, on a statistical basis, of the over-all picture that the present book makes available. In the meantime, I am convinced that the sense of intimate acquaintance with working-class life that this book engenders in the reader will do much to help the city planner, the person engaged in social action, and particularly members of the health professions in coming to grips with the planning and implementation of community services.

ERICH LINDEMANN, M.D.
Professor of Psychiatry,
Harvard Medical School
Psychiatrist-in-Chief,
Massachusetts General Hospital

PREFACE

This book is a report of a participant-observation study of an inner city Boston neighborhood called the West End, and, in particular, of the native-born Americans of Italian parentage who lived there amidst other ethnic groups. The area I studied no longer exists. Declared a slum in 1953, it was torn down under the federal renewal program between 1958 and 1960, and its residents dispersed all over the metropolitan area. At this writing (January, 1962), the first residents of the new West End—a luxury apartment house complex—are just beginning to move in.

I lived in the West End from October, 1957, to May, 1958, just before the onset of redevelopment. My main research interests were two: to study a slum and to study the way of life of a low-income population. Contemporary city planning and professions such as education, social work, public recreation, public health, medicine, and psychiatry, which Erich Lindemann has aptly described as caretakers, use middle-class values to help low-income populations solve their problems and improve their living conditions. As a sociologist and city planner, I wanted to test the validity of this approach. I wanted to know what a slum was like, and how it felt to live in one, because many planners and caretakers believe that it is the source of much of the low-income population's problem. I wanted to study the way of life of a low-income population because planners and caretakers act on the assumption that this way of life is simply a deviant form of the dominant American middle-class one, that it is born partly of deprivation and lack of access to the improved living conditions and other services provided by these professions.

Since I was also interested in other aspects of class and ethnic group behavior, my study developed into an extensive analysis of the Italian-American society and culture. At the end, I concluded that by and large, the planners and caretakers were wrong. The West End was not really a slum, and although many of its inhabitants did have problems, these did not stem from the neighborhood. More important, the West Enders were not frustrated seekers of middle-class values. Their way of life constituted a distinct and independent working-class subculture that bore little resemblance to the middle-class. Consequently, I concluded that the behavior patterns and values of working-class subculture ought to be understood and taken into account by planners and caretakers.

In some ways my book is an instance of what David Riesman and Nathan Glazer have called the continuing conversation between the upper and lower levels of our culture. Actually, most of the talking has usually been done by the upper level; the people of the lower one sit by quietly, and even sullenly, often without listening. Thus, although I came to the West End from the upper level, I have tried to describe the way of life of lower level people as they might describe it themselves if they were sociologists. In a sense, then, I am reporting to the upper level for them and urging that they be given more consideration when policy decisions are made.

Partly for this reason, I have tried to write this book as much for the planners, caretakers, other policy makers, and the general public who influence them, as for my colleagues and for students of sociology. And in doing so, I have violated several canons of sociological research reporting: I have described as findings what are properly speaking only hypotheses; I have occasionally generalized beyond the evidence; I have not qualified these generalizations as being based on a single population, or noted other limitations to their applicability elsewhere; and I have not fully related my conclusions to the work of other sociologists. Conversely, I have suppressed—somewhat—the desire to contribute to the theoretical discussions and arguments that go on inside sociology but that are of little interest to the nonsociological reader.

The book begins with two introductory chapters: one to describe the West End; another to introduce the Italian West Enders. Chapters 3 to 9 then go on to describe their way of life in detail, using chapter headings that follow the sociological and anthropological traditions of the community study and also reflect what I take to be the West Enders' social structure. Incidentally, I should note that since I describe people rather than the neighborhood, and since their way of life goes on even though their old neighborhood is no more, I have written these chapters largely in the present tense.

Chapter 10 looks at the West Enders from a more dynamic perspective, going back to their ancestors in Southern Italy and forward to the next generation. One of the purposes of this analysis is to determine whether ethnicity or class is a more relevant concept for understanding their way of life. This issue is resolved in Chapter 11, where I relate my findings to previous sociological studies to show that the West Enders' way of life resembles that of other working-class populations. This conclusion in turn leads to some observations about the nature of class as subculture; the differences between working-class, lower-class, and middle-class subcultures and finally, in Chapter 12, to some proposals as to how these subcultures ought to be treated by planners and caretakers.

A two-chapter Epilogue deals with the redevelopment of the West End. Chapter 13 describes the redevelopment process and its impact on the West Enders. Chapter 14 is a critique of this process, of the conventional definition of slum, and of the planning that was done—and not done—for the relocation of the West Enders. An Appendix describes the methods of the study, and some of the limitations of its findings.

My study was one component of a larger research project, entitled "Relocation and Mental Health: Adaptation under Stress," which is investigating the nature and dynamics of working- and lower-class society and culture, and the impact of redevelopment and relocation on the West Enders. This study, based primarily on intensive interviews with a sample of West Enders before and after relocation, is still in process, and will provide more systematically collected data on many of the subjects I have discussed. It is being conducted at the Center for Community Studies, affiliated with Harvard Medical School and Massachusetts General Hospital, by a staff headed by Dr. Marc Fried. The study was initiated by Dr. Erich Lindemann.

Acknowledgments

My research was supported—as part of the larger study just described—by PHS Grant 3M-9137 from the National Institute of Mental Health, United States Public Health Service. This book, based on an earlier report I made to the Center for Community Studies, was written in my present position as a staff member of the Institute for Urban Studies, University of Pennsylvania.

Many people helped to bring the study to fruition. Dr. Leonard J. Duhl, of the Professional Services Branch, National Institute of Mental Health, initiated the process that led me to do the study and encouraged me in many ways. Dr. Erich Lindemann and Dr. Marc Fried made it possible for me to conduct the actual research and gave me the freedom to do it in my own way.

Many colleagues and friends also provided helpful advice during the field work: in addition to Drs. Duhl, Fried, and Lindemann, there were Laura Morris, Lois Paul, and Edward Ryan of the Center for Community Studies; and Martin Meyerson, Walter B. Miller, David Riesman, John Seeley, Ezra Vogel, and William F. Whyte, Jr. Iris Lezak, to whom I was then married, helped in the field work, and a number of the observations in the book are hers. Joseph Caruso, Nathan Glazer, Ira Glick, Victor Goscia, Helen Icken, Barbara Schwartzman, Denise Scott-Brown, and Anselm Strauss commented on earlier versions of this manuscript. I am especially indebted to Martin Meyerson, who reviewed the final version and offered much helpful criticism. The optimum working conditions that I have enjoyed at the Institute for Urban Studies also aided me in writing the book. For these I must thank Dr. William L. C. Wheaton, the Institute's Director. Mrs. Mary Ellison typed most of the manuscript; Mrs. Marjorie Roberts and Mrs. Amy Morris, the rest.

The major contributors to the book, however, were the people of the West End—those who staffed its various institutions, and most important, those who lived there. They provided the data, many of the ideas, the cooperation and the companionship which enabled me to do the research and made me want to write this book.

H. J. G.

CONTENTS

PART ONE Introduction

CHAPTER 1 The West End: An Urban Village

An Historical and Ecological Overview

To the average Bostonian, the West End was one of the three slum areas that surrounded the city's central business district, little different in appearance and name from the North or the South End. He rarely entered the West End and usually glimpsed it only from the highways or elevated train lines that enveloped it. From there he saw a series of narrow winding streets flanked on both sides by columns of three- and five-story apartment buildings, constructed in an era when such buildings were still called tenements. Furthermore, he saw many poorly maintained structures, some of them unoccupied or partially vacant, some facing on alleys covered with more than an average amount of garbage; many vacant stores; and enough of the kinds of people who are thought to inhabit a slum area. If he ventured inside the area, he saw some old people who looked like European immigrants, some very poor people, some who were probably suffering from mental illness, a few sullen looking adolescents and young adults who congregated on street corners, and many middle-aged people who were probably mainly Italian, Russian Jewish, Polish, and Irish in parentage.

To the superficial observer, armed with conventional images and a little imagination about the mysteries thought to lie behind the tenement entrances, the West End certainly had all the earmarks

3

of a slum. Whether or not it actually was a slum is a question that involves a number of technical housing and planning considerations and some value judgments. I felt that it was not, but I will postpone the discussion of this question until Chapter 14. For the moment, the West End can be described simply as an old, somewhat deteriorated, low-rent neighborhood that housed a variety of people, most of them poor.

In most American cities there are two major types of low-rent neighborhoods: the areas of first or second settlement for urban migrants; and the areas that attract the criminal, the mentally ill, the socially rejected, and those who for one reason or another have given up the attempt to cope with life.

The former kind of area, typically, is one in which European immigrants—and more recently Negro and Puerto Rican ones—try to adapt their nonurban institutions and cultures to the urban milieu. Thus it may be called an *urban village*. Often it is described in ethnic terms: Little Italy, The Ghetto, or Black Belt. The second kind of area is populated largely by single men, pathological families, people in hiding from themselves or society, and individuals who provide the more disreputable of illegal-but-demanded services to the rest of the community. In such an area, life is comparatively more transient, depressed if not brutal, and it might be called an *urban jungle*.[1] It is usually described as Skid Row, Tenderloin, the red-light district, or even the Jungle.

In sociological terminology, these are ideal types, and no existing neighborhood is a pure example of either. Moreover, since the people who occupy both types are poor and at the mercy of the housing market, they often may live in the same neighborhood, erecting physical or symbolic boundary lines to separate themselves. In some areas, especially those occupied by the most deprived people, the village and the jungle are intertwined.

The West End was an urban village, located next to Boston's

1. These are purely descriptive terms, and should not be taken too literally. They are not ecological concepts, for neither in economic, demographic, or physical terms do such areas resemble villages or jungles. They are terms that describe the quality of social life, but do not definitively identify social structure or culture.

original and once largest skid row area, Scollay Square. During the early nineteenth century, the West End had been an isolated farm area, almost inaccessible from the North End and the central business district area that then constituted Boston. Later, some streets were cut through and developed with three-story single family homes of various price levels. Following the arrival of Nova Scotian and Irish immigrants, other streets were built up with three- and five-story tenements, until, by the turn of the century, the five-story tenement became the main building type. The structures built in the latter half of the nineteenth century were intended, like those in the North End, for the poorest tenants. Apartments were small and several units had to share bathroom and toilet facilities. The buildings constructed around the turn of the century, however, were intended for a somewhat higher income group. Instead of three- and four-room apartments, there were five- and six-room ones, each with private bath and toilet, and kitchens equipped with a large combination heating and cooking stove. The new and the old apartments were built at high densities—more than 150 dwelling units per net residential acre—as compared today with the 5 to 8 units in the average middle-income suburb. Land coverage was high, 72 per cent of the land being covered with buildings, and, in a quarter of the blocks, buildings comprised over 90 per cent of the land.[2] Some of the streets were shopping blocks with small stores on the ground floor of the tenements. A few industrial lofts that attracted small manufacturing and wholesale establishments were scattered through the shopping streets.

Physically, as well as socially, the development of the West End followed a typical ecological process. The West End is located at the bottom of one slope of Beacon Hill. At the top of this hill are the apartments and townhouses inhabited by upper- and upper-middle-class people. As one descends the slope, the status of buildings and people decreases. The "Back of the Hill" area, once occupied by servants to the Hill aristocracy, now is inhabited by families who moved up from the bottom of the slope, and, increasingly, by young middle-class couples in modernized tenements

2. Boston Housing Authority, "West End Project Report," Boston: The Authority, 1953, p. 5.

or converted townhouses who are gradually erasing the social differences between the Back of the Hill, and the Hill itself.[3]

The West End is at the bottom of the slope. At one time, when the Back of the Hill was a low-income settlement, both it and the area below were called the West End. Then, with the widening of Cambridge Street in the 1920's, a physical boundary was created between the two areas that eventually led to the symbolic separation as well. Within the West End, the area nearest to Cambridge Street and the Back of Beacon Hill contained the better apartment buildings, and the two major institutions in the area—Massachusetts General Hospital and St. Joseph's Roman Catholic Church. The hospital, traditionally an extremely high status institution, is one of the teaching hospitals for the Harvard Medical School. The church, originally Congregationalist, later became one of the higher status Irish churches, which served Beacon Hill as well.[4] The area closest to Cambridge Street and that fronting on the Charles River was known as the "upper end." Then, as one descended to what was called the "lower end," dwelling units became older and the people, poorer. At one corner of the lower end, the West End fronted on the Scollay Square skid row, and provided rooming houses for the people who frequented its bars and eating places. At another corner, there were small commercial buildings which were part of the industrial and wholesaling area that separated the residential portions of the West End from the North End.

Several times during its existence, the population of the West End has changed in a pattern typical of other urban villages. The North and the South End were the primary areas of first settlement for Irish, Jewish, and Italian peoples, in that order. The South End also served the other ethnic groups that settled in Boston, especially Chinese, Greek, and Syrian. The West End had somewhat more distinctive functions. First, it was an overspill area for those who could not find room in the North End; later, it became

3. For descriptions of this area, see Walter Firey, *Land Use in Central Boston,* Cambridge: Harvard University Press, 1947; and H. Laurence Ross, "The Local Community and the Metropolis," Unpublished Ph.D. Dissertation, Harvard University, 1959.

4. At one time, it was the church of the Kennedy family, and President Kennedy attended it as a boy.

an area of second settlement for some of the groups who began their American life in the North End. Thus, the West End underwent approximately the same ethnic succession pattern as the North End. In the late nineteenth century, it was primarily an Irish area, with Yankees scattered through the upper end.[5] Then, around the turn of the century, the Irish were replaced by the Jews, who dominated the West End until about 1930. During this era, the West End sometimes was called the Lower East Side of Boston. In the late twenties, Italians and Poles began to arrive, the former from the North End, and they joined a small Italian settlement that had existed in the lower end of the area since the beginning of the century. Throughout the 1930's and early 1940's, the Italian influx continued until eventually they became the largest ethnic group in both the upper and lower portions of the West End. The changes in population are reflected in data taken from library registration cards.[6] In 1926, the area was estimated to be 75 per cent Jewish. In 1936, however, the library users were 35 per cent Italian, 25 per cent Polish, 20 per cent Jewish, and 20 per cent "miscellaneous." [7] By 1942, the Italians were in the majority.

A Polish church that had been established in 1930 quickly enrolled 250 families. Although it later lost some of these, the congregation was replenished by displaced persons who came into the West End after World War II. Also there were small Greek, Albanian, and Ukrainian settlements, the latter served by a Ukrainian church located in a tenement. Consequently, proud West Enders were able to claim that twenty-three nationalities could be found in the area. In recent years, small groups of students, artists, and Negroes had come into the West End, some from the Back of the Hill as rents there had begun to rise.

5. For a detailed description of the West End around the turn of the century as it appeared to Yankee settlement house workers, see Robert A. Woods, ed., *Americans in Process,* Boston: Houghton Mifflin, 1902. For a fictional description of Jewish life in the area in the second decade of the twentieth century, see Charles Angoff, *In the Morning Light,* New York: Beechhurst Press, 1952.

6. From unpublished reports in the files of the West End Library.

7. *Ibid.* Registration figures do not reflect the population distribution with complete accuracy. In all likelihood, Jews are overrepresented among library users; and all other ethnic groups, underrepresented.

Numerically, the West End was at its height around 1910, when it had 23,000 inhabitants. In 1920, it had 18,500 residents; in 1930 and 1940, 13,000; and, in 1950, 12,000.[8] In 1957, the population was estimated to be about 7000 individuals in about 2800 households. The long-range population decline could be attributed to decreasing family size among the descendants of immigrant groups, and to the gradual reduction in dwelling units as the hospital expanded its facilities, and as deteriorated buildings became vacant. Between 1930 and 1950, the population remained constant, at least in total number. After that time, it decreased, partially because young families moved out to raise their children in lower density urban and suburban areas, and because of the announcement in 1951 that the area would be redeveloped.

At the time of the study, then, the population of the West End consisted of the following major groups:

1. *Second- and First-Generation Italian Households*. They included the surviving immigrants—most of them elderly—and the much larger group of second-generation people who were their children, or who had come into the area from the North End. The Center for Community Studies survey indicated that the Italians constituted 42 per cent of the West End's population.[9]

2. *First-Generation Jewish Households*. By 1930, the main Jewish population contingent had moved on to Roxbury and Dorchester. But some of the Jews who had come to America in the final wave of European immigration, 1918–1925, did remain in the West End, maintaining two synagogues, a Hebrew school, and a number of stores.[10] Most of them, however, lived in retirement—some in poverty—and spent their time in visiting, in synagogue social activities, and with their children. The Jews accounted for 10 per cent of the West End population.[11]

8. Boston Housing Authority, West End Project Report, *op. cit.*, p. 18.

9. Marc Fried, "Developments in the West End Research," Center for Community Studies, Research Memorandum A 3, October 1960, mimeographed, p. 5. This, and other estimates from the Center's survey reported in this chapter and the next are based on interviews with a 473-person random sample of the West End female population aged twenty to sixty-five.

10. Most of the West End stores were owned by Jews, as were the medical, dental, and legal offices. These were largely run by second-generation Jews who no longer lived in the West End.

11. Fried, *op. cit.*, p. 5.

3. *First- and Second-Generation Polish Households.* This group consisted of immigrants who came before and during the depression, of second-generation families, and of displaced persons. They comprised 9 per cent of the population.[12]

4. *An Irish Residue.* A small number of Irish families, most of them old people, stayed either because they owned buildings in the area, or because they were active in the Catholic church and parish. They constituted 5 per cent of the population.[13]

5. *Other Ethnic Groups*—Albanians, Ukrainians, Greeks.[14]

6. *Pathological Households.* Each major ethnic group left behind a residue of families or individuals whose social and residential mobility had been aborted either by extreme poverty, or by physical or psychological disability. In addition, a part of the area served to house some of the Scollay Square transients.

7. *Postwar Newcomers.* When young residents left after 1950, landlords no longer could replace the vacancies left by them with tenants from their own ethnic group. In order to fill the buildings, they rented them to anyone who came along. Thus the West End attracted people who came because of its low rents—Gypsies, groups of single men, broken families subsisting on Aid to Dependent Children, and people who fled from the New York Streets Redevelopment project in the South End. Some were squatters who tried to live rent-free in vacant buildings.

8. *Middle-Class Professionals and Students.* The presence of the hospital and the availability of clean, low-rent, and conveniently located apartments attracted a number of nurses, interns, and doctors as well as students from various colleges in the city. They provided a smattering of professional middle-class culture to the area.

9. *Other Hospital Staff.* A number of hospital service workers also lived in the area because of the low rentals and the convenience. Some of these were women, wives of Italian or Polish

12. *Ibid.*

13. *Ibid.* The rest of the population was almost equally distributed among "Other Latin," "Other Slavic," English, American, and "Other" ethnic groups. Only 7 per cent of the West End sample was of American background.

14. The Center for Community Studies survey shows 8 per cent of the sample to be "Other Slavic," a category which includes some of the above. Fried, *ibid.*

residents, who worked in the cafeterias, kitchens, and laundries. Some were homosexuals who worked as male nurses in the hospital, and were able to practice their deviant ways in an area which disapproved of them, but which tolerated them grudgingly.

10. *The Artists and Bohemians.* A small but highly visible group of artists, would-be artists, and bohemians was scattered throughout the parts of the West End closest to Cambridge Street. While some of these were students, others worked in low-status jobs and took advantage of the low cost of living in the area.

Some other characteristics of the West End population in 1958 are available from data gathered by the Center for Community Studies survey.[15] Like the Italians to be discussed in later chapters, the largest single group of West Enders—50 per cent—was native born of foreign parentage. A third were European immigrants, and the rest were children of native-born parents. Seventy per cent of the women were married and living with their spouses, and 10 per cent had never married. About a fifth of the sample was twenty to twenty-nine years old, half was between thirty and forty-nine, and the remainder between fifty and sixty-five.

The population's socio-economic level was low. Indeed, the sample's median income was just under $70 a week. About a quarter earned less than $50 per week; a half between $50 and $99; and the top category, slightly less than a fifth, between $100 and $175. Most of the household heads were unskilled or semiskilled manual workers (24 and 37 per cent, respectively).[16] Skilled manual workers, semiskilled white-collar workers, and skilled white-collar workers (including small businessmen) each accounted for about 10 per cent of the sample.

15. These data, and additional figures on the second-generation Italians reported in Chapter 2, are from preliminary tabulations by the Center for Community Studies. I am grateful to the Center, and to Chester Hartman of its staff, for making them available to me. Since the Center's survey is based on a sample of women respondents age twenty to sixty-five, these distributions do not report on single men of all ages, and on households of people over sixty-five. They are, however, a negligible proportion of the West End population.

16. These figures report the occupation of the past or present household head. In 18 per cent of the cases, the woman's occupation is reported, either because there was never a male household head, the husband was not in the labor force because of illness, or because his occupation was unavailable.

Data on years of schooling are available only for women respondents. The median educational level was about 10.5 years: 40 per cent had had eight years of school or less, 30 per cent had nine to eleven years, 19 per cent had graduated from high school, and 10 per cent had attended college for a year or more.

Life in the West End

As a neighborhood is more than an ecological or statistical construct, some of its qualities can perhaps be captured only on paper by the sociologically inclined poet or artist. Typical aspects of West End life and the "feel" of the area can best be described by an informal sketch of what so often struck me as an urban village.

To begin with, the concept of the West End as a single neighborhood was foreign to the West Enders themselves. Although the area had long been known as the West End, the residents themselves divided it up into many subareas, depending in part on the ethnic group which predominated, and in part on the extent to which the tenants in one set of streets had reason or opportunity to use another. For example, the social distance between the upper and the lower end was many times its geographical distance.[17]

Until the coming of redevelopment, only outsiders were likely to think of the West End as a single neighborhood. After the redevelopment was announced, the residents were drawn together by the common danger, but, even so, the West End never became a cohesive neighborhood.

My first visit to the West End left me with the impression that I was in Europe. Its high buildings set on narrow, irregularly curving streets, its Italian and Jewish restaurants and food stores, and the variety of people who crowded the streets when the weather was good—all gave the area a foreign and exotic flavor. At the same time, I also noticed the many vacant shops, the vacant and there-

17. One resident who had lived for thirty-five years about two blocks away from the upper end, and who had supper with relatives there at least twice a week for more than a decade, said that he knew very few people in the upper end.

fore dilapidated tenements, the cellars and alleys strewn with garbage, and the desolation on a few streets that were all but deserted. Looking at the area as a tourist, I noted the highly visible and divergent characteristics that set it off from others with which I was familiar.[18] And, while the exotic quality of the West End did excite me, the dilapidation and garbage were depressing, and made me a little fearful of doing a participant-observation study.

After a few weeks of living in the West End, my observations—and my perception of the area—changed drastically. The search for an apartment quickly indicated that the individual units were usually in much better condition than the outside or the hallways of the buildings. Subsequently, in wandering through the West End, and in using it as a resident, I developed a kind of selective perception, in which my eye focused only on those parts of the area that were actually being used by people. Vacant buildings and boarded-up stores were no longer so visible, and the totally deserted alleys or streets were outside the set of paths normally traversed, either by myself or by the West Enders. The dirt and spilled-over garbage remained, but, since they were concentrated in street gutters and empty lots, they were not really harmful to anyone and thus were not as noticeable as during my initial observations.

Since much of the area's life took place on the street, faces became familiar very quickly. I met my neighbors on the stairs and in front of my building. And, once a shopping pattern had developed, I saw the same storekeepers frequently, as well as the area's "characters" who wandered through the streets everyday on a fairly regular route and schedule. In short, the exotic quality of the stores and the residents also wore off as I became used to seeing them.[19]

The attractions that the West End had for the people who had

18. For some of the characteristics of the tourist view of the social and physical landscape, see Kevin Lynch, *The Image of the City*, Cambridge: Technology Press and Harvard University Press, 1960; and Herbert J. Gans, "Diversity Is Not Dead," *New Republic*, vol. 144 (April 3, 1961), pp. 11–15, at p. 14.

19. A similar change of perspective over time has been reported by a student of a working-class municipal housing estate in London. See Peter Willmott,

lived there for a long time became evident quickly. Apartments were extremely cheap. I paid only $46 for a six-room apartment with central heating. Long-time residents paid as little as $35 for one like it, and $15 to $25 for a similar unit without central heating. The rooms were large and the apartments comfortable. In buildings without central heating, the apartments were heated with the large combination cooking and heating stoves placed in the kitchen.

At first, I thought that the buildings without central heating were slums, but I soon learned otherwise. The kitchen stoves freed the West Enders from dependence on the landlords and their often miserly thermostats. Moreover, people with stoves could heat their apartments to their own specifications, making them as warm as they liked. In a cold spell, the kitchen stoves were less desirable, for the rooms furthest away from the kitchen were cool, and, when the temperature went down to 10 degrees above zero, the outside bedroom was icy. Some people placed smaller oil or kerosene stoves in these rooms, and these occasionally caused fires, although the kitchen stove was completely safe. Needless to say, central heating was cheaper in the long run, for people had to buy oil to heat the stove. Usually, the oil was purchased in quantity, and stored in the cellar. Poorer people had to buy it in smaller amounts. The apartments also were equipped with gas water-heaters, which required West End families to heat their own water, but also assured independence from landlord whims.

The apartments did, of course, have a number of faults. The buildings were old and not easy to keep clean. Windows leaked and the plumbing had its quirks. There were rats in many of the cellars—although they rarely disturbed anyone except the janitor. No one liked these faults and almost everybody wanted a modern apartment that lacked these disadvantages. However, people were happy with the low rents they were charged in the West End; modernity is not much of an advantage when it depletes the family budget.

Of course there were people, especially the very poorest, who lived in badly substandard housing where the toilets were shared or

"Class and Community at Dagenham," London: Institute for Community Studies, 1960, mimeographed, Chap. 1.

broken, the rats were a danger, the oil stove did not heat properly, and the leaks in the windows could not be sealed. Such people, who were probably also paying higher rents, suffered from all the ills of poor housing. When it comes to livability standards, there is little difference between the classes. Although poorer people do not have as high expectations as the well-to-do, they are no more willing to live with defective plumbing than anyone else.

Everyday life in the West End was not much different from that in other neighborhoods, urban or suburban. The men went to work in the morning, and, for most of the day, the area was occupied largely by women and children—just as in the suburbs. There were some men on the street: the older, retired ones, as well as the young and middle-aged ones who either were unemployed, worked on night shifts, or made their living as gamblers. In the afternoon, younger women could be seen pushing baby carriages. Children of all ages played on the street, and teenagers would "hang" on the corner, or play ball in the school yard. The West End's lone playground was fairly dilapidated, and usually deserted. Many women went shopping every day, partly to meet neighbors and to catch up on area news in the small grocery stores, and partly to buy foods that could not be obtained in the weekly excursion to the supermarket.[20] On Sunday mornings, the streets were filled with people who were visiting with neighbors and friends before and after church.

The average West End resident had a choice between anonymity and total immersion in sociability. A few people had moved into the area to hide from the world, and, while visible to their neighbors, could discourage contact, and thus feel anonymous. Generally speaking, however, neighbors were friendly and quick to say hello to each other, although more intense social contact was limited to relatives and friends. Deviant behavior, as displayed by the area "characters," the bohemians, or the middle-class residents was, of course, highly visible. As long as the West Enders were not affected personally, however, they were tolerant. Yet this tolerance

20. There were no supermarkets within the West End, but one was located just outside it. Many of the West End families with cars went supermarket shopping in outlying neighborhoods, often combining this with a visit to relatives or friends.

was ambivalent: people objected to deviants grudgingly but explained that such kinds of people must be expected in a low-rent neighborhood. At the same time, they found deviant behavior a lively and readily available topic of conversation, which not only provided spice and variety for gossip, but also an opportunity to restate and reaffirm their own values. The bohemians and the schizophrenic characters also served as sources of community amusement, although the latter usually received friendly greetings from other West Enders, even if they did laugh at them once their backs were turned. On the whole, however, the various ethnic groups, the bohemians, transients, and others could live together side by side without much difficulty, since each was responsive to totally different reference groups. Also, at various points, the diverse cultures had common values. For example, everyone liked the low rents, the cheapness of the cost of living generally, and the convenience to downtown. Moreover, as Italians like to stay up late, and to socialize at high decibel levels, the bohemians' loud parties were no problem, at least to them.

The sharing of values was also encouraged by the residential stability of much of the population. Many West Enders had known each other for years, if only as acquaintances who greeted each other on the street. Everyone might not know everyone else; but, as they did know something about everyone, the net effect was the same, especially within each ethnic group. Between groups, common residence and sharing of facilities—as well as the constant struggle against absentee landlords—created enough solidarity to maintain a friendly spirit. Moreover, for many families, problems were never far away. Illnesses, job layoffs, and school or discipline problems among the children occurred regularly. Alcoholism, mental illness, desertion, the death of a loved one, serious financial difficulties, and even violence were familiar to everyone. If they did not take place in one's immediate family, they had happened at some time to a relative or a neighbor. Thus when emergencies occurred, neighbors helped each other readily; other problems were solved within each ethnic group.

For most West Enders, then, life in the area resembled that found in the village or small town, and even in the suburb. Indeed, if differences of age and economic level among the residents were eliminated, many similarities between the life of the urban neighborhood and the suburb would become visible.

Age and class differences are, of course, crucial; they, rather than place of residence, shape the lives of people. That West Enders lived in five-story tenements and suburbanites occupy single-family houses made some—but not many—differences in their ways of life and the everyday routine. For example, although the West Enders were less than a mile from the downtown department stores, it is doubtful whether they used these more than the average suburbanite who has to travel 45 minutes to get to them. Not all city neighborhoods are urban villages, of course, and there are few similarities among the urban jungle, the apartment hotel district, and the suburb, or for that matter, the urban village.[21]

Although it is fashionable these days to romanticize the slum, this has not been my purpose here. The West End was not a charming neighborhood of "noble peasants" living in an exotic fashion, resisting the mass-produced homogeneity of American culture and overflowing with a cohesive sense of community. It was a run-down area of people struggling with the problems of low income, poor education, and related difficulties. Even so, it was by and large a good place to live.

21. Similarities and differences between city and suburb are discussed in more detail in Herbert J. Gans, "Urbanism and Suburbanism as Ways of Life: A Re-evaluation of Definitions," in Arnold Rose, ed., *Human Behavior and Social Processes*, Boston: Houghton Mifflin, 1962, pp. 625–648.

CHAPTER 2 The Italians of the West End: Place, Class, Culture, and Social Structure

Introduction

The remainder of this study deals with the Italians of the West End.[1] This chapter locates them in the area, describes their socio-economic and ethnic characteristics, and outlines the nature of the social structure that will be examined in detail in subsequent chapters.

As previously noted, this study concerns second-generation Italians [2]—the American born children of parents who came from Italy—some from the Southern Italian provinces, others from Sicily.[3] They now are adults, mainly in their late thirties and forties, who are raising their own children.

At this time some terminological and other qualifications are also in order. I have used the shorthand term "Italian" to refer to people who should properly be called Italian-Americans. Also,

1. The Epilogue, however, describes all of the people in the West End.
2. The Center for Community Studies survey indicates, as already noted, that they made up 42 per cent of the West End population. They comprised 55 per cent of all second-generation residents.
3. The Sicilians came primarily from Eastern Sicily; many from the town of Augusta.

I have made no distinction between Italian- and Sicilian-Americans. Although considerable differences do exist between Southern Italian and Sicilian society—and between their emigrants—such differences will not be considered in this study, mainly because most of them have disappeared in the second generation.[4] And from this point on, the term "West Enders" will be used to refer to the second-generation Italian-Americans who lived in the West End.

Whether the West Enders are typical of all second-generation Italians in America is difficult to say without comparative studies in other communities. Some second-generation Italians, having moved far from downtown tenement districts, working-class jobs, and Italian culture, are now living almost like their neighbors in the lower-middle-class suburbias that surround the cities. Others, who have remained in the neighborhoods in which their parents settled after they landed, are more Italian than the West Enders. The majority, who probably have a higher proportion of skilled blue-collar jobs than do the West Enders, have moved to somewhat newer areas further from the center of the city. In social structure and culture, however, I suspect that they are much like the people I am describing.[5] Thus the West Enders are almost, but not entirely, representative of the mainstream of second-generation Italian life in America.[6]

4. At least they are not visible to the non-Italian observer. Also, the differences are less relevant to this study, which compares West Enders to other Americans, than they would be to a more detailed ethnographic survey of the group.

5. This typology is based on, but not entirely in agreement with, that of Paul J. Campisi, "Ethnic Family Patterns: The Italian Family in the United States," American Journal of Sociology, vol. 53 (1948), pp. 443–449. See also Francis A. J. Ianni, "The Italo-American Teenager," The Annals, vol. 338 (November, 1961), pp. 70–78. My notions about the majority of second-generation Italians are based on informal observations in Boston, Philadelphia, and Chicago, and on Nathan Glazer, "The New York Italians," in his forthcoming book, The Peoples of New York (tentative title).

6. The West Enders also differ from the second-generation Italians studied by Child. They are not as threatened by assimilation to exhibit either the rebel or in-group reactions he describes. Most West Enders would probably be identified with what he calls the "apathetic reaction," although that term is inappropriate because it implies the desirability of a more nationalistic reaction.

Patterns of Residence

To most of the West Enders, the area had been home either since birth or marriage. Some were born in the West End because this was where their parents had settled when they first came to America or where they had moved later in life. Others came as adults in the Italian "invasion" of the West End during the 1930's. Many of them had grown up in the North End and had moved at the time of marriage in order to take advantage of better and larger apartments in the West End. In any case, almost all of the West Enders came to the area as a part of a group. Even their movements within the West End—that is, from the lower end to the upper—had been made together with other Italians at about the same time.

Almost all West Enders were tenants. Some of the immigrants had purchased tenements in the Thirties, and offered apartments to their children, to relatives, and to friends.[7] Thus, in many buildings, tenants had more than a purely economic relationship to the landlord. In later years, when increasing costs forced landlords to cut down on services and maintenance, this was often done at the cost of broken friendships with their tenants. Indeed, when West Enders moved as individuals, rather than as part of a group move, it was usually because of a fight with the landlord.

Although West Enders were in the West End because this is where they "belonged," they also found it convenient and economic to live there. Many of the men who worked in the North End or in the central business district walked to work to save carfare. Then, too, they were very much in favor of a short journey to work; understandably so, since, as blue-collar workers, they had to be

---

Irvin L. Child, *Italian or American? The Second Generation in Conflict,* New Haven: Yale University Press, 1943, Chaps. 4–6.

7. A survey of nominal owners listed on West End deeds showed that 37 per cent of the owners had Italian names. Thirty-four per cent had Jewish names; 7 per cent, Slavic; and the rest were split almost equally between Anglo-Saxon and diverse ethnic names. The ethnic background of 10 per cent was not ascertainable on the basis of names.

at their jobs very early in the morning. In addition, the women liked the closeness of the West End to the food stores of the North End, and the shopping and window shopping opportunities of the downtown retail area. Also, people were so used to paying low rents that their whole mode of life was adjusted to them. Any apartment that rented for more than $50 for five or six rooms was thought to be outrageously expensive. Thus, when people had to start looking for new dwellings, they had difficulty in realigning their expenditures to the rent levels outside the West End.

The apartments were kept spotlessly clean, and, although the living room and bedroom furniture was often that purchased at the time of marriage, kitchen equipment and other appliances were usually modern. The kitchen was normally the main arena of social activity. The living room was used mainly to house the television set, and, when visitors came, to allow the men to separate themselves from the women and carry on their own conversation.

West Enders did not think of their area as a slum and resented the city's description of the area because it cast aspersions on them as slum dwellers.[8] They were not pleased that the apartment buildings were not well kept up outside, but, as long as the landlord kept the building clean, maintained the mechanical system, and did not bother his tenants, they were not seriously disturbed about it. People kept their apartments as up-to-date as they could afford to, and most of the ones I saw differed little from lower-middle-class ones in urban or suburban neighborhoods.

Attitudes toward the density, physical layout, and social reputation of the West End were different, however, from typical middle-class ones. If West Enders did not have to live on a fourth or fifth floor, they found little fault with the densely built tenements. For one thing, regardless of where they live, they have little interest in the type of privacy demanded by middle-class families. While they do want to be left alone, they are not averse to the aural or visual closeness of their neighbors. As everyone knows everyone else's activities and problems anyway, they know that it is impossible to hide anything by physical privacy. As one West Ender put it:

8. For more detail on these topics, see Chapters 13 and 14.

I like the noise people make. In summer, people have their windows open, and everyone can hear everyone else, but nobody cares what anybody is saying; they leave their neighbors alone. In the suburbs, people are nosier; when a car comes up the street, all the windows go up to see who is visiting whom.

While the image of the suburb is overdrawn, it is true that in the West End, where people knew so much about each other, there was no need for prying. A feeling of privacy could be maintained in the midst of high density.

In addition, hearing and seeing their neighbors' activities gave the West Enders a share in the life that went on around them, which, in turn, made them feel part of the group. As later chapters will show in detail, West Enders, living mainly in the group, have an insatiable appetite for group experience. Also, since they, like most other working-class people, invite only relatives and close friends into the apartment, much of the other daily social life took place on the street. Watching this social life from the window—elbows on a pillow—was a popular spare time activity in the West End.

Housing is not the same kind of status symbol for the West Enders that it is for middle-class people. They are as concerned about making a good impression on others as anyone else, but the people to be impressed and the ways of impressing them do differ. The people who are entertained in the apartment are intimates. Moreover, they all live in similar circumstances. As a result they evaluate the host not on the basis of his housing, but on his friendliness, his moral qualities, and his ability as a host. Not only are acquaintances and strangers invited less freely to the home than in the middle class, but they are also less important to the West Enders' way of life, and therefore less significant judges of their status. Thus, West Enders, unlike the middle class, do not have to put on as impressive a front for such people, and there is no need to have "an address" or a well-manicured yard in a carefully zoned neighborhood. Indeed, the people who had to satisfy such status needs through housing could not live in the West End, and had to move. Such a move meant leaving the group, and subjecting themselves to criticism, for it implied that the old neighborhood and the neighbors were no longer good enough.

Not all people who left the West End, however, were criticized.[9] Families that moved because the apartments were unsatisfactory or because they wanted a new house were complimented. They were also pitied if the move isolated them involuntarily from old friends, or if they were not accepted in the new neighborhood. But there was no rigid commitment to the tenement district. Indeed, many West Enders indicated that they would be glad to move to a new house in the suburbs, if they could do it together and maintain the old social ties and the old social climate. One of my neighbors wanted to have a single-family house right in the West End.

Whereas most West Enders have no objection to the older suburban towns that surround the Boston city limits, they have little use for the newer suburbs.[10] They described these as too quiet for their tastes, lonely—that is, without street life—and occupied by people concerned only with trying to appear better than they are. West Enders avoid "the country," by which they mean not only rural and vacation areas, but also the lower density suburban towns. They do not like its isolation and, even at vacation time, they go to the densely populated resort areas where the crowds and entertainment facilities of the city prevail. The younger children like the country because there is more play space around single-family houses. As they grow older, however, they play in the city streets as did their parents before them, and their interest in the country vanishes. I was told by one social worker of an experiment some years back to expose West End children to nature by taking them on a trip to Cape Cod. The experiment failed, for the young West Enders found no pleasure in the loneliness of natural surroundings and wanted to get back to the West End as quickly as

9. I am referring here to people who left the West End voluntarily in the years before the urban redevelopment program forced them to do so.

10. The older towns are suburbs only because they are outside Boston's city limits. They are built up with apartments as well as houses. West Enders liked them because they contain Italian neighborhoods, and because they had friends and relatives there. Many West Enders eventually moved to these towns when redevelopment came.

possible. They were incredulous that anyone could live without people around him.

The smaller children's preference for open space made little impression on the parents, for, in the West Enders' family system, the wishes of the children have less priority than those of the adults.[11] A young West Ender, however, might have moved to the suburbs at the urging of his wife, in order to make it easier for her. Indeed, taking two- and three-year olds down several flights of stairs a few times a day is strenuous and time-consuming work for a busy mother. Certainly one of the reasons for the recent suburban exodus has been the ease of rearing small children in one- or two-story dwellings with private yard space. Not only does this eliminate stair-climbing, but mothers then can let their children stay outside without constant supervision. Middle-class mothers, who supervise children closely, feel that it is impossible to raise children in city apartments.

The younger couples who moved from the West End earlier in the 1950's might have left for just this reason. But those West Enders who stayed behind indicated that as they had grown up in tenements, their children could do likewise. For many of them, moreover, a suburban house was financially out of reach. Perhaps they would have preferred one a few years earlier, but most of the mothers I observed had some older children, and found raising them in an apartment to be no problem. Girls, from about age ten, are expected to help with household tasks and to watch over the younger children on the street. Boys of that age are given considerable freedom to be outside without supervision.

Many West Enders impressed me as being true urbanites, with an empathy for the pace, crowding, and excitement of city life that one finds only in upper-middle-class cosmopolites. They are not cosmopolites, however; the parts of the city that they use and enjoy are socially, culturally, and physically far different from those frequented by the upper-middle class.[12] And, as already noted, the

11. See Chapter 3.

12. This does not mean that all Italians are urbanites. Some of the Italian immigrants moved out of the city as soon as they were able, and built themselves modest homes with large yards in the towns surrounding Boston, where

West Ender would gladly exchange his apartment for a detached house, as long as it cost no more, was located near the center of the city, and allowed his relatives, friends, and present neighbors —or similar ones—to live near him.

The Class Divisions

Classes are strata-with-subcultures that grow out of the structure of the national economy and society.[13] This structure not only sets up the opportunities and range of choices available to the members of the society, but also reacts to their ability to make specific choices from the range of alternatives.

The major strata among the West Enders will first be described by the distribution of opportunities—especially income, occupation, and education—and then by how West Enders use this distribution to differentiate people. Subsequently, I will outline the major subcultures, as suggested by variations in life-styles.

Although the participant-observer method is not suited to the collection of statistical data about occupation, income, and education, intensive observation may result in fairly correct estimates of actual frequency distributions. More reliable data about the West Enders, however, are available from the survey conducted by the Center for Community Studies.[14]

The Center's survey shows that the majority of West Enders are employed in manual occupations.[15] Eighteen per cent are un-

they were able to own some of the land they could not have in the old country. I remember talking once to an old Italian immigrant who was visiting in the West End, who could not understand how people could live in apartment buildings, and at such a density.

13. This definition of class is discussed more fully in Chapter 11.

14. Actually, my estimates were surprisingly accurate. In the initial analysis of the data I had overestimated the median income, but the review of my field notes for the preparation of this book indicated that I had been generally correct, underestimating only the number of people earning less than $50 a week; and the number who had graduated from high school.

15. These data report on a sample of 128 second-generation Italian respondents, age twenty to sixty-five. The age limitations of the Center's data reported in Chapter 1 do not apply here, since few second-generation households would be either under twenty or over sixty-five.

Age data for female respondents show 15 per cent to be twenty to twenty-

skilled workers; 39 per cent, semiskilled; and 20 per cent, skilled. Sixteen per cent are in semiskilled white-collar jobs; 6 per cent are skilled clerical workers and small businessmen; and 1 per cent fall into the large business, professional, semiprofessional, and managerial category.[16]

Incomes range from less than $25 to $175 weekly, with the median at about $80. The Center's survey shows that 24 per cent earn less than $50 weekly; 29 per cent, between $50 and $74; 28 per cent between $75 and $99; 13 per cent between $100 and $124; and 6 per cent between $125 and $175.

Most West Enders have completed elementary school or the first two grades of high school, but the high-school graduate is in the minority. Data on female respondents indicate that 30 per cent had 5 to 8 years of schooling; 40 per cent, 9 to 11 years; and that 26 per cent had completed high school. Two per cent each had no formal schooling, and 2 per cent had one or more years of college. My observations would suggest that the number of male high-school graduates is lower because some West Enders have had to leave school to contribute to the family income, and because women often take more readily to education than men.[17]

If class is defined by these criteria, the large majority of West Enders are clearly working class. Some few have risen into the lower-middle-class stratum; and others who, for a variety of reasons, have remained in unskilled and often temporary jobs, must be considered lower class.

Although the categories that West Enders devise to describe these strata differ little from the researcher's, they do make more subtle distinctions in the major strata, or elaborate them by other criteria which are more useful for differentiating people.

For example, the major income divisions were described by one West Ender as follows: "There are our kind, the people who live

nine; 34 per cent to be thirty to thirty-nine; 36 per cent, forty to forty-nine; 11 per cent, fifty to fifty-nine; and 4 per cent, sixty to sixty-five.

16. These figures report the occupation of the past or present household head. Where there was no male household head, or where the husband was not in the labor force, or his occupation was not available, the woman's occupation is reported. Only 8 per cent of the women were never married; 76 per cent were married and living with their husbands.

17. See Chapter 6.

from week to week; people who manage to save money, to put a little away each week; and people who don't have enough coming in every week, whose income is not certain." This description excludes the handful of West Enders above and below—people who are comfortably off by their own standards and can afford some luxuries as well as savings, and the destitute. The former, however, were rarely found in the West End, and had usually left the area because their style of life would have made it difficult for them to find friends. As one family who had moved out of the West End into an aging lower-middle-class town explained: "People don't visit us here; they think we're rich." The ones who remained did so probably because they occupied a special niche in the West End, as in the case of a local gambler who gave some of his profits to West End institutions and Italian charities.

The major occupational distinctions are made between employment and self-employment. The latter, valued for its independence, is a rarity. Among employed people, West Enders distinguish less between blue- and white-collar jobs than between clean and dirty ones. The latter denote physically exhausting unskilled, as well as dirty, labor which is of such low status that it is performed only by Negroes or by "greasers," the recently arrived Italian immigrants.

Education is not usually considered a criterion for distinguishing between people. West Enders are conscious only of differences between highly educated people—such as professors, lawyers, or doctors—and people like themselves "without much schooling." Education is primarily valued as a source of access to clean jobs for the children. Realizing that a grade-school education is no longer sufficient for employment, they urge their children—especially the boys—to graduate from high school and possibly even to go to college.[18]

These are the West Enders' views of the major determinants of class. Having little control over the incomes, occupations, and years of schooling they can obtain, however, they feel it would be unfair to evaluate people by these criteria. Instead, West Enders use other criteria that reflect behavior patterns over which they believe each person can have some control. Should he fail to meas-

18. See also Chapter 6.

ure up to these, he can be judged equitably, and his compatibility for the all important social life of the group can be determined.

The major criteria for ranking, differentiating, and estimating compatibility are ingroup loyalty and conformity to established standards of personal behavior, as well as interpersonal relations. West Enders expect each other to maintain prevalent social practices and consumer styles, to marry within the ethnic—or at least the religious—group, and to reject middle-class forms of status and culture.

Since they do not know each others' incomes, they base their evaluations on expenditures and style of life. Thus, the breadwinner is expected first to take care of his family needs, and then to set a good table for friends and relatives. Women evaluate their peers in a similar way. Material possessions are not important, for these depend on income. What matters—and what can be controlled—is their ability as wives, mothers, and housekeepers. For this reason the neatness of the apartment and cooking and baking skills are of primary importance.

Most important, however, are the characteristics of interpersonal behavior. Honesty, responsibility, and reliability are all highly valued. Should one mistreat a relative or friend for economic gain, or save his money for purely selfish purposes instead of benefiting family and friends, he will be evaluated negatively, although the latter less so than the former.

The most significant criterion of interpersonal behavior is *behavior control*—the ability to regulate one's own needs and wishes and to defer to the needs of the group when necessary. The highest status accrues to the person who makes the most material and nonmaterial contributions to the group, without using these to flaunt or to indicate his economic or cultural superiority. Conversely, the lowest status is reserved for the "bum," a person who cannot or does not want to function properly within the group. This term may be applied to an adolescent who does not pay for his share of the peer group's activities, to an adult who fails to take care of his family, to one who does not pay his debts, or to one who spends his money on luxuries before taking care of necessities. A woman who harasses her husband, who lets her children run around unkempt and at odd hours, or who is unfaithful is described similarly. The mentally ill person who is incapable of following the rules of the group also may be called a bum.

From the list of controllable and uncontrollable criteria of class, it is possible to isolate four major behavior styles that predominate among West Enders and separate them into strata and subcultures. These are: the *maladapted,* the *middle-class mobiles,* and—the two most important ones—the *routine-seekers* and *action-seekers.* The former is based on the search for a routine life, and the latter, on the pursuit of adventurous episodes, or what West Enders call "action." They will be described first.[19] The two terms distinguish between conceptions of living and between ways of responding to opportunities and of making choices. These, in turn, result in differences in rhythm of life, in the patterns of family relationships, work, leisure, religious behavior, attitudes toward authority, and, indeed, in the very purpose of human existence.

The routine-seekers are people whose aim is the establishment of a stable [20] way of living, in which the economic and emotional security of the individual and of his family are most important. Their way of life is marked by a highly regular and recurring scheduling of behavior patterns, and nearly all their activities are organized into a routine. There may be a regular menu for every day of the week, which differs little from one week to the next. And the same people may be visited or entertained on the same evening every week. A similar regularity is observable in the celebration of holidays, giving of gifts, and in many of the other spheres of life in which the middle-class person strives for novelty

19. The distinction bears some resemblance to that drawn by English sociologists between "respectable" and "rough" members of the working class. Kuper, for example, distinguished respectables by their high standards of domestic and personal cleanliness, speech and manners, personal appearance, and upkeep of the home; roughs, by the absence of these criteria. Leo Kuper, "Blueprint for Living Together," in Leo Kuper, ed., *Living in Towns,* London: Cresset Press, 1953, pp. 1–202, at pp. 78–82. Kuper's criteria would also distinguish between routine- and action-seekers, but what he describes are the most visible elements in a pattern that can be traced to the more fundamental differences I have suggested.

20. This term I have taken from S. M. Miller and Frank Riessman, "The Working-Class Subculture: A New View," *Social Problems,* vol. 9 (1961), pp. 86–97, at p. 91.

and variety. As this regularity is especially striking among West Enders, I have therefore used the term "routine." [21]

For the action-seeker, life is episodic. The rhythm of life is dominated by the adventurous episode, in which heights of activity and feeling are reached through exciting and sometimes riotous behavior.[22] The goal is action, an opportunity for thrills, and for the chance to face and overcome a challenge. It may be sought in a card game, a fight, a sexual interlude, a drinking bout, a gambling session, or in a fast and furious exchange of wisecracks and insults. Whatever the episode, the action-seeker pursues it with a vengeance, and lives the rest of his life in quiet—and often sullen—preparation for this climax, in which he is usually said to be "killing time."

In most instances, routine-seekers are more likely to have stable jobs, which require more skills and pay higher wages than do those of action-seekers. But this is not always so. Indeed, should society not make stable jobs and adequate income available in sufficient amounts, people may try to achieve a routine life style, but be unable to overcome the many obstacles to it. When work, income, and education equivalent to working-class status are available, those who seek routine can usually find it, unless their desire for it is frustrated by personal or familial disabilities.

Among the West Enders, action-seekers generally occupy jobs of minimal stability, skill, and pay. This is partly cause and partly

21. I do not use the term deprecatingly, for there is more than enough spontaneity and surprise in everyday life to counteract the regularities. West Enders do not seem to be unwilling slaves to a routine, or to be bored by it. In fact, I did not really develop the concept until after I left the West End, and owe it to a middle-class informant in another community, married to an Italian, who complained bitterly that her in-laws had a set and never deviating menu for every day of the week.

22. The conception of action-seeking and the episodic rhythm of life struck me one night early in the field work, after I had spent an evening in a tavern, listening to a West Ender's riotous life history. The concept of episode comes from Nelson N. Foote, "Concept and Method in the Study of Human Development," in Muzafer Sherif and M. O. Wilson, eds., *Emergent Problems in Social Psychology*, Norman: University of Oklahoma Press, 1957, pp. 29–53. For a detailed description of action-seeking which has clarified my own conception, see Walter B. Miller, "Lower Class Culture as a Generating Milieu of Gang Delinquency," *Journal of Social Issues*, vol. 14, No. 3 (1958), pp. 5–19.

effect. As their upbringing has not prepared them for work or interest in work, they often gravitate into the least satisfying jobs. This, in turn, encourages them even further to find gratifications in episodes of action.

The search for action is a male prerogative. As children reach school age, the boys are allowed to roam the streets and to look for childhood adventures, more so in lower-class than in working-class families. Girls, however, are expected to stay home, and thus are less likely to want action—at least overtly.

Action-seekers also are more apt to be found among adolescents than adults, for adolescence, especially in the working and lower class, is peculiarly suited to the episodic life. The routine portions of existence, such as school and work, are usually based on adult rules, and unsatisfying to the adolescent. Thus, the teenage boy can be himself only during adventurous episodes that are interspersed between periods of time-killing. Most adolescents graduate into the routine pattern when they marry, and develop stable family relationships. Others, however, may marry, and then pay little attention to their families, spending their nonwork hours with male companions and "playing around" with other women on the side. These, West Enders describe as being "unable to get off the corner."

The differences between the two styles range over many areas of life. Routine-seekers are more likely to be regular churchgoers, to live by the ethical norms of the religion, and to favor moderation in all pursuits. They will accept the authority of the more powerful as long as it is wielded equitably, and they are willing to grant the possibility that the government may act with good intentions, although they believe that it does not do so often. The action-seeker goes to church mainly to seek absolution from sins committed during episodes, is belligerent in the presence of authority, and is certain that government is always exploitative and corrupt.

Routine-seekers are thrifty; they spend extra funds on the family, or save it for emergencies. Action-seekers spend the same monies on nightclubs, new clothes, appliances, automobiles, or gambling sprees, even if their impulsive spending leaves them no funds for what they consider to be necessities. Routine-seekers also spend money for impulse goods, but they buy clothes only for the holidays and postpone more expensive items until the need or desire for them becomes pressing. When they gamble, they set a limit on their losses and stop playing when it is reached.

Although the action-seekers are less concerned with behavior control than the routine-seekers, they must be distinguished from a third group, the maladapted—people who are entirely unable to control their behavior because of alcoholism or other personal difficulties. To the middle-class observer there may be little difference between them and the more impulsive action-seekers. But whereas the latter pursue episodes within a context of rules, and do not cut themselves off from family and peers, the maladapted may be mentally ill, and lack the self-control and contact with reality to function in these groups. If these people behave in nonthreatening ways, West Enders often call them "characters." And, as noted earlier, they also may call them "bums," although routine-seekers use this term as well to describe action-seekers.

For the most part, the action- and routine-seekers are socially nonmobile. Another set of West Enders, however, is mobile. Bearing a superficial resemblance to the routine-seekers, these people strive to move themselves—or, more often, their children—into the middle class. But since West Enders reject the middle class, as I shall show in Chapters 10 and 11, those who seek to rise into it must do so either as individuals or as individual family units. Moreover, since no middle-class culture exists among West Enders, the mobile have to model themselves on outsiders. As a result, they must detach themselves from relatives and old friends and are often rejected by these.

Placing the West Enders into classes depends on the definition of class that one uses. If working class is equated to the holding of a relatively stable skilled or semiskilled job, and lower class, to the holding of an unstable, unskilled one, most West Enders can be described as working class. This holds true both for the routine- and action-seekers. If a class is defined by life-style, however, action-seekers can be described as lower class; routine-seekers, as working class. But not all action-seekers are lower class. The analysis of the American class system in Chapter 11 will clarify this qualification by showing that action-seeking is a prevalent but not the distinguishing characteristic of lower-class culture.

For the purpose of summarizing this discussion, however, the West Enders can be divided into four major strata: the lower-lower-class maladapted, the lower-class action-seekers, the working-class routine-seekers, and the middle-class mobiles.

Sociologists rank the classes in terms of their economic, social, and political influence in the larger society, and on that basis, the middle-class mobiles are most important, followed by the routine-seekers, the action-seekers, and the maladapted. But while West Enders would accept the notion of a class hierarchy, they would reject this ranking. Generally speaking, each group—except the last—considers itself to be most desirable, using criteria of evaluation that would support its judgment. Thus, while the routine-seekers deplore the impulsive behavior of the action-seekers, the latter are scornful of the routine-seekers' inability to have fun, as well as for the dullness of their lives. Both see the middle-class mobiles as snobs or renegades.

In terms of number of people in the West End, the routine-seekers are most important, followed by the action-seekers, the middle-class mobiles and the maladapted. The chapters that follow will concentrate on the initial two, especially on the first. In Chapter 10, I will deal more specifically with patterns of mobility, and in Chapter 11, with the processes by which mobile people move into the middle class. This chapter also will compare lower, working-, and middle-class subcultures in America, in order to develop some hypotheses regarding the essential differences between them. At that time, I will also deal further with the unresolved question in the present chapter—whether classes ought to be defined in terms of occupation, income, and education, or in terms of life-styles.

Ethnicity

A third way of describing the West Enders is in terms of ethnicity. By this, I mean their ethnic—that is, Italian—characteristics, as well as the impact of acculturation on the Italian culture, and of assimilation on the social structure.

Generally speaking, the Italian and Sicilian cultures that the immigrants brought with them to Ameria have not been maintained by the second generation. Their over-all culture is that of Americans. A number of Italian patterns, however, have survived, the most visible ones being food habits. In all European ethnic groups, traditional foods and cooking methods are retained long after other aspects of the immigrant culture are given up. This is true also among West Enders. Most of the women still cook only Italian dishes at home, and many of them still make their own "pasta," especially for holiday dishes. They do not care for what they call the "American" types of spaghetti, macaroni, and other pasta products.

The pattern of heavy eating and light drinking, found in most Latin and Mediterranean cultures, also persists among the West Enders. Thus, rich food rather than alcohol is used to counteract deprivation or to celebrate. Entrees are strongly spiced, and desserts are very sweet. Even so, the food is milder and less spicy than that eaten by their parents. Moreover, West Enders have also given up the immigrant pattern of preparing olive oil and wine at home, and buy the weaker commercially made ones.[23]

The durability of the ethnic tradition with respect to food is probably due to the close connection of food with family and group life. Indeed, food patterns are retained longer than others because they hold the group together with a minimum of strain. Also, there seems to be some association between food and the home. Food preparation serves as an example of the woman's skill as a housewife and mother. When company is present, it enables her to display her skills to relatives and peers.

Another pattern that has persisted into the second generation is language. Most of the West Enders I met could speak Italian—or, more correctly, the special patois of their locality—because they had learned it from their parents, and had to use it to communi-

23. These and other changes in Italian eating and drinking practices in America are described in detail in G. Lolli, E. Serianni, G. Golder, and P. Luzzatto-Fegiz, *Alcohol in Italian Culture,* New York: The Free Press of Glencoe and Yale Center of Alcohol Studies, 1958.

cate with them. Their children—that is, the third generation—are not being taught the language, however. Also, Italian names are slowly being Anglicized. Surnames are changed by people whose work brings them into contact with Americans, so that their names will be more easily understood. Given names are being changed for esthetic reasons, English ones being described as "nicer" than Italian ones. Thus, second-generation West Enders named Giuseppe by their parents introduce themselves as Joseph, and give only the English name to their children.[24]

There is little, if any, identification either with Italy or with the local areas from which the immigrants came originally. Second-generation people know their parents' birthplace, but it is of little interest to them. Excepting a handful of Italian intellectuals and artists, I encountered no identification with Italian culture or Italian symbols. Even those Italians who had made a name for themselves in sports or in entertainment were not praised solely because of their ethnicity. In fact, when a local Italian boxer lost a fight to his Negro opponent, I was told scornfully about a West Ender who had mourned this as a loss of Italian pride. Likewise, there seemed to be no objection to a Jewish singer who had made several hit records of bowdlerized Italian folk songs. "After all," people said, "most of us work for a Jewish boss." Whereas West Enders were more likely to vote for an Italian politician than any other, this was so only because they felt all politicians to be crooked. An Italian, being one of their own, would perhaps be less evil, and, if not, he at least would be more accessible to them than others.[25]

Acculturation thus has almost completely eroded Italian culture patterns among the second generation, and is likely to erase the rest in the third generation.[26] In fact, the process seems to have begun soon after the arrival of the immigrants. One West Ender told me that his Italian-born mother had saved for years for a visit to Italy, but that when she was finally able to go, came back

24. In a lower-middle-class suburb near Philadelphia that I studied after the West End, people of Italian background sometimes gave their children names such as Lynn or Mark.

25. See Chapter 8.

26. For a similar description of second-generation Italian ethnicity, and how it is changing, see Child, *op. cit.*, especially Chap. 2.

after a month, saying that she could not live among these people because she was not like any of them. The woman, even though she had never learned to speak English properly, had become Americanized in the West End. Such rapid acculturation is not surprising, for the Italians who came to America were farm laborers whose life had been an unending round of much work and little leisure. As the patterns associated with rural poverty that they brought to America were jettisoned quickly, the ensuing vacuum was filled by things American.

Assimilation, however—the disappearance of the Italian social system—has proceeded much more slowly. Indeed, the social structure of the West End, to be discussed in the next section, is still quite similar to that of the first generation. Social relationships are almost entirely limited to other Italians, because much sociability is based on kinship, and because most friendships are made in childhood, and are thus influenced by residential propinquity. Intermarriage with non-Italians is unusual among the second-generation, and is not favored for the third. As long as both parties are Catholic, however, disapproval is mild.

The relationship to the church is also similar to that of the immigrant generations. West Enders are religious, but they minimize their ties to the church. And while the traditional Italian emphasis on the Virgin Mary and the local saint continues, the superstitions based on the anthropomorphizing of nature have faded away.[27]

Judging by the nostalgia of the West Enders for the past, it would appear that the Italian group is no longer as cohesive as it was in the previous generation. They say that in those days, people were friendlier and more cooperative, and that there were fewer individual wants, especially on the part of children.[28] But while they mourn the loss of cohesion, they do not pursue it. For example, the redevelopment gave West Enders an opportunity to return to a more cohesive community in the nearby North End, which is still entirely Italian.[29] None of the West Enders seemed

27. See Chapter 5.
28. Attitudes toward the past are considered further in Chapter 10.
29. This is the society described in William F. Whyte, Jr., *Street Corner Society*, Chicago: University of Chicago Press, 1943; 2nd ed., 1955.

to be interested, however, largely because of the poorer quality of the housing. The ethnic homogeneity and cohesion of the North End were never mentioned either positively or negatively; for most people it was a place to shop for Italian food, and to visit relatives.

Relationships with members of other ethnic groups are friendly but infrequent. These groups are characterized by traditional stereotypes, to which exceptions are made only in the case of specific individuals. For example, the fact that the Irish husband of an Italian woman was an alcoholic occasioned no surprise, because all Irishmen were suspected of being drunkards. The social distance between ethnic groups was illustrated by one West Ender, who was on friendly terms with her Jewish neighbor. When she spoke of the woman, however, she did not use her name, but called her simply—and entirely without malice—"the Jew."

The Structure of West End Society: An Introduction to the Peer Group Society

While residence, class, and ethnicity may locate the West Ender in ecological and social space, they tell us little about how he lives his daily life. As has already been noted in passing, life for the West Ender is defined in terms of his relationship to the group. The nature of this group, that is, the social organization of West End life, will be the principal subject of all but the concluding chapters of this study.

The life of the West Ender takes place within three interrelated sectors: the primary group, the secondary group, and the outgroup. The primary group refers to that combination of family and peer relationships which I shall call the *peer group society*. The secondary group refers to the small array of Italian institutions, voluntary organizations, and other social bodies which function to support the workings of the peer group society. This I shall call the *community*. I use this term because *it*, rather than the West End or Boston, is the West Ender's community. The outgroup, which I shall describe as the *outside world*, covers a variety of non-Italian institutions in the West End, in Boston, and in America that impinge on his life—often unhappily to the West Ender's way of thinking.

Although social and economic systems in the outside world are significant in shaping the life of the West Ender, the most important part of that life is lived within the primary group. National and local economic, social, and political institutions may determine the West Ender's opportunities for income, work, and standard of living, but it is the primary group that refracts these outside events and thus shapes his personality and culture. Because the peer group society dominates his entire life, and structures his relationship with the community and the outside world, I shall sometimes use the term to describe not only the primary relationships, but the West Enders' entire social structure as well.

The primary group is a peer group society because most of the West Enders' relationships are with peers, that is, among people of the same sex, age, and life-cycle status. While this society includes the friendships, cliques, informal clubs, and gangs usually associated with peer groups, it also takes in family life. In fact, during adulthood, the family is its most important component. Adult West Enders spend almost as much time with siblings, in-laws, and cousins—that is, with relatives of the same sex and age—as with their spouses, and more time than with parents, aunts, and uncles. The peer group society thus continues long past adolescence, and, indeed, dominates the life of the West Ender from birth to death. For this reason I have coined the term "peer group society."

In order to best describe the dominance of the peer group principle in the life of the West Ender, it is necessary to examine it over a typical life cycle. The child is born into a nuclear family; at an early age, however, he or she—although girls are slower to do this than boys—transfers increasing amounts of his time and allegiance to the peers he meets in the street and in school. This transfer may even begin long before the child enters school. Thus, one West Ender told me that when he wanted his two-year-old son to attend an activity at a local settlement house, bribery and threats were useless, but that the promise that he could go with two other young children on the block produced immediate assent.

From this time on, then, the West Ender spends the rest of his life in one or another peer group. Before or soon after they start going to school, boys and girls form cliques or gangs. In these cliques, which are sexually segregated, they play together and learn the lore of childhood. The clique influence is so strong, in fact, that both parents and school officials complain that their values have difficulty competing with those being taught in the peer group. The sexually segregated clique maintains its hold on the individual until late adolescence or early adulthood.

Dating, the heterosexual relationship between two individuals that the middle-class child enters into after puberty—or even earlier—is much rarer among West Enders. Boys and girls may come together in peer groups to a settlement house dance or a clubroom. Even so, they dance with each other only infrequently. Indeed, at the teenage dances I observed, the girls danced mostly with each other and the boys stood in the corner—a peer group pattern that may continue even among young adults. A West End girl in her twenties described her dates as groups of men and women going out together, with little social contact between individual men and women during the evening. Individual dating takes place not as part of the group activity, as in the middle class, but only after the group has dispersed. Judging from the descriptions given by young West End men, the relationship then is purely sexual—at least for them.

The hold of the peer group is broken briefly at marriage. During courtship, the man commutes between it and his girl. Female peer groups—always less cohesive than male—break up even more easily then, because the girl who wants to get married must compete with her peers for male friends and must be at their beck and call. At marriage, the couple leaves its peer groups, but after a short time, often following the arrival of the first child, they both re-enter peer group life.

Among action-seeking West Enders, the man may return to his corner, and the woman to her girl friends. But most often—especially in the routine-seeking working class—a new peer group is formed, consisting of family members and a few friends of each spouse. This group meets after working hours for long evenings of sociability. Although the members of the group are of both sexes, the normal tendency is for the men and women to split up, the men in one room and the women in another. In addition, husband and wife also may belong to other peer groups: work colleagues or childhood friends among the men, informal clubs of old friends that meet regularly among the women. In the West End, friendship ties seem to be formed mainly in childhood and adolescence, and many of them last throughout life.

But the mainstay of the adult peer group society is the *family circle*.[30] As already noted, the circle is made up of collateral kin: in-laws, siblings, and cousins predominantly. Not all family members are eligible for the peer group, but the rules of selection—which are informal and unstated—are based less on closeness of kinship ties than on compatibility. Family members come together if they are roughly of the same age, socio-economic level, and cultural background. How closely or distantly they are related is much less important than the possession of common interests and values. Even among brothers and sisters only those who are compatible are likely to see each other regularly.

This combination of family members and friends seems to continue to function as a peer group for the rest of the life cycle. Thus, each of the marriage partners is pulled out *centrifugally* toward his or her peers, as compared with the middle-class family in which a *centripetal* push brings husband and wife closer together.

The West End, in effect, may be viewed as a large network of these peer groups, which are connected by the fact that some people may belong to more than one group. In addition, a few individuals function as communicators between the groups, and thus keep them informed of events and attitudes important to them all.

As will be shown in detail in later chapters, the hold of the peer group on the individual is very strong. Some illustrations of this can be given here. Achievement and social mobility, for example, are group phenomena. In the current generation, in which the Italian is still effectively limited to blue-collar work, atypical educational and occupational mobility by the individual is frowned upon. Children who do well in school are called "sissies," and they cannot excel there and expect to remain in their peer group. Since

30. I have borrowed this term from Michael Young and Peter Willmott, *Family and Kinship in East London*, London: Routledge and Kegan Paul, 1957.

allegiance to any one group is slight at this stage, however, the good student can drift into other peer groups until he finds one with compatible members. Should such peers be lacking, he may have to choose between isolation or a group that does not share his standards. Often, he chooses the latter. This is well illustrated by children who have intellectual skills but who find that out of fear of peer group pressures they cannot summon the self-control to do well in school.

Life in a peer group society has a variety of far-reaching social and psychological consequences. For example, the centrifugal pressure on man and wife affects the family structure, as does the willingness—or resignation—of the parents in relinquishing their children to their own peer group at an early age. The fact that individuals are accustomed to being with—and are more at ease with—members of their own sex means that their activities are cued primarily to reference groups of that sex. This may help to explain the narcissistic vanity among West End men, that is, their concern with clothes, and displays of muscular strength or virility.[31] It also may help to explain the chaperoning of unmarried women, in fear that they will otherwise indulge in sexual intercourse. Not only does the separation of the sexes substitute for the development of internal controls that discourage the man from taking advantage of the woman, but they replace, as well, those controls that allow the woman to protect herself.

The peer group principle has even more important consequences for personality organization. Indeed, the role of the group in the life of the individual is such that he exists primarily in the group. School officials, for example, pointed out that teenagers were rough and active when they were with their peers, but quiet and remarkably mild and passive when alone. Their mildness is due to the fact that they exist only partially when they are outside the group. In effect, the individual personality functions best and most completely among his or her peers—a fact that has some implications for independence and dependence, conformity and individualism among the West Enders. In some ways the in-

31. It is thus not necessary to use explanations invoking latent or manifest homosexuality, although latent homosexuality is also present. Vanity is not limited, however, to the latently homosexual. See Chapter 3.

dividual who lives in a peer group society is more dependent than the middle-class person. This is true, however, only on a superficial level. In Chapter 4, devoted to a consideration of this problem, it will be shown that both types are independent but that their independence is expressed in different contexts, and varies in a number of other characteristics.

My emphasis on the role of the peer group should not be taken to mean that it is distinctive to the West End, or even to second-generation Italians. Other studies have suggested that it is a fairly universal phenomenon in working-class groups.[32] Nor does its influence end at this point. Peer groups are found in all classes, but in the middle and upper-middle-class, they play a less important role, especially among adults. In the lower-middle-class, for example, peer groups are made up of neighbors and friends, and exist alongside the nuclear family, but usually they do not include members of the family circle. Moreover, dependence on the peer group for sociability and mutual aid is much weaker. Also, there is much more interaction among couples and groups of couples. Nevertheless, social gatherings usually do break up into male and female enclaves, and voluntary associations are segregated by sex. In the upper-middle-class, social relationships take place primarily among couples, and voluntary associations are less frequently segregated by sex. Even so, social gatherings and activity groups may break up into male and female subgroups. Upper-middle-class women often resent the fact that concentration on the mother role creates handicaps to job or organizational activities in which the sexes work together.

In the lower-middle-class, and more so in the upper-middle-class, people move in a larger number of peer groups, often formed to pursue specific interests and activities. The West End pattern, in which people spend most of their spare time within the confines of one peer group, is not found here. Consequently, the influence of the peer group on the life of the middle class is much less intense.

32. See Chapter 11.

PART TWO The Peer Group Society

CHAPTER 3 The Family

Family Types

Sociologists and anthropologists generally distinguish between the *nuclear* family, made up of husband, wife, and children but separated from other relatives; and the *extended* family, in which a group of nuclear families and related individuals from several generations act together as a virtual unit. The extended family is found most often in agricultural or hunting societies, where such groups are functioning economic units. The nuclear family is associated with the urban-industrial society in which family members cannot be employed together, and in which, because of rapid social change, cultural differences between the generations and the resulting conflict between young and old make life together difficult.

West Enders fall squarely between the two ideal types. The nature of the family, however, can best be understood if one can distinguish between households and families. West End households are nuclear, with two qualifications. Married daughters often retain close ties with their mothers and try to settle near them. They do not share the same apartment, because however close the ties, there are differences between the generations—or at least between husband and mother-in-law—that are likely to create conflict. Some households take in close relatives who would otherwise be alone, especially unmarried brothers, sisters, or even cousins, because of feelings of obligation, love, and the desire to reduce the loneliness of the single person. Pitkin, observing a similar pattern in his study of a Southern Italian village, described this family as *expanded*.[1] Since rents were low in the West End, unmarried siblings often had their own apartments. Much of their spare time, however, was spent with married brothers or sisters, and they often participated in child-rearing as quasi-parental aunts and uncles.

But although households are nuclear or expanded, the family itself is still closer to the extended type. It is not an economic unit, however, for there are few opportunities for people to work together in commercial or manufacturing activities. The extended family actually functions best as a social circle, in which relatives who share the same interests, and who are otherwise compatible, enjoy each other's company. Members of the family circle also offer advice and other help on everyday problems. There are some limits to this aid, however, especially if the individual who is being helped does not reciprocate. For example, one family I met in the West End had a member who suffered from spells of deep depression. The family circle visited him frequently to cheer him up, to give advice, and to urge him to join in family activity, but when he failed to accept their ministrations, his relatives became impatient. They continued to visit him, but did so grudgingly. As one of his relatives put it: "He has no interests, why should anyone care about him?"

The extended family system is limited generationally, for relationships between adults and their parents—the immigrant generation—are fewer and less intimate than those between adults of the same generation.[2] Visits with parents are exchanged, but parents

1. Donald Pitkin, "Land Tenure and Farm Organization in an Italian Village," Unpublished Ph.D. Dissertation, Harvard University, 1954, p. 114.

2. Others have reported the lack of contact between the generations and the frequency of contact within them among second-generation Italians. See Philip Garigue and Raymond Firth, "Kinship Organization of Italianates in London," in Raymond Firth, ed., *Two Studies of Kinship in London*, London: Athlone Press, 1956, especially pp. 74, 82. Comparative studies of Italian and Irish populations have also reported this pattern, noting the difference in the Irish family, where old people are venerated and powerful. See M. K. Opler and J. L. Singer, "Ethnic Differences in Behavior and Psycopathology," *International Journal of Social Psychiatry*, vol. 2 (1956), pp. 11–22; and Ezra F. Vogel, "The Marital Relationships of Parents of Emotionally Disturbed Children," Unpublished Ph.D. Dissertation, Harvard University, 1958, Chap. 6.

are generally not part of the continuing social life of the family circle. Widowed parents do not live with their children if other alternatives are available. While old people are allowed to function as grandparents, they are freely criticized for spoiling their grand-children, or for insisting on outmoded ideas. Compared with the middle class, in fact, the older generation receives little respect or care. Social workers in the West End told of families who sent old people to welfare agencies even when they could afford to support them, although this is not typical. The lack of respect toward the older generation is especially noticeable among children, who tease and insult old people behind their backs, including their own grandparents.

The only exception to this pattern is the previously mentioned tie between mother and married daughter, and a more infrequent one between mother and unmarried son. Even so, mothers tend to assist rather than guide their married daughters. They help out in the household and in the rearing of children, but they have neither the power nor authority of the "Mum," the ruling ma-triarch of the English working-class family.[3]

The expanded family that I have described is common to both the routine-seekers and the action-seekers. The analysis of family life in the following pages will deal principally with male-female and parent-child relationships among the routine-seekers. As al-ready indicated, most West Enders are routine-seekers—or become so when they marry—and families in which the husband is an action-seeker are relatively few in number.

Male-Female Relationships

I pointed out in Chapter 2 that West Enders socialize primarily with people of their own age and sex, and are much less adept than middle-class people at heterosexual relationships. In many working-class cultures, the man is away from the house even after work, taking his leisure in the corner taverns that function as men's clubs. But, since the Italian culture is not a drinking one,

3. The role of the "Mum" has been described in many studies of English working-class life. See, for example, Michael Young and Peter Willmott, *Family and Kinship in East London*, London: Routledge and Kegan Paul, 1957. See also Chapter 11.

this is less frequent among West Enders. Consequently, much of their segregation of leisure takes place within the home: the women sit together in one room, the men in another. Even when everyone gathers around the kitchen table, the men group together at one end, the women at the other, and few words are exchanged between them. Men are distinctly uncomfortable in the company of women, and vice versa, but the men find it harder to interact with the women than the women with the men. At social gatherings I attended, whenever women initiated conversations with men, the men would escape as quickly as possible and return to their own group. They explained that they could not keep up with the women, that the women talked faster and more readily, turning the conversation to their own feminine interests and that they tried to dominate the men. The men defended themselves either by becoming hostile or by retreating. Usually, they retreated.

The men's inability to compete conversationally with women is traditional. Second-generation Italians grew up in a patriarchal authority system with a strictly enforced double standard of behavior for boys and girls. The boys were freer to indulge their gratifications than the girls. In order to be able to do what they wanted, the girls thus had to learn early how to subvert the male authority by verbal means—"how to get around the men"—and what they did not learn elsewhere, they learned from the mother's wile in getting her way with her husband. As will be noted subsequently, the father enforces discipline and administers punishment; he does not need to talk. The mother can influence her husband only by talking to him, reinterpreting the child's deeds so that he will not punish the child any more than she feels desirable. Talk is the woman's weapon for reducing inequities in power between male and female.

With unrelated women, the male reaction sometimes resembles fear. The men are afraid that the women will overpower them through their greater verbal skill, and thus overturn the nominal dominance of the man over the woman. In a culture that puts great stress on what David Riesman has called "male vanity," placing a man in an inferior position is thought to impugn his masculinity. In other situations, his fear is based on an opposite motive, that undue contact with a woman may produce sexual desire that cannot be satisfied. Among West End men, the unrelated woman is conceived mainly as a sexual object. At the same time, the strict double standard makes her sexually inaccessible. Consequently, while men are freely aggressive, both sexually and verbally, with a "bad" girl, they must control themselves with an inaccessible "good" girl. Among unmarried people, for example, when a "good" girl enters an all-male group, profanity and sexual talk are immediately halted, and the men seem momentarily paralyzed before they can shift conversational gears.

What the men fear is their own ability at self-control. This attitude, strongest among young, unmarried people, often carries over into adulthood. The traditional Italian belief—that sexual intercourse is unavoidable when a man and a woman are by themselves—is maintained intact among second-generation West Enders, and continues even when sexual interest itself is on the wane. For example, I was told of an older woman whose apartment was adjacent to that of an unmarried male relative. Although they had lived in the same building for almost twenty years and saw each other almost every day, she had never once been in his apartment because of this belief.

As a result, the barriers between the sexes are high, and they are crossed mainly by deviant types. The only men who carry on a consistent social relationship with women are "ladies' men," who are in varying degrees effeminate. Likewise, the only women who carry on such a relationship with men are likely to be those with strong masculine tendencies. Some of my neighbors used to anger their wives by sharing sexually connotative jokes and indulging in sexual banter with a young woman who appeared to be masculine in some of her ways. They were able to do this because the girl did not represent a potential sexual object. Although she still saw herself as a potential bride, and expressed great, though false, embarrassment at the men's behavior, she was a safe target for the expression of the sexual hostility of the males toward the women. At the same time, she never discouraged these attacks because they were the only kinds of advances she was likely to get from men, and perhaps because she was masculine enough to be able to enjoy the joking. West End women indulged in sexual banter, too, but only among themselves.

The male fear of "good" girls was vividly portrayed one evening when a group of men in their twenties were pursuing another man who had slashed one of the group in a tavern brawl. The man ran into his apartment building, leaving the entrance blocked by his mother and his sister. Armed with sticks, the men pushed the mother—a women in her sixties—out of the way. The girl, however, was able to stop them from coming into the building. While they did attack her verbally, they did not touch her, and then, promising to carry out justice at some other time, they eventually withdrew.

Husband-Wife Relationships

The general pattern of male-female interaction carries over into the relationship between husbands and wives. The barriers between male and female are translated into a marital relationship that can be best described as *segregated,* as distinguished from the *joint* relationship that characterizes the middle-class family.[4] Bott's description of this phenomenon among English families applies to the West Enders as well:

> Husband and wife have a clear differentiation of tasks and a considerable number of separate interests and activities. They have a clearly defined division of labor into male tasks and female tasks. They expect to have different leisure pursuits, and the husband has his friends . . . the wife hers.[5]

While the husband's main role is breadwinning, the wife is responsible for all functions concerning home and child, even the finding of an apartment. Women speak of the family apartment as "my rooms"; husbands speak to wives about "your son." Responsible for overseeing the rearing of the child, the mother may even administer discipline, although this is usually left to the father when he comes home from work.

On the surface, this pattern differs little from the middle-class

4. These terms are taken from Elizabeth Bott, *Family and Social Network,* London: Tavistock Publications, 1957, pp. 53–54.

5. Bott, *op. cit.,* p. 53.

one. In middle-class society, as in most societies, most of the tasks connected with home and child are also the mother's duty. In the West End, however, the boundary between tasks is quite rigid. As one West End housewife put it, "when my husband comes home with the pay, I can't ask him to help in the house." Whereas the middle-class husband expects to help out in the household, and to share the responsibilities of child-rearing, the West End husband does not expect to do so, and will help out only in unusual situations. It is not that he rejects the possibility of joint action; it is simply something outside of his experience.

The segregation of functions is more clearly visible in the emotional aspects of the husband-wife relationship. Although young West Enders are as much concerned with romantic love as other Americans, and although couples do marry on the basis of love, the marital relationship is qualitatively different from that of the middle class. Not only is there less communication and conversation between husband and wife, but there is also much less gratification of the needs of one spouse by the other. Husbands and wives come together for procreation and sexual gratification, but less so for the mutual satisfaction of emotional needs or problem solving. Among my neighbors was a bachelor. When I asked one of his relatives whether he would ever marry, it was explained that he would probably not, since his work brought him into contact with women who satisfied his sexual needs. In addition, his frequent visits to his married sister's household provided the opportunity for the little relationship with children expected of the man.

Thus the marriage partners are much less "close" than those in the middle class. They take their troubles less to each other than to brothers, sisters, other relatives, or friends. Men talk things over with brothers, women with sisters and mothers; each thus remains on his side of the sexual barrier.

I can best illustrate the nature of the marital relationship anecdotally. Most of the small stores in the West End were family enterprises. Two of the Italian stores that I frequented were each run by a man and a woman who I knew to be related, and who I thought were either brother and sister, or cousins. In both cases, my assumption was based on the man's lack of interest in the woman's children when they were in the store, as well as her total lack of interest in his business. One day, when I raised the question of relocation plans in one of the stores, the woman replied curtly, "I don't care about the store, it's his; it's his business to make a living, not mine." This was said matter of factly, without a trace of anger or malice. If the woman did interfere in the man's activities, especially in one of the many extracurricular ones that commonly took place in small stores,[6] she was rebuked and told to mind her own business. In both stores, the lack of communication convinced me that the relationship was that of two individuals who were brought together by economic necessity and by kinship ties, but who otherwise were not close. My assumption that they were siblings or cousins had been based on my middle-class expectations, and I was much surprised to discover that, in both places, they were husband and wife.

The segregated conjugal pattern is closely associated with the extended family, for the functions that are not performed by husband and wife for each other are handled primarily by other members of the extended family. In a society where male and female roles are sharply distinguished, the man quickly learns that, on many occasions, his brother is a better source of advice and counsel than his wife. The recruitment of the family circle on the basis of compatibility enhances this pattern, for those relatives who provide helpful advice are also likely to be compatible in other ways, and thus to be part of the circle.

Although the middle-class observer may find it hard to imagine the absence of the marital closeness that exists in his own culture, this pattern has been functional for people like the West Enders. Until recently, they have lived under conditions in which one of the spouses could easily be removed from the household by mental or physical breakdown, or premature death. In years past more than today, job insecurity, occupational hazards, and poor living conditions meant that every wife might have to reckon with the incapacitation or removal of the breadwinner—even though male desertion was and is rare. Likewise, illness or death in childbirth might remove the woman before her time. The lack of closeness, however, makes it easier for the remaining parent to maintain the household, raise the children—usually with the help of members

6. See Chapter 5.

of the extended family—and to overcome the emotional loss of the spouse. For example, a West Ender I met had lost her husband, with whom she was said to have been exceptionally close, a few months earlier. With her children married, however, she began to think of herself as a single woman again, and participated in social activities with a number of unmarried women of whom she said— only half in jest—she would join in "man-catching" endeavors. At the same time, however, she was able to talk about events which she had shared with her husband as if he were still alive. She did not have to shut him out of her mind in order to overcome the pain of her loss.

Although the segregated conjugal pattern is clearly dominant among the West Enders, signs of its eventual disappearance are making themselves felt.[7] Between the first and second generation, the major change has been that of bringing the men into the house for their evening activities. While Italians have never been frequenters of neighborhood taverns, the immigrant generation did set up club houses for card playing and male sociability that kept some men away from the house after work. These have disappeared, however, and, as already noted, second-generation men now segregate themselves from the women inside the home, and spend only one or two evenings a week in activities "with the boys." The women also have begun to conceive of their husbands as helping them in the home, although they are not yet ready to insist or even to ask for their aid. The move to the suburbs is probably one indication of the ascendancy of the wife to greater equality, for in these areas, where the joint conjugal pattern is dominant, it is somewhat harder for the man to maintain the old pattern. West Enders occasionally mentioned couples in which the wife, shortly after marriage, had persuaded the husband to move out of the West End in order to "get him away from the boys." But this does not always work; some men, even after twenty years of living elsewhere, return to the West End for evening visits to male friends. One man I knew, who used to come back for male companionship, was kidded about being dominated by his wife, and this has driven him further away from his old peers.

7. These changes are discussed further in Chapter 10.

Child-Rearing

In the West End, children come because marriage and God bring them. This does not mean that West Enders believe children to be caused by God, but that the Catholic church opposes birth control, and that this is God's wish. There is some planning of conception, either through the use of the church-approved rhythm method, or, more rarely, through contraception. But while the sale of contraceptives is illegal in Massachusetts, this does not prevent their acquisition. West Enders, however, do reject their use—or at least talking about their use—on religious grounds. The major method of family planning seems to be ex post facto. Should the wife become pregnant after a couple has had what they deem to be enough children, she may attempt to abort herself, using traditional methods that she has learned from other women. If the attempt fails, as it probably does in many cases, the new child is accepted fatalistically—and usually happily—as yet another manifestation of the will of God. Even so, families are smaller among second-generation Italians than among their parents. The couple with six to eight children, which seems to have been prevalent among the first generation, now has become a rarity. A large family is still respected, however, because children themselves are still highly valued.

The fact that children are not planned affects the way in which parents relate to them, and the methods by which they bring them up. Indeed, American society today is characterized by three types of families: the *adult-centered*—prevalent in working-class groups—run by adults for adults, where the role of the children is to behave as much as possible like miniature adults; the *child-centered*—found among families who plan their children, notably in the lower middle class—in which parents subordinate adult pleasures to give the child what they think he needs or demands; and the *adult-directed*—an upper-middle-class pattern—in which parents also place lower priorities on their own needs, in order to guide the children toward a way of life the parents consider desirable.[8]

8. S. M. Miller and Frank Riessman have used similar terms—parent-centered and child-centered—to distinguish working-class families from middle-

In the lower middle class of the present generation, husband and wife are likely to have finished high school, perhaps even the same one. This shared background helps them to communicate with each other, and creates some common interests, although much spare time still is spent with peers of the same sex. The most easily shared interest is the children, and the parents communicate best with each other through joint child-rearing. As a result, this family is child-centered. Parents play with their children—which is rare in the working class—rear them with some degree of self-consciousness, and give up some of their adult pleasures for them. Family size is strongly influenced by educational aspirations. If the parents are satisfied with their own occupational and social status, and feel no great urgency to send their children to college, they may have as many children as possible. For each child adds to their shared enjoyment and to family unity—at least while the children are young. Sometimes, the child will dominate his parents unmercifully, although child-centered parents are not necessarily permissive in their child-rearing. Rather, they want the child to have a happier childhood than they experienced, and will give him what they believe is necessary for making it so. One of their child-centered acts is the move to the suburb, made not only for the child's benefit, but also to make their child-rearing easier for themselves, and to reduce some of the burdens of child-centeredness. They give the child freely over to the care of the school, and to organizations like the Scouts or Little League, because these are all child-centered institutions.

Among college-educated parents, education and educational aspirations shape family life. College education adds immeasurably to the number of common interests between husband and wife, including activities other than child-rearing. Consequently, these parents know what they want for their children much more clearly than does the child-centered family, and their relationship to the children is adult-directed. Child-rearing is based on a model of an

class ones in "The Working-Class Subculture: A New View," *Social Problems*, vol. 9 (1961), p. 92. For a different typology of family organization, using somewhat the same terms, see Bernard Farber, "Types of Family Organization: Child-Oriented, Home-Oriented, and Parent-Oriented," in Arnold Rose, ed., *Human Behavior and Social Processes*, Boston: Houghton Mifflin, 1962, pp. 285–306.

upper-middle-class adulthood characterized by individual achievement and social service for which parents want the child to aim. As a result, the child's wants are of less importance. Such parents devote much time and effort to assuring that the child receives the education which will help him to become a proper adult. For this purpose, they may limit the size of their families; they will choose their place of residence by the quality of the school system; they will ride herd on the school authorities to meet their standards; and, of course, they will exert considerable pressure on the children to do well in school.[9]

The West End family is an adult-centered one. Since children are not planned, but come naturally and regularly, they are not at the center of family life. Rather, they are raised in a household that is run to satisfy adult wishes first. As soon as they are weaned and toilet-trained, they are expected to behave themselves in ways pleasing to adults. When they are with adults, they must act as the adults want them to act: to play quietly in a corner, or to show themselves off to other adults to demonstrate the physical and psychological virtues of their parents. Parents talk to them in an adult tone as soon as possible, and, once they have passed the stage of babyhood, will cease to play with them. When girls reach the age of seven or eight, they start assisting the mother, and become miniature mothers. Boys are given more freedom to roam, and, in that sense, are treated just like their fathers.

But while children are expected to behave like adults at home, they are able to act their age when they are with their peers. Thus, once children have moved into their own peer group, they have considerable freedom to act as they wish, as long as they do not get into trouble. The children's world is their own, and only within it can they really behave like children. Parents are not expected to supervise, guide, or take part in it. In fact, parent-child relationships are segregated almost as much as male-female ones. The child will report on his peer group activities at home, but they are of relatively little interest to parents in an adult-centered family. If the child performs well at school or at play, parents will praise

9. For an example of what I call adult-directed child-rearing, see J. Seeley, R. Sim, and E. Loosley, *Crestwood Heights,* New York: Basic Books, 1956, especially Chaps. 7–9.

him for it. But they are unlikely to attend his performance in a school program or a baseball game in person. This is his life, not theirs.[10]

Schoolteachers and social workers who dealt with West End children often interpreted the family segregation patterns from a more child-centered perspective, and assumed that the parents had lost interest in their children or were ignoring them. But this is not the case. At home, they are still part of the family circle, and continue to play their assigned roles. In fact, West End children continue to attend family gatherings at ages at which middle-class children are usually excused from them. They also sit in on social gatherings from which middle-class children might be excluded altogether. But then West Enders do not make the same distinction between family and social gatherings, since they usually involve the same people.

There are parents among the West Enders who do ignore their children, and take no interest in them. Usually, these are people who for one reason or another are incapable of playing a parental role, and most West Enders consider them to be immoral, or pathological.

The departure of the children from home to peer group functions to support the adult-centered family. When the adults have complete authority over what goes on in the home, the children's need to behave like children must take place outside the view of adults. In the case of an acculturating ethnic group, the segregation of children and adults also reduces some of the conflict that would otherwise result from culture clashes between the children and the parents. At the same time, the children are able to bring home some of the dominant American culture patterns, and thus to act as an acculturating influence on the parents.

The children's movement into the peer group proceeds gradually, with the latter taking up more and more of their time as the

10. Covello reports that immigrant Italians criticized their children for participating in such childish activities as school sports, and tried to prevent their playing. They were expected to behave like grown adults by the time they reached the age of eight, and to have outgrown the need for play. Leonard Covello, "The Social Background of the Italo-American School Child," Unpublished Ph.D. Dissertation, New York University, 1944, p. 467. Changes in the conception of the child's role are discussed further in Chapter 10.

children become older. As already noted, boys are allowed more freedom than girls, but when girls reach their teens, they also move into peer groups outside the home, performing their household functions grudgingly. Although parents would like to keep the girls closer to home, they find it difficult to fight the peer group attractions that draw their daughters out of the household. By adolescence, then, children spend little time in the parental home.

Mothers do attempt to teach their departing children rules of proper behavior, namely, the rules of the adult-centered and routine-seeking home, and urge them to adopt these in peer group activities. During this time, however, the child is also learning what are called the rules of the street, that is, those of the peer group. Thus, for some years, parents fight the ascendancy of street rules over home rules, especially if the former appear in his behavior at home. When a boy reaches the age of ten to twelve, however, parents feel that he is now responsible for his own actions. If he gets into "trouble," through behavior bringing him to the attention of the police or the priest, the blame must be attached to the influence of bad companions. Having done their best by urging him to follow home-rules, parents hope that he will do so. Should he fail to do so, however, the consequences are ascribed fatalistically to his peer group and his own moral failings. But whereas parents are concerned about the results, they neither feel the same responsibility for the child that is found in the middle-class family, nor develop the same guilt feelings should he get into trouble.

Interestingly enough, the home-rules that are preached to the child differ little from those held by the middle class. Mothers are more likely to be routine-seeking than action-seeking, and their desire for stability creates values which are also found in the middle class. The extent to which these rules are enforced, however, varies between action-seeking and routine-seeking or mobile families. The former, for instance, seem to surrender earlier, with less resistance to the child's inevitable adoption of the rules of the street. Moreover, the child himself reacts differently to the enforcement of these ideals. The child of a routine-seeking family, discovering that there are home rules and street rules, soon learns therefore to act accordingly in both places. In an action-seeking family, however, the child learns that the rules which the parents preach and those which they themselves practice diverge sharply. Thus he is more likely to reject the preached rules, and behave according to the street rules both at home and on the street.

The predominant method of child-rearing is punishment and reward. Children are punished when they misbehave, and rewarded —though not always—when they are obedient. Punishment is both physical and verbal: mothers slap and beat their children, tell them not to do this or do that, and threaten to tell the fathers when they come home. Indeed, to a middle-class observer, the parents' treatment often seems extremely strict and sometimes brutal. There is a continuous barrage of prohibitions and threats, intertwined with words and deeds of reward and affection. But the torrents of threat and cajolery neither impinge on the feelings of parental affection, nor are meant as signs of rejection. As one mother explained to her child, "We hit you because we love you." People believe that discipline is needed constantly to keep the child in line with and respectful of adult rules, and that without it he would run amok.

West Enders raise their children impulsively, with relatively little of the self-conscious, purposive child-rearing that is found in the middle class. Parents tell their child how they want him to act without much concern about how he receives their message. They do not weigh their words or methods in order to decide whether these are consistent with earlier ones, or with the way they want to raise the child. Since the child is viewed as a little adult, parents do not think much about how he reacts qua child. Nor do they worry whether too strict a punishment or too permissive rewarding will have subsequent detrimental consequences. Even while they are conscious of the possibility of children being "spoiled," especially by relatives, they mean by this only that the child may get more attention than is compatible with an adult-centered family system.

Impulsive child-rearing is possible because West Enders are not concerned with *developing* their children, that is, with raising them in accordance with a predetermined goal or target which they are expected to achieve. Unlike adult-directed or even child-centered families, West Enders have no clear image of the future social status, occupational level, or life-style that they want their children to reach. And even when they do, they do not know how to build it into the child-rearing process.

West Enders want for their children what they want for themselves—a secure existence as persons who are both accepted and somewhat envied members of their family circle and peer group. They hope that their children will seek a better education and obtain a better job than they, but the children are not pushed hard toward this goal. If a child does not achieve the parental wishes, he is pressed no further. Indeed, the parents' greatest fear is that the child will become a "bum." The worry about downward mobility is stronger than any desire for upward mobility. Consequently, the major hope is that in education, occupation, and general status, the child will not fall below that of his peers.

The impact of these child-rearing patterns on the child himself is less confusing than one might imagine. As the child learns largely by imitation, parents often try to behave as models—in censoring their own profanity, for example. But as they cannot long keep up such behavior, the child soon learns what is considered normal. He accepts the unending mixture of physical or verbal reward and punishment in the same way. Public reactions, of course, are no index to possible deeper impact, but judging by what is visible to the observer, the child is guided by the torrent of words to avoid behavior that results in punishment. He pays less attention to the rest of what is said. He reacts similarly to the verbally stated norms which he is asked to follow, but which he sees are being violated by his parents and the world around him. The child, thus becoming aware of the inconsistencies between word and deed, soon learns that what people say is less significant than what they do. Although he neither rejects the words, nor the norms they state, he quickly learns to dichotomize between what is and what ought to be.

These conclusions not only color his later life, but many of them stand him in good stead. The child learns the morality imbedded in the stated rules, but seems to internalize little of it. Instead, he accepts it as an ideal guide by which to judge the reality he faces, and to measure the deviation between the two. This allows him to justify his own failure to act in terms of the ideal, and to develop a protective cynicism, especially toward the stated norms of the outside world. In turn, this skepticism protects him from the deprivations and disappointments he encounters as a member of a low-income population. But it also blinds him to people's good intentions. When such intentions might result in desirable innovations, his failure to respond to them other than cynically often deprives him of the benefits offered by the outside world.[11]

The child's pragmatic outlook impresses him with the need to obey authority that can implement power and to ignore that which cannot. The dichotomy between word and deed allows him to develop a posture of respect for authority and the cunning to subvert it for his own aims. At first, he uses this to negotiate between the conflicting rules of street and home. Later, it will allow him to develop strategy to maneuver through the intricate mixture of words and deeds in the peer group. Words, he learns, are meant to impress people, but deeds and only deeds count.[12]

The Mother's Role in Child-Rearing

As noted previously, child-rearing is the mother's function; the father provides mainly the formal discipline. The father is also a behavior model for the male child, and, as in all cultures, the boys learn male behavior by watching him and other males in the family circle. The mother also refers to the father as a model of masculinity, and identifies him with male authority as well. More important, she frequently reminds the boy that he is male, and lets him know when his behavior deviates from what she considers to be properly masculine. In this, she is supported by other male and female members of the family circle. Mothers and aunts will point out instances of the slightest "girlish" or "sissy" behavior even in the men that the boy sees. In one family, for example, the reluctance of one of the men to watch the fights on television, and his

11. This creates problems in community participation and in relationships with the outside world generally. See Chapters 5 and 7.

12. Thus, words are used as means to an end, rather than as conceptual tools. This may explain why the Italian-American community has produced so few analytically inclined intellectuals, but a larger number of critical and moralizing polemicists. For they also have come out of working-class parental backgrounds similar to those in the West End.

interest in dramatic programs was interpreted as a deficiency in maleness, and pointed out as such to the boys in the family. Mothers also become as much concerned as fathers when their boys are called sissies by their peers. Sometimes, boys may be punished with taunting signs of femaleness. For example, I was told that when students in the West End parochial school forgot to wear ties, the nuns punished them by making them wear bows in their hair.

A number of observers of working-class life have pointed out that the mother's dominance in child-rearing and the lack of a consistently present male figure in the household can result in the boys' concern about their maleness and a tendency toward latent or overt homosexuality.[13] Although West End adolescents exhibit similar behavior, it cannot be attributed to the absence of the father from the home.

Actually, what matters is not the husband's physical presence but his family role, and how this is interpreted by the mother. In the Negro population described by Walter Miller, long-term male employment instability, coupled with the availability of stable employment for Negro women and the long history of matriarchy in Negro society, have practically pre-empted the male's family role. Thus, he is often a weak or absent father, for he may desert the family when he is unemployed, or he may be asked to leave by the woman. Under such conditions, the mother becomes the dominant member of the family, and has little respect for the man —or men—around her.[14] The children not only see evidence of male weakness, but are also exposed to the mother's never-ending complaints of male failure.

Among the West Enders, however, the man is not usually weak. Italian peasant society was always patriarchal, and, although there are many families in which the woman is actually stronger than the man, the nominal power is still acknowledged to belong to him. Yet, while the men have suffered from layoffs and unemployment in periods of national or local depression, there has been no history of continuous unemployment. When full-time jobs have been

13. See, for example, Walter B. Miller, "Lower Class Culture as a Generating Milieu of Gang Delinquency," *Journal of Social Issues*, vol. 14, No. 3 (1958), pp. 5–19, at p. 9.

14. *Ibid.* This family type is discussed more fully in Chapter 11.

scarce, West Enders seem to have found some part-time employment, often with relatives who were better situated than they. Even in times of unemployment, however, Italian men have been less likely to abdicate from the household, either through desertion or breakdown. As a result of all these conditions, women have not needed to turn against their husbands, or men in general, as has been the case in the Negro population. Moreover, as I noted earlier, the women themselves are active in supporting by word and deed the authority of the father, and in urging the child to act in ways defined as male by Italian culture.

Many Italian men, of course, do evince the kind of vanity regarding their physical and sexual powers, and the concern with their physical appearance and dress that is usually identified with latent homosexuality. But whether or not this display of male vanity is always an index of homosexuality—as is often the case in middle-class culture, where such displays are out of the ordinary—cannot be answered conclusively by the data collected in the West End. It should be noted, however, that in a low-status, uneducated population whose life proceeds largely within a relatively cohesive primary group, individualistic behavior by men and women alike is normally expressed in personal and verbal display.[15] This, in fact, is the main way of expressing individualism. Consequently, observers from a culture that provides a variety of opportunities for individualistic behavior may thus be culture-bound in their unilateral identification of display with latent homosexuality.

Even so, instances of latent as well as overt homosexuality can be found. Indeed, among a small group of action-seeking young men whom I observed sporadically, joking and semi-serious accusations of homosexual desires or escapades were often expressed. Their conversation dealt even more frequently, however, with heterosexual adventures. While these men had little respect for women, they spoke in only the most deferential tones about their mothers. Perhaps they had experienced the maternal overprotection that has been suggested as a cause of latent homosexuality.

Maternal overprotection seems to be found in families in which the father is unreasonably authoritarian toward his children. Adult

15. See Chapter 4.

West Enders, who sometimes described their fathers as having been excessively strict, explained that, since they were immigrants, they could not understand or tolerate the children's American ways. Under these conditions, mothers protected their children as much as they possibly could from severe paternal punishment, by lying to their husbands about the children's activities and hiding their misdeeds. This may well have led to the maternal veneration and paternal hatred expressed by some West End men, especially among the action-seekers.

From Adolescence to Adulthood

As the child grows into an adolescent, he is home less and less often, until parents begin to think of him—and, to a lesser extent, her—as only a boarder in the home.[16] Relationships with parents become more tenuous, and often result in conflict. For while the child has some difficulty in conforming to the rules of the adult-centered household, the adolescent finds it much harder. The source of conflict may be found in the changes in family structure and family concept that accompany acculturation. In Italy, and among the immigrants, there was no such concept as adolescence. Childhood, as noted earlier, was a brief period, which ended about or even before the age of ten. From then on, the young person occupied an adult economic role, but remained in the household, contributed to the family income, and obeyed the patriarchal regulations until he married. In America, where compulsory school attendance lengthened the period of functional childhood, the immigrants had some difficulty in accepting the American concept of a longer childhood, and often felt that their children should leave school to go to work.[17]

Second-generation parents have accepted the need for education through high school, but they—like their own parents—have continued to maintain the traditional demand that within the house-

16. Most of the analysis that follows concerns the adolescent boy; adolescent girls are harder to talk to in a society like the West End, and their activities are less visible to the male observer.

17. The cultural conflict over the school is described fully—and skillfully—by Covello, op. cit. See also Chapter 10.

hold the child must obey parental rules.[18] The adolescent, however, does not accept the traditional pattern. He feels that he too has reached adulthood, and that the household should respect his own style of life.

The West End adolescent, as noted before, is alive only with his peer group; outside it, he exists as a quiet and almost passive individual. With adults, he is likely to be lethargic and sullen, seeking always to minimize contact with them. In the peer group, however, the style of life is one of action-seeking. Much of the conflict between adolescent and adult therefore is that between the action-seeking and the routine-seeking patterns.

In the adolescent peer group, manifesting the episodic search for action in an almost pure, ideal-typical form, life alternates between killing time and searching for action. Some of it takes place right within the group, in a dialectic of conformity and competitiveness through which the individual realizes himself.[19] Most satisfying, however, is the search for action by the group as a whole. In this activity the adolescent achieves a kind of personal autonomy that he gets nowhere else. "Action" generates a state of quasi-hypnotic excitement which enables the individual to feel that he is in control, both of his own drives and of the environment. Also, it allows him to forget that he is living in a routine-seeking world, where "they," that is, the routine-seeking adults, make and enforce most of the rules. As previously noted, this state may be achieved through a card game, an athletic contest, a fight, a sexual adventure, or through an attack on the adult world. Whereas most of these attacks are in the nature of petty mischief—taunting adults, stealing fruit from a push cart, writing angry exclamations on public walls, or breaking windows in an empty building—some are more serious, and are defined by the adult world as delinquency. There was some disagreement about the amount of delinquency in the West End; city officials claimed that it was high, while West Enders and the local police insisted it was low. I encountered little evidence of delinquency while I lived in the West End.

Many explanations have been offered as to the causes of ado-

18. Attitudes toward education are discussed in Chapter 6.
19. This is discussed in greater detail in the next chapter.

lescent delinquency. Bloch has argued that it results from the tensions of the transitional adolescent stage; Walter Miller, that it is simply an expression of lower-class cultural values such as toughness, the search for excitement, and maleness; and Matza and Sykes, that it implements leisure values pursued also by the middle class —which the latter is unwilling to admit or recognize.[20] Cohen, and Cloward and Ohlin have stressed the gap between aspirations and reality.[21] Cohen argues that delinquency is an overcompensation against middle-class goals that the lower-class child cannot implement because of social and economic deprivation. Cloward and Ohlin propose a similar hypothesis but describe the goals not as middle class but as "conventional." Finally, Paul Goodman explains delinquency as protest against the unwillingness of adults to give teenagers a viable function in the society.[22]

The behavior of West End adolescents would suggest that there is some truth in all of these hypotheses. The strains between teenagers and adults, noticeable in relationships with adults, were most often expressed by sullen withdrawal. As already indicated, school officials in the West End pointed out that in school their charges were unexpectedly quiet and well-behaved. Outside the school, however, the teenagers expressed the kinds of cultural values that Miller has identified. Some of their doings that differ little from the hell-raising activities of middle-class groups—notably school fraternities—were more noticeable to the adult world because West Enders, like other working- and lower-class groups, could not carry them on behind the closed doors of fraternity houses. Most of the time, they had to meet on street corners, in tenement hallways, settlement houses, or in and around the small soda-

20. Herbert Bloch and Arthur Neiderhoffer, *The Gang*, New York: Philosophical Library, 1958. Walter B. Miller, "Lower Class Culture as a Generating Milieu of Gang Delinquency," *op. cit.;* David Matza and Gresham Sykes, "Juvenile Delinquency and Subterranean Values," *American Sociological Review,* vol. 26 (1961), pp. 712–719.

21. Albert Cohen, *Delinquent Boys: The Culture of the Gang,* New York: The Free Press of Glencoe, 1955; Richard A. Cloward and Lloyd E. Ohlin, *Delinquency and Opportunity,* New York: The Free Press of Glencoe, 1960. These hypotheses are in turn based on Durkheim's and Merton's work on anomie.

22. Paul Goodman, *Growing Up Absurd,* New York: Random House, 1960.

shops and groceries that dot areas like the West End. After vacancies began to increase in the area, some of the groups set up "cellar clubs"—clubrooms located in a basement, an empty store, or apartment that could be rented cheaply. The clubroom, obtained if the group had money to pay the rent, was vacated when the money ran out, at which time the group returned to the corner. Within the cellar clubs the activities were not too different from those of a fraternity house: card-playing, stag conversation, and informal weekend dances, with beer, whiskey, and profanity flowing freely.[23] After hours, individuals might return for sex play. While the police did keep an eye on the clubs, they intervened only if the neighbors complained, or in cases of extreme drunkenness and violence. When the groups had no clubrooms, they frequented the settlement house on "club nights," but restrained themselves in activities and language to conform more to the routine-seeking culture.[24]

Of course, all adolescents, whether they be middle class or working class, are at times attracted to mischief and vandalism, although their desires are not always expressed in action. Generally speaking, such activities are directed against the institutions that the mischief-makers feel to be most oppressive at the moment, especially those from another social stratum. Thus, whereas middle-class adolescents are more often aggressive toward the police, working-class ones leave the police alone, and direct their energies toward the school or the recreation center. In the West End, for example, there was considerable breakage of windows, but mostly in the school and only rarely in stores or in the hospital. The adolescents did not like the police, but they were not aggressive toward them. Conversely, the police were not as hostile toward them as they are in some middle-class communities I have observed, where the resident has higher status than the policeman. The working-class teenager probably will do more damage than the middle-class mischief-maker. Moreover, he carries it out with a toughness that makes it more visible and more threatening to the larger society, and he does seek out middle-class institutions as a target.

23. The girls, having no cellar clubs, had to meet on the corner or in tenement hallways.

24. Settlement house activities are described in Chapter 7.

There is no doubt that the West End teenager's withdrawal in school and his protest against the routine and aims of the school are based on a gap between aspirations and reality. Indeed, some of the after-school destructiveness is a more active form of expressing this gap. My impressions of West End teenagers would suggest that their protest is directed less against middle-class values than against what Cloward and Ohlin call conventional ones—what I identify as the values of the routine-seeking society—some of which overlap working and middle class. But there is no indication that West Enders are seeking either the goals usually sought by middle-class children, or, for that matter, the manly, manual, and craftsman-like forms of work proposed by Goodman. In early, or even late, adolescence, they have not thought seriously about their future as adults, and, since the peer group does not encourage career aspirations, they are not yet anticipating the trauma of low-status employment and the dead-end job. Rather, they want the material appurtenances of modern life—especially cars and spending money—and they want to be freed from the routine-seeking society which "bugs"—or imposes on—them. Yet, at home, school, church, and in public recreation facilities, action-seeking is strictly forbidden to them. Their protest, then, is directed diffusely against the parental and adult demand for conformity to routine as defined by adults.

Why should teenagers be addicted to the action-seeking life style? The main reason, perhaps, lies in their inability to accept routines that adults propose to them, and their lack of any self-defined routine as a substitute. For this reason the most important adult routine, that of school, is anathema to many. Emerging from homes in which learning has not been encouraged, they have been brought up in such a way that their attention span is very short. This makes studying and learning difficult. Moreover, the school—a middle-class institution—seeks to train them for a way of life that in many ways is diametrically opposed to the one which they have so far experienced. Also, they are being taught by women, which, especially after the onset of puberty, can be an insult—if not a threat—to maleness. But, if school has no meaning, there are no other functions which society permits them to perform. Moreover, as the peer groups in which they gather have no substantive function, they must therefore find things to do in a world hedged by adult restrictions. As a result, adolescent groups represent a form of the leisure class, sharing some of the ways of the departed aristocratic leisure class but lacking the power, status, and resources that would legitimize such behavior.[25] This is not to imply that adolescents would necessarily welcome the opportunity to pursue routines developed on their own. Action-seeking episodes are, after all, a source of fun and excitement, as well as an opportunity for exploring one's identity as an individual and group member.

Yet no explanation of adolescent behavior or delinquency can ignore the fact that these patterns do cease abruptly with marriage. Although it was difficult to determine numbers, few West Enders graduated from adolescence to a career in crime. Moreover, many West Enders did regret their lack of interest in school, and their failure to graduate from high school, as soon as their occupational function in society had been established. Consequently, the transitional nature of this behavior and the close relationship it bears to the adolescents' lack of viable function in the society cannot be ignored in theories of adolescent conduct.

Although the teenage way of life seems to coincide more often with the action-seeking than with the routine-seeking values, there is, of course, considerable variety among teenage groups. Some are embroiled in continuous conflict with the adult world, and it is they who become most visible to the middle-class eye. More participate—at least part of the time—in school and in settlement house activities, and thus are on the way to becoming routine-seekers. A rare few become middle class in the way in which the school and settlement house want all of them to be. Thus, the teenager may chose from a variety of groupings although the choice does become numerically more limited toward the middle-class end of the scale.

While the teenage groups were sexually segregated, girls' groups in the West End met near the corners where the boys hung out. Occasionally, the two groups joined forces for an evening outing. Likewise, girls were invited to weekend dances at the male cellar

25. Edgar Friedenberg, *The Vanishing Adolescent,* New York: Beacon Press, 1959, especially Chap. 1.

clubs—usually those girls who were attached to the boys' group in a more or less steady, though informal, arrangement.. These were group get-togethers. But the hold of the group is so strong that only rarely did the boy have an individual date. West Enders noted that boys rarely left the group for a girl, and that a male group seldom broke up because of conflicts over a girl. They did indicate, however, that female peer groups were much less stable, and often collapsed if two girls became interested in the same boy. If a boy should leave the group for a girl, he is likely to be accused of disloyalty, and must either give her up or leave the group. I am distinguishing here between a date with a "good girl" who may be a potential wife, and the continuous search for sexual relations with compliant "bad girls." It is dates with the former that result in accusations of desertion. Dating the latter, however, is a much sought after experience. It is a form of action that is subsequently described to the group—with proper embellishment— and provides a source of conversation many times over.

Eventually, as group members reach the end of their teens, boys will leave to court, and at that time many of the peer groups break up. Subsequently, new ones form among those boys who are not yet ready to get married, and those who may never marry.

Marriage is a crucial turning point in the life of the West End boy. It is then that he must decide whether he is going to give up the boys on the corner for the new peer group of related siblings and in-laws—a decision related to and reflected in his choice of a mate. If he marries one of the girls who has hung nearby on the same corner, he may interrupt the life on the corner only during the early months of marriage. Should he fall in love with a girl who has spent her adolescence closer to the family, he is likely to move into a family circle on marriage. He may even be attracted to a mobile girl who wishes to leave the peer group society entirely. But should he fail to agree with her, his married life is likely to be marked by ambivalence and marital tension. This is one instance where the lack of communication between men and women is a real drawback in married life. In most cases, the West Ender leaves the corner on marriage, and from then on participates in a not altogether different peer group existence in the living room and kitchen of his own home.

That the man may or may not make the move from the corner to the apartment is one index of his future choice between routine and action, and is evaluated as such by West Enders. Indeed, routine-seeking people feel that adult men who return to the corner "never grow up," and remain adolescents. There is considerable truth in this observation, for the boys who stay with the corner and the episodic life are continuing adolescent, or what Bennett Berger calls youthful, patterns.[26] They are apt to participate only sporadically in married life and continue as long as possible to maintain the attitudes and values they held during adolescence.

Needless to say, life on the corner is often routine, and the meetings of the family circle are interrupted by weekly nights out in male company. Moreover, even in the family circle the search for action is not given up, but frozen in time. Much of the talk is given over to recalling exciting episodes of adolescence and early adulthood that are relieved vicariously, over and over again.[27]

This emphasis on the past is not only nostalgia, but an index to the real importance that childhood and adolescence have in the life of the West Ender. As these were the times when he was most alive, when things happened, and when he could make things happen, his adventures are remembered fondly as pranks, and are retold frequently, if only to show that the person has not really given in to the requirements of responsibility or the routine. The stories reinforce the belief that one can fight back, outsmart, and even defeat the outside world. Adolescence is also a period of achievement, especially for the talented boy. Thus, within the small world of the neighborhood, he may have been the best boxer, baseball player, or the most successful gambler, and as an adult he will bring out trophies, pictures, and other evidence of his past accomplishments.

26. Bennett M. Berger, "On the Youthfulness of Youth Cultures," Urbana: University of Illinois, 1961, mimeographed. He makes a distinction between adolescence and youthfulness, noting that young people who conform to the routines set by the adult world are hardly youthful, and that adults may continue the behavior patterns falsely identified as limited to adolescence.

27. The Italian ability to recollect past events vividly has also been noted by G. Lolli, E. Serriani, G. Golder, and P. Luzzatto-Fegiz, *Alcohol in Italian Culture*, New York: The Free Press of Glencoe and Yale Center of Alcohol Studies, 1958, p. 65.

Childhood and adolescence are also the time when enduring friendships are made.[28] Some of these, which last for the rest of the person's life, are maintained alongside the friendships that exist between brothers and other relatives. I was constantly amazed at the continued contact which adults maintained with the people whom they had known as children or adolescents. Not all of these become friends, but they do remain acquaintances for life, and, when they meet, childhood events are recalled with pleasure. Most of the adult friendships outside the family circle are established in childhood or adolescence, and probably outnumber those formed during adulthood. Of course, this is encouraged by the fact that West Enders are not mobile, and that most of them will occupy a similar social—as well as physical—space throughout their lifetime. Consequently, they are likely to have enough in common to remain friends. The converse was brought out by one West Ender who told me that he had had a number of close Jewish friends in childhood, but that he had lost them in adolescence, as they went off to a college preparatory high school and he did not. Because of the lack of mobility among most of the Italian West Enders, ties between childhood friends remained strong even when one moved out of the West End, especially since the move usually was to a neighborhood easily accessible to, and in continuing contact with, the West End.

Although the adults limited their reverence for adolescent behavior mainly to the nostalgic memories, they did occasionally indulge in activities that resembled adolescent ones in deed and spirit. For example, they gambled behind the priest's back in church organization meetings, went on sprees that wreaked havoc with the family budget, or enjoyed a stag night out on the town. And while they did not recognize them as regressions into adolescence, these adventures were talked about in such a way as to suggest that they do bear some similarity to adolescent behavior.[29]

Middle-class observers of working-class life around the turn of the century often described their adult subjects as child-like or

28. For a similar observation among the North End "corner boys," see William F. Whyte, Jr., *Street Corner Society,* Chicago: University of Chicago Press, 1943; 2nd ed., 1955, p. 255.

29. This behavior is not restricted to the West Ender, but can, at some time, be found among all classes.

happy like children. Some of these interpretations reflected the cultural difference and the social distance between a reserved Yankee middle class and a less inhibited working class. They also were meant—or at least reported—in a somewhat patronizing fashion. But they seem to have had some truth to them, in that they did touch on the strong identification with childhood and adolescence that is found much less among the middle class. Obviously, West End adults are neither childlike, nor are they children, but as they do place such great emphasis on the early years, an outsider might possibly arrive at this conclusion.

Observers of working-class life, here and in the underdeveloped areas, have called attention to the fact that for girls, the high point of life is adolescence—especially the courting period—and that they age quickly after marriage and childbearing, becoming old and passive much earlier than do middle-class women. Although men go through much of the same rapid cycle, their greater freedom of movement all through life does reduce this difference between adolescence and adulthood. They also age somewhat more slowly unless their work is so strenuous as to drain them physically.

Rapid aging was more prevalent among the immigrants than it is among the West Enders, since life is no longer a constant struggle for survival for the men, or an endless succession of childbirths for the women. It is still true, however, that for the West Ender—and perhaps for all working-class people—childhood and adolescence are the most gratifying phases of life, and that adulthood only rarely attains the same level. Conversely, the middle-class adult— and especially the upper-middle-class one—is likely to view the periods prior to adulthood as less happy times, with real fulfillment found only as family and the career are firmly established. I am not implying that adult life is a period of dull decline for the West Ender, as the next chapter will testify. The absence of interest in a career, the lack of identification with work, the fatalism about deprivation inflicted by the outside world, and the vitality of peer group life—all combine to minimize feelings of resignation and decline, perhaps more so among Italians than among other working-class groups.

CHAPTER 4 The Peer Group and the Individual

Peer Group Life

The basis of adult West End life is peer group sociability. By sociability I do not mean the entertaining and party-giving of the middle class. Nor do I mean the informal conversational activity that the middle class ranks well below occupational, familial, and self-improvement activities in importance. For the West Ender, sociability is a routinized gathering of a relatively unchanging peer group of family members and friends that takes place several times a week. One could almost say that the meetings of the group are at the vital center of West End life, that they are the end for which other everyday activities are a means.

Membership in the group is based primarily on kinship. As already noted, brothers, sisters, and cousins of the husband and wife —and their spouses—are at the core. The group also includes godparents and friends who may come less regularly. Godparents are friends who, because of their closeness, are given quasi-familial status. Godparentage is awarded to best men at a wedding or to the children of one's godparents, as well as to true godparents; in short, to people who become "friends of the family" in middle-class American kinship terminology.[1] It is also used as a way of cementing rela-

1. This is one of the few instances in which West Enders still use an Italian term to describe a phenomenon. They refer to their "compares" (male)

tionships. For example, one West Ender asked his neighbors, with whom he had long been friendly, to be godparents for his newborn child, in order to maintain contact between the two families after redevelopment. In adult life, West Enders have little contact with their actual godparents, since the older generation is not part of the peer group social life.

Included among other unrelated individuals are friends of long duration, as well as more recent friends. Though the latter may be newcomers to the group, they are likely to have been known to the group before, because, as already noted, everyone knows of everyone else. Consequently, nearly everyone is a potential friend who can join a peer group at any time. This happens most often after people have extended help to each other, met at ceremonial occasions, or have had prolonged contact, for example, as hospital patients. Recruitment is not deliberate, however, and self-conscious "mixing with people" is explicitly rejected. A mobile woman who had left the West End suggested to West End relatives one night that women should get out of the house and mix with people. But her relatives, discussing it afterwards, thought that this belief was a result of her being childless, for which they pitied her. Similarly, when a relocation official spoke to a West Ender about the new social experiences he would encounter in a new neighborhood, the West Ender replied angrily: "I don't want to meet any new people. I get out quite a bit all over Boston to see my brothers and sisters, and, when they come over, we have others in, like neighbors. You can't do that in the suburbs."

Neighbors also may be included in the group if they are friends, but they are not eligible merely because they live next door. As neighbors, they may have frequent physical contact that might facilitate the social contact prerequisite to friendship.[2] But it also might reveal differences in background and behavior that could

---

and "commares" (female), perhaps because the term godparent is not quite the same, and because there is no other English word that quite describes the relationship.

2. In most of the tenements, neighbors were residents of adjacent buildings who faced on a common fire-escape or airshaft. In the building in which I lived, kitchens faced each other, thus giving housewives frequent opportunity for visual contact. There was less contact with people on other floors of one's own building, since they were seen only fleetingly when using the stairs.

preclude friendship.[3] In the West End, neighbors quite often were also socially close because of the previously noted tendency of landlords to rent apartments to relatives or friends.

Potential peer group members are many, but their number is effectively reduced by the requirement that people must be relatively compatible in terms of background, interests, and attitudes: what they have to say and what they want to listen to must be of common interest. They also must hold somewhat similar attitudes toward marriage, child-rearing, religion, politics, taste, and other important issues, because West Enders cannot cope effectively with disagreement.[4] As a result, the group is limited to people of similar ethnic background and class. There is no formal exclusion, but since the conversation may be unkind to other ethnic groups, they do run the risk of being antagonized. Even within the Italian group itself, those who are more or less acculturated than the rest stay away. The former are uncomfortable because they are "too American"; the latter, because they become embarrassed when the group makes fun of old-fashioned people. A woman with old-fashioned ideas is more acceptable than a man, since she is likely to keep quiet and not upset the group. Also, being old-fashioned is more of a virtue for women. The people who are mobile are kidded so much about their wealth that they come only rarely. Very mobile women are likely to be antagonized by references to wild or unwomanly ways, or by scornful stories about "society ladies." Those of lower status than the rest of the group are not rejected unless they are "bums," but remain away because they may be weighed down by problems that do not concern the others.

Single individuals often are part of the group even if they do not meet the standards of compatibility. Included because they are alone—a dread scourge in Italian culture—they nevertheless remain on the fringes of the group's conversational and other ac-

3. The role of physical propinquity and background homogeneity in friendship is discussed further in Herbert J. Gans, "Planning and Social Life," *Journal of the American Institute of Planners*, vol. 27 (1961), pp. 134–140, at pp. 134–136.

4. The reasons are discussed on pp. 79, 94.

tivities even though they are likely to be present more often than people with familial responsibilities. Our own participation in one of the peer groups was due in part to the fact that we were new to Boston and, having few friends in the city, were thought to be isolated somewhat like the single people in the group. The initial invitation was extended, however, because we were neighbors, and because the wives, who had met across the fire-escape, took a liking to each other.

The peer group meets regularly in the kitchens and living rooms of innumerable West End apartments. There are no formal invitations or advance notifications; people arrive regularly one or more evenings a week. Generally speaking, the same people come the same days of the week. Certain evenings are thus reserved for being with the peer group, and the gathering is called off only for unusual events.

While a few people may come for dinner, the gatherings usually begin shortly afterwards and others may drop in all through the evening. The talk goes on for hours—often past midnight—even though the men have to be at work early the next morning. As noted earlier, the sexes remain separate most of the evening, and, even when they gather around the kitchen table for coffee and cake, the men often sit at one end, the women at the other. Some people bring their children, especially if they do not have older ones who can stay home with the younger ones. The children sit and listen until they become sleepy, and then are sent off to the bedrooms until their parents leave.

The peer group conversation covers a relatively small number of topics: accounts of the participants' activities since the last gathering; news of people they all know; plans for special events such as weddings, showers, and other celebrations; current topics of interest; stories and anecdotes; and memories of younger days or highlights of the more recent past. Quite often, a current happening will set off talk about the past, and people contribute stories of parallel events that took place earlier. From there, it is easy to drift into talk about the good old days. The conversation also may turn to reports—and judgments—of deviant behavior. In addition, advice is exchanged, but there is little systematic attempt at problem-solving. Usually, people discuss problems encountered by others, especially those who are not present at the gathering. Problems common to the group as a whole also enter the conversation. I was always surprised, however, that what I thought to be the most pressing problem—redevelopment and relocation—received relatively little attention. Most West Enders felt that as there was not much they could do about this, there was little sense in discussing an unpleasant reality. This principle also covers the discussion of problems in general. The men talk about current happenings at work, in sports, in the area, and occasionally in the city and the country. But there is little concern with politics, except when events have occurred that illustrate once again the West Enders' belief that politics is corrupt. The women talk about housekeeping, child-rearing, and other subjects relevant to their occupational role.

Much of the conversation is devoted to the exchange of reportage—and gossip—about people known to the group. As noted earlier, every peer group is tied, through kinship, friendship, or other connections to many other groups and individuals in a giant network that extends far beyond the West End. Thus, someone may have a report about someone else, even if he does not know the individual personally. For example, one evening, the conversation concerned a woman who had recently had a child, many years after having the last one. One of the women at the table reported that she had heard about the blessed event, though she had never met the mother, and did not know that she was the hostess' neighbor. As it turned out, she was friendly with a relative of the new mother, and had heard about it from her. That she did not know the mother personally was irrelevant; knowing her sister and some other relatives was quite sufficient.

The exchange of news has a number of functions. It keeps people up-to-date on what is going on among present and potential peer group members, and defines or redefines the place of the reporter and his audience in this large group. It also provides for social control, since deviant behavior is reported and evaluated quite fully. And, at the same time, it considers new ideas that might be useful to the group. Moreover, it supplies information about services and "experts" in a culture that suspects or rejects the professional expert provided by the outside world.[5] Thus the constant flow of news holds the network of peer groups together and makes it easier for West Enders to do without formal community organizations—either their own or those of the outside world. Finally, the reportage and gossip provide entertainment and drama about one's own group of the kind that is available about other groups in soap operas and similar mass media fiction.

As the hours pass, the talk shifts back and forth. And while there are people who dominate the conversation, and others who contribute little, there is generally an opportunity during the long evening for everyone to talk, either to tell a story or to deliver an opinion. Conversation is interspersed with discussion and argument, although the arguments are generally over matters of current or past history rather than over opinions. Should there be radical disagreement about a substantive topic, say, race relations or birth control, the conversation comes to a sudden halt and the subject is changed. For reasons that will become apparent, West Enders are not attuned to the give-and-take of discussion, and, since the expression of highly diverse opinions on important issues could split the group, this is thus avoided by changing the subject.

The conversation therefore is cued to topics that will keep exchange and individual contributions flowing; those that do not lend themselves to this social function are quickly dropped. Midway in the study, for example, we spent two weeks in Puerto Rico, and, after our return, were invited to tell about the trip. As it turned out, however, there was little interest either in the trip, or in descriptions of Puerto Rico; West Enders were more curious as to how it felt being back in the group. The story that my wallet had been stolen on the last day of the trip did arouse great interest, and, for more than an hour afterwards, people talked about thefts which they had experienced or heard. This topic in turn led to some anecdotes about the honest poor, who gave rewards for the return of lost or stolen items, and the greedy rich, who did not.

On ceremonial and holiday occasions, the gathering of the group is more formal. On birthdays, saints' days, other religious

5. See Chapters 6 and 7.

holidays, and of course at weddings, christenings, and first communion celebrations, everyone in the entire family circle tries to be present, including members of the parental generation. At such times, the food is more lavish and gifts may be given. During the year, the group also may go out to restaurants or night clubs to watch a popular performer.

Peer group life also extends beyond the family circle, and some West Enders participate in informal cliques and in clubs made up of unrelated people. For example, unmarried men may spend their evenings at clubs in which they play cards during the week, and hold dances and parties on the weekends; married men may go out once or twice a week for a night with the boys. In addition, many women belong to informal—and nameless—clubs that meet weekly, biweekly, or monthly at each other's houses on a rotating basis, and hold dinners at downtown restaurants on special occasions. Some of the clubs, many of whose members have known each other since adolescence, were formed after the women became wives, and have continued to meet regularly for more than a decade since then. In number, and in the amount of time devoted to them, however, these groups are much less important than the family circle. The remainder of the chapter refers mainly to the latter.

The Individual and the Group

Although peer group sociability is prevalent in middle-class society, it is not as important as it is in the West End. I have already indicated the central role of the peer group throughout the life cycle, and I have hinted repeatedly at the emotional as well as social importance of the group in everyday life. One fact, then, should be obvious: West Enders live within the group; they do not like to be alone. Thus, what has been noted earlier about teenagers—that they are quiet and passive by themselves and burst into activity only with their peers—is true almost as much among adults. Indeed, for most West Enders, people who have been trained from childhood to function solely within the group, being alone brings discomfort and ultimately fear. The discomfort was expressed by housewives who got their housework done quickly so as to be able "to visit." It was expressed more strongly by people who feared that the destruction of the West End would tear them away from their group and leave them isolated. It was expressed perhaps most vividly by a corner boy who explained to his friends that a prison sentence was bad "because it separates you from friends and family."

Yet the peer group is important not only because it provides this much desired companionship and the feeling of belongingness, but because it also allows its members to be individuals, and to express that individuality. In fact, it is only within the peer group that people can do so. In the middle class, people can exist as individuals outside a group, and enter a group to accomplish personal as well as shared ends. Among the West Enders, however, people grow up within a group and use it to be individuals, with the result that this group cannot work together. This is the basic paradox of the peer group society. In unraveling it below, I hope to show also some of the differences between West End and middle-class social structure and personality.

Although the peer group is the most important entity in the West Ender's life, he is not merely a robot whose actions are determined by the group or the cultural tradition. In fact, peer group life in many ways is just the opposite of the cohesive and tightly-knit group that has served as a model for descriptions of primary relations in other societies. It is a spirited competition of individuals "jockeying" for respect, power, and status. Indeed, to the outside observer, West Enders appear to be involved in a never ending dialectic: individual actions take them out of the group momentarily and are followed by restraints that bring them back, only to be succeeded by more individuating talk or behavior. Peer group members act as if they were held together by ties of rubber, which they alternately stretch and relax, but rarely break.

This is most visible among the teenage and young adult action-seekers. Within the group their behavior is a series of competitive encounters intended to assert the superiority and skillfulness of one individual over the other, which take the form of card games, short physical scuffles, and endless verbal duels. Through bragging, teasing, wisecracking, and insulting, individuals express their own verbal strength and skill, while denigrating the characteristics and achievements of others. Only when there is a common opponent does the group coalesce, but even then this is not always likely to happen. For example, among the young adults whom I observed at a tavern where they hung out nightly, a basketball team broke up because the better players did not want to play on a team with the poorer ones, who would deny them the opportunity to display their individual talents.

While there is no physical competition among the adult groups, and even card games are rare, similar competition does exist, although in considerably muted form. One of the women's clubs in the area made an explicit agreement that members should not compete among each other in the purchase of house furnishings and furniture. At the same time, however, one of them told me that she spent more than a day to bake and clean house when the club met at her apartment. She did not consider this competitive activity. Most of the competitive play takes place in conversation, through an exchange of anecdotes that display the story teller's exploits, and of jokes and wisecracks that entertain the group while making one person stand out. The exchange is not vicious, nor is it used by self-centered people to call attention to themselves, or to make others look bad. In fact, any attempt by an insecure person to build himself up in the group at others' expense is considered out of place. It is politely ignored in his presence, and harshly criticized when he is out of earshot.

Group members—be they adult or adolescent—display themselves to the group, to show their peers that they are as good if not slightly better than the rest, but then they yield the floor to the next person and allow him to do likewise. The purpose of this is to create mild envy among the rest of the group. The settlement house worker who pointed this out to me was in charge of a kindergarten at the time, and illustrated her point by noting that whereas Jewish mothers came to find out how their children were doing, and what help the teacher could give them, Italian parents came to find out how well their offspring were doing compared with others, and to get praise about them from the teacher.

Individual display takes place not only in group interaction, but also in many other ways. One is conspicuous consumption. West Enders of both sexes like to display themselves in new clothes, which are bought regularly at Easter and Christmas and for other special occasions. The men do the same with their cars, either by purchasing new ones, or by continuously polishing the old ones. The women like to display their cooking and baking skills. And the most talented of both sexes try to become entertainers. Thus, although an interest in art is considered effeminate, there is nothing wrong if boys want to become singers of popular music, for this is an opportunity for self-display. In fact, most of the successful white singers today are Italians, and it is no accident that they are as much creators of a distinctive personal image as they are purveyors of songs. Italians have done well in contemporary popular music because it emphasizes the development of an individual image and style more than technical musical skill.[6]

The need for display within the group is so strong among West Enders, in fact, that they find themselves unable to save because of their high expenditures of food, clothing, and other expenses of group life. I heard some criticism of recent Italian immigrants who failed to participate in this pattern, and who saved their money to buy a house after living only a few years in America. Although redevelopment would force many renters to become homeowners, and the need to save money for the future had become apparent, the native-born West Enders were unable to withdraw sufficiently from the group display to put any money aside. Nor would they have seriously considered this alternative.

It should be noted that what I have called conspicuous consumption and display is not to be equated with the kind of consumption competition which has been noted among the *nouveau riche*, or among the American Indian tribes given to pot-latches. The West Enders do not seek to outdo all others, and thus be the best or numerically the greatest in these displays. Rather, they want to show themselves off, without questioning the right and ability of everyone else to do much the same.

Two other expressions of West End individualism are the rejection of formal dependence on the group, and the emphasis on the mutual nature of obligations. Despite the fact that West Enders

6. Incidentally, despite the popular stereotype, there was little interest in opera among the West Enders. If such interest had existed among Southern Italians and Sicilians, it disappeared with the first generation.

live so much within a group, they feel that they cannot and do not want to depend on it for help. People say that "in the last analysis, you have to depend on yourself." They are loath to ask for favors from others, even within the family circle, and much more so from organized charity. The emphasis on independence is based partly on a realistic appraisal that others can extend only a limited amount of help, and that it would be unrealistic to depend on them. When economic deprivations strike one member of a low-income population, they are likely to hit others as well. Moreover, if other troubles arise, such as illness, they are apt to be serious ones. Although West Enders will offer and accept help, they do not cherish being dependent on others. They want to remain independent, for accepting aid is thought to reflect on the strength of the individual, and is thus a reflection on self-respect which places the dependent person in an inferior position.

Moreover, giving and receiving—of help or gifts—involves the individual in a spiral of reciprocatory obligations. The obligation may be latent, in which case people feel a desire to give and receive, and enjoy the resulting reciprocity. Or it may be manifest, thus becoming a duty. In this case reciprocity can turn into a burden, and people try to escape involvement. This happens most often with representatives from the outside world, like welfare agencies and settlement houses, who want to give aid in exchange for deference or loyalty to institutions.[7]

Among close friends and relatives, goods and services are exchanged freely and obligations remain latent, unless one or the other person falls seriously behind in reciprocating, or unless the exchange becomes competitive. Should someone reciprocate with a more expensive gift than he originally received, he may be suspected of showing off, or of trying to make the other person look bad. If it continues, this can lead to an eventual alienation from the group.

When relationships are not close, obligations are manifest. For example, after a man had done some electrical work for his sister, she invited him to dinner several times as payment for the work —which he had done for nothing. Although she was not formally required to reciprocate, since he was her brother, she wanted to do

7. See Chapter 7.

so because she felt it to be the proper thing. This brother had married an upwardly mobile woman, and was not part of the immediate family circle.

When obligations concern authority figures and hierarchical relationships, the rejection of dependence becomes stronger, and often evolves into fear of domination. Thus, whereas West Enders will subordinate themselves to someone whom they recognize as a leader, they will bitterly reject the individual who is imposed as a leader from the outside—or who tries to impose himself.

As relationships within the peer group society are expected to be equalitarian, no one is permitted to dominate anyone else. Someone who attempts to do so is suspected of wanting to exploit, to get something that he does not deserve and cannot get in any other way. This attitude, which governs almost completely relationships with the outside world, also crops up in dealings with other West Enders. For example, one morning, two cars approached each other on a West End street temporarily restricted to one lane and came so close that neither could pass the other. A five-minute discussion then followed of who would back up to let the other through. At the height of the argument, one said to the other, "we've been friends for years but you can't command me." Such struggles are frequent when West Enders relate to each other in roles that are outside the normal range of those encountered in peer group relations. Thus, if landlords who invited friends to take apartments in their buildings had to act as landlords, by raising the rent or by cutting down on maintenance, it was often done at the cost of broken friendships.

Although the peer group is a theater for individual expression, it is also characterized by strict control of deviant behavior. This is all the more important when individualistic striving is central to the group, for there is always the possibility that the group may be disrupted, which in turn would shut off further opportunity for individual display. The major mechanisms of social control are criticism, the expectation of criticism, and the not always successful attempts by individuals to maintain self-control.

Since everyone knows everyone else, life is an open book, and deviant acts are hard to hide. This means that such acts are committed either outside the reaches of the group—as in the case of adolescents who do their misbehaving outside the West End—or that they are not committed at all. As noted earlier, much of the group conversation is devoted to judging behavior, and any unusual behavior, whether deviant or innovating, is likely to be criticized. Jokes and wisecracks, a polite way of questioning deviant behavior, usually suffice to bring the individual back into line. Similarly, the individual is expected to keep up with the activities of the group, and the pattern of individual display. The person who is too noisy or dominating is suspect, but so is the one who is too quiet. The hostess who sets too lavish a table is criticized, but even more so is the person who is unwilling to entertain or feed the group in the style to which it is accustomed.

But as so much of life is based on routine, there is little incentive for nonconforming behavior. Thus most conformity is quite voluntary. But West Enders also regulate their conduct by involuntary conformity of the type expressed in the phrase "what will the neighbors think." Indeed, the expectations of what other people will think are extremely harsh; they assume the blackest thoughts and deeds possible. For example, a neighbor who had recently had a baby carried the baby carriage up several flights, rather than leaving it in an empty store that served as storage room for several adjacent apartment buildings. She justified her behavior by explaining that, since the storage room was not in her own building, people might think she was going in there to steal something. Similarly, the woman described earlier who had never entered her relative's apartment because she felt people would suspect them of having sexual relations, was certain that they believed this to be the case anyway. Politicians complain that they, too, are believed to act only on the basest motives. While the exaggerated expectations do constitute a potent control against deviant behavior, they create, at the same time, an unspoken atmosphere of mutual recrimination, in which everyone is likely to expect the worst from everyone else. It must be noted, however, that such expectations are usually not held about peer group members, but only about people who are less close—neighbors, for example.

It is clear that the ascription of evil motives and deeds stems not from observations of the neighbors' behavior or inferences from their conversations, but from the individual himself. He projects on the neighbors his underlying fear that he himself might do evil things or harbor evil motives. For although West Enders believe that fate regulates actions over which they have no say, their own behavior is thought to be self-determined. For example, crime, such deviances as homosexuality, overt forms of mental illness—and even fits of depression—are thought to be caused by lack of self-control.

The West Ender therefore is frequently concerned over his ability to control himself.[8] Among the adolescents and the action-seeking adults, the main concern is to stay out of "trouble"—which means not only to avoid getting caught by the police or by other agents of social control, but also not going out of control in episodic behavior, for this might detach the individual from the group. Among routine-seeking people, uncontrolled behavior is less of a problem. Their concern is to avoid getting into situations that could be misinterpreted. In short, the individual must control himself so that he cannot be suspected of negatively evaluated behavior, either by the group or by himself.

The definition of deviant behavior comes initially from the group itself, and the group encourages individuals to shame each other into conformity through overt criticism. As in all other groups, this criticism is often anticipated by expectations in the individual. Thus, one West Ender said one night, when he was eager to leave the female half of the family circle: "If I don't go back to the living room [and the male company] they'll start talking about me." West Enders seem to differ from middle-class people in that the individual's own preoccupation with self-control

8. The concern with self-control is graphically illustrated in Joseph Caruso, *The Priest*, New York: Popular Library, 1958. This novel, written by a West Ender, deals with a priest whose unsuccessful attempt to control impulses of lust and violence drives him into renouncing his post. In the end, he returns to his duties because of peer group pressure. For empirical studies of Italian-American self-control problems, see M. K. Opler and J. L. Singer, "Ethnic Differences in Behavior and Psychopathology," *International Journal of Social Psychiatry*, vol. 2 (1956), pp. 11–22; and Ezra F. Vogel, "The Marital Relationships of Parents of Emotionally Disturbed Children," unpublished Ph.D. Dissertation, Harvard University, 1958, Chap. 6.

results in highly exaggerated—and sometimes unwarranted—expectations of what others think of him. This in turn is an effective device for limiting deviant behavior.

But whether social control is imposed from within or without, the middle-class stereotype of working-class society is in error. What the neighbors think is just as important to the West Ender as to the newest recruit to suburbia. If anything, social control is more strict than in the middle class, and nonconformity is not as easily excused.

In view of the severity of social control, it would be easy to caricature peer group life as a prison for its members. To the outsider, the concern with social control and self-control might indeed seem oppressive. But he must also take into account that there is little desire for voluntary nonconformity, and, consequently, little need to require involuntary conformity. Nor do people seem to be troubled by fears about the breakdown of self-control, or about the possibility that they may be suspected of misdeeds. Although these potentialities do lurk under the surface, they do not usually disturb the positive tenor of group relations. Such fears, of course, may be private preoccupations, less visible to the sociologist than they would be to the clinical psychologist. Moreover, the people who are seriously troubled by these fears shun the kind of group I have discussed.

Tensions and problems exist in the peer group, as in every other group, but they are overshadowed by the gratifications that it provides for the individual. Perhaps the best illustration of this was given by a young man who was suffering from an ulcer, and was faced with a choice between his health and his group. As he explained it: "I can't stop drinking when I'm with my friends; I eat and drink like they do and when I'm alone I take care of my ulcer. But I don't care if it kills me; if it does, that's it."

In summary, social relationships within the peer group follow a narrow path between individualistic display and strictly enforced social control. The group is set up to provide its members with an opportunity for displaying, expressing, and acting out their individuality, as long as this does not become too extreme.

As a result, the peer group is unable to work together to achieve a common goal unless it is shared by all members of the group.

Since the main function of the group is to provide an area for individual display, the members are less interested in activities that require working together than in impressing each other. Moreover, if group tasks, especially those of a novel nature, are suggested, people become fearful that they will be used as pawns by an individual who will gain the most from this activity. Consequently, the inability to participate in joint activities does inhibit community organization, even when it concerns the very survival of the group, as it did in the clearance of the West End.[9] This, perhaps, is the peer group society's most serious weakness.

Person-Orientation and Object-Orientation

I have tried to show that peer group life is characterized by a paradox: that the group is used by its members to express and display individualistic strivings and that these strivings prevent the group from acting in concert. A more detailed analysis of the West Ender's individualism will try to explain this paradox and will also shed some light on his character and personality structure.

By individualism or independence, I mean the attempt by the individual to express his personality or idiosyncratic character, to achieve what he believes to be his own aspirations, and to feel himself to be a distinct entity apart from the group. At one level of analysis then, there is a separation—and sometimes conflict—between individual and group. At another level of analysis, however, it can be shown that the patterns with which individualism is expressed are themselves group products, that is, roles whose content is part of a shared culture.

In order to describe the relationship between peer group and individual—and to compare it to the group-individual relationship in the middle class—it is helpful to contrast two kinds of individualistic modes of behavior, *object-oriented* and *person-oriented*.[10] The distinction between them can best be described by differences in aspirations. Object-oriented individualism involves striving to-

9. See also Chapters 5 and 13.

10. These are ideal types, and also polar ones. Ideal types oversimplify reality; polar ones exaggerate differences between people to fit the dichotomous pattern. Despite these faults, however, the distinction is a useful one.

ward the achievement of an "object." This may be a moral object, for example, a principle; an ideological object, such as "understanding"; a material object, such as level of income; a cultural object, such as a style of life; or a social object, such as a career or a status position. Although people strive after a variety of objects, they tend to verbalize ideological and moral ones more than the material and social ones.

What unites this diverse set of aspirations is that each is aimed toward an object or object-goal that can be conceptualized in a self-conscious and deliberate manner. In order to achieve it, the individual may have to detach himself from some groups, or attach himself to others. For example, if he is seeking a career, he may have to give up childhood friends who are not pursuing one, and join with other individuals who share with him only this common object.

Person-oriented individualism also strives, but not for object goals. Here, the overriding aspiration is the desire to be a person within a group; to be liked and noticed by members of a group whom one likes and notices in turn. Now, wanting to be liked and noticed is also an object, and people join groups for this purpose. The difference between object-orientation and person-orientation is that whereas the former exists prior to and apart from a group, the latter is intrinsically tied to, and is itself a product of, participation in the group. Object-oriented people may enter secondary groups or reshape primary ones in order to achieve their object goals; person-oriented ones develop their aspirations within a primary group in which they are members, and which they are not interested in leaving. Without such a group, they have no aspirations, and for them, being alone is undesirable precisely because aspirations are so closely tied to the group.[11] The object-oriented people will join a group in order to achieve a common purpose; the person-oriented ones need the group to become individuals. Consequently, when a set of person-oriented people must act together, they lose interest; they become "selfish," that is, con-

11. In Parsons' conceptual scheme, object-oriented people move into universalistic groups in order to achieve; person-oriented ones are tied ascriptively to particularistic ones. See, for example, Talcott Parsons, *The Social System*, New York: The Free Press of Glencoe, 1951, pp. 102–104.

cerned about what common action will do to them as individuals. Thus the two kinds of aspirations are radically different.[12] To the object-oriented, person-oriented people seem to be without aspirations, to lack ambition, and to be unable to defer gratification. Conversely, to the person-oriented, those who strive for object-goals seem cold and inhuman, pursuing selfish aims at the expense of others, and unable to enjoy life as a result. Both perceptions are limited. Person-oriented people do have aspirations for which they strive in their group—where these are not very visible. But these gratifications are precisely those which the object-oriented think should be deferred for object-goals. Object-oriented people choose their groups more deliberately—which makes their striving more visible—but once they do, they too develop affectional ties, and derive enjoyment from the group much like their opposites. If anything, their group behavior is more altruistic, precisely because they do not need to rely on any one group to express their individuality.

Person- and object-orientation are modes of behavior; they can

12. The distinction between person-orientation and object-orientation is a somewhat different way of dealing with phenomena described by such traditional sociological dichotomies as Gemeinschaft-Gesellschaft, mechanical-organic, emotional-rational, and ascription-achievement. It has been inspired most directly, however, by Merton's distinction between "locals" and "cosmopolitans." In developing his dichotomy, Merton suggests that for locals, social relationships are the principal aim, and that ideas are used as means to them. For cosmopolitans, on the other hand, ideas are central, and social relationships follow, mainly with people who share the same ideas. See Robert K. Merton, "Patterns of Influence," in his *Social Theory and Social Structure*, New York: The Free Press of Glencoe, 2nd ed., 1958, pp. 387–420, especially at pp. 396–399. Needless to say, the two dichotomies are dissimilar in many ways. Person- and object-orientation may also be compared with Ephraim H. Mizruchi's distinction between "means-valuation," and "ends-valuation," "Social Structure, Success Values and Structured Strain in a Small City." Paper read at the 1961 meetings of the American Sociological Association, mimeographed, p. 5. Mizruchi associates means-valuation with the lower class, ends-valuation with the middle class, especially in connection with attitudes toward education. Unless the distinction is used carefully, however, it runs the risk of characterizing lower class people as lacking ends, rather than seeking ends which differ from those pursued by the middle class. My dichotomy may also be compared with Riesman's concepts of other-direction and inner-direction. This comparison is made in Chapter 11.

be thought of as sets of related "propensities-to-act," or as systems of choices that guide behavior when all other conditions are held constant. Thus, within the same social situation or set of opportunities, a person-oriented individual will act differently from an object-oriented one. For example, the distinction might predict how two persons will react to job offers which will take them away from relatives, friends, and neighborhood for a considerable time. All other conditions being equal, the object-oriented individual is likely to accept the job if it will help him achieve his career goal. The person-oriented individual is likely to reject it because the move would take him out of his peer group, and because he has no career goal. When all other conditions are not equal, however, the two concepts are not applicable. For example, a person-oriented individual who is out of work might take the job whatever its disadvantages.

This qualification calls attention to the fact that the pressures and opportunities created by the social structure have as much of a motivating force as do the cultural and characterological ingredients of the two modes of behavior. To put it another way, these two modes are exercised only in some situations. When a person needs work and has little job choice, being person-oriented or object-oriented cannot affect his choice, although it may affect his adjustment to the job he must take. In addition, there are prerequisite objects that are sought by person-oriented people—notably income—while even the most object-oriented individual needs to belong to a group that will accept him for what he is, without requiring that he strive for an object. Likewise, both types seek affection, but they do so in different ways. The object-oriented individual may pursue it in a purposive manner, when seeking compatible friends or a mate; the person-oriented one expects it to come to him in the normal course of peer group relationships. Thus, no individual is ever entirely person- or object-oriented, but in roles which provide the opportunity for choice, his response may tend more to one mode than to the other.

It should be apparent by now that West Enders try to be person-oriented and that they seek a minimal number of object-goals.[13]

13. S. M. Miller and Frank Riessman have recently described the working class as being person-centered. See their article, "The Working Class Subculture: A New View," *Social Problems*, vol. 9 (1961), p. 93.

Moreover, they seek these primarily outside the peer group, and, whenever possible, from people identified with the outside world. West Enders, for example, are not interested in careers, but in jobs that pay the most money for the least amount of physical discomfort, because they want to make money and save their energy for person-oriented behavior within the peer group. They do not seek status by clearly identified and universally accepted status symbols, but want to be able to shine as individuals within their own group. Similarly, they do not strive to live up to moral or ideological principles, but want to act in a way that earns no opprobrium from the group, and that fits group beliefs.

West Enders treat each other, and expect to be treated, in a person-oriented mode by actual and potential peer group members; those who do not do so are rejected. I have already noted that tenants treat landlords as peer group members and expect to be treated in the same way. Should the landlord raise the rent or fail to make needed repairs, however, the relationship becomes object-oriented, and the landlord is treated as an outsider. One West Ender has never forgiven his landlord for announcing a rent increase in a tone of voice which suggested to him that he was being treated as a tenant rather than as a peer group member. This encounter took place shortly after World War II.

A similar process was described by a West Ender in connection with his work. As a commercial photographer, he was often asked by friends and relatives to take pictures at weddings and other family affairs. Although he could have used the money, he refused to accept such assignments because they would have placed him into a business role vis-à-vis potential peer group members who would, however, demand to be treated in a person-oriented fashion. Expecting him to reduce his prices to a level at which he could not provide his services, they would suspect him of exploiting them if he did not do so. Thus, in order to maintain the peer group relationship, he sacrificed the potential income.

The priority of person-oriented responses is apparent also in relation to moral objects. One evening, a group of West Enders whom I was visiting became embroiled in a lengthy discussion about whether one should tell the truth to a person when the truth might hurt him or his feelings. The consensus was that one should not do so if the other person felt badly as a result. Since he would eventually find out the truth anyway—if only by other people's silence—he should be told a white lie that would make him feel good. As one person explained, "If I can't say anything good, I don't say anything." Only one individual favored telling the truth or being honest with the other person regardless of how this affected the personal relationship. He did admit, however, that this policy often offended people, and that it might even be dangerous. To illustrate, he reported the story of a man who killed his brother-in-law for telling him that his wife was "a tramp." "But I'd still tell the truth, ninety-nine times out of a hundred," he concluded. Holding back on the truth is a special case of a more common occurrence that I have already described: when people disagree about an issue on which there may be contradictory opinions, the subject is changed in order to maintain the relationship on an even keel.

Another instance of the priority of personal relationships over truth was exemplified after a minor accident on a West End street. The brother of the man who was responsible for the accident asked one of the relatives of the victim—a boy whose bicycle had been damaged—not to tell the police what she had seen, because they might revoke his brother's driving license. In a quite matter-of-fact tone, he tried to argue that the woman's first duty was to him—evidently an acquaintance—rather than to the boy, the police, or the truth.

As these examples suggest, West Enders are not always successful in keeping peer group relationships person-oriented. If the striving for basic object-goals such as money should force West Enders to treat one another in an object-oriented fashion, broken relationships and conflict are the result. This is something over which West Enders do not always have control. In periods of economic depression, for example, they must compete against one another for jobs. Likewise, when the generations become embroiled in cultural differences, relations between them often diverge considerably in the direction of the object-oriented, until they are based on little more than feelings of duty.

As often as possible, object-goals are sought in the outside world, where people can be more easily treated in an object-oriented mode, mainly because West Enders expect to be treated the same way. This choice is based on bitter experience. For even in the outside world, the West Ender begins with the assumption that life proceeds by peer group rules. When he learns otherwise, he is deeply hurt and describes people as self-seeking and exploiting. He thus feels free to treat them in this fashion if and when it is to his advantage to do so. Since, according to West Enders, business, politics, and government bureaucracies are run by and large by men who are "out to get theirs," they feel justified in acting likewise. They develop a kind of cunning and sensitivity to the visible strengths and weaknesses of others, which stems directly from the aggressive give-and-take of peer group competition. For those who can act in this manner, this behavior pattern is useful for success in the outside world, especially in politics and in the highly competitive economy of small, marginal entrepreneurs. But as most West Enders cannot act in this way, they shrink from unnecessary contact with the outside world.

Active or passive, the West Ender has considerable difficulty in understanding object-oriented behavior. He is unable to visualize people organized in cooperative group activity toward a common goal. Although he can see, observe, and describe this activity, he cannot see himself in such a role, and therefore cannot quite understand how others carry it out. Similarly, he has difficulty in comprehending the nature of administrative procedure, and the rules of bureaucratic government. He can explain these only by concepts based on individual motivation and morality, for example, by honesty, selfishness, and greed. Thus, he personalizes all of what are in part, at least, impersonal relationships. This leads to the belief that governments are themselves honest or dishonest, usually the latter. Consequently, West Enders feel themselves to be exploited or even persecuted by government. In extreme situations, their view of government and the entire outside world may appear to be paranoid, even though its origin is dynamically quite different from paranoia. Also, West Enders, like other low-income populations, have been exposed to sufficient exploitation by more powerful groups in the city to justify some of their suspicions. Even so, not all governmental activities can be explained by personal greed or corruption.[14]

14. This question will be discussed in more detail in Chapter 8.

Part of the difficulty lies in the West Ender's unilateral adherence to a religious morality that provides guides mainly for person-oriented behavior and for relationships between individuals. Norms such as equality, justice, independence, charity, reciprocity, and personal honesty are conceived as they apply to peer group relationships. The West Ender also applies these norms to the outside world, without, however, making adjustments necessary for secondary-group relationships. Businessman-client or government-citizen encounters are expected to follow peer group norms. But the businessman who seeks a legitimate profit cannot treat all his customers as friends. Nor can the politician who must satisfy a diverse constituency give the West Enders' wishes the priority to which they feel they are entitled. Similarly the bureaucrat who must follow legislative regulations cannot depart from them because of the personal attention that the West Ender thinks his case deserves. Nor can the doctor who must maintain affective neutrality take over the patient's suffering as his own. But the West Ender, viewing all of these as potential peer group members rather than roles, is bitterly disappointed when they do not act by peer group norms. Not understanding their object-oriented behavior, he believes them to be immoral, and acts the same way in self-defense. But underneath his pragmatism and cynicism, he retains his belief in the rules of person-oriented morality, and waits for the day when the outside world will abide by them. As one slum landlord once put it, and quite seriously: "If we had an honest mayor, I'd be honest too."

West Enders thus impose their peer group society on the outside world, and on their relationships with it. Having few object-goals themselves, it is possible for them to conceive of an entirely person-oriented world in which all groups are primary and peer-like, acting on the basis of person-oriented morality.

By identifying the outside world with object-goals, West Enders are thus able to restrict their own desire for its social and material objects. They are familiar, of course, with the possibilities of social mobility and high prestige, with luxury consumer goods and costly entertainment facilities, and with college and career opportunities to which children can be exposed. But they are also able to reject any temptations that these images might raise by associating them with the outside world and its defects. For example, the desirability of homeownership—mostly because it frees one from relations with the landlord—is neutralized by the belief that suburbanites are cold and lonely people who use each other as objects in the struggle for status. Similarly, the value of a college education is balanced against the belief that having an education is no guarantee to a better job, and may lead to disappointment and unhappiness.

It would be easy to label these reactions as renunciations, and to conclude that West Enders reject the attractions of the outside world as sour grapes because they are inaccessible. While it is true that West Enders have never had any real opportunity to come within touching distance of these attractions, it is also true that they see them—and find them wanting. Having grown up without them, they have developed a style of life that offers many other satisfactions. Thus, they feel no great temptation for the attractions of the outside world. The fact that the rest of the peer group does not desire them either also makes it easier to ignore them. Had the West Enders grown up under different circumstances, with more opportunities to achieve object-goals and with parents who urged them to strive for these, they undoubtedly would have a different reaction.[15] But as it stands now, these goals are associated with people who are thought to be lacking in the human qualities prized by West Enders.

Person-Oriented Individualism and the Structure of the Self

The peer group's central position in West End life, its function of providing for individual expression, and the person-oriented mode of behavior that it encourages all have implications for the West Ender's personality structure. Some limited characteristics of this personality structure will be explored here through a consideration of the *self,* using George Herbert Mead's classic formulation as a take-off point.

According to Mead's central hypothesis, a person's self is formed, in part, out of the conceptions which other people have of him, the attitudes they display, and the actions that they take.

15. The West Enders' rejection of middle-class mobility is discussed in more detail in Chapter 10; the sources of object-orientation, in Chapter 11.

This process, begun in childhood, eventually allows the individual to see himself as others see him. Thus his conception of their views is systematized into a "generalized other," which then becomes "society's representative in the individual." [16] The self is a result of this process, and of the individual's response to it. For this reason, Mead distinguishes between the "me" and the "I." The former is "the organized set of attitudes which one himself assumes," and the latter is "the response of the organism to the attitudes of others." [17]

Since the "me" is created out of group activity, the total self is naturally affected by the nature of this activity. Thus Mead's model of group endeavor—for adults, at least—derived from that deliberately organized cooperative activity that is dedicated to the achievement of specific goals, in baseball teams, clubs, political organizations, and civic activities.[18]

This is the society of voluntary organizations and purposive community participation that often requires the kind of behavior I have previously described as object-oriented. In order to participate in this type of group life, the individual must develop some detachment and self-consciousness about his activities and about himself, which leads to the creation of a *self-image*. This self-image is often imperfect, and may be restricted only to those roles and personality characteristics which are required for participation. But it does allow the individual to confront new kinds of people and new experiences without too much difficulty or feeling of threat.

The person-oriented West Ender, however, does not live in this society. His social life takes place in peer groups that are not given to cooperative activity or purposive goal-seeking. Indeed, much of his behavior is based on impulsive, but time-tested, reactions to the people he has known since childhood—a type of social life that does not encourage or require the detachment demanded in volun-

16. Anselm Strauss, ed., *The Social Psychology of George Herbert Mead,* Chicago: University of Chicago Press (Phoenix Books) 1956, p. xiv. This book is a compilation of Mead's writings, notably his *Mind, Self and Society.*

17. Strauss, *op. cit.,* p. 243. Quotations are from Mead.

18. *Ibid.,* pp. 232–234.

tary organizations. Thus, the West Ender develops a different "me," with a different type of "generalized other," and operates without a self-image. Settlement house workers in the West End described this as "a lack of inner self," conceiving their mission to be the development of such a self in their clients.

The West Enders' lack of a self-image can be illustrated by various examples. While they do give of themselves as freely as do other people, they cannot conceive of themselves doing so. Whereas the object-oriented person can give of himself to his children, bring himself to a social gathering, or "contribute" to a meeting, the West Ender cannot conceive the self that he gives. Therefore, he brings gifts when he goes visiting. He shuns meetings and has considerable difficulty in giving of himself consciously to his children. Settlement house workers frequently mentioned that mothers would ask them to teach their young children behavior patterns and values with which the mothers themselves were quite familiar, but which they felt unable to transmit consciously. Similarly, adults are ill-at-ease with people who try to take their point of view, for example, with well-meaning social workers or doctors who assume the West Enders to have a sense of identity to the benefit of which they can contribute. It is for this reason that West Enders prefer "to look out for themselves," as if to say that others cannot know us, since we do not know ourselves. The fear of being alone stems from the same source, for confrontations with the self are perplexing in the absence of a self-image.

The object-oriented individual develops a self largely from the experience of perceiving how others see him. West Enders, however, are not very adept at judging others' conceptions of them. As already noted, they have highly exaggerated notions of what the neighbors think. And insofar as they have developed a generalized other, it is based less on empirical observation of how others see them, than on how they *feel* others see them. Instead of developing expectations from the actions of other people, they develop such expectations from projections. The evil thoughts they believe others to harbor about them stem from their own fears concerning loss of self-control. And the preoccupation with self-control, in turn, is encouraged by the lack of a self-image.

Difficulties in perceiving the actions and attitudes of others create problems in contacts with people who are not already well known, and who operate on the basis of unfamiliar norms. This encourages the West Ender to limit his interaction to peer groups in which everyone is well known, and in which the dangers of exaggerated perception are minimized. It also explains the faithful adherence to a routine among so many West Enders.

Because of the difficulties in the perception of others, the person-oriented type is particularly sensitive to being hurt by them. In order to defend himself, he is therefore quick to detect selfishness in others and to respond with selfishness himself. This, of course, impedes cooperative activity. For when the individual cannot define himself and his self-interest, he "plays it safe," and rejects any group activity which might impinge negatively on the self. He is fearful of being "taken," especially by people whom he does not know. This helps to account for the conception that the outside world is exploiting, and that he must either defend himself against it, or stay out of it entirely.

In actual practice, then, West Enders shrink from involving themselves in roles that will take them out of their familiar social context. The disinclination to venture into new roles was reflected in attitudes toward leaving the West End; people were genuinely frightened at the thought of going into other neighborhoods. I was told of two West End women, both elderly, who had moved to Brookline, a middle- and upper-middle-class suburb, before redevelopment actually began. Although they had felt safe on West End streets at night, they were certain that the streets of the suburb were full of dangers, and it took some time before they would venture out on them. The disinclination toward new roles is also reflected in the great nostalgia people have for their childhood and adolescence, for these were periods when roles seemed few and simple.

My view of the West Enders' self bears considerable similarity to the findings of a study made by Daniel Lerner and his associates among Middle Eastern peasants. Lerner described this population as lacking the ability to empathize, to place themselves into the positions of others. As he put it, "empathy . . . is the capacity to see oneself in the other fellow's situation. This is an indispensable skill for people moving out of traditional settings." [19] His interview respondents could not conceive of roles other than their own, and of having opinions on matters relevant to strange roles. West Enders have gone a step further. They can place themselves into other roles, but if they have to empathize, they redefine the role so that it fits a familiar situation. Thus, whereas the Middle Eastern peasant would not be able to see himself as mayor of his town, a West Ender can describe what he would do if he were mayor of Boston. He would redefine the job, however, into that of the mayor of the West End.

In short, the object-oriented individual can be described as having a dualistic self, which allows him to be sensitive to the actions of others as they become part of himself. He is able to be self-conscious and develops a self-image or sense of identity. When the communication process between the "I" and the "me" is disturbed, he becomes self-centered. The person-oriented type, on the other hand, develops a monistic self, which makes it difficult for the individual to differentiate between his own and others' view of him. The lack of a clear self-image encourages and requires display. Thus the communication process between the "I" and other people is limited as much as possible to routine behavior among intimately known people. When this process is disturbed, the individual becomes selfish.

In describing the West Ender as lacking a self-image or sense of identity, I do not mean to suggest that he feels himself to be impaired, for he moves in a society in which self-consciousness is not so urgent. He is at a disadvantage only if and when social conditions force him to become a full participant in the outside world.[20] At present, he is able to participate minimally in that world, and he can protect himself from it by suspicion and rejection, as well as by the support he can get from the peer group society.

Conversely, from a different value position, an object-oriented person could be described as impaired, because he lacks such abilities as belonging totally to a group, retaining childhood friends,

19. Daniel Lerner, *The Passing of Traditional Society*, New York: The Free Press of Glencoe, 1958, p. 50.

20. This possibility will be discussed in Chapter 12.

and expressing one's individuality among such people. He would also find it difficult to exist in a peer group society, since it pursues so few activities aimed at object-goals. Needless to say, he is not asked to do so.

The object-oriented self is geared to a society in which people are able and need to place themselves in the roles of others. The person-oriented self, found in a social system in which social intercourse is restricted to familiar persons, has less need to be empathic. Indeed, the pattern of projecting one's own expectations on others is possible only in a social group in which behavior and attitudes are similar; otherwise there would be disastrous consequences. The inclination toward selfishness and away from self-consciousness seems to be functional in a low-status group where survival cannot be taken for granted, and where solutions are beyond the control of the individual or group. In such a milieu selfishness enables the individual to keep up in the struggle for survival, and the lack of self-consciousness minimizes preoccupation with insoluble difficulties. Instead of melancholy there is acting-out behavior; neurosis is rare; and difficulties that cannot be surmounted conclude with a psychotic breakdown instead, extruding the individual out of the group entirely. Although this may not be beneficial for the individual, it does protect the group, at least over the short range. If social conditions result in the breakdown of a large number of individuals, the group itself will eventually fall apart.

The origins of the person-oriented self can be related—and perhaps traced—to child-rearing practices. As I noted in Chapter 3 the West End child is brought up impulsively and according to adult values. Parents do not recognize that he has individual needs, nor do they react to him in ways that would make him conscious of these needs. Also, they do not behave self-consciously toward the child, nor expose him to situations in which they try to see things from his perspective, as do child-centered parents. Thus, the child is not likely to see people take someone else's point of view. Since there is little deliberate teaching by parents, and since the child therefore learns mostly by imitation, he has few opportunities to learn self-consciousness, or to develop a self-image.

Needless to say, the explanation of the person-oriented self cannot terminate in child-rearing practices. As I have tried to suggest in Chapter 3, and will show in more detail in Chapter 10, there are broader social and cultural forces that shape the parents who administer the upbringing of the children, and that encourage them to use this particular mode of child-rearing rather than another.

CHAPTER 5 The Community

The Nature of Community

Sociologists generally use the term "community" in a combined social and spatial sense, referring to an aggregate of people who occupy a common and bounded territory within which they establish and participate in common institutions. I shall employ the term in a purely social sense, however, to describe the set of institutions and organizations used by the West Enders to perform functions that cannot be taken care of within the peer group society. While these institutions are located in the neighborhood, this only puts them within reach of their users. Their functions otherwise have little to do with the area or neighborhood. For this reason the role of the institutions in the lives of the West Enders can be described almost without reference to the spatial community or neighborhood.[1]

In fact, the West End as a neighborhood was not important to West Enders until the advent of redevelopment. Early in my study, for example, when asking people why they liked the West End, I expected emotional statements about their attachment to the area. I was always surprised when they talked merely about its

1. In this chapter, as elsewhere, I shall use the present tense to describe patterns that are associated with the way West Enders live wherever they reside, but I shall use the past tense to describe institutions that no longer exist.

convenience to work and to downtown shopping. Then, after I had lived in the area a few weeks, one of my neighbors remarked that I knew a lot more about the West End than they did. This led me to realize that there was relatively little interest in the West End as a physical or social unit. West Enders were concerned with some of the people who lived in the area, but not with the entire population. Their interest in the physical features of the area was limited generally to the street on which they lived, and the stores which they frequented. This fact was illustrated by the fact that during past election campaigns, politicians made a somewhat different speech on each street, filled with promises of what they would do for the street if elected.

Indeed, only when the outside world discovered the West End and made plans to tear it down did its inhabitants begin to talk about the West End as a neighborhood, although, of course, they never used this term. And yet some felt sure until the end that while the West End as a whole was coming down, *their* street would not be taken, which helps to explain the lack of protest about clearance until it was too late.[2] Only after it was too late did people begin to realize that they did have some feelings about the entire area.[3] Even then, however, they talked mostly about losing their apartment, and being torn from the people with whom they had been close so long. It is for these reasons that I use the term "community" in a more limited, nonspatial sense.

The specific institutions that constitute the community are the church; the parochial school; formal social, civic, and political organizations, some of them church-related; and some commercial establishments.[4] These institutions—predominantly Italian—exist outside the peer group society, but are linked with it if and when they can be used to meet group and individual needs. The peer

2. This is discussed further in Chapter 13.

3. This has been reported about the entire West End population by Marc Fried, "Developments in the West End Research," Boston: Center for Community Studies Research Memorandum A3, October 1960, mimeographed, p. 7. For a more detailed analysis of how this population felt about the West End, see Marc Fried and Peggy Gleicher, "Some Sources of Residential Satisfaction in an Urban 'Slum,'" *Journal of the American Institute of Planners,* vol. 27 (1961), pp. 305–315.

4. These will be described in subsequent sections of this chapter.

group society so dominates West End life, however, that the community is relatively unimportant. Excepting the church, the success of the remaining institutions therefore depends on the extent to which they are allied and subservient to peer group needs.

The community must be distinguished from still another set of functions and institutions which may be of more importance to the West Ender, but which he views either as necessary evils required by the larger, non-Italian society, or as services offered him by that society which he uses selectively and with little enthusiasm. These include work, education, health services, welfare agencies, government, and the mass media of communications. Because these institutions are, in differing degrees, imposed upon the members of the peer group society, I have described them as the outside world.[5]

Patterns of Community Participation and Leadership

In the middle class, people are viewed as participating in community activities. That is, they enter organizations because they share the values and aims fostered by them; or because they find organizational activities—such as the acquisition of prestige, leadership experience, or social and business contacts—useful for their own purposes. Since for the West Ender, parallel functions can be satisfied within the peer group, participation in the community is ancillary. Sometimes, however, a single peer group does become active in an organization to help out a friend who has become an officer. But most of the more active individuals are either socially marginal or mobile.

West Enders usually will belong only to those organizations which offer opportunities for peer group activity that are not available elsewhere. For example, the Holy Name Society of the parish church gave the men an opportunity to take communion as a group, and to bowl together. When one of the members decided to run for office—undoubtedly at the urgings of his friends—and was elected, he brought in family members and friends to help run the organization. Peer group ties obligated people to help the officer; and the group, in effect, ran the organization. Politicians followed

5. These institutions will be analyzed in the following four chapters.

somewhat the same procedure. In the West End, they called on relatives and close friends to form a campaign staff, who, if their man was elected, became an informal kitchen cabinet that advised him. Since a peer group's competence to counsel on city-wide affairs was limited, the politician used the group to unburden himself, and to test the advice he got from experts.

Most of the remaining participation was handled by the socially marginal and a few community-minded West Enders who are middle-class mobiles. For example, Italian participation in the Save the West End Committee—the group organized to protest the area redevelopment—was limited to a handful of intellectuals and artists. Although they were active within their own peer groups, their career and creative interests separated them from these groups psychologically, and also caused them to be treated with some suspicion. As a result, they developed a strong symbolic identification with the West End, which provided a feeling of belongingness, and, at the same time, allowed them to express feelings of protest about the redevelopment which could not be expressed as easily by their neighbors. Partially because of their skills and their marginality, they were able to develop a holistic concept of the West End as a neighborhood.

Community participation also provided an entree into the peer group society. For example, one of the most active participants turned out to be a man of Baltic descent whose activity helped him become part of the Italian group. Most people were unaware that he was not of Italian origin, and those who did know believed him to be French. His entry into the peer group society was aided by the fact that he had no brothers or sisters in the West End, and that he had married an Italian girl. His skill in carrying out activities in which other West Enders had no interest or ability helped him in becoming part of a male peer group. Another active West Ender used participation to remain in the peer group. He explained that his activity was motivated by his desire to be a model of respectability for his children. Since he was also an inveterate gambler, I suspect he used his organizational activity to counteract this failing, and to maintain his standing in the routine-seeking peer group to which he belonged.

Most of the other active people—and they were few—were mobile, some with white-collar jobs, and all of whom were seriously thinking about sending their children to college. Several had been asked to participate in the community by the church, or by settlement houses which typically attracted such people.

As already noted, many West End women belonged to informal and nameless clubs that were actually peer groups. Adolescents and young adult peer groups were organized as clubs for a variety of reasons. Adolescents formed them so as to be admitted into the settlement houses for "club night." Young unmarried men, scattered geographically and few in number, needed clubs in order to come together. Within the clubs, however, activities differed little from informal peer group pursuits. Thus, such groups were not really part of the community.

The remaining West Enders, that is, the large majority, did not participate in the community at all. The reasons for non-participation are to be found in the peer group society. As I noted in the previous chapter, West Enders are not adept at cooperative group activity. The peer group must, above all, give life to the individual, and cooperative action directed toward a common end detracts too much from this central purpose. Moreover, West Enders are reluctant to place themselves in a leader-follower, officer-member relationship, which would detract from the individuating function of the group and would also require members to assume a subordinate, if not dependent, role toward the leader. Consequently, only a highly charismatic leader seems to be able to attract followers and retain their loyalty for any length of time.

Leadership itself is sought, however, because it provides considerable opportunity for individual expression. In fact, one of the reasons for the inability of the Save the West End Committee to function was the desire of most of the participants to be leaders and their unwillingness to carry out the routine tasks required. The familiar complaint of community organizations everywhere—"too many chiefs and no Indians"—is perhaps nowhere more true than among people like the West Enders.

Now, leadership requires some detachment from the group. But any such act of detachment from the group immediately lays the leader open to suspicion that he is out for personal gain. This suspicion dogs every political leader, particularly since his activities take him into the outside world where he is free from peer group control. Consequently, he is expected to participate in the exploitative relationships thought to be dominant there.[6] Milder forms of this suspicion also greet the leader of local organizations. In fact, the only people who seem to escape it are religious figures. Even then, this is true only as long as they are concerned with purely religious activities. The moment a priest involves himself in worldly affairs, such as city politics or even church building plans, the halo is removed, worldly motives are imputed, and suspicion reigns. Thus, even in the absence of any real evidence, West Enders were sure that the leadership of the Boston archdiocese had a set of venal motives for the destruction of the West End.

The suspicion of leadership can frustrate community participation only because the majority of the people see no need for such participation. As West Enders see it, problems are solved either by the individual, the peer group, or by going to the politician to ask for a favor. Should these methods fail, they resign themselves to the problem's insolubility, and attribute the lack of action to the immorality of those in control. For example, West Enders were quite upset about poor municipal services and the disrepair of local streets, but aside from complaints to the politicians, no further action was taken. During the late 1930's and early 1940's the West End did have a Citizen's Planning Board that took such complaints to City Hall and that was fairly successful in having them corrected. This Board, however, had no citizen members, and was run by three Jewish settlement house workers, only one of whom lived in the West End.

Because of the absence of citizen participation, leaders do not even think in terms of citizen activities. Nor are organization programs designed to involve them as participants. For example, the Save the West End Committee, after endless meetings to discuss ways of meeting the redevelopment threat, acted mainly by publishing leaflets which documented the immorality of the city. These offered no opportunity for citizen action, and the anger that they expressed was only repeated—and dissipated—in peer group discussions. One West Ender who shared fully the beliefs of the Committee argued that it should not "get people all stirred up, because

6. This will be discussed further in Chapter 8.

they do not unstir easily." He felt that this would only incite useless riot, and did not even consider the possibility of group action.
In fact, among the West Enders of Italian background who participated in the Committee, violence against the mayor, or burning
him in effigy was the mode of action most often and most enthusiastically proposed. The only group action scheme to get beyond
the talking stage was a mothers' march on City Hall, planned in the
belief that even the immoral men who had decreed the destruction
of the West End could not remain deaf to the plaints of mothers,
especially old ones. But although such a march was actually
scheduled, only its planners showed up, and it had to be cancelled.

The behavior of West End leaders appears irrational—and
threatening—to outsiders. Thus, settlement house people viewed
the protests against redevelopment as rabble-rousing, and local
politicians as demagogues. The leaders—especially the politicians
—are caught in a difficult dilemma. Even when they do not share
the West Enders' personalized view of events—and quite often they
do—they know that West Enders will become interested only when
their anger is aroused. Moreover, West Enders expect their leaders
to arouse them, and to express for them their own anger at the
outside world. Should a politician fail to do so, he is suspected of
having sold out. Thus, he must often function in ways that the
outside world interprets as rabble-rousing, even though his in-
flammatory appeals are not likely to produce much citizen action.

Leaders of all kinds always labor under some suspicion. They
are expected to produce results, and, if they do not, someone is
sure to suggest that they have been paid off. If they do succeed,
they may be suspected of having profited handsomely in the process. Even if a leader does remain above suspicion, he receives little
reward for his efforts, for West Enders are fundamentally uninvolved in community activities.

The Church

The most important formal institution in the West End was
St. Joseph's Roman Catholic Church, which provided West Enders
with a facility for religious worship and for the parochial education of their children. Its Holy Name and Catholic Women's

Societies accounted for most of what little "rank-and-file" community participation did occur.[7]

Even so, West Enders were not closely identified with the church. There are a number of reasons for this. Southern Italians, and especially Sicilians, have been traditionally anticlerical because the church, in the past, had sided with the large landowners against the peasants and farm laborers. And although events in the Sicilian past are of little interest to the American-born West Ender, they have created a tradition of nonidentification which the American church has had to overcome. This, it has failed to do, at least in the West End.

Yet, West Enders are a religious people, and accept most of the moral norms and sacred symbols of the Catholic religion. They believe that the church ought to be the source and the defender of these norms, and expect it to practice what it preaches. At the same time, they observe that it is in reality a human institution that often fails to practice what it preaches. Thus, they identify with the religion, but not with the church, except when it functions as a moral agency. For example, most West Enders attend Sunday Mass because it is a religious duty—and absence a sin—rather than because of any identification with the local parish.[8] Men see the conflict between religion and church more sharply than women; and the action-seeking group, more than the routine-seeking one. It is reflected in lower male and action-seekers' church attendance. Men also are more impatient than women with religious ritual. A small Italian-Protestant church on the edge of the West End was scorned because its members took too great an interest in religion. One West Ender described them as "holy jumpers," not because they acted out their religious feelings physically, but because of the emotional intensity of Protestant congregational participation.

The male attitude toward the church is based in large part on lack of respect for the priesthood. For while priests are expected

7. I use the past tense here because although the present church has survived the redevelopment, most of the parishioners were West Enders, and have been dispersed.

8. Attending Mass also provides an opportunity to dress up, to see people and be seen, to promenade after church, and to socialize with friends and neighbors.

to be morally superhuman, they also are suspect for being not quite human enough, because they have chosen a way of life that requires celibacy. They are criticized for playing parish, diocesan, or city politics, for having favorites among parish members and choosing them so often among the more well-to-do, and for personal "vices" such as drinking. Thus, they are scorned for acting like normal men, even while they cannot perform the one act that would prove their masculinity. The priesthood is felt to be a suitable role for those uninterested in sex and unwilling to marry. This was underscored by a rumor that one of the few priests who had gained the affection of the West Enders some years back was said to be keeping a mistress. This rumor was told me with relish and pretended disapproval that reflected respect for the priest's manliness. Conversely, West End men have considerable regard for the nuns who teach in the parochial school, because the nun's virginity and her total dedication to whatever duty she is assigned by the male leadership of the diocese implement to perfection the male ideal of the good woman.

In his moral role, the priest is respected. He functions as judge and jury on all religious matters and on moral transgressions. The police in the West End, for example, took juvenile delinquents not to the station house but to the priest in order to mete out punishment for initial offenses; only when a boy became a habitual delinquent was he booked and judged by secular law. When a priest did cross over what West Enders defined as the line between sacred and secular concerns, however, legitimate authority ended, and he was either openly chastised by the parishioners or his transgression was reported to the pastor. Similarly, the Archbishop was severely criticized for taking a stand on the clearance of the West End—he was for it—and for permitting the destruction of the area's Polish church.[9]

Part of the lack of identification with the local church must

9. West Enders were upset because the Polish church building was only fourteen years old, while the parish church, which was spared from destruction, was over a hundred years old, and considered by its congregants to be an ugly and drafty old barn. Built in 1844 as a Congregational church, it was preserved for its architectural value.

be ascribed to an ethnic conflict. The parish had been founded at the time when the West End had been predominantly Irish. And, although the Irish had long ago moved out and the congregation was now overwhelmingly Italian, the pastor, many of his priests, and most of the lay leaders still were Irish. West Enders referred to the parish church as "the American church." Even so, they were not visibly bothered by the dominance of the Irish, if only because the church did not really engage them strongly. Perhaps they were also resigned to the inevitable, for the church has always been under Irish control in Boston. As the Catholic church does permit its adherents to attend mass outside the parish, some West Enders went to the Polish church because its schedule of masses suited them better. They also could have gone to one of the Italian churches in the North End, but only some of the old people did so, mainly for language reasons.

The West Enders' detachment from the church may also be a result of the differences between the Irish and the Italian concept of the Catholic religion. Italian Catholicism emphasizes the worship of the Virgin Mary; the source of authority is matriarchal. Indeed, West Enders displayed pictures and statues of the Madonna and Child in almost every room of their apartments. Irish Catholicism stresses, among other things, the Trinity, which is male, and its source of authority is patriarchal. But as Italians are notably resistant to patriarchal authority, those who did give any thought to the matter had little sympathy for the stern and less permissive Irish Catholicism being taught to their children at church and in the parochial school.

A factor distinctive to the West End was the pastor's policy that the church should minimize church-related social and neighborhood activities. The pastor himself had little contact with his parishioners, leaving this function to the other priests. The ones who were assigned to the West End parish during the time of my study had little interest in, and sympathy for, the neighborhood. In fact, the two members of the church staff whom I interviewed described the area as a slum in which it was not safe to walk at night and viewed its residents as mostly transient and socially undesirable people. They looked forward to the redevelopment of the West End, and hoped for a more middle-class group of parishioners.[10] Their attitudes resembled those of the church's Irish lay leaders. Most of these, living on the Back of Beacon Hill, felt that the West End had deteriorated significantly when it had become predominantly Italian.

Although the pastor did permit the Holy Name Society and the Catholic Women's group to function, these and the St. Vincent de Paul—a group of laymen who administered charity to a small number of parishioners—were the only groups attached to the church. By contrast, the Polish church, which served a smaller congregation, had ten such satellite organizations.

The Catholic Women's Society, dominated by Irish parishioners until the area was torn down, functioned as the main social circle for the Irish women of the church, and enrolled few Italian parishioners. The Holy Name Society leadership, however, had been taken over by Italians during the 1950's. The Society's program was a fairly representative one: the group took communion together once a month, and held meetings afterwards at which films or speakers on male topics were presented. There was also a weekly bowling league. In 1958, 30 per cent of the male parishioners were said to belong to the Society, although most of them were inactive.

The parochial school was run in conjunction with the church. Having once had sixteen grades, it had since been cut to eight grades, and, in its last few years of existence, only first graders were accepted as new students. Thus, it was difficult to estimate how many West Enders sent their children to the parochial school. There was general agreement that the parochial school was better than the public ones, mainly because it expelled students with discipline problems, who then wound up in the public schools. I believe that most West Enders who could afford the tuition fee sent their children to the parochial school.

This choice was based neither on identification with the church, nor on a belief in the school's Catholic curriculum, but on the

10. Some time ago, the church carried on its staff a priest who was deeply involved in the community, and who ran athletic programs for the adolescents. He was evidently much liked in the community, and the fact that he was Irish did not detract from his influence. The central character in Joseph Caruso's novel, *The Priest,* New York: Popular Library, 1958, bears some resemblance to this man.

ability of the nuns to obtain and maintain discipline. Indeed, West Enders often suggested that the main purpose of school was to train the children in self-control, obedience to female and religious authority, and submission to discipline generally. As one mother explained, "Education teaches [my son] to keep away from bad boys." Parents respected the nuns for their dedication and sternness, and hoped that their methods would help keep the children out of trouble as they became adolescents. The students were exposed to a classical academic curriculum, but little rubbed off on them beyond the fundamentals. Dutifully learned by rote methods, it was all forgotten when the examinations were over.[11] Conversely, some West Enders who were dedicated to Italian Catholicism complained that the school was indoctrinating their children in Irish Catholicism, but whether this indoctrination takes hold cannot be judged fully until the children reach adulthood. Observations of Italian families in the suburbs, however, would suggest that third-generation adults have continued to keep themselves aloof from church activities other than attendance at mass.[12]

Formal Organizations and Associations

By 1958, the only West End organizations with members of Italian origin were the American Legion post and the Augusta Society. The Legion post, located just outside the West End, had been founded when the community was predominantly Irish, but was now largely composed of Italians.[13] It was, however, almost defunct, and was run by a West End barber who assailed his customers with complaints about the lack of cooperation he was getting to his appeals for help in reviving the post. In 1958, the post came alive only before St. Patrick's Day and Christmas, when about two hundred women attended the "penny sales"—lotteries in

11. General attitudes toward education and the public school are discussed in Chapter 6.

12. This impression is based on comments by Michael Parenti, of the State University of New York at Oyster Bay, and on my own observations in suburban communities. This problem is also discussed by Nathan Glazer, *Peoples of New York,* forthcoming.

13. Another post, located within the West End, was frequented by Polish legionnaires.

which nearly a hundred prizes were raffled off at the cost of one cent a ticket.[14] These sales, like the church bazaars and card parties, provided a religiously legitimated opportunity for the gambling that the men—and some women—pursue day in and day out by betting on the numbers and on sporting events.

The Augusta Society, open only to Sicilians who have come from the village of Augusta in eastern Sicily, attracted mostly immigrants. I was told that less than half of its members still lived in the West End, and that most of these came from a three-block area of the West End that had not been included in the slum clearance project.[15]

Another organization based on residential origin is the Old-Time West Enders club, which meets in a downtown hotel once a year. It was started about 1950 by some Irish and Jewish men who had grown up in the West End between 1900 and 1915. Limited to men who were born and raised in the area, the organization attracts about three hundred men to its annual gatherings. The main event of the annual meeting is a speech by a prominent person who grew up in the West End. The meeting which I attended was addressed by a railroad president, who attributed his occupational mobility and worldly success to lessons learned "at the university of hard knocks" in the West End of his childhood. He also contrasted the heavy responsibility of his current social status with the simpler, if more poverty-stricken, way of life of a slum child. I was told that other speakers stressed similar themes, and that there was much nostalgia about the good old days and the joy of life in the West End. Most of the members are middle-class men who now live in the suburbs of Boston. Although the West Enders who I have been describing in this book were eligible to belong to the group, only a few ever came. The handful who did attend the meeting at which I was present had little sympathy for the speaker's feeling about the West End, and pointed out acidly

14. Just before the 1958 St. Patrick's Day penny sale, the Legion commander decided that it should be associated with Easter rather than with the Irish holiday. Since the post had been predominantly Italian for many years, he confessed sheepishly that the change should have taken place at least ten years earlier.

15. This area has since been scheduled for clearance as part of the Scollay Square redevelopment project.

that the group had not opposed the redevelopment of the area.

Just after World War II, the West End also boasted a number of young men's social clubs, which were formal organizations only to the extent that they had names and constitutions. This enabled them to hire meeting rooms, and to extract tribute from politicians at election time in exchange for an endorsement. Although the clubs took little or no part in the campaigning, I was told that if the candidates had not contributed funds, club members would have entered the campaign by maligning them.[16] Members met nightly for card games, and held informal parties on weekends. The club rooms also provided an opportunity for peer group sociability, inexpensive entertainment, and privacy for dancing and drinking, as well as for after-hours sexual activities with whatever girls could be persuaded to stay after the dance was over. The clubs seemed to have divided on somewhat the same college-boy–corner-boy basis that Whyte had observed in the North End.[17] By 1958, only one such club still survived, consisting primarily of young men who had attended college or who held white-collar jobs. Most of its members no longer lived in the West End, but returned to the area to meet childhood friends, or because they could not find compatible associates in their new neighborhoods.

Commercial Establishments

The West End's taverns, stores, and restaurants were part of the community because, like most of the previously discussed organizations, they served the peer group society in a variety of special functions. Some provided meeting places for groups that had no other home, and others served as ganglia in the area's extensive communication network.

The West End was also dotted with lunch counters and "variety

16. The West End clubs seem to have been less important politically than those which Whyte described as operating in the North End. In the 1940's and 1950's, the candidates of Italian background came primarily from the North End, and evidently felt that the West End was less important to their political fortunes. For an analysis of the political club in the North End, see William F. Whyte, Jr., *Street Corner Society*, Chicago: University of Chicago Press, 1943, 2nd ed., 1955, Chaps. 2 and 5.

17. Whyte, *op. cit.*, Part I.

stores," the latter selling newspapers, magazines, candy, school supplies, a small stock of groceries, soft drinks, and sandwiches. These places too—as well as the taverns and barber shops—provided hangouts for men who were not visibly employed, and for others who stopped by after work. Since Italians drink less liquor than other working-class populations, the taverns tended to attract few of the West Enders. Several of the smaller ones, however, were taken over entirely by young men who spent their afternoons and evenings there, and who drank enough beer to pay the rent. They so dominated these taverns, in fact, that other West Enders rarely entered. In the tavern which I visited occasionally, the bartender was part of the peer group, and participated in the card games and conversational competition as an equal. Much of the time he did not even function as bartender; the regular customers came behind the bar to serve themselves, and put their own money in the cash register. Similarly, in one of the luncheonettes where I sometimes drank coffee, the regular customers did not give orders to the owner, for he knew exactly what they wanted. Women did not "hang out," of course, but they did combine shopping with socializing, mostly in the small groceries.

Teenagers also frequented some of the stores, but most of them congregated on corners near one of the variety stores or small groceries, where their presence was met with mixed felings. For although they did buy ice cream, candy, and cigarettes from the stores, they also expressed their hostility toward the adult world to the adult customers. The owners occasionally would try half-heartedly to chase the teenagers away. But they had little success, for, in most cases, the same corners had been used for "hanging out" for two generations.

The owners and managers of the bars and luncheonettes were kept busy also in taking and passing along messages for their regular customers. The latter, who frequented the stores at regular and unchanging times during the day, often received phone calls there. Moreover, as many of them did not seem to have telephones at their own homes, they could best be reached at their regular hangout. In addition, the establishments served as centers for the exchange of news and gossip. Since the West End did not have its own newspaper, and since West Enders placed little trust in the city press, the commercial establishments thus played an important communication function in the area.[18]

Some of the commercial establishments also served as hangouts and communication centers for *sub-rosa* activities. A number of the men who could be seen in the area during the day made their living as petty gamblers, or by working for more organized gambling endeavors. Some of the luncheonettes and variety stores had installed special pinball machines equipped for gambling, with payoffs increasing with the amount of money put into the machine. With the right combination of skill and luck, investments of several dollars in nickels could pay a 50 to 200 per cent return to the player. I use business concepts to describe the play, because the men who played these machines regularly approached them with the same amount of deliberation and care that a middle-class person would use in playing the stock market. Less dedicated gamblers generally stayed away from the machines.

Most of the extrabusiness activities that I have described took place in establishments owned or managed by people who lived in the West End, and who were socially and culturally like their customers. Indeed, they were able to compete against the more modern stores outside the West End only because they could attract regular customers whom they treated as peer group members rather than as customers.[19] Many of them probably earned little more from their establishments than the employed West Enders. Some of the luncheonettes were perhaps able to stay in business only because of income derived from the ancillary gambling activities. Maybe this is why they had been opened in the first place.

18. See Chapter 7.

19. In addition, the food stores retained their customers by giving credit and by being near at hand to West Enders who were restricted in their movements, especially the elderly and the people without cars.

CHAPTER 6 The Outside World: Work, Education, and Medical Care

The Structure of the Outside World

To the West Ender, the organizations and institutions that constitute the community are an accepted part of life, since their functions are frequently auxiliary to those of the peer group society.

Other organizations and institutions, however, which play an equally if not more necessary role in the life of the West Ender, are less freely accepted. Added together, these make up what I have called the *outside world*. Although the term is mine, it reflects what West Enders describe as "they" or "them." This is the world beyond the peer group society and the community: the world of employers, professionals, the middle class, city government, and—with some exceptions—the national society. Although the outside world is almost entirely non-Italian, it is not defined by its ethnic characteristics. Thus, even Italians who adopt its values are scorned by the West Enders. In short, then, it consists of those agencies and individuals who interfere with the life of the peer group society.

The agencies which I have grouped under this rubric differ widely, both in function and the way in which West Enders relate to them. At one extreme, for example, are the worlds of work and health care, which are so vital to the individual and the peer group society that they have little choice but to accept them. Then, there are the services that social agencies from outside the West End offer to West Enders, notably the settlement houses.[1] These are treated with a mixture of curiosity and suspicion. But, since they are not necessary for peer group life, they are essentially ignored—at least by adults. In between is education, especially at the high school level, which most West Enders now accept as being necessary, although they are still ambivalent as to its usefulness. At the other extreme are the law, the police, and the government. Conceived as agencies that exist to exploit West Enders, they are thus viewed with considerable hostility.[2] If possible, contact with them is minimized, and relegated to the politician. Off to one corner is the world of consumer goods and the mass media of entertainment,[3] whose products are welcomed into every West End home, albeit with considerable selectivity. Even so, the mass media do constitute one of the major ties to the outside world.

These diverse agencies can be discussed together because they are external to the peer group society. Since they are manned by nonmembers, who are expected to treat West Enders in object-oriented ways, the rules of behavior that govern the peer group society are not applicable to them. The services of the outside world are to be used if they are desirable and to be ignored or fought if they seek to change or injure the individual or the peer group. As I noted in Chapter 4, the West Ender always expects to be exploited in his contact with the outside world, and is ready to exploit it in return. If he is treated in a person-oriented fashion, he is pleasantly surprised and ready to do likewise. But he still remains on guard, and the burden of proof rests with the outside world.

Attitudes toward the outside world are not homogeneous. Action-seeking people, for example, are much more suspicious and hostile than the routine-seeking. Likewise, men are more hostile than women, mainly because they have frequent contact with the

1. See Chapter 7.
2. See Chapter 8.
3. See Chapter 9.

outside world, and more often need to defend themselves against it. Even so, everyone shares the basic gulf that exists between the peer group society and the outside world—a gulf that must be crossed by one or the other before the West Ender will become a part of the larger American society.

The World of Work

The parents of the West Enders were farm laborers in Italy, and were employed as unskilled factory or construction laborers in America. While the second generation's fortunes have improved considerably, most West Enders still are employed in unskilled and semiskilled blue-collar jobs. Although the bureaucratization and unionization of employment have vastly increased job security, the West Ender continues to think of employment as insecure and expects layoffs—temporary or permanent—to come at any time. There are good reasons for his suspicion. Since Boston has not experienced the large immigration of Negroes that has taken place elsewhere, Italians occupy a "lower" position in the Boston labor market—and in the city's division of labor—than they do in New York, Chicago, and other large cities.[4] Moreover, they work in more marginal industries, where layoffs, the disappearance of jobs, and the closing down of firms are not unusual. West Enders also told me that discrimination against Italians still occurs occasionally.

These conditions help to define the West Ender's attitude toward work. Work is thought of as a necessary expenditure of time and energy for the purpose of making a living, and, if possible, for increasing the pleasure of life outside the job. Thus, West Enders work to make money, and they want to make money to spend on themselves, the family, and the peer group. Since most of them must work for other people, their jobs often take them outside the peer group society and the community. It is for this reason that I have classified work as part of the outside world.

For the West Ender, work means manual labor, and the expenditure of physical energy under frequently unpleasant work-

4. See, for example, Irvin L. Child, *Italian or American? The Second Generation in Conflict*, New Haven: Yale University Press, 1943; and Nathan Glazer, *Peoples of New York*, forthcoming.

ing conditions. Nonmanual jobs are not considered to require work. Thus, white-collar people are described as not really working, but as being able "to sit on their can." Similarly, executive and supervisory work is seen as consisting of giving orders and talking, neither of which is considered work by voluble West Enders.

The ideal job is thought of as one that pays the most money for the least physical discomfort, avoids strenuous or "dirty" physical labor, demands no emotional involvement, such as "taking the job home with you," requires no submission to arbitrary authority, and provides compatible companions at work. Taxing and dirty jobs are associated with the parental generation. West Enders today feel that such jobs should go to Negroes, Puerto Ricans, and immigrants who have recently arrived from Italy. They do not, however, reject physical labor as such, especially if other working conditions are pleasant. Some of the young West Enders, for example, who work in the food markets of the North End spoke with satisfaction of the unregimented nature of their work, and of the ability to see friends and continue the peer group conversations during working hours.

Indeed, West Enders expect to work hard, and they derive satisfaction from doing a good job. Although they may talk freely about the pleasures of loafing, a few days' illness or a vacation spent at home quickly convinces them that life without work would be unbearable. Because most West Enders work in small firms, and because they do not find it easy to accept authority of any kind, one of the most important criteria for job satisfaction is having a good boss. The good boss treats his employees as close to equals as possible, works hard himself, and does not unduly exert his authority, especially in matters unrelated to work. As the West Ender's most intimate contact with the outside world is with the boss, his behavior is thus watched closely. Should he act unreasonably, he will quickly lose his employee's respect and good will. Further, should the West Ender feel that he is being exploited, he will exploit his employer in turn wherever and whenever he can —short of losing his job.

The expectation of exploitation comes most often from those working in large firms, and, when it does occur, considerable satisfaction is derived from fighting back. One West Ender, who had once worked as a sweeper in a company that cleaned office buildings, spent considerable time in "goofing off," and methodically violating the rules set by management, because the wages were low, and the union was in a strong position. He intimated that the pleasure of his revenge reimbursed him for the poor wages. During the war, he also had worked in a government-owned defense installation, and described the ways in which his colleagues stole time or materials from the government. Mainly because the federal government had done nothing to exploit him, he had not participated in this activity. He was highly critical, however, of the hasty cleanups that took place when visiting dignitaries came to the plant, and tried his best to minimize his share of what he considered to be fraudulent activity. A younger West Ender, who had recently been mustered out of the Army, took great pride in the wholesale evasion of work and rejection of authority he practiced against the Army to get even for being separated from his friends in the West End.

Even when work is well paid and satisfying, the West Ender will try to minimize any involvement in it beyond that required of him. Work is a means to an end, never an end in itself. At best, single-minded dedication to work is thought to be strange, and, at worst, likely to produce ulcers, heart trouble, and the possibility of an early death.

Thus while the West Ender has developed skills which he seeks to practice, and in which he takes some pride, notions of a career are still rare. Indeed, the difference between the West Ender and the middle-class person is perhaps nowhere greater than in this attitude toward the career. The idea that work can be a central purpose in life, and that it should be organized into the series of related jobs that make a career is virtually nonexistent among the second generation.

This is best illustrated with respect to professionalism. Middle-class professionals see themselves as striving to bring their own activity into line with an idealized conception of their calling and to refine their work method so as to be professionals in the best sense of the word. Although a few West Enders have moved into professional occupations—especially in law and accountancy—their work is devoted less to the achievement of professional perfection and recognition from fellow professionals than to the application of skills—and contacts—in behalf of the peer group society. Thus, lawyers become politicians and agents of the Italian community in the outside world. Consequently, their legal practice consists primarily of cases to help Italian clients get what is theirs from the outside world. They also use their legal skills and contacts for business dealings. But while these lawyers do want to maximize both income and status, their primary reference group is still the peer group society. As a result, they are person-oriented service agents, and have no desire to be object-oriented practitioners of "the law." It should be noted, of course, that as "the law" is largely in the hands of high-status individuals of Yankee Protestant origin, lawyers of Italian or other ethnic origin have little access to the more prestigeful types of legal practice, even should they want these.

Similar orientations can be found among other Italian professionals. The singer, for example, aims to achieve a personal style of delivery, rather than technical virtuosity. The artist and writer want to portray their society to the outside world, and to come to terms with both of them personally. Thus, most of the novels written about Italian-American life are at least partly autobiographical. The photographer works for "effects" that will please the client. In short, all of them give lower priority to the formal esthetic and technical concepts of their craft.

The attitudes that stand out most clearly among the first Italians to enter the professions are present among other workers as well. For example, as most of the semiprofessional people came to their work without the educational background usually associated with it, they have a less secure foothold in their occupation than middle-class colleagues. As a result, they are less embued with the beliefs and goals of their craft. The only West Enders who could be said to think in terms of a career were lawyer-politicians. Yet, even they were quite ambivalent about pursuing politics as a career and were not sure that they wanted to advance on the rungs of the political ladder. It should be noted, however, that the insecurity of political life does not encourage career aspirations.

People who work in low-skill white collar jobs, or in blue-collar ones, cannot really begin to think in career terms. Such thinking assumes the existence of broad opportunities and a moderate assurance of job security. I have already noted that West Enders believe, with some justification, that jobs are scarce and that job security is nonexistent. With luck an individual may get one job that he can define as good, but this is not likely to happen twice in a row. Even workers with specific skills do not expect that they will always be able to find jobs in which they can practice them.

The lack of identification with work is hardly surprising. Second-generation Italians, it must be remembered, were raised by parents whose occupational skills and choices were few, and for whom work usually mean backbreaking labor at subsistence wages. But although the immigrants encouraged their children to escape this kind of work—if they needed any encouragement—they had no reason or precedent to urge them toward any identification with work, or to expect any satisfactions from it. Unlike the Jews who came to America with something approaching middle-class occupational aspirations and who passed them on to their children, the Italians had only a tradition of farm labor with no hope for anything else. And given the conditions they encountered in America, it would have been foolhardy for the immigrants to encourage their children to seek emotional involvement in work. Instead, they prepared them to work hard, and to accept job loss and temporary unemployment as inevitable.

The second generation, in turn, encourages its children to equip themselves for better jobs, and urges them to get as much education as they can for this purpose. Although West Enders are interested in job mobility for their children, they have not yet begun to encourage career thinking, for they have not had the job security that would enable them to do so. The children listen to the parental urgings about education, but they also observe the attitudes toward work that are expressed all around them day after day, and they share the group's lack of interest in thinking about the future. Parents are disappointed if their children announce that they will not continue their education beyond the legal minimum, and that they have no interest in better jobs than their parents', but this disappointment is not intense. After all, work is not a fundamental purpose in life, and if they have gotten along, so will their children.[5]

West Enders are employees more from necessity than choice. Indeed, the peer group society, by developing people who compete with each other for emotional satisfaction within the group, tends to encourage what Miller and Swanson have called "entrepreneurial personalities." [6] Because of this, many West Enders are predisposed to self-employment—an attitude they share with many other ethnic and working-class groups.

The desire for self-employment is also closely related to the West Ender's conception of work. As already noted, work means manual labor, and self-employment may permit him to make more money without such labor. Also, the self-employed person does not have to take orders; he is independent and free from authority. Moreover, he may even be able to limit his contact with the outside world, and, if he cannot do so, he has considerable opportunity to exploit it, and to get even for the actual or imagined exploitation to which the peer group society is exposed. One self-employed West Ender described with glee the satisfaction he derives from creating "short cuts" in his work that are not visible to his customers, but that give him the feeling that he is putting something over on them.

The hostility toward the outside world also allows the West Ender to condone illegal work activities. Consequently, little disapproval is expressed toward gamblers, and even racketeers, as long as their activities do not hurt the peer group society. Thus, West Enders usually had only words of praise for a well-known gambler —one of the wealthiest men in the West End—because he gave lavishly to local organizations and to charities. And while the bootleggers and racketeers who had lived in the area during the days of prohibition were not praised, even they were thought to have done no harm, because their illegal activities had been aimed at the outside world, and their violence had been restricted to their own associates and competitors. Since the parents of West Enders made

5. Attitudes toward education will be discussed further in the next section.
6. Daniel B. Miller and Guy E. Swanson, *The Changing American Parent,* New York: Wiley and Sons, 1958, Chap. 2.

their own wine for family use—in the bathrooms and cellars of their tenements—they also had little sympathy for the prohibition laws that forbade this activity.

The preference for self-employment, however, still stops far short of entrepreneurial ambition. West Enders have little capital, and not much interest in risk-taking. They say that when a Jew goes out of business, he will open another place and try again, but that an Italian, in the same circumstances, will go to work for someone else. Entrepreneurial activity, unless it is a group venture, invites failure or success, both of which are likely to separate the individual from the peer group. Also, whereas the immigrant generation saved its money to buy land or an apartment building, their children, who have embraced American standards of living, find it difficult to save. Moreover, as they are not imbued with peasant values, the ownership of land as an end in itself has less meaning to them. Apartment buildings can no longer be bought cheaply, and West Enders have no desire to become landlords or their own janitors, a kind of work that is considered to be undesirable.

Consequently, self-employment opportunities that require little capital and allow the owner to use family members are preferred, and the West Enders naturally gravitate toward service functions. Opening a garage is sometimes mentioned, as are services that involve display or the management of display of others—being a barber, for example, or a tailor, or owning a clothing store. Running a luncheonette or a restaurant is still liked, partly because the owner can have peer group company on the job. Contracting, on the other hand, once a popular avenue for self-employment among Italians, now requires too much capital; and grocery store ownership lost its attractiveness with the coming of the supermarkets.

Most of the talk about escaping employee status, however, is at the level of dreams rather than goals. Few West Enders are either able or willing to think about such a change in status. In effect, work is simply not that important. And as the small owner becomes more and more marginal, even the dreams about self-employment become more infrequent, and are not passed on to the next generation.

Work, of course, is entirely a male pursuit. Husbands do not want their wives to work after marriage, nor do the women themselves. They are expected to be ready to work if the husband is laid off, or if the family budget requires their help. I encountered no women who worked because they wanted to, however, or because they wished to obtain money for individual and family luxuries, or for that matter, because they wanted to compete with their husbands for economic mastery of the household. Even childless wives preferred to be housewives and aunts. For the women, then, work itself holds even fewer attractions than it does for the men.

Education

West End children can go either to the parochial or public elementary schools, but most of them must go to public ones for their high-school education. Although their parents prefer parochial to public institutions, the distinction that is of most significance to them and that creates uncertainty about schooling is between person-oriented and object-oriented education. Person-oriented education teaches children rules of behavior appropriate to the adult peer group society, and stresses discipline. This is identified with the parochial school. Object-oriented education teaches them aspirations and skills for work, play, family life, and community participation.[7] Rightly or wrongly, this type of education is identified with the public school. It is also the source of West End ambivalence, and accounts for the placement of education in the outside world.

On the one hand, West Enders do recognize that education is needed to obtain employment, and urge the children to get as much schooling as is required for a secure skilled blue-collar or white-collar job. On the other hand, parents are suspicious that education will estrange the children from them, and from the peer group society as well. Consequently, they are somewhat fearful

7. In some ways, this is the traditional Southern Italian peasant distinction between "buon educato," being well-mannered or well brought-up, and "buono istruito," being well-instructed in book learning, which was considered of little importance. R. A. Schermerhorn, *These Our People*, Boston: D. C. Heath and Co., 1949, p. 242.

about the public education to which the children are exposed in high school.

These fears are best illustrated by the West Enders' conception of the public-school teacher. They see her as a woman who has little interest in teaching, and who is more concerned with making money, chasing men, or "boozing" after hours. As one West Ender pointed out, the nun who teaches in the parochial school is unpaid, and her work is motivated solely by religious dedication. Consequently, her life is limited to teaching and prayer, and she is likely to be in bed by 9 P.M. The public-school teacher, however, is either working at an extra job, or drinking in a tavern during the evening hours when she should be resting or preparing herself for the next day's teaching. Therefore, she is not fit to teach self-control to the children, and is thought to be too tired even to keep order.

This fantastic conception stems partly from the public-school's reputation as a haven for incorrigibles who cannot accept parochial discipline.[8] It also reflects the considerable social distance between the West Ender and the school. Public-school officials claimed that parents took little interest in their children and even less in the school. Over the years, several attempts to develop Home and School associations in the West End failed because only a few parents showed up. As might be expected, the parents of children with scholastic or behavioral difficulties were least likely to come to school, whereas those whose children were doing well did take an interest.

Parental lack of interest in the school is a function of the segregation between adults and children in the adult-centered family, a process that begins just about the time that the child starts attending school, and that increases with age. The public school is keyed, of course, to the child-centered family in which parents do involve themselves in their children's lives; the parochial school accepts the adult-centered family, and does not expect or encourage parental participation, except when the child gets into trouble.

From the parents' perspective, then, education is useful only for behavior training and for obtaining a job. They see no need

8. This is ironic, because I noted earlier that public-school principals found their students to be surprisingly quiet and well-behaved.

for subject matter that does not contribute directly to this aim. As one skilled worker told me: "What good is archeology in a mechanical arts high school? You want to learn it if you're a teacher, but not for other things. I am a working man." Some West Enders are not yet convinced that additional schooling will be useful even occupationally. For example, they point out that depressions and layoffs take no notice of education, and that whom you know rather than what you know is still the key to occupational success in many places. This attitude is voiced mainly by those who are satisfied with their own occupational achievements. Other West Enders, especially those who are not satisfied with their jobs, and those in white-collar positions, realize only too clearly that they would have done better had they been able to stay in school beyond the elementary grades or the first years of high school. Most West Enders of the present generation, however, had little choice in the matter, for they were expected to go to work as early as possible. It is these people who urge their children to finish high school.

By and large, full-blown skepticism as to the value of education now centers on college attendance, especially at a private liberal arts school, which West Enders consider to be playgrounds for the idle rich. They delight in telling stories of college-educated people who hold jobs no better than their own, or who are total failures. One story, for example, concerns a West End "character" with several university degrees who now makes a living by scavenging through area garbage. The implications of the story are clear: college education does not assure occupational success, and over-education may lead to mental illness. Yet the same people who tell such stories will also speak of their hopes that their boys will continue their education after high school so as to get a better job. At the same time, they sense that college attendance can estrange parents and children. Consequently, they question the desirability of a liberal arts or academic education, explaining that "college is only for the very brightest boy." Indeed, academic skill is viewed as a kind of virtuosity, much like musical ability and is thought to be desirable—and attainable—only for the rare youngster who is intellectually gifted. Lower-class West Enders, on the other hand, retain some of the traditional hostility toward the high school and consider it as keeping the child from going to work at the earliest opportunity.

Attitude differences also exist between mothers and fathers, and between their aspirations for boys and for girls. Generally, mothers are more favorably inclined toward the school, partly because of their concern that the child learn behavior control. Fathers, however, are less interested in behavior control, and are more fearful that boys will become "sissies or girl scouts" if they become too identified with the ways of the school. Moreover, since most of the teachers are women, fathers see education as a feminine undertaking that might endanger their boys' maleness.

Girls are thought to need less education than boys, since they will get married soon after leaving school. Responsibility for the girl's educational decision is therefore left up to the mother. If the girl does well in school, she has her mother's approval to continue as long as she wishes; and, if family finances permit it, her father's silent acquiescence. But the father is primarily interested in the boy's education. If a boy does not do well in school, and wants to drop out, he is likely to get support from his father, especially should the latter be satisfied with his own occupational fortunes. His mother may object, but will probably resign herself to the alliance of father and son. Whenever possible, West End parents will express their doubts and negative feelings about education only in adult company. As they have enough respect for the value of schooling as a means to occupational success, they try to speak only favorably of it to the children.

Despite these parental efforts, many of the children do not take to education. Even though family finances permit them to stay, they often drop out of school at the earliest opportunity. The general picture drawn by the school officials with whom I spoke was that the majority of children displayed little interest in learning, that many had learning difficulties, and that even more were waiting only to reach the legal school-leaving age. The West End principals estimated that about half of the students—from all ethnic groups and class levels in the area—completed senior high school. During the 1950's, 3 to 5 per cent of the junior high-school graduates had been sent to Boston Latin, the city's college preparatory senior high school, but only some of these eventually got to college. The junior high-school principal's main problem was truancy, and the parental acquiescence concerning this. Boys were more likely to be truant than girls, and to be poorer students as well.

The reasons for the failure to respond to education—especially on the part of boys—can be found in the influence of the peer group society. Success in school depends to some extent on student motivation, and this is largely absent. In part, this lack can be traced to the parental ambivalence about the usefulness of education, and to the absence of books and other intellectual stimuli in the home. Class differences between student and teacher are also crucial. But other factors come into play even before the child is old enough to develop motivation for school learning. For one thing, educational achievement depends largely on the ability to absorb and manipulate concepts, to handle the reasoning processes embedded in the lesson and the text, and to concentrate on these methods to the exclusion of other concerns. West End children are adept at none of them.

The peer group society trains its members to be sensitive to people, rather than to ideas. Words are used, not as concepts, but to impress people, and argument proceeds by the use of anecdotes rather than by the common sense forms of logic. The rhythm of peer group life, the impulsive approach to child-rearing, the stress on the episodic—whether in the form of action or anecdote—and the competitive nature of peer group conversation—all encourage a short attention span. It is this very shortness of attention and the inability to concentrate that seem to accompany, if not cause, many of the learning difficulties. Certainly it is not a lack of native or acquired intelligence. For even in their early years, West End children—like children everywhere—are sensitive to the ins and outs of interaction with parents, and they quickly learn how to use words and acts to bend people to their wishes.

The school also conflicts with the many and opposing attractions of the children's peer groups. In fact, it tries to break up these groups, although not always consciously, and expects the children to act as independent individuals. But as many are either unable or unwilling to act in this way, they respond with passivity. The moment they leave the school building and the teacher's control, they coalesce quickly into peer groups to spend the afternoon learning the lore of the streets.

Neither children or teachers get much help from parents. Most of them, having left school before the tenth grade, find the material strange. Although parents tell their children to learn, and to do homework, there are still people like one West Ender who castigated his eight-year-old daughter for wanting to go to the library again after just having been there the previous day. Bright children are encouraged by their teachers, but have peer group difficulties, unless they can find like-minded colleagues. I was told that this had been much easier before the Jews moved out of the West End, since the occasional Italian who was interested in learning then could have attached himself to a Jewish group, at least through elementary school age.

For the child with learning difficulties, school is probably a real torture. By the time this child has reached adolescence, he usually has accepted his handicap with sullen passivity. But as soon as the activities of the peer group are stepped up, and require more pocket money, there is little incentive to stay in school. Thus, if the parents permit it—and even if they do not—the teenager may become a habitual truant until he reaches the school-leaving age. His departure from school is experienced as a release from prison. Later on, when these boys become aware of the limited choice of jobs to which their decision to leave school has sentenced them, they wish they had remained to graduate. But then it is too late.[9] Actually, the drop-outs that occur at the legal school-leaving age are only a formality, the outcome of factors that have estranged such boys from school for many years prior to their physical departure.

The people who staffed the West End schools seemed to be resigned to the students' lack of interest in education. I should explain here that I spoke only to principals, but not to any teachers, and that my observations are limited by this gap in my research.

9. It would be highly desirable if a far-sighted government allowed these youngsters to leave school when they wanted to and provided them with scholarships and subsistence for their families so that they could return to school when they become so motivated in their mid-twenties.

Nor was I able to evaluate the quality of the teachers, although I was told by people inside and outside of the West End that most of them were older women who were serving out their years in the system without much enthusiasm for or understanding of their students. Whether or not this judgment is accurate, it is true that there was little incentive for a bright young teacher to work in the West End, since it was known as a slum area by the average Bostonian.

I was able to interview two of the three public school principals in the area. One, who had been in the West End school only a few years, liked his students and accepted their lack of interest in learning with stoic resignation. He prided himself on being one of the first Irish Catholics to become a principal—the Boston public school system is still largely under Yankee Protestant control—and looked back nostalgically on the intellectual rewards of teaching in a predominantly Jewish school before becoming a principal. He also looked forward to the redevelopment of the West End, with the expectation that the new student body would be more interested in education.

The other principal, with a similar social and ethnic background, had been in the West End for many years, and had adapted himself to the values of his students. He argued that occupational success was to be ranked above learning, for, as he put it, "dollars are more important than IQ's." He also noted that some of his poorest students had gone on to well-paying jobs, or now owned profitable enterprises. Both principals, aware of the cultural differences between school and students, viewed these as problems residing in the latter, and in the economic position of the students' parents. Both were also surprised but grateful that their charges provided no serious discipline problems.

Yet the picture is not as black as I have painted it here. The third generation does stay in school much longer than the second generation, if only because students do not have to leave to support their families, and because child-labor laws, as well as changes in the labor market entrance age, have encouraged their staying in school. This is especially true of the girls, who not only remain in school longer, but seem to absorb more of its offerings. The girls find it easier to identify with the female teacher than the boys, and, as noted earlier, receive more encouragement from their mothers to stay in school. In addition, the school culture is more congruent with the routine-seeking working-class culture norms that mothers defend and pass on to their daughters, and with the functions girls perform at home. They are expected to learn to sew, cook, and help in child-care—duties that are more akin to school requirements than are the peer group activities of boys as they roam the streets. The girls may not go on to college after they graduate, but they are more likely to work in a store or office until marriage, while their brothers will probably gravitate to blue-collar jobs. The girls who do go to college often find husbands there and leave areas like the West End. Since the number of mobile girls exceeds that of boys, I suspect that some of the girls have trouble finding a husband in the Italian group and will intermarry or stay single as a result. Neither is considered desirable by the peer group society. Boys who go to college also may fail to return to the West End, but they are much less likely to shed West End associates and ways of behaving. Even if they work in the middle-class world, they often revert to the style of the peer group society when they come home at night—to the chagrin of their wives.

Early marriage may abort college even when the desire and the financial resources are present. This was illustrated dramatically by the son of a well-to-do West Ender who had made plans to attend law school at one of the better universities in the Northeast. His plans were interrupted by marriage, however, and he decided instead to go to a local night law school. The middle-class practice of being supported by his family or his wife while in school was out of the question. After marriage, he went to work as a law clerk and his wife stayed home; occupational aspirations were quickly relegated to a lower priority, and seemingly without regrets.

Medical Care and Health

Medical care is another necessary function for which the West Ender must go into the outside world, at least in cases of serious illness. Minor ailments are treated by patent medicines and home remedies. These represent a modern folk medicine that has largely replaced the Italian equivalent brought over by the immigrants.[10]

The care of more serious illness has been classified as part of the outside world for two reasons. First, since there are no doctors in the peer group society, West Enders must use outsiders. Second, their conceptions of illness and care differ from those of the doctors. Consequently, the West Enders have not embraced the latter's medical care wholeheartedly. Rather, they have resigned themselves to it because they have none of their own. They accept it with some hesitation and suspicion, and this in turn affects their attitude toward doctors, as well as the nature and efficiency of the care process.

Medical care in the West End was provided by two sets of outsiders, the local practitioners and the Massachusetts General Hospital. While the hospital was held in affectionate regard by many West Enders, it was nevertheless viewed as part of the outside world, mainly because of its affiliation with Harvard University, and the absence of Italian doctors on the staff. West Enders used the hospital freely, especially its out-patient clinics, but they perceived the hospital as an organization of extremely high status, endowed with economic and political influence of gargantuan proportions. Its high status image stemmed from its association with Harvard, which is regarded as a university for the upper class. Since few West Enders have attended Harvard, or know anyone who has, they consider it as totally inaccessible, and regard it with a mixture of respect and suspicion. The hospital's power was ascribed to the presence of many of Boston's social and power elite on the board of trustees and administrative staff, and to its success in obtaining West End land and other privileges from the city. For example, West Enders noted wryly that whereas they were ticketed frequently for parking violations, hospital staff members had only to go down to the police station to register their license plate numbers in order to avoid this. The hospital also was thought to have had considerable influence in the decision to redevelop the West End, and some people were sure that the area was really being cleared for hospital expansion and parking

10. I did not collect any data on the number of Italian home remedies still being used by the West Enders, or on the proportion of illnesses which are treated without the aid of a doctor.

lots. Although their view of the hospital's status and influence was somewhat exaggerated, it was essentially accurate.

Most of the time, West Enders turned to the local practitioners for their medical care. These were older men, most of them Jewish—and none Italian—who had been born in the West End or had come to it when it was predominantly Jewish. Although they had taken part in the Jewish residential exodus, they had also kept their practices in the area. One of the few who had not moved his home lived in a huge townhouse on the best street in the West End and was probably the area's last owner-occupant of a free-standing house.

The local doctors continued to practice in the West End because they had become accustomed to their patients and were not highly motivated—or skilled enough in the latest techniques—to set up a new practice amidst younger and mobile people. They provided medical care in a fairly authoritarian manner, treating their patients almost as children who could not be expected to understand their own illness or the treatment for it. This approach is in sharp contrast to a middle-class practice, where the patient is treated as a more active participant in the care process, is informed about the diagnosis and the methods of care, and may even be told when the doctor is uncertain as to either the diagnosis or the efficacy of the treatment.

The West End doctor derived much economic and emotional security from his authoritarian role, but it was not entirely a matter of his own choosing. The West Enders came to the office with their own beliefs about illness and medical care and with a considerable lack of confidence in the medical profession. Their suspicions in turn led the doctor to command in an omniscient and dogmatic style, hoping thereby to persuade his patients to follow his recommendations for treatment.

The West Enders view illness as resulting either from a breakdown in self-control, or from conditions beyond the individual's control. The first type is thought to require self- or group-inflicted punishment as part of the treatment. In the second type of illness, the doctor's services may be used, but the possibility of a cure rests to a considerable extent on the workings of fate.

Psychosomatic and mental illnesses are attributed to lack of self-control. Ailments such as ulcers and high blood pressure, which seem to occur frequently, are ascribed to "hot-bloodedness." Hot blood is conceived as a physiological characteristic of Italians, which is not easily amenable to self-control. Heart attacks, however, are thought to be the result of overwork that is brought on by the inability to control ambition. Mental illness, whether expressed by deviant behavior or depression, is thought to stem from the individual's unwillingness to control his impulses, and is described in moral, rather than pathological, language.

As the lack of self-control is considered a personal failing, treatment thus must be punishing as well as therapeutic. For example, an ulcer patient with whom I talked refused to follow the diet prescribed by his doctor. He felt it would do no good, and that a more painful treatment—he did not specify what—would be needed. Although deviant behavior may be described as illness by West Enders, they reject any treatment of it that does not include strict punishment, especially if the act should be in any way antisocial. For example, depression is at first treated with sympathy, but should the individual fail to respond, he is then punished by social isolation.

Illnesses and disabilities such as respiratory diseases, cancer, arthritis, or broken bones are not thought to result from lack of self-control. Some illnesses are ascribed to the negative effects of the outside world. For example, many of the heart attacks and deaths among elderly people in the area were ascribed to the shock of redevelopment, thereby justifying West Enders to accuse the city administration of murder.

The cure of uncontrollable diseases is assigned to the removal of hostile forces in the outside world, to fate, and, last and least, to the doctor. West Enders will call the doctor, and expect him to deliver a cure, but they are skeptical that he can meet their expectations. If they do recover, the doctor's role is acknowledged grudgingly, but someone is sure to voice the suspicion that his treatment had nothing to do with it. Should the illness continue, people suspect that fate has willed it so, and that doctors are unable to provide proper treatment.

Such attitudes allow West Enders to postpone or even to avoid treatment of serious illness. Frightened of hospitals and even more so of operations, they will cite cases of people who have died on the operating table, usually because of medical incompetence. Fatalism reinforces their skepticism. One of my neighbors, for example, a factory worker, had suffered a head injury on the job. He had then gone to the hospital for an examination, was told that his injury might be serious enough to require an operation, and was given an appointment for further treatment. He failed to keep the appointment, however, and, although he suffered from recurring headaches, did not go back to the doctor. The fear of an operation and his fatalistic assumption that if his condition was serious, nothing could be done, prevailed over arguments—mine included—to get him to make another hospital visit.

Milder illnesses, especially those that are experienced by members of the peer group at the same time, such as viral infections, are not associated with fate. A doctor is called to treat influenza, for example, but once recovery is achieved, his role is minimized. People point out that he merely administers penicillin, and thus credit is given more to the magic of the wonder drug than to the doctor.

The West Ender's fatalism in the face of illness is due neither to superstition or helplessness. Indeed, the fabled belief in the evil eye that his parents brought over from Italy no longer exists. Fate is rather a reflection of a determined universe, the sacred portion of which is controlled by God, the secular portion by the powers-that-be of the outside world. It is this belief in fate that allows the West Ender to face illness and even death with resignation when there is little chance for recovery, and that softens the blow for his survivors, allowing them to continue to function. It is not an exclusively pessimistic belief, however, for the fatalistic attitude also permits the possibility of recovery, and explicitly recognizes the fact that sick people sometimes do get well without medical care. But although the West Ender is healthier than his parents or his Italian ancestors, physical or emotional breakdowns, serious injuries at work, and early deaths still do happen frequently and suddenly enough to justify the persistence of the traditional fatalism.

Thus the doctor plays a marginal role in medical care. West Enders do not like to consult him in the first place, and when they do, they have difficulty in describing their symptoms. Moreover, they may ignore his recommendations and fail to fill the prescriptions he gives them, especially when these are costly. Often he is described with considerable hostility as a man who takes poor people's money without exerting much physical effort or offering any sympathy. West Enders are not convinced that he is really working, for he does not like to make house calls, and even when he does come, he only prescribes rest, or gives shots. For this he collects fees that strike the West Ender—who has little contact with any other kind of fee-charging professional—as much too high. Actually, the fee for a house-call and a shot of penicillin was $4 in 1958. But since the doctor is extremely rich by area standards, West Enders still suspect that they are being exploited. Thus they love to tell scandalous stories about free-spending doctors, and about patients who were not helped by them, or who improved without ever calling one of them.

In many ways attitudes toward the doctor are similar to those toward the public-school teacher. The doctor is expected to be a selfless and monastically dedicated individual who should guarantee results but should not earn more money than the average West Ender. In short, he is expected to be a saint. Were he a member of the peer group society, these specifications would no doubt be reduced, but precisely because he is not, West Enders set an impossibly high moral standard by which to judge him, and thus to control his behavior. His inability to live up to sainthood creates and justifies their hostility and rejection.

The doctor-patient relationship therefore is incredibly difficult. Middle-class doctors who seek to incorporate the West Ender into the treatment process find that they cannot get a reliable account for their diagnosis, and that their recommendations are frequently ignored. For this reason, local doctors have resigned themselves to a detached role; they neither confide in the patient, nor expect him to obey their prescriptions. As class differences add to the conflict of expectations, there is little feedback between patient and doctor. This in turn only increases patient hostility and lack of confidence. Not only do few practitioners know how to overcome the obstacles to communication, but fewer still have any incentive to do so.

CHAPTER 7 The Caretakers: Missionaries from the Outside World

The Caretaker–Client Relationship

Every society has what Erich Lindemann calls "caretakers"—institutions and individuals who offer various kinds of care to its members. The term "caretaker" can thus be applied broadly to anyone who provides services to people, including salesmen who offer advice while selling a product. It can also be narrowly defined to include only those who give therapeutic care to patients. The definition used here will be midway between these alternatives. It shall refer to agencies and individuals who not only give patient care, but other kinds of aid that they think will benefit the client, and who offer aid as an end in itself, rather than as a means to a more important end. Caretakers thus include those people and agencies who offer medical and psychiatric treatment, case work, occupational, social, and psychological counseling, economic assistance, technical aid or information, advice in general, and educational and quasi-educational programs intended to benefit their users. This definition excludes the salesman whose advice is given to sell a product, while including the relative or neighbor who helps out in an emergency.

Caretaking is not an altruistic act, but a reciprocal relationship in which the caretaker gives his services in exchange for a material or nonmaterial return. The doctor receives a fee; the social worker, deference. Most caretaking functions today are carried out by non-profit agencies who are supported by public funds, and the client is asked only to request care. By doing so, however, he contributes to the institutional strength of the caretaking agency, which, in turn, enables the agency to show that it performs a function for which it can request public funds. For the larger its case-load or attendance, the more funds it may request. Caretakers also may ask clients to adopt the beliefs or norms of the agency. Thus, the settlement house tries to convert its members to middle-class norms, and the library hopes to make enlightened citizens out of its readers.

The caretaker's portion of the exchange can take at least three forms, differing in the demands made on clients. The *service-oriented* caretaker helps the client to achieve goals that he cannot achieve by himself, as in the case of the doctor who aids the patient in regaining his health. The *market-oriented* one gives the client "what he wants," as exemplified by the recreation director who schedules activities preferred by his youthful clients, or the doctor who tells his patient what he wants to hear, and not only what makes him well. This exchange bears some resemblance to a commercial one, and therefore is considered undesirable by most caretakers. The *missionary* caretaker wants clients to adopt his own behavior and values. Thus, character-building agencies such as settlement houses seek to persuade working-class clients to develop middle-class patterns of behavior. Or the doctor may try to persuade patients to adopt his own methods of personal maintenance and illness prevention.

In all events, the client comes to the caretaker because he wants something, and exerts some pressure on the caretaker to be market-oriented. Thus most caretaker-client relationships are a combination of the market-orientation and the service or missionary one. The recreation director is market-oriented, for example, in order to attract clients for missionary purposes.

The service-oriented and especially the missionary relationship often require clients to behave in unaccustomed ways, or to do things they are unwilling to do. For example, the working-class youngster who comes to use settlement house sports facilities must observe the house's rules of decorum that are imposed in order to encourage middle-class behavior. Partly for this reason, caretakers ask clients to adopt a quasi-dependent role. Thus the doctor expects the patient to remain in his care until the end of treatment, rather than go from doctor to doctor in the hope of finding a market-oriented one. Or the settlement house registers its clients and asks them to be loyal to the agency. The caretaker also asks his clients to defer to his superior expertise—and status—thus placing them in a subordinate position during the care process.

Clients are not always, or entirely, bound by these demands. Rather they can select from them, responding to those which satisfy their own goals, and rejecting those which do not. For example, the settlement house user may come to use the athletic equipment, but he will simultaneously resist efforts to make him act in middle-class ways. Even when caretaker demands are compulsory, the client can observe them in form rather than in spirit. For example, the student may have to be physically present in school, but can remain intellectually and emotionally uninvolved. Conversely, if the caretaker-client relationship is not compulsory, the caretaker can reject clients who do not accept his guidance. But as most caretakers are dependent on fees or public funds for support, they must therefore take on some clients who do not entirely accept their requirements.

For this reason, the caretaker-client relationship is considerably more complex than that between the buyer and seller of other services. It may be further complicated by cultural differences between the caretaker and his clients. I shall describe the caretaker as *external* if he represents a culture different from that of his clients; *internal,* if he comes from the same culture. This distinction has nothing to do with geographical origins. That is, caretakers may come from the West End and still be external. Since they are usually middle class or upper-middle class, however, low-income areas like the West End are generally served by external caretakers. In fact, caretakers often come into such areas as missionaries in order to convert their residents to the behavior and beliefs of the outside world, and bring with them services which their clients can use, or which they cannot afford to provide themselves.

Finally, it is useful to distinguish between the *formal* and *in-*

formal caretaker. Whereas the formal one, trained for his function, is usually employed or self-employed, the informal caretaker is an untrained, or occasionally self-trained, amateur. He is an ordinary resident who has gravitated into a caretaking role among relatives, friends, or neighbors because of his special skills, or because of a "therapeutic personality" that allows him to give help and to derive satisfaction from doing so. Nor is he paid for his work in money, although sometimes he may be paid indirectly. For example, if he is a storekeeper, he may be patronized for his caretaking skills. Most often, however, the informal caretaker is paid with social funds, such as prestige or appreciation. He is usually more market-oriented than the formal caretaker, and is, of course, internal in cultural origin.

External Caretakers in the West End

The West End, like other low-income areas, was richly blessed with external caretakers, including governmental and private welfare agencies, such as the Department of Public Welfare, the Visiting Nurses Association, and the Salvation Army; character-building agencies, such as the settlement houses; and quasi-educational institutions, including the settlement house kindergarten, the Salvation Army nursery school, and the public library.[1] The schools, the doctors, and the hospital, which were discussed in the previous chapter, are also external caretakers.[2]

Many of these caretakers came into the West End in the late nineteenth and early twentieth century, primarily as missionaries, but also to give service- and market-oriented care. Some of the agencies had been established when the West End was predominantly Irish, but the character-building and educational agencies came with the arrival of the Jewish immigrants. Here, they found an enthusiastic set of clients among the young people, who wanted to learn American ways, and who used these agencies to aid them in their social and occupational ascent into the middle class. Two

1. This list is intended to be illustrative rather than complete.
2. They were discussed in the previous chapter because they play almost as important and essential a role as work, and thus seemed to belong there as well as in the present chapter.

of the three settlement houses, as well as the local branch of the public library, were founded by civic leaders from the Beacon Hill aristocracy. One of the settlements was staffed from the beginning by Jews, and the public library developed in the 1920's as Boston's main center for Jewish book collections. They were internal caretakers while the West End was predominantly Jewish.

When the main body of Jews left the area, and was replaced by Italian and Polish newcomers, the caretaking agencies made relatively few changes in staff or program, and thus became external vis-à-vis their new clients. The role of the missionary caretakers among Italian West Enders will be discussed primarily with reference to the four agencies which I learned to know best: the three settlement houses, and the public library.

Elizabeth Peabody House, or Peabody House as it was called, was the largest settlement house in the area, its eight floors overtowering the tenement blocks it served. Although its program had been cut sharply in the 1950's, in 1958 it still conducted activities for children of all ages, adolescents, and adults. For the children, the House provided arts and crafts, athletics, dramatics, scouting, cooking classes, and game room activities, as well as a variety of activities for sexually segregated peers who were organized into clubs formed by the House staff. For the adolescents, there were similar activities, as well as dances, and a teen-age lounge in which they could dance or play a variety of games. The women had a Mother's Club and sewing and cooking classes. The men were also invited, but, since they never came, there were really no activities for them. The policy-making board and most of the staff came from outside the neighborhood. The board itself was made up largely of upper-class businessmen, most of them Yankee Protestants. The staff consisted of professionals as well as students from Harvard and Massachusetts Institute of Technology. There were also a few volunteers from the neighborhood. Although the building was one of the first to be torn down in the redevelopment process, the House remained in the West End, functioning on a limited scale in an old residential building, until most of the people had moved out.

The West End House, located just outside the redevelopment project area, still stands today. It serves boys exclusively, primarily with athletics, games, and some arts and crafts. Although started by a Yankee civic leader, the House is now run by a board of Jewish alumni, people who grew up in the West End but who moved out in the 1920's and 1930's. In some cases, board members are descendants of adults who grew up in the West End. Even though there is now only an occasional Jewish boy among its clients, the Jewish alumni have continued to support the House. Until the late 1950's, the House was run by professional directors, one of whom served in that capacity for over two decades. In recent years, the directorship has been held by a retired salesman, himself a board member and alumnus, who runs the House with some professional and semiprofessional aid.

The third settlement, the Heath Christian Center, was a Baptist mission housed in an old Episcopal church, that served both sexes and all ages, regardless of religion. It also conducted a popular kindergarten for the area, social and athletic activities for older children and adolescents, and some clubs for women. The Center was staffed by a Baptist minister and a number of professionally trained people—also Baptist—who had dedicated their lives to denominational service. Since most of the clients were Catholics, the program had very little religious content. Although West Enders felt that the local pastor did not approve of the Center, this did not significantly deter Catholic users. The Center ceased its operations shortly after relocation began.

The public library, housed in an old church building, was used both as a neighborhood facility for the West End and a city-wide library of Judaica. This latter function was created for it by the head librarian who ran the library from the early 1920's until her retirement in 1958. She had come to the post as the city's first Jewish head librarian, only to find the Jewish exodus from the West End in full swing. The newcomers were much less interested in using the library, and out of her bitter disappointment at the loss of the Jewish clientele came the idea to make the library into a repository of Yiddish and Judaic materials in Boston. Although the branch was closed when the West Enders departed, plans were made to restore the building to church use and to construct a new branch library for the new population.

The Missionaries and the West Enders

The caretakers who staffed the welfare agencies, settlement houses, and the library were, as noted, missionaries, who hoped to change the behavior of their West End clients. Although they never put it in these terms, they wanted to break up the peer group society with its person-orientation, and transform West Enders into object-oriented individuals who could participate in purposive groups, especially in the neighborhood and in the city. For example, one group worker who worked mostly with boys saw his function as teaching the children "activities," and getting them interested in undertaking and completing "tasks," which would discourage them from killing time in the peer group. A settlement house teacher explained that she wanted to develop within her children what she called a "personal or inner self" that would reduce dependence on the peer group. Another settlement house worker told me that the most important single achievement in her career had been her success in converting a delinquent into a "pillar of the West End community." This man now holds a responsible white-collar job, and has spent much of his spare time in helping out with settlement house activities.

For adults, the missionary aim was "to prepare adults for participation in neighborhood life," and "to strengthen family life and help in the growth of healthy neighborhoods." [3] By strengthening the family, the caretakers meant to reduce the segregation between husband and wife, to increase the status of the wife in the family, and to encourage the husband to help in the household. They also sought to bring parents and children closer together, to have the parents take a greater interest in their children's activities, and to reduce the adult-centered focus of the household. Participation in neighborhood life meant being active in formal organizations like the settlement houses, Home and School associations, and the public library—in short, to become clients and associates of the missionary caretakers. The nature of the caretaker concept of participation emerged most clearly when the Redevelopment Authority began to make its land takings in the area. At that time,

3. Elizabeth Peabody House, *Annual Report, 1958,* p. 2.

some of the West Enders finally began to participate in the protest movement of the Save the West End Committee. Some of the settlement house workers were upset by the militancy of the protest, even those who opposed the redevelopment. To them, this was not neighborhood participation but mob action.

Although the caretakers were first and foremost missionaries, they were genuinely interested in providing service to their clients, and in satisfying their demands. These aims required an insight into and empathy for West End life, however, which was lacking among the caretakers. They were conscious of differences between themselves and their clients, but they viewed these as the involuntary consequences of slum residence. The West Enders were what they were, it was argued, because they lived in the West End, and if they could have been encouraged to leave it they would have adopted the behavior patterns and attitudes urged on them by the caretakers. As a result of this reasoning, many caretakers were ambivalent about the redevelopment. On the one hand, they saw that moving would disrupt family life, disperse friends and relatives, and impose heavier financial burdens on slim budgets. On the other hand, they were sure that leaving the West End would produce the behavioral changes for which they had worked so earnestly. For this reason, most caretakers favored the redevelopment, hoping only that the relocation would proceed with justice and a minimum of pain.

The caretakers could not see that West Enders had their own social system and culture that existed independently of physical conditions in the area. Ultimately, West End behavior was always explained as an individual and essentially arbitrary reaction to deprivations created by the physical environment. This physical bias was well illustrated in a description of the West End that appeared in a settlement house memorandum for the training of new staff:

> The West End is a multi-cultural, predominantly residential area. . . . The difficulties of inadequate housing, tenement buildings, dirt, disease, and lack of recreational space have caused tensions and strains in the lives of the West End residents. . . .

Despite these lacks and pressures, the West End holds a charm and a security for its residents, and outsiders can quickly sense the warmth and friendliness of the area. The stability of long-time residence, the nearness of the river, and its parks and pools, the familiarity bred of close living conditions, the richness of the variety of cultures—these are some of the pleasurable aspects of life here which serve to draw the people more closely together.

This is essentially a tourist's picture of the West End. While it would interest the visitor from middle-class suburbia who might come to the area for vicarious identification with exotic culture and the dense street life, it made no reference to the important but less visible facets of West End society and culture. West Enders themselves were not interested in the ethnic variety of the area, except when they praised their neighborhood to outsiders. And although they did use the riverbank and swimming-pool, most West Enders thought of these facilities as being outside the area: physically, because they were separated by a busy expressway; and socially, because they had been put there by people from the outside world. The river was rarely mentioned. And no West Ender in his right mind would have described the neighborhood as having charm.

Nor did the caretakers have much understanding of the West Enders' needs and perspectives. For example, just after the city announced that it had taken over the West End, and that relocation was imminent, one of the settlement houses scheduled a meeting to help the West Enders with redevelopment and relocation problems. The main speaker, a social worker from outside the West End, was not even familiar with the area. Describing the communities to which West Enders might move, she evaluated them not on the basis of availability of housing, rent levels, population characteristics, or resident attitudes to low-status newcomers, but by the number and quality of social agencies in each. Instead of discussing the problems of relocation, she catalogued the social agencies that would make West Enders feel at home in their new areas. In answer to a question about hospital facilities, she described the quality of the staff and the availability of specialized treatment facilities. The

West Enders in attendance, however, were interested in out-patient clinics but about these the speaker knew nothing. At the end of the meeting, a woman who had already moved to a new neighborhood spoke up to complain that the schools were crowded, the teachers poor, and the students inhospitable to newcomers. Then, a teacher at this school who happened to be present talked about the high quality of foreign language instruction, and the availability of modern teaching equipment, such as television and a camping program. Finally a ten-minute debate ensued, at which the mother and the teacher each spoke about those aspects of the school program that interested her, without ever talking about the same ones.

Another example of the failure to understand the West Enders was demonstrated by a settlement house amateur drama group. As its final program, the group decided to put on selections from three plays about family tensions which might help the West Enders solve some of the problems engendered by relocation. Two of the plays, *The Glass Menagerie* and *All My Sons,* were chosen to illustrate mother-child and father-child relationships respectively.[4] Despite the good intentions of the group, however, it would have been difficult for West Enders to find parallels between Tennessee Williams' play about a downwardly mobile mother's attempt to marry off her daughter or Arthur Miller's drama about the war profiteer father whose defective goods lead to the death of his son, and their own problems of losing their neighborhood and finding a new place to live.

The caretakers' blindness to the nature of West End life stemmed in part from their being middle-class people who did not live in the area, but even more so from their missionary outlook. Most of the caretakers were trained professionals from middle-class backgrounds, who worked but did not live in the West End. Only a few staff members were Italian in background. Most of the caretakers, however, had worked in the West End for a long time.[5] These were people with deep feelings of affection for the area and

4. The third was a selection from a Thornton Wilder comedy.
5. In fact, several agencies were at one time or another headed by persons who had served as directors for many years, so that their values and personality characteristics practically shaped the institution. When such people left, or died, their successors often had some difficulty in carrying on the work.

its people, whose interest in professional prestige or in agency growth was much less than in that of serving the West End. In fact, their feelings toward the people often were pseudofamilial in character.[6] Many of the caretakers were single women without families. Moreover, because of their belief that wives were being neglected by their husbands, and children by their parents, they were encouraged to assist as quasi-family members, to sympathize with the women as quasi-siblings, and to treat the children quasi-maternally. Indeed, some caretakers talked about their youthful clients as "their children," and assumed a protective if not almost possessive attitude toward some of the women who came to them with problems.

People who want to be missionaries must believe that human beings are amenable to drastic change. They can believe this, however, only by ascribing present behavior to conditions that are themselves subject to drastic and deliberate change. Thus, the caretakers had to believe that the West Enders' refusal to follow object-oriented middle-class ways was pathological, resulting from the deprivations imposed on them by living in the West End. They could not admit that the West Enders acted as they did because they lived within a social structure and culture of their own. Such an admission not only would have required the realization that change was much harder to bring about, but also that they had little or no control over the primary causes of such change. Consequently, regardless of how long the caretakers had been in the West End and how many of its people they knew well, they found it difficult to shed their professional perspective.[7]

Thus, although the caretakers approached the West Enders with the best of intentions and with open arms, the latter did not respond in kind. Generally speaking, they used the agencies selec-

6. This observation stems from Erich Lindemann. He has also suggested that such feelings color the caretaker-client relationship generally, and can be found in clients as well as in caretakers.

7. Most of what I have written about the caretakers, and what I write below about the West Enders' reaction to them, duplicates quite closely Whyte's observations about the North End settlement houses twenty years earlier. See William F. Whyte, Jr., *Street Corner Society*, Chicago: University of Chicago Press, 1943, 2nd ed., 1955, pp. 99–104.

tively, coming for those services and facilities which interested them and ignoring or rejecting all others. This reaction conflicted with the theory of missionary caretaking, that is, to be market-oriented in order to attract clients into the agency, but then to motivate them into an acceptance of the services and missionary aims for which it exists. For example, the settlement house provided athletic and game facilities to bring people into the house with the hope that the people so attracted would absorb the social and cultural norms by entering into a relationship with the caretaking staff.

West End children generally behaved according to this theory. And, since they were too young to notice the cultural and other differences between caretakers and clients, they were the most enthusiastic users of the agencies. They were also too young, however, to absorb much of the normative instruction aimed at them. The adolescents, on the other hand, came to use the facilities but kept their distance from the caretakers. They streamed to the settlements to use the gyms, club rooms, game equipment, and dance floors they could get nowhere else, but they had as little contact as possible with most of the staff. Settlement house "cultural" activities they ignored almost entirely.

The caretakers' attempts to involve the adolescents in the social climate of the settlement house brought them into conflict with peer group rules. Some of the resulting tension was expressed in hostility toward the staff, noisy use of profanity, and occasional destruction of settlement house property. Adolescents also came to the settlement house in groups and watched each other to see that no one became too friendly with the staff. I was told that those who did so were sometimes beaten up afterwards.

The adult West Enders viewed the settlement houses and the library as places for children that could help keep them out of trouble. Thus some of the mothers asked the settlements to teach their children the home rules that they could not teach themselves. For their own lives, however, the settlement house programs had little relevance. With almost no West Enders on the staffs, the agencies were automatically classified as part of the outside world, and, since the staff members were mainly women, men were never seen inside the agencies. For example, when the settlement house held its previously mentioned meeting on redevelopment and relocation, one of my neighbors who had received a personal invitation indicated that she had not even considered going. As she explained, it had never occurred to her that "the place had anything to do with me." She meant this not as an indication of the agency's lack of interest in her, but of its lack of relevance to her life. A male neighbor expressed surprise that the agency was even interested in relocation, but when I urged him to come with me, he did so. The meeting only confirmed his preconceptions. He, I, and a professional community organizer who came to listen were the only men in an audience of fifty women. Not only was the speaker a woman, but as already noted, she was also not acquainted with the West Enders' problems and needs. At the end of the meeting, the community organizer spoke to my neighbor about the advantages of relocation, noting the joys of suburban living, of meeting new people, and making new friends. His remarks did not sit well. My neighbor—involved in a hyperactive peer group—pointed out acidly that he had no time or desire for new contacts. He was too proud to add that he could not possibly afford to move to the suburbs even if he should want to do so. That was his last contact with the settlement house, and provided him—and subsequently the rest of his peer group—with advance warning that they could not expect much useful help from caretaking agencies when they would have to move.

The settlement houses attracted two types of women—the socially mobile and the marginal.[8] As the agencies' aims and programs were congenial to the small group of West End women who were favorably predisposed to middle-class culture, they, like their Jewish predecessors, used the agencies to help acculturate themselves to it. The settlements also provided a meeting place for women who were left out of the peer group. One Mothers Club,

8. Marc Fried has recently shown that, among West Enders of all ethnic backgrounds, social agency use is highest for people with one foreign-born and one native-born parent, and for those who married spouses more or less acculturated than they. Moreover, these users diverge most sharply from typical West End behavior patterns and attitudes. Marc Fried, "A Social Science Approach to Health and Welfare Problems," paper delivered at the Harvard Medical Society, January 9, 1962, mimeographed.

for example, seemed to enroll women who had intermarried: primarily Jewish women who had married Italian men, and Italian women who had married Jewish men.

The settlement houses also attracted troubled people of all ages, and devoted considerable time and effort to help them. For example, one of them drew to itself a group of homosexual adolescents, girls as well as boys, and tried hard, although unsuccessfully, to encourage one of the boys to develop his dancing talents and enter ballet school.

The Cultural Barrier between Caretakers and West Enders

The caretakers and West Enders related to each other across a system of cultural and emotional barriers that prevented the development of satisfactory interaction. The nature of the barrier can best be illustrated by a description of a weekly "lounge" night at one of the settlements. Every Tuesday, the settlement held open house for the area's adolescents, at which they could play cards and other games, dance, or sit around and talk. Because the teenagers had no other place to go, the lounge was always well-attended. But they made it clear that they would rather have been elsewhere. They came with a mood of sullen hostility, which expressed itself every so often in spurts of destructiveness. At such times, they would tear up playing cards, break phonograph records or throw them out of the window, and upset furniture.

Although the house staff attempted to guide lounge activities in an informal, permissive manner, they could do little more than join a card game if they were invited. Most of the time, the teenagers ignored or rejected them. Thus, the staff members stood on the sidelines, hoping to quell the mischief if it grew to unmanageable proportions. While some of them had been trained in group work, they did not know how to deal with their unruly charges. Approving neither of the teenagers' choice of games nor their dance styles, they reacted negatively to almost everything their charges did. They were also afraid of their clients, as well they might be. No amount of cultural relativism, or sociological explanation of group conflict could overcome their fear or disapproval.

The adolescents, recognizing the caretakers' discomfort, and being well trained in competitive interaction, took advantage of it. When they broke phonograph records or the phonograph itself, the caretakers would argue that they were only depriving themselves of dance music. The teenagers knew, however, that the phonograph would always be repaired again, and that new records would be acquired. Thus they exploited what they interpreted as the softness of the caretakers, and took pleasure in making them as uncomfortable as possible.

At one time, the settlement house seemed to have solved the problem by excluding the unruly teenagers. By 1957, however, the more restrained ones had either left the West End or had joined the unruly groups. Of course, the house staff could have abolished the lounge nights altogether, but as missionaries, they had still not given up hope of reforming their clients. Also, they realized that the teenagers did want to come. In turn, the teenagers, sensing that the caretakers needed and wanted them, tried to see how far they could go in destructive activities before being ejected.

It seemed to me that the teenagers came to the lounge partly to express their hostility to the outside world. By their actions, they hoped to taunt the caretakers into giving up their middle-class standards, and into resorting to revenge. Knowing that the caretakers neither could nor would do so only increased the teenagers' pleasure. More important, it provided them with evidence that their own ways of behaving were superior, and that the outside world could be defeated.

Only one staff member was able to deal with the teenagers. This he did essentially by adopting peer group competitiveness. Able to return wisecracks or hostile taunts, he even invited them, thus giving the teenagers an opportunity to measure their skill against his. At the same time, he never surrendered his allegiance to the settlement house and did not cross over to their side. While the teenagers did not always obey him, they did respect him, and were attracted to the relationship he offered. He respected them in turn, partially by not being afraid, and by not retreating either from them or from his values. He took the role of an older brother, who shared some of their ways—at least for the moment. In doing so, he was able to insist on limits to their hostility and destructiveness.

Had the rest of the staff resembled him, the settlement could have allowed the teenagers to express their hostility without as much destruction and discomfort. It might even have been able to channel the teenagers' energy into more constructive activities of their own choice. The settlement might also have been able to reduce the social distance between itself and the neighborhood. Many group workers and other caretakers, however, are trained only in techniques. They learn neither the detachment from middle-class standards nor the imaginative synthesis of caretaker and client culture that seems to be necessary to communicate with people like the West Enders.

Those West End caretakers who could not cross the cultural barrier adapted themselves in other ways. The settlement houses and the library concentrated considerable effort, for example, on the younger children, who, because they were too young to choose sides, gave hope—false, to be sure—that they would later adopt the caretakers' point of view. With respect to adolescents, the settlement houses stressed the number they attracted, rather than the way they behaved once they came. This not only assured board members that their settlement house was earning its keep, but reassured its staff that, despite all of the frustration, it was performing a useful function. Although adult members were numerically the scarcest, the settlements took pride in the loyalty and fairly intense participation of those who did come. They convinced themselves—out of ignorance as well as need—that these women were representative West Enders, and that the settlements thus were a part of the neighborhood.

Some of the individual staff members avoided the cultural barrier by minimizing contact with the West Enders, and by delegating it to those people who were most successful at establishing rapport. For example, one settlement house illustrated its close ties to the neighborhood by relying on one of the senior staff members who had been born in the West End and who had lived there all her life. At meetings with professionals from outside the area, she was often described as "Miss West End." Indeed, this woman was deeply attached to the West End, and knew—or knew something about—most of the people in it. Her closest contacts, however, were with the people with whom she had grown up. Many of them were

Jews who, like herself, had remained behind in the general Jewish exodus from the West End. Her contact with the rest of the population—the large majority—was much less close, and many of the younger and middle-aged Italians knew her only by reputation. Nevertheless, her presence on the staff did allow the house to feel itself to be in intimate contact with the neighborhood. This in turn allowed the other caretakers to minimize their relationship to the West End, and to spend more time with middle-class professionals in or outside of the area.

The heads of the West End House and the public library devoted most of their time and energy to their Jewish clients. In the West End House this was difficult, since the House was used mainly by neighborhood children. The staff member with whom I spoke, however, felt that most of them were either mentally retarded or "no good," and gave his attention to the Jewish alumni group that supported the House. As a result, most of my interview with him was devoted to his recalling the days when the House had served a more appreciative Jewish clientele, who had been more interested in the cultural activities than in the athletic ones demanded by the present clients.

The library, as already noted, served both the neighborhood and the city-wide Jewish population. Consequently, while most of the library's clients were children and old people from the West End, the head librarian threw herself into caring for and promoting the Jewish collection. In this connection, she instituted a number of lectures and festivals at the library. Although these were open to the neighborhood, all but a handful of the people who came were Jews from other parts of Boston. The adult West Enders, who would have taken little interest in the library even had it served them with more determination, watched its disassociation from the neighborhood with good-natured amusement. At the time of the annual Christmas-Chanukah festival, which had become a well-publicized library tradition, one of the West Enders said smilingly, "F—— is giving another party for her friends."

Because of the cultural barrier, a mixture of lack of understanding, resignation, and occasional fear of clients seemed to hover over most of the caretakers in the West End. This helps to explain why most of them were in favor of the redevelopment project and why they hoped to be able to work with more compatible clients in their new assignments.

Even though the external caretakers created only a minor impact on the West End, it would be wrong to conclude that they were not needed in the area. Many of their goals may have been inappropriate for the clients they sought to attract, but the West End would have been a poorer place without them. They were perhaps most helpful to the people who were marginal to the peer group society, and to those few trying to break out of it. Indeed, if they failed to function in an optimal manner, it was only because their goals bade them provide services to all of the West Enders.[9]

The Internal Caretakers

Since the West Enders associate the external caretakers with the outside world, the cultural barrier between the agencies and themselves are of little concern. Even the fact that the caretaking agencies were in favor of the redevelopment came as no surprise. One reason for this detachment stems from the fact that the West Enders have their own internal caretakers, who provide some, though not all, of the needed care.

Most of the care functions are performed within the peer group, and members are willing to help each other in a variety of ways. As I indicated in Chapter 3, aunts and uncles aid in rearing children, and take over when parents are ill. Relatives also care for each other as best they can, especially if they can thus avoid calling a doctor. For example, one of my neighbors made frequent calls on a relative who was suffering from recurring episodes of depression. The family made these visits with deliberate therapeutic intent, hoping that they would cheer him up. They also struggled to find new ways of helping him, and finally advised him to make a trip to Florida, arguing that the change of scenery would do away with his moods.

Neighbors also seem to be willing to help each other should no one in the peer group be available for that role. One West End mother, who functioned as a "visiting nurse" on an informal and

9. A more explicitly evaluative analysis of the caretakers is developed in Chapter 12.

unpaid basis, took care of neighborhood families if one of the adults were ill or in the hospital. She derived considerable pleasure from such acts, in addition to the feelings of satisfaction they gave her for living up to Christian precepts. Since she had a somewhat greater ability to empathize than most West Enders, she was also able to listen to other people's troubles as well, and function as an informal counselor. Of course, caretaking roles such as she performed are not distinctive to the West End, and can probably be found in all communities.

In addition, there are a number of institutionalized internal caretakers, notably the church. In the West End, for example, the Catholic priests acted as confessors, interpreters of the moral code, and buffers between the West End and the outside world. I noted earlier that when Catholic teenagers in the West End got into trouble and were picked up by the police, they were taken to the priest, who kept their delinquent behavior off the police record, and punished them himself. The priests also functioned as advice-givers in familial and peer group conflicts. Although politicians were sometimes called in to do this, they hesitated to give advice, especially if doing so might alienate one or the other party of the dispute. The priests did not need to worry about votes. Being outside the peer group society, and possessed of supernaturally legitimated authority, they were able to pass judgment without fear of antagonizing anyone.

The church also carried out some welfare functions, and the priests made house calls as amateur caseworkers. The St. Vincent de Paul Society, for example, offered financial and other help to West Enders in need so that they did not have to go to outside agencies. Their help was short-range, and, if the need was of longer duration, the case was transferred to the Catholic Welfare Bureau, or to the public welfare agencies. The Society, operating with diocesan rules which were not distinctive to the West End, gave out money under conditions of strict secrecy, so that no one in the neighborhood knew who was receiving aid. It also restricted its funds to those people who showed some willingness to help themselves.

Store owners and bartenders have often been described as internal caretakers in ethnic and working-class neighborhoods. In the West End, they functioned in this capacity mostly because—and when—they were also peer group members. Strangers thus were excluded from such consideration. Bartenders performed both care and control functions, for instance, by refusing to serve peer group members if they became so drunk as to lose their self-control. Since every bartender knew the capacity of his peer group customers, as well as their reaction to too much alcohol, he thus could tailor the refusal to each drinker. A persuasive demonstration of the bartender's caretaking functions was illustrated by the following incident. A young man had just come back from the hospital after an ulcer operation, and the peer group was divided as to whether he should drink with them. The bartender, who had already decided that he should not do so, was surreptitiously serving him shots of cola and water. When one of the young man's friends objected to what he thought were real drinks, the bartender announced with a straight face that he was not responsible for his customers, that he did not care whether they should drink or not, and besides, "so what if he dies, one more Polack bastard gone." At this, the friend who objected became quite angry, and said that the bartender would not drink like that if he himself had an ulcer. The bartender, replying that as a matter of fact he did have one, invited the man to join him in a free drink. He then served him the cola and water combination. The entire group enjoyed the joke, after which the bartender announced that, of course, he would not serve anyone who had an ulcer.

Politicians also function as caretakers, but since their role places them in the outside world, they are, strictly speaking, not internal caretakers. Their activities will be described in the next chapter.

The internal caretakers are usually market- or service-oriented, and consequently the care they provide has a number of limitations. Whenever possible, they try to do what will please their peer group "clients," even when this is not the wisest course. They do not necessarily act in this fashion to be ingratiating, but because they share the same beliefs. For example, if a person is ill and refuses to see a doctor, the internal caretaker who has similar feelings about doctors may reinforce the patient's hesitation. Also, they may cut off further care should the client refuse to follow their advice. Most important, since they often have no more knowledge than their clients, the care they give is not always what is needed.

The internal caretaker functions most successfully when the client's need is for group support—be that financial or psychological —and least successfully when the need is for expertise that can be found only in the outside world. If the care cannot be supplied by internal caretakers, as is the case with medical or dental treatment, West Enders will eventually visit the external caretaker, although they may postpone it as long as possible. But if the treatment needed is psychological in nature, West Enders may feel that it can best be supplied internally by affection and advice from the peer group, in which case the visit to an external caretaker may be postponed indefinitely.

CHAPTER 8 The Politicians: Ambassadors to the Outside World

Government and the Citizen

The West Enders become most suspicious of, and hostile toward, the outside world when they must deal with government and the law. Most West Enders are convinced that the police, the government bureaucracy, the elected officials, and the courts are corrupt and are engaged in a never-ending conspiracy to deprive the citizens of what is morally theirs. Although suspicion of government and politics can be found among all social strata, in smaller communities as well as in the city, the West Enders' feelings on this subject are more intense and less open to change. Consequently, they try to have as little to do with government as possible and pass on to the area politician the task of dealing with it in their behalf.

By government, West Enders mean city government. There is almost no interest in state government, even though the State House is located less than half a mile from the West End, and even though an Italian occupied the governor's chair during the time of my study.[1] There is even less interest in the doings of the federal government. In 1958, the local congressman was an Irish-

1. He was not, however, of working-class origins.

man who lived in East Boston and paid little attention to the West End. At that time, John F. Kennedy was a United States Senator, and even though people sometimes mentioned that he was a West End boy—because he had attended the parish church as a child—he was too far removed from the area by his high office and took no direct interest in it. There was occasional criticism of the then President Eisenhower, but the comments were much like those made about mass media personalities, and dealt with rumors about his personal life. State and federal government are far removed from the concerns of most West Enders; their existence is noticed only when some issue develops with relevance to them.[2]

The West Enders' conception of government and its officials also sheds further light on the dominating role of the peer group society. As already noted, West Enders think of government primarily as an agency that should be an arm of the peer group society to satisfy their needs. Moreover, they conceive the governmental process to be much like personal relationships in the peer group society. Thus, government agencies are identified with the individuals who run them, and agency behavior is explained in terms of their personal motives. During the time of my study, for example, West Enders were naturally concerned with redevelopment, which brought the Housing Authority and the Mayor into their view. The West Enders, however, spoke not of agencies but of individuals in them, notably one leading Authority official and the Mayor. They felt that these two men were in the pay of the private redevelopers, and were tearing down the West End for personal gain.

Government agencies have no reality; the city is seen as a congeries of individuals, most of whom are corrupt. Although West Enders know bribery to be wrong, for instance, they do not hesitate to bribe a policeman to prevent a traffic ticket. They believe that in either case the money they pay goes into someone's pocket. To them, there is thus no difference between the payoff to the policeman and the fine that is paid to the traffic court, and both go to the outside world.

The personalization of government operations stems in part

2. These observations were made during a time in which there were no major elections; interest undoubtedly rises somewhat during a presidential vote.

from the West Enders' inability to recognize the existence of object-oriented bureaucracies. The idea that individual officials follow rules and regulations based not on personal morality but on concepts of efficiency, order, administrative hierarchy, and the like, is difficult to accept. For example, when the redevelopment agency initiated its procedures for taking title to the West End properties, and for relocating people and demolishing houses, West Enders refused to believe that these procedures were based on local and federal regulations. They saw them only as individual, and individually motivated, acts. Taking title to the land was described as a land grab to benefit the redeveloper. Relocation was explained in terms of the desire of the redeveloper and his governmental partners to push West Enders out of their homes as quickly as possible, so that the new buildings could be put up. The protests of redevelopment officials that they were only following standard operating procedures went unheeded.

Since the government is viewed as consisting of individual actors, West Enders evaluate it on the basis of the same moral code that they apply to each other. Government officials are expected to act on the basis of absolute and unvarying principles, to treat West Enders as equals, and to respect the patterns of mutual obligation that operate in the peer group. As a result, West Enders hold to a conception of "good government" that is as strict if not stricter than that of the middle-class reformer. Their conception differs only in substance. Middle-class reformers define good government by the extent to which it follows business concepts of efficiency, fairness and honesty in contractual relations, and the allocation of resources by middle-class priorities—be these liberal or conservative in ideology. West Enders judge good government by peer group rules and by the extent to which its allocation policies fit their interests. Thus, they described middle-class reform movements in Boston as nothing more than a shifting of the graft from the pockets of politicians to those of bankers and businessmen.[3] Conversely, the regime of Mayor James Curley, long considered as one of the most corrupt by the middle class, was generally praised by

3. It should be noted that the reform movement which flourished briefly in Boston during the first half of the 1950's was dominated by business elements more than by the liberals.

the West Enders because it respected and benefited the poor people. Evidence of graft and corruption in his administration were not denied; they were simply compared to the much larger amounts of profit made in the assignment of contracts to private business when government was run by businessmen. This they called "legal graft." Since West Enders judge the law by the extent to which it benefits or hurts them, the fact that the business reform administration acted within the limits of the written law was not considered relevant.

West Enders see that, most of the time, government does not act as they would wish it to and that it is exploiting or depriving them of their rights. This, they also explain in peer group society terms. Thus, the people who conduct government business are individuals gone wrong, motivated by greed and ambition, and unable to control their desires. They have been corrupted by the object-goals of the outside world. As I noted in Chapter 4, West Enders are disappointed that individuals in government do not act like peer group members, and they express great admiration for the honest cop or government official. Such individuals are rare, however, for few can act as West Enders would wish them to.

Since West Enders think that the majority of government officials are out to exploit them, they feel justified to do likewise if and when the need arises. They avoid contact with the government as much as they can, but should it threaten to exploit them, they feel free to retaliate. For example, when the city took over the West End and, in effect, became its landlord, West Enders demanded that redevelopment officials rehabilitate buildings that had just been declared a slum. Some refused to pay rent in order to get even with the city.

Such a conception of the governmental process, and of government-citizen relationships, may indeed seem irrational to the middle-class person who learns early in life to understand bureaucratic organization and behavior.[4] And, as I have already noted, it also may appear to be paranoid. Only a clinician can make judgments about individual pathology. But given the West Enders'

4. Daniel B. Miller and Guy E. Swanson, *The Changing American Parent,* New York: Wiley and Sons, 1958.

status in the larger society, their view of the outside world is neither irrational nor a sign of group paranoia. No group can long retain a conceptual system that does not stand up against experience. For while the West Enders' explanation of governmental behavior may be distorted, it fits the phenomena they observe more often than not.

There are several reasons for the "fit" of the West Enders' theory. In the first place, most of them have had little direct experience with bureaucratic organizations. Few of them work in offices, either in private industry or in the government. Moreover, since Boston's political life is still firmly in the control of the Irish population, few Italians have even tried to find jobs in government offices. They described sardonically the experience of a North Ender who had tried and failed for years to get a job in a city department —until he changed his long Sicilian name to Foley. Consequently, West Enders see the bureaucracy only from the position of the client. And, since bureaucracies do not generally explain the reasons for their actions to clients, there is little opportunity to learn how they work.

In addition, many of the actions of the government do tend, whether intentionally or not, to hurt them and to benefit the more well-to-do citizens. The clearest case in point is the redevelopment of the West End itself, which took their homes to construct apartments for the wealthy few. In earlier years, West Enders could see that the city tore down part of the nearby North End—where some West Enders had grown up—in order to build an expressway that aided the suburban residents who drove downtown to work or shop. They also saw that the quality of municipal services on Beacon Hill was much better than in the West End. In 1958 they had only to read the papers to learn that the Mayor was planning to accept a well-paying position with a local insurance company after his retirement, and that this company, which was planning a huge redevelopment project elsewhere in Boston, had been able to get a liberal tax reduction as an incentive.

Moreover, despite the inroads of civil service, city governments still are run to a considerable extent by methods that seem to validate the West Ender's conceptions. This is particularly true in Boston, where traditional political machine methods have not given way to reform, and where nepotism and graft are still accepted as normal and inevitable. Even where reform movements have taken over control of government operations, they rarely have time to do more than make changes at the higher echelons. West Enders, however, come into contact with only the lowest echelons of the government. Whereas they do not know department heads or police commissioners, they do know, or know of, policemen, building inspectors, and laborers who work for the city. For example, many West Enders play the numbers, and since "policy" is controlled by Italian elements, they have fairly reliable evidence that payoffs are made to allow the policy wheels to operate. Also, they know that some policemen sell parking spaces on downtown streets at regular monthly rates. Consequently, it is not difficult to understand why they believe the police to be "legal racketeers" who take payoffs whenever they can. The final proof of the correctness of their view is that the higher graft payoffs go to the top police echelons, and that the men who walk the beat get little or nothing from the large amounts of money that are distributed. In government, as in business, the big money goes not to the little man but to the boss.[5]

Middle-class people have a much different type of contact with their city governments. They rarely find themselves inside a police station, and, if they work for the city, they are employed in the middle or higher levels of the bureaucracy. Most of the time, they see only the performance of civic progress and democracy that the government puts on for their benefit. Rarely do they go behind the scenes where the operations that actually keep the city running are taking place. Even when they do, they are able to maintain the kind of detachment that allows them to pay small bribes to a traffic policeman without feeling guilty or outraged about corruption. Not only do they have little direct contact with corruption, but most important, their contact is limited to those times when they are the beneficiaries.

The West Enders more often are found behind the scenes, either as employees, or as friends and relatives of employees. They

5. I am reporting what West Enders told me. I did not check on the validity of the stories or of the motives that were attributed.

are hired or turned down for patronage jobs, and may work on city construction projects. Thus, when bribes are passed, illegal influence employed, and shoddy materials used in construction, they are closer to the evidence than the middle-class person. They confront corruption every day, and see others gain by it, without reaping any benefit from it themselves.

Consequently, the West Enders' theory of government is frequently supported because they are closer to the seamy side of city operations. Nevertheless, they also hold to the theory even in the absence of such evidence. Thus, they not only expect to find corruption and wrongdoings before the evidence is available, but may reject contrary evidence even when it is available. For example, the city's decision to give the aforementioned insurance company a tax reduction was an incentive to still the company's doubt about proceeding with the project—not a result of the job offer made to the Mayor. Likewise, most of the city's actions in the redevelopment process reflected federal and local regulations, rather than the immoral motives of city officials.

As a result, the belief that the outside world is harmful can blind the West Enders to its beneficial acts. In the West End for example, they failed to see that the police often kept adolescent misbehavior off the police blotter, and that caretakers genuinely wanted to be of assistance. Nor did they see, during the redevelopment, that relocation officials sometimes went out of their way to help people who could not help themselves. This blindness has had undesirable consequences for both parties. The West Enders play it safe by minimizing relationships with government officials. The latter interpret this hesitancy—and the distorted view of motives—as insult or personal rejection, and consider West Enders to be ungrateful citizens.[6]

Middle-class people may be equally sensitive to the corruption of government and the dishonesty of its representatives, but they can be convinced by evidence to the contrary. Moreover, they believe in the possibility that government and politics can be reformed. The West Enders, on the other hand, are nigh well certain that one cannot fight—or change—city hall.

6. The communication problems between government officials and the West Enders are considered in more detail in Chapters 13 and 14.

The Politicians: Ambassadors to the Outside World

If the government is run, or thought to be run, by universally known and publicly visible rules, the citizen need only to know these rules and deduce from them his rights, obligations, and the proper posture toward its officials. When the government is, or is thought to be, personalized, capricious, and depriving, however, the citizen feels helpless, and must call on an influential person who can intervene in the government on his behalf. For the West Ender, this person is the politician.

The major functions of the "pol"—as West Enders call him—is to do favors for his constituency, to keep them informed of what is going on, and to represent their point of view in the legislative and executive chambers. For these functions, West Enders turned to the state representative—the state "rep"—and the city councilor. Until 1950, city councilors in Boston were elected from wards, and thus functioned as local politicians. Since then, they have been elected at large, and no longer represent any single ward. But West Enders were still able to contact one of the city councilors, because he lived in the West End, and had his political roots in that area and the nearby North End. As a result—and because he was an Italian—West Enders continued to consider him their local politician, and used him for this purpose. He was available to do favors, and could function as an informant, but since he was elected at large and had to represent the entire city, he could no longer think purely of his home ward when it came to legislation.

With the change in the city council, the representative to the State House, who is still elected by wards, became more important as a local politician. Consequently, West Enders treated their two "state reps" as their representatives to the city, even though the two men had no official standing at City Hall. They did, however, have some political influence. Moreover, since Boston does not have home rule, a considerable amount of municipal legislation is enacted in the State legislature. As a result, the state representatives could act as local politicians.

Doing favors is the local politician's most important function. And since this is his most frequent reason for contact with his constituents, it is their most important index for evaluating him. Should the politician be unwilling to do favors or unable to obtain what he has promised, he will lose the confidence and the votes of those who asked him for favors. In addition, he will get a reputation for being unable "to produce." Such a reputation can mean loss of an election.

In a government that is perceived as a system in which selfish individuals seek to maximize their takings, favors are viewed as a normal device by which constituents get their rightful share. Most of the favors are requests for jobs and for welfare payments. But these are usually covered respectively by civil service regulations and eligibility criteria over which the politician has no control. He can only find out the results of bureaucratically made decisions, and transmit these to his constituents. The politician thus functions mostly as an ambassador to the outside world. He handles the West Enders' dealings with an impersonal bureaucracy which they cannot understand, or are afraid to face. Moreover, by acting as a go-between, he allows his constituents to retain their personalized image of government. He does not do this purposely, however. In fact, he wishes he did not have to do it at all. Politicians often complain about the amount of time they must spend on what to them are time-consuming and superfluous errands, although they also realize that doing such favors raises their batting average for being able to produce.

The politician is also asked to do favors that require the application of his political influence. The most common request is for jobs that are not covered or only partially covered by civil service. For example, when a number of men have made equal scores on a civil service test, political influence can evidently help to place a constituent at the top of his equals. It also can help to get one of several equally qualified applicants into a public housing project, especially one with a long waiting list.

Although the social welfare functions have shrunk considerably since the days of the New Deal, the politician is still, to some extent, a caretaker. He offers advice on how to deal with the outside world, and acts as a middleman between the external caretaker and the client. He has retained a caretaking function partially because he is market-oriented, and because he abstains from missionary activities. He provides a service to voters in exchange for political loyalty. In return, he is able to spare them contact with missionary caretakers who want to change their behavior, or who ask questions which imply to West Enders that they ought to change their behavior. Thus, he shelters them from discomfort and rejection by the outside world.

Another of the politician's important functions is that of providing reliable information. West Enders often do not believe much of what they read in the newspapers. They consider the press to be an agency of the outside world that usually defends, and sometimes fronts for, the city government—a belief for which there is some justification. Newspapers, at least in Boston, seem to be written on the assumption that poor people, like the West Enders, do not read them. They either present the news from a middle-class perspective or leave out the kinds of information that would be of most interest to the West Enders. For example, the Boston press not only favored the redevelopment of the West End in repeated and enthusiastic editorials, but also covered the news only from the point of view of the Redevelopment Authority. Press releases or interviews with officials about the West End were never complemented by the West Enders' version of the situation, or, indeed, by their feelings about the matter. Features, moreover, depicted the West End as a vice-ridden set of hovels in which respectable human beings could not be expected to live, thus insulting the West Enders and making them feel like outcasts.[7] As stories about redevelopment or relocation procedures generally were written from the point of view of the casual bystander, West Enders had difficulty in understanding what was happening next.

The press bias was not necessarily intentional, except in the editorial columns which generally reflected the businessman's point of view on most topics. The newspages were written by people who simply expressed their preconceptions about slum areas—often of a quite falsely stereotyped nature—and who then applied them to the West End. The West Enders, of course, were convinced that the distortions were intentional, and had been dictated by City Hall in order to discredit and drive them out of the West End.

7. See Chapter 13.

They were not surprised by the patterns of news coverage. This is what they expected from the outside world.

Because of such situations as these, the politician is asked to provide information, not only to fill the news vacuum, but to deliver unpublished information about behind-the-scenes activities and about motivations so that West Enders may interpret the news according to their own theory of government. Since politicians operate on the basis of a similar theory to explain City Hall politics, they have no difficulty in providing the desired facts, rumors, motives, and interpretations.[8] During the tense period preceding the start of redevelopment, however, some politicians tried to scotch the more outrageous rumors and interpretations when they had facts to the contrary. By this time, however, they had little success, for the West Enders were ready always to believe the worst; and, since the redevelopment officials did not understand the informational role of the local politicians, and often failed to keep them abreast of events, the politicians frequently knew little more than did their constituents.

The politician's third major function is that of representation. Not only must he vote according to local directives, he must also carry out what middle-class people call citizen participation, and develop a public image of the West Enders for the outside world. As already noted, West Enders are not given to political participation any more than to other forms of civic activity. Their only personal participation in the political process is to ask for favors, to express occasional opinions to politicians if they happen to run into them, and to vote. Any other political duties are expected to be carried out by elected officials; after all, that is what they were elected for. Thus West Enders did not protest the redevelopment to City Hall more systematically because, among other things, they conceived this to be the job of their elected politicians.

This apparent passivity carries over from Italian society, for the West Enders' ancestors were not encouraged to participate politically. Among the immigrant generation, moreover, there was no incentive for change in the tradition, because from about 1900 to 1925 the West End literally ran the city. During this time a

8. See p. 180.

political machine headed by Martin Lomasney, which represented a ward consisting of the North, West, and South Ends, had its headquarters in the West End. Lomasney, then the most powerful figure in Boston politics, was thus able to see that his constituents received their share, or more, of the political spoils. He also passed out the jobs, the loans, the welfare, and the Christmas baskets that his constituents needed.[9] Even had the West End not been so well represented, it is doubtful whether the immigrant generation would have become politically active. For neither they nor the second generation seemed willing or able to participate effectively in politics as a group, and could not carry the ward even though they outnumbered the Irish population in later years. Shortly after Lomasney's death the machine began to break up—thanks partly to the welfare measures of the New Deal. But his Irish followers continued to retain control over its remains throughout the 1930's and 1940's. Even though the North End section of the ward had long been predominantly Italian, Irish candidates still stood regularly for election, and, more often than not, they won.[10] I was told that the Irish domination had finally been eliminated when quarreling Italian factions realized that until they made peace, they would never elect someone of Italian origin to city office. Italian politicians—most of them from the North End—finally took over the ward after World War II.

The rarity of participant motivations and skills among the West Enders has meant, among other things, that the politician who represents them does not have the benefit of citizen groups that can demonstrate to his legislator colleagues or to the Mayor the extent of his political influence. In short, he is required to be his own pressure group—a fact that does not enhance his political effectiveness. In addition, West Enders expect their politician to

9. For a description of Lomasney's organization, see Lincoln Steffens, *The Autobiography of Lincoln Steffens,* New York: Harcourt, Brace, and World, 1931, Chap. 36. Steffens used Lomasney and his organization as the model in his arguments in behalf of political machines.

10. The Irish nominees, of course, were frequently tied in with Italian political groups, and even controlled by powerful Italian figures. For an analysis of one of the Irish victories in the North End during the 1930's, see William F. Whyte, Jr., *Street Corner Society,* Chicago: University of Chicago Press, 1943, 2nd ed., 1955, Chap. 6.

develop a public image of them, depicting them as proud citizens fighting for their rights against the hostile outside world. He is encouraged to make fiery speeches that condemn the powerful for criminal or negligent behavior, and threaten them with violence or political reprisals by an aroused electorate. Luckily for the politician, West Enders are more interested in having this image presented to themselves than to his colleagues or superiors. Nevertheless, as I suggested earlier, political speeches in the West End appeared to the outside world as demagoguery and rabble-rousing. The more successful politicians learn to make speeches that will satisfy their constituents without alienating the powerful agencies or individuals with whom they must work.

What little political activity there was took place mainly before elections. West Enders are Democrats and, however skeptical they may be of that party, they would not think of voting Republican. Consequently, local elections in the West End were decided in the Democratic primary. The election for city councilor and for state representatives that took place during my study created little interest. The candidates put up posters, gave a few speeches before the remaining social clubs, and made themselves generally visible at church and in the neighborhood. The most effective campaigning, however, was done through word-of-mouth, as families and friends of the candidates tried to get support for them from the neighborhood—exploiting the system of obligations within the peer group society, and promising favors when they were needed. In the election campaign which I observed, there was, of course, only one issue—redevelopment—and all the candidates opposed it strongly. The major emphasis in the campaign was on the moral and cultural attributes of the candidates themselves, especially on their honesty and their ability to fight on behalf of the West End.[11] The two major opponents represented the routine-seeking and the action-seeking points of view, respectively. Both candidates vowed to fight City Hall. But whereas one implied that he would use his intelligence, citing his college education, the other stressed his ability to defend himself and his constituents against exploitation

11. I was told that in past decades, candidates campaigned largely by "mud-slinging"—casting doubt on their opponents' honesty and qualifications with slanderous, and often fictional, details of their personal and political misdeeds.

and his willingness to use his fists if necessary. The college-educated candidate also appealed to the lower-class group by playing down his educational achievements in his campaign literature.

Once a candidate is elected, he is relatively independent of his constituents. As long as he is willing to do favors and to vote properly on the few issues that concern them, he is free to act as he sees fit. He can vote his conscience, and make alliances that will help him politically and financially. At the same time, however, people soon begin to wonder about his activities in the outside world, and before long he is suspected of acting like an outsider. If his votes hurt any West Enders or noticeably benefit some persons or areas outside the West End, he is suspected of having been "bought." If he fails to attend a local meeting, people wonder if he has deserted them or has sold out to an enemy. Once the suspicion arises—and it always does—even his actions in behalf of his constituents may be explained as an attempt to seek personal gain.

The voters' suspicions stem in part from the fact that politicians use their office to enhance their business activities or law practices. Since salaries paid to municipal and state lawmakers are low, the elected official needs an additional source of income. Success in business or legal practice, therefore, can quickly lead to suspicions that political influence has been used or that the politician has been corrupted. Given Boston politics, the suspicions were sometimes justified. Even if they were not, they would be bound to crop up anyway, simply because the politician's work takes him into the outside world—tacit evidence that he has adopted its exploitative behavior patterns. Moreover, as the politician moves into the outside world, his activities do change, if only because he must adopt some of its styles in order to function effectively. This in turn increases the social distance between him and his constituents. If he is elected on an at-large basis, and must represent interests other than those of his home district, suspicion develops almost automatically that he has become a renegade.

Thus the politician is caught between conflicting pressures. On the one hand, he must participate in the outside world in order to be effective, even if only in the service of his constituents. On the other hand, as his constituents display little interest in his activities, he cannot explain them fully. As a result, he is suspected of having deserted the peer group and of having become a crook. Moreover, since the suspicion exists regardless of whether or not he has done anything to deserve them, he may himself become cynical, and conclude that he should use his office to advance his own fortunes. This does not necessarily hurt his political future. Voters who are convinced that he is dishonest simply because he was elected may not cast their ballot for him again anyway. Conversely, others will vote for him either because they believe all candidates to be dishonest, or because he is an Italian or a "neighborhood boy," or simply because they think that the outside world deserves to be exploited by a self-seeking politician.

The image of the working-class politician as a beloved neighborhood figure is largely fiction. West Enders feel that politics is intrinsically and inevitably corrupt, and that few politicians can resist the temptations. Consequently, they must be watched so that the constituents come out ahead in the exchange of votes and favors. I was told that this view had prevailed also in the days when Martin Lomasney was the boss of the West End and when his organization had a much more frequent, direct, and visible impact on the voters' everyday life. Although Lomasney's contributions to the area's economic welfare were freely acknowledged and his personal honesty rarely questioned, informants agreed that he had been ruthless in manipulating his constituents for his own political needs. It was said that young men who were interested in a political career had to join his organization and that if they refused, he would see to it that they were politically blacklisted. Sometimes, a fledgling politician's first assignment was to run as a dummy opposition candidate to the organization nominee. If he performed that service properly, he then would be rewarded by nomination as an organization candidate in a subsequent election. Although Lomasney was reported to have been very generous in helping people in need, he did dictate in turn how they should vote. He was respected because he could produce, and many West Enders felt sure that had he still been alive, the area would never have been proposed for redevelopment.

Personal Characteristics of the Politician

Voter suspicions—and the social distance between citizens and politicians—are supported by the fact that the local politician is often socially mobile. Political life has traditionally served as a channel for social mobility to ethnic group members who lack the social background and investment capital necessary to success in other occupations. Thus, it is not surprising to find that many of the local politicians who served the West End were mobile people. This was not true of all of them. Some were in politics because it had become a family occupation, or because it was a useful adjunct to business activities. For example, among Italians, funeral directors often will enter politics because their work provides them with the necessary free time, and because it is good advertising for their establishment. This was true also in the West End.

Even so, three of the four local politicians with whom I talked were using their political careers to move themselves or their children into the middle class.[12] One of them was the man who, under the pseudonym of Chick Morelli, played a central role in Whyte's *Street Corner Society*.[13] An ambitious young man when Whyte knew him in the North End, his political fortunes had risen when I met him to the point where some West Enders thought that he might someday become Boston's first mayor of Italian background.

The three men, Chick Morelli included, were quite ambivalent, however, about their mobility. Two had married women from middle-class families, but they themselves retained considerable al-

12. I interviewed only about a third of the dozen or so men who were politicians in the ward in which the West End was located. I suspect that the majority of those to whom I did not talk were less mobile than my respondents.

13. Whyte, *op. cit.*, especially Chap. 2, and Appendix, pp. 344–349. The fact that he was Morelli came out one evening at his house when he asked me my opinion of *Street Corner Society*. Subsequently, I learned that during one of his previous election campaigns, a Boston newspaper had reported that "his struggles to overcome boyhood disadvantages . . . are pictured in a well-known college textbook entitled *Street Corner Society*." The story was given to the paper by one of his associates the day before election. Many of Morelli's companions in *Street Corner Society* were still his friends, and functioned as his political advisors.

legiance to the peer group society in which they had grown up. The wives were uncomfortable in these surroundings, and put considerable pressure on the men to leave the ward, so that their children could be raised in higher status surroundings—a move the men resisted, both for personal and political reasons. The clearance of the West End did provide one of the men with an excuse to move into a middle-class neighborhood, but since he left somewhat earlier than the rest of the population, the West Enders interpreted his move as a sign that he had sold them out. Although the other man did not have to move right away, he did not know how long he could hold out against his wife's insistence that they leave the area. Both men liked the neighborhood, and were reluctant to give up the peer group ties, although they also enjoyed their contacts with the middle-class world. The wives, however, who were not raised in the peer group society, wanted their husbands to spend more time with them and the children, and resented the childhood friends and other men who invaded the household almost nightly. The third of the mobile politicians was torn between his enjoyment of politics and the low status of his position. Having at one time considered becoming a doctor, he was now sorry that he had not entered the medical profession, because of the higher prestige and respect accorded it.

The politicians' status ambivalence also reflected itself in their political behavior. When I talked with them, for example, two of the men were struggling to decide what to do after the loss of their West End constituents—whether to continue as working-class politicians in other parts of the district, or to become reformers and serve a more middle-class group of voters. One of the men had already begun to take the latter path. Consequently, he adopted two political styles, one for West Enders and other Italian voters, another for the middle-class reform groups. In the privacy of his own home, however, he has remained a West Ender. While his speeches and some of his actions are cued to middle-class reform, his thinking about city problems differs little from that of other West Enders. Favoring impulsive action at the expense of analysis, he still talks about resorting to violence to get things done, and his solutions tend to be authoritarian, with little concern for the rights of those who disagree. His proposals for reform call not for structural changes in city government, but for moralistic crusades against the men whom he believes to be corrupt.

As his political career advances, he has moved into the powerful and statusful sectors of city life, but he is still quite insecure about mixing with upper-middle-class people. His reports of his social activities to the peer group, for example, are full of anecdotes in which he confronts prominent people with the fact that he is now their equal despite his lowly origins in the Boston slums. He enjoys such encounters, and feels that he is making fools of high-status individuals. In short, although he has entered the outside world and has become successful within it, he has retained the peer group society's hostility toward it.

In many ways the politicians' own view of the power structure coincides with the peer group society's person-orientation. Politicians see issues in terms of their appeal to voters, and the power structure as a group of individuals competing for personal political advantage. They describe the decision-making process, whether in politics or in government, in terms of the goals of the competing decision-makers: power, money, and prestige. These are traced in turn to motives of political ambition and greed. The goals and motives are, moreover, interpreted in moral terms, and political life is thus evaluated as a struggle between heroes and villains. The local politicians fail to see that many of their own actions and those of their colleagues are determined by the requirements of the political party system and by the diverse demands of their respective constituencies. In short, the "pols" interpret political events with the same theory of government as their West End constituents and lack the detachment and insight that is common among the party leaders. This is probably one reason that they are local politicians.

CHAPTER 9 Consumer Goods and the Mass Media: Selective Acceptance of the Outside World

Italian and American Culture

West Enders do not reject the outside world in its entirety. Indeed, some of its features are chosen freely and with considerable enthusiasm to enhance peer group life. Principal among these are consumer goods and the entertainment provided by the mass media of communications. West Enders have enjoyed the products of American popular culture since they were children, when they frequented the dozen or so vaudeville and movie theaters then located on the edge of the West End.[1]

A number of critics of American society have argued that its people are flooded with the goods and ideas of mass production, and are powerless to resist their temptations. This is not the case among the West Enders. Just as their lack of money and distrust of installment buying limit the purchase of consumer goods, so the preference for company and conversation outdistances the pleasures

1. At one time, nearby Scollay Square was Boston's major entertainment center.

of television or the movies. Solitary forms of entertainment, such as reading or listening to music, are virtually unknown. Advertisements are studied, but with considerable skepticism. Also, as West Enders are not placed on mailing lists because of their low income, they thus escape the flood of money-saving offers and special bargains in goods and ideas that fill the mailboxes of the middle class.

Moreover, the West Enders—at least the adults—make highly selective use of the popular culture. Among the vast variety of available consumer goods, movies, television programs, and reading matter, their choices are structured so as to filter out themes that do not support or enhance the life of the peer group society. Whatever cannot be enjoyed within the confines of the peer group society is ignored or rejected. As is the case in settlement house use, the artifacts made available by the outside world are accepted, but the social arrangements and ideas that accompany them are sidestepped. The choice of goods and entertainment is also regulated by a set of esthetic principles that guide West Enders into accepting only what they think beautiful or pleasurable. While these principles are used unconsciously, and terms such as taste, culture, or art are never heard, West Enders still know what they like, and whenever possible, choose accordingly.

Although these principles partake of the tradition which the immigrants brought over from Italy, the West Enders bear no particular allegiance to Italian culture. Nor do they think of choosing between Italian and American culture. Some features of the outside world are described as "American"—for example, restaurant cuisines—and the term is often used to classify things West Enders do not like. However, movies or television programs are not thought of as American, for there is no Italian equivalent for them.[2]

Consumer Behavior

A visitor to West End apartments might have been surprised to learn that they belonged to second-generation Italians, since the

2. West Enders do not go to see the Italian films that come to Boston "art theaters."

visible artifacts were largely American. To understand this it is important to remember that the immigrants came to America with comparatively few items of material culture. Moreover, much of what they did bring was given up as soon as there was an opportunity to choose American goods. It is in this context that the second generation grew up.

Years of postwar prosperity have allowed West Enders to purchase the furnishings, appliances, clothing, and other consumer goods that mass production has made available. This is most noticeable in the kitchen, because even the most traditional West End housewife is likely to prepare her Italian dishes with the latest appliances and kitchen utensils, if her husband can afford to buy them for her. Television sets are also likely to be of recent vintage. In some families, the man's wish for a late model car may take priority over everything else. Living room and bedroom furniture, on the other hand, is usually older and often dates back to the time of marriage. Many West End housewives hoped to buy some new furniture when they moved—perhaps the only silver lining in the otherwise dark cloud with which relocation threatened to cover their lives.

Some observers have interpreted the purchase of modern appliances and automobiles as signs that people like the West Enders have thereby accepted American middle-class culture. But there is no evidence for this observation. Appliances are culturally neutral artifacts that can be adapted to almost any culture. The decision to buy them means only that West Enders and other working-class people now can afford to enjoy the comfort and convenience that these appliances supply. In short, the desire for comfort and convenience cuts across all classes. For example, West Enders—like their parents before them—place great value on fresh meat and produce, and the refrigerator is useful for eliminating daily shopping trips. But this fact has not encouraged the use of more American dishes, or frozen and canned goods. Refrigerators can be used to store the foods of any culture, and require no changes in basic patterns of living.

Indeed, the outside world has had only a partial influence on the purchase and use of foods. As noted earlier, West Enders have maintained the Italian cuisine, and do not like "American" fare. Their actual diet, however, bears little resemblance to that of their Italian ancestors, for they have adopted American items that can be integrated into the over-all tradition. For example, although their ancestors could not afford to eat meat, West Enders can, and thus spend considerable amounts for it. Typically American meats such as hot dogs, hamburger, and steak are very popular indeed, but they are usually prepared with Italian spices, and accompanied by Italian side-dishes. The role of American culture is perhaps best illustrated by holiday fare. Turkey is eaten on Thanksgiving, but it is preceded by a host of Italian antipastos, accompanied by Italian side-dishes, and followed by Italian desserts. This amalgamation of ethnic and American food products is of course not distinctive to the West Enders, but can be found among all groups of foreign origin.

The choice of most other consumer goods is unencumbered by Italian tradition, for such goods were not available to the West Enders' Italian forebears. Even so, the selections which West Enders make from the vast variety of alternatives does reflect a distinctive esthetic that is partially working class and partially Italian. Moreover, the functions to which goods are put also reflect the needs of the peer group society.

The automobile, for example, serves as an important mode of self-expression to the male West Ender—as it does to many other working-class Americans: it displays his strength and his taste. When the man has the money—and the freedom to spend it—he thus will buy the most powerful automobile he can afford, and will decorate it with as many accessories as possible. The size of the car and the power of its motor express his toughness; the accessories, the carefully preserved finish, and chrome are an extension of the self he displays to the peer group. This was illustrated one night when a drunk damaged a young West Ender's car with a beer bottle. The West Ender was enraged, not because of the violence done to the finish nor because of the cost of repairing it, for the damage was slight. He was angry, rather, because of what he called "the principle of the thing," that someone had hurt him —through his car—without cause. The object is an extension of the person, and it is important only insofar as it represents that person.

Not all West End men pay so much attention to their cars, and routine-seekers do so less than action-seekers. For some of the latter, the car provides an opportunity to express male vanity, and is cared for punctiliously. Sometimes it is washed and polished every weekend. The women display themselves similarly in the kitchen; in the West End the stove was kept shiny, and copper hot water heaters were polished to maximal brilliance.

The desire for display can also be observed in the choice of clothing. Like most working-class groups, West Enders are enthusiastic clothes purchasers, and celebrate the major holidays by the acquisition of new outfits. The display of self through clothing is as important for men as for women, and young adults of both sexes spend considerable amounts for it. Expenditures diminish after marriage, but only so that the money may be spent to outfit the children, and to show them off to the peer group society.

West Enders have no more influence in the decision of clothing designers than anyone else and accept changes in fashions without much protest. They are not fashionable, however, and do not need to be the first to display new styles. Rather, they choose from what is available that which fits their esthetic: bright and cheerful colors, color contrast just short of color clash, and emphatic rather than subtle texture. Men prefer darker colors than do the women, but the immigrant black disappeared long ago. The choice of styles can be best described as informal and jaunty. At the time of the study, for example, the "Ivy league" style was beginning to be seen among the young men of the West End. Their version of this style, however, bore little resemblance to that worn on the Harvard campus: flannel colors were darker, shirts and ties were much brighter, and the belt in the back of the pants was more significant in size if not in function.

Home furnishings reflect the same esthetic. When the women talked about what furniture they would like to buy in their new homes, they spoke in terms of modern styling. Having grown tired of the overstuffed and highly ornamented pieces, they looked forward to the easier-to-clean simple styles of today. At the same time, they wanted bright, cheerful colors, strong textures, and enough "body" to provide comfort and the feeling of comfort. "International-style contemporary" thus evoked no enthusiasm; it was described as cheerless, much too small for comfort, and too delicate for long heavy wear. The preference was for what stylists often call "moderne."

Much the same esthetic is reflected in the religious objects that could be found in every room of the West End apartments. Most of these were Madonnas and Child: large and gaily colored paintings or statues expressing the joyfulness of the mother-baby relationship. Crucifixes were fewer and smaller, and the tragic religious themes were underplayed.

Patterns of spending for consumer goods reflect the same careful exuberance as the West Enders' esthetic principles. They do so because the outside world's appeals for saving and for installment buying both fall on deaf ears. Not only do West Enders have little money to save, but there is also little they want to save for. As I noted previously, the immigrant belief in the need to find security in landownership has disappeared. Being a landlord now means only hard work, complaining tenants, and little profit. Whether or not children will go to college is not decided until it is clear that they will finish high school. Thus, there is no incentive to put money aside for educational purposes. Saving for emergencies is thought to be useless, for although emergencies are expected to come, there is no sense in anticipating them. In any case, the outlays they require are always much more than the little money that people can save. As one West End housewife told me: "When I have money, I want to spend it, and enjoy life, not worry about the future. . . . I admire people who can save, though."

The lack of interest in saving, however, is not accompanied by profligacy. West Enders do not believe in living beyond their means, and installment buying is kept to an absolute minimum. They distrust the outside world, and therefore are skeptical about a method of buying which would put them in debt to that world for a long time. Moreover, they recognize that installment buying increases the cost of what they buy. Whenever possible, then, they use cash; and, since households are long established, expensive items are rarely needed. Only cars are financed by monthly payments, and even they, I was told, are sometimes bought for cash. As most West Enders do not have such cash reserves, I suspect that those who paid cash for automobiles were using *sub-rosa* income.

Money earned is to be spent on making daily life more pleasant and to contribute to the enjoyment of the group. One West Ender, in explaining why he rejected installment buying, described the prevalent pattern: "I want to live my way, with a full table, beer and whiskey, a full choice when people drop in. Also, I like fine clothing and my children all do, too." The goods which contribute to the enjoyment of the group and the display of the individual ought to be the best that can be obtained; but the quantity and quality of food, drink, and clothing that are purchased leave little else for other expenditures or savings. West Enders explain that life is too short for any other way of behavior.

As gambling provides an opportunity to enhance the daily expenditure pattern, and to earn money for presents or for special treats for the family and the peer group, many West Enders play the numbers and some, the horses. Although the amounts they wager are small, an occasional win not only adds excitement to life, but also brings in money that can be used for a night out on the town, or for a party. Among young men, unless they make their living by gambling, a "hit" on the numbers must be spent within the group. Adults use their winnings to buy things for the family, or for out-of-the-home spending money. An adolescent neighbor bought clothes for her younger siblings with her winnings. Few West Enders rely on gambling as a steady source of income, but for most of them, it is a source of periodic pleasure and, should they win, an occasion for impulse buying.

The Mass Media

Of all the ideas which come from the outside world, the most avidly received are those transmitted by the mass media. Although West Enders read little, adolescents and young adults are frequent movie-goers, and the adults keep the television set on all evening long. Young and old alike are much interested in the media personalities, and follow closely the details of their private and public lives. Preferences in mass media programming and performers, however, are highly selective. West Enders accept themes that mirror their own values, and reject others as illustrating the immorality and dishonesty of the outside world. Since the media offerings present both themes in considerable quantity, the West Ender thus feels that his point of view is supported by powerful American institutions. In short, the media can be used to justify both the peer group society and its rejection of the outside world.

The choice of mass media content is restricted to a few favorite types, and these differ sharply between the sexes. Among the men, the favorite movies or television programs are those which contain "action"—the mysteries, adventure stories, and westerns that emphasize plot and minimize dialogue. These, the West Enders call "stories." Sports programs are liked for their abundance of action; and slapstick comedy, because it is filled with horseplay, that is, "comic action." Musicals, musical comedies, drawing-room comedies, serious plays, and all "stories" which take place in middle-class surroundings or deal with the problems of middle-class people are rejected.

The women prefer just the opposite. They like musical programs, soap operas, and other stories that deal with romance or with family situations and problems, even middle-class ones. Men who choose stories popular with women are described as sissies. Indeed, one West Ender was accused of "going soft" and becoming a "half-woman" because he was not interested in watching sports events.

Whereas both sexes use the media for entertainment, the women may occasionally watch dramas and even documentaries that show them how family problems are to be handled. News and other informational programs that deal with the outside world are ignored, however, except for the weather report. Television does not cover local news that would be interesting to West Enders, and other news is of little concern to them. Moreover, West Enders prefer to get their information from peers. For example, one night I was watching television in a local bar about the time that an area boxer was fighting in the nearby Boston Gardens. The young men present asked that the television set be turned off when the news came on because they wanted to hear the outcome of the fight from friends who were in attendance and who were expected momentarily to return and give their report.

For the West Ender, the most important components of the popular movie or television program are "action" and the performer.[3] He is concerned first and foremost with the movement of the plot. This is illustrated not only by program choices but by the way in which people watch television. At home, the set is always on—even when company is present—and dials are turned to the station that offers the favorite programs. But viewing itself is intermittent. People watch the beginning and the end of the program—when the dramatic tension is established and when it is resolved. The other twenty minutes of the half-hour drama— the form prevalent at the time of my study—are ignored in favor of the conversation, although heads turn to the set at those times when something important seems to be happening.

Action programs are popular because they allow the West Ender to see his aspirations portrayed by the outside world. The action story usually centers on the adventures of a hero—the epitome of maleness—fighting and conquering the forces of evil. He is a moral man who defeats the immorality in the outside world. He is also a virile and handsome man, who is proud of his virility and dresses well. While his class background is usually not defined, many of the norms and methods he uses to produce social benefits and to achieve personal success are those of the working-class culture. For example, he is loyal to his buddies, and will not desert them for a woman. His tools are cunning, physical strength, and courage; and the *deus ex machina* that arrives just in time at the end proves that fate and luck are on his side.[4]

Thus the action drama provides an opportunity for the West Ender to see himself as he would like to be. This is even more clearly illustrated by specific preferences among action heroes. The hero with middle-class characteristics is rejected, for example, as is the educated man who displays his education. Policemen are disliked unless they are sympathetic to working-class characters, and are willing to ask them for help. Thus the haughty Sergeant Friday

3. Most of the observations that follow apply to the men in the West End media audience.

4. This content analysis and the prevalence of working-class norms in mass media action content are described in more detail in Herbert J. Gans, "American Films and Television Programs on British Screens: A Study of the Functions of Popular Culture Abroad," Philadelphia: Institute for Urban Studies, 1959, mimeographed, Chap. 5. See also, "Hollywood Films on British Screens," *Social Problems,* vol. 9 (1962), pp. 324–328.

of "Dragnet"—a television program that earned high national ratings at the time of the study—was scorned by West Enders both because he was a policeman and because he had no sympathy for the working-class people with whom he came into contact. Conversely, McGraw, a private detective and the hero of "Meet McGraw," was liked because he had little respect for the police, and used newsboys and other working-class types to help him solve the crime. He was a smart person who inevitably outwitted the police, but did so only with the help of people like the West Enders, thus acknowledging their importance in society.

The hero's relationships with women and children are also watched closely. While the Western or detective hero who is able to attract a good-looking woman and to conquer her without becoming involved is admired, the hero who is conquered by the woman is scorned. The young men with whom I watched television in the bar were quite explicit on this point: the hero who can "love 'em and leave 'em" was admired; but if he was caught or dominated by the heroine, the program was angrily dismissed as "mush," in much the same way that children will reject a romantic interlude. Although it may appear from these reactions that the young adults have retained childish attitudes, this is not the case. They rejected only those romantic situations in which men were shown to be powerless. Moreover, if the hero was not sufficiently ardent in his pursuit of the heroine, he was egged on by the viewers with frequent and vivid descriptions of what they would do if they could only spend some time alone with her.

Among married men, romantic scenes evoke no salacious comments—at least when they are at home—and they may even protest off-color material on television because they feel it should not enter the home. At the same time, they are bored by television comics whom they know to use such material in night clubs, for they feel that such performers are not operating at top peak in television. For sexually connotative material, West End men go to night clubs or burlesque theaters, although the married ones do so only infrequently.

When the mass media depict family relationships, West Enders approve those which support their values and reject those which do not. For example, men do not like family-situation comedies in which the husband is shown as a weak or stupid pawn of his wife and children, or those in which teenagers are shown evading or circumventing parental demands because they have more worldly wisdom than their parents. A program upholding paternal authority and wisdom, such as "Father Knows Best," receives more favorable response.

The other major attraction of the mass media is the performer. West Enders are very much interested in the stars of movies, night clubs, and television, and are knowledgeable about their activities. Frequently they choose a movie or a television program to see a favorite performer, and even when they do not choose content on this basis, they pay attention to the cast. "If I watch something on TV, I want to know who's playing in it." When people describe a movie or a television drama, they explain the events in it as having happened to the actor himself, not to the character he is playing. Thus, while they may begin by saying that John Wayne plays a cowboy in the movie under discussion, the action is explained from then on in terms of what Wayne did or what was done to him.

Among the men, the most popular actors are those who concentrate on action roles, such as John Wayne and the late Humphrey Bogart. They are liked because of the roles they play, and also because their private lives—or at least those portions which are known to the public—maintain the image they create in their roles. Should there be some disparity between roles and private lives, West Enders quickly lose interest in the actor; a man who plays action roles on the screen, for example, but who is rumored to have homosexual inclinations is disparaged in no uncertain terms. The performer is first evaluated by the roles he plays, but his private life must coincide with them. As he becomes a favorite, he is liked because he is playing himself.

Watching a favorite entertainer provides an opportunity to establish—and maintain—what Horton and Wohl have called a parasocial relationship with the performer.[5] Thus, West Enders keep track of their favorites, and will point out whether or not an actor is looking better or more poorly than the last time they

5. Donald Horton and R. Richard Wohl, "Mass Communication and Parasocial Interaction," *Psychiatry*, vol. 19 (1956), pp. 215–229.

saw him. They also keep tabs on what kinds of parts he is getting, in order to judge whether the powers who rule the media are using his talents properly and giving him his due. Yet there is little adulation in all of this among the older West Enders, for they react not as fans but as quasi-colleagues or peers. For example, one night a neighbor who came into the room to bring coffee to the men watching television spotted a popular actress in one of the roles. "She's doing her hair a new way, and doesn't it look nice," she said—in much the same tone as she would comment about a neighbor or an old friend.

Interest in the performer is strongest when he or she displays characteristics valued by the West Ender. Perhaps the most popular performer—at least at the time of my study—was Frank Sinatra. Among young adults, he was almost worshipped. The reasons for his popularity illustrate the kinds of values which the young West Ender wants to see in the outside world. Sinatra is liked first because he is an Italian who is proud of his lowly origin, not so much because of his ethnic background per se—although it is not disparaged—but because he is willing to admit and defend it. Unlike some other performers of Italian parentage, he has neither changed his name, nor rejected his background and the people who helped him get started. Many Italian singers are—or are said to be—aided by racketeers who invest in their careers and pay the costs that accrue on the road to success. Some of the singers turn their back on their underworld sponsors once they have achieved success. Sinatra, however, has continued to associate with childhood friends and early supporters even though some may be racket figures and though the association may hurt his career. He has become rich and famous, but he has not deserted the peer group that gave him his start. Nor has he adopted the ways of the outside world. Still a rebellious individual, he does not hesitate to use either his tongue or his fists to fight those who seek to deprive him of what is rightfully his. Also, he shows his scorn for those aspects of the outside world that do not please him, and does not try to maintain appearances required by middle-class notions of respectability. Making headlines regularly for his sexual escapades, he is said to be unwilling to become emotionally involved with his sexual partners.[6] He is loyal to his male friends, and may indulge in action-seeking adventures with them when the mood strikes him.[7] He gambles, plays the horses, and sits up all night for card games. As an actor, he often plays the kind of rebellious roles with which West End men can identify. As a singer, the inflection he gives to the tune and the lyrics is interpreted as arousing his audience to action. As a West Ender said, "He gives you a little dig in his songs." At the same time, his singing style has a teasing quality which suggests to West Enders that he is making fun both of the song and of the outside world. To them, he seems to be putting something over on the outside world, while at the same time taking its money and attractive women. He has risen to the top, failed, and come back again to even greater fame, to prove that downward mobility is not inevitable, that the "bum" can return to even greater heights than he achieved before. And, despite his success, he has not given up the old values; he has remained what he was originally—a seeker of action with peer group values.

The West Ender's interest in performers, his identification with their problems, and his response to them as a near-colleague may be related to the similarities between them. The performer is an individual who displays himself to an audience. Moreover, he does so in a highly competitive situation; his status depends on his ability to display himself and his talents so as to obtain people's approval. In some ways his job is only a more extreme version of the display that takes place within the peer group.

Values and the Mass Media

In using the mass media, West Enders are accepting themes from the outside world. Whether or not they are also accepting its

6. He is also said to make the traditional Italian distinction between the "good" and the "bad" girl.

7. In recent years, he has become known as the leader of a predominantly male group of entertainers that indulges in impulsive forms of "action," and is known as "the clan," or the "ratpack." In some ways, the men are a group of Hollywood corner boys. According to one reporter, their motto is "Where's the action?" Richard Gehman, *Sinatra and His Ratpack,* New York: Belmont Books, 1961.

values, however, is doubtful. The consistent choice of content and performers suggests that West Enders are careful to select from the large variety of themes those which support their own values— many of which originate within the peer group society.

In addition, the intrusion of outside values is controlled by the maintenance of some detachment toward the content of the movie and television screen. For example, excessive television watching is discouraged, but among adults more than among children. The latter are allowed to watch whenever they feel like it, although they are not home often enough to be tied to the set. In the evenings, adults control program choices. Adults who spend too much time in the movies or in front of the television set are ridiculed, often to their face. Moreover, if they take what they see too seriously, they are said to be childish.

The major source of detachment, however, is the knowledge that the mass media are part of the outside world, and that there-fore they cannot be trusted. West Enders enjoy making fun of the media as much as they enjoy the programs. As one of my neigh-bors put it, "We heckle TV just like we used to heckle the freaks at the circus when we were kids." Television commercials are some-times watched raptly, and then bombarded with satirical comments which question exaggerated or dishonest claims and meaningless statements. West Enders do not enjoy watching satire, but they do enjoy creating their own in response to what they see. They also are sensitive to media content which allows them to demonstrate the hypocrisy of the outside world. Thus programming which praises politicians as honest, which implies that middle-class char-acters who talk about morality also act that way, or which suggests that businessmen are more interested in community service than in profit is debunked in no uncertain terms.

Although West Enders are strongly attracted to "the stories," they also remember that what they see is fiction. When anachro-nisms or mistakes appear in the plot, the scenery, or the dress of the characters, people comment upon the stupidity or dishonesty of the media. Thus they note the six-shooter that is fired seven times, or the heroine whose coiffure remains unruffled throughout the wildest adventures. If programs are monotonous, considerable enjoyment is derived from isolating and criticizing the standard clichés that dominate television stories. Thus, West Enders can enjoy the fantasy even while debunking some of its elements.

A similar detachment is maintained toward the performers. West Enders know that much of the material disseminated about them is pure fiction, and cannot be believed. For example, they may cheerfully admit that many of the stories about their favorite performers are probably manufactured by a press agent. While this does not prevent them from feeling rapport toward the performers, it does allow them, at the same time, to maintain some suspicion as to the honesty of the mass media. Any inconsistency, for example, between the role played by the performer and his personal characteristics is spotted, and used to reduce the rapport. One of my neighbors, who had considerable contact with performers who visited Boston, was often teased by his relatives about watching television when he knew what the performers "were really like." People accuse each other of being taken in by what appears on the screen, and thus protect each other from too close an involvement in the fantasy. Comments are made such as: "How can you watch this man play a cowboy when you know he can't even ride a horse?" or "How can you watch young actresses play mothers when you know what they really are?"

In effect, the mass media are approached with some of the same ambivalence as other features of the outside world. This in turn allows the West Ender to interpret the media content so as to protect himself from the outside world and to isolate himself from its messages unless he wishes to believe them. Because of his suspicion of the mass media as an institution, the appearance of people and values of which he approves demonstrates that they are there because they are superior and cannot be held back. If Sinatra is in much demand by the media entrepreneurs and yet can act like a quasi-West Ender, he must be better therefore than his employers.

The defenses which West Enders set up against the undesired themes and values are strong. Whether some of the values get through in spite of the defenses is impossible to say without much more intensive study. The West Enders who are adults today were avid movie goers in their youth, but they do not parrot the values that dominate Hollywood movies. Even so, the people who grew up in immigrant households are American and not Italian in culture. That this change can be traced to the mass media—or, indeed, to any single agent—however, is doubtful.

CHAPTER 10 The Peer Group Society in Process

Introduction

The description of the peer group society so far has been static, resulting in a cross-sectional view at one point in time. In order to move from description to explanation, a more dynamic perspective is required. A glance backward at the immigrant generation and its ancestors, and a look forward at changes now taking place in the second and third generations will isolate the factors that shape the peer group society. This in turn will make it possible to outline some essential differences between it and middle-class America in the next chapter.

Although the antecedents of the present West Enders can be studied in several ways, perhaps the best approach would have been to consult their parents and other immigrants who were still living in the West End. This would have required a knowledge of Italian —and of regional dialects—which I did not have. It also might have created a picture distorted by faulty memories and nostalgia for the past. There are also two other possible approaches: to discover what West Enders themselves report about their parents and the generations in Italy; and to consult existing sociological studies of Italian immigrants and of Italian society before the exodus to America. Such studies also can be backed up by research in present-day Italian communities.

Both approaches are fraught with considerable danger. The West Enders know the past only from their experience, most of which was collected in childhood.[1] The use of other sociological studies, on the other hand, requires the assumption that the ancestors of the West Enders are like the people in the Italian communities where the research took place. Moreover, the attempt to describe people by generations assumes that generations are cultural units, and that Italian, immigrant, and second-generation groups in one place and time will be roughly similar to those of another place and time. But the society and culture of any generation are affected and altered by the social and economic conditions within which they exist.

As it turns out, however, the studies made among immigrants and of Italian society at the time of the major exodus, as well as those made recently in Southern Italy, have reported many similar findings. Moreover, these findings do not diverge significantly from the picture which I have drawn of the West Enders. It would seem, therefore, that not only are Italians much the same everywhere, but that there is a clearly identifiable Italian social structure that has changed remarkably little in the passage of time and place from Italy to America. This stability can be traced largely to the uniformity in social and economic conditions under which the several generations have lived.

From the types of change that have taken place between the immigrant and the second generation, and from behavioral patterns visible among the more mobile West Enders and their children, it is possible to project some of the changes that will be likely to take place when the third generation reaches adulthood. Observations about the West Enders' resistance to change, and especially to the middle class, would suggest, however, that the family circle and the other institutions basic to the peer group society will continue to exist in the third generation. Thus, the children of the West Enders will neither move—nor be swept—into the institutions of middle-class American society nor adopt its value premises.[2]

1. Consequently, their comments about the past will be used only sparingly.
2. It must be remembered of course that the West Enders are not entirely representative of all second-generation Italian-Americans. See Chapter 2.

The Southern Italian Society

Southern Italian society—that is, the provinces below Rome and in Sicily—was agrarian, feudal, and static when the exodus to America began at the turn of the century. Most of the land was owned by a relatively small number of large absentee landowners —some of them of the nobility—who either leased their land to peasants, or had it farmed by landless day laborers under the supervision of resident managers. The local community consisted typically of four major social strata, each rigidly separated from the other: the "galantuomini," or gentry, including the nobility, other large landowners, the professionals, and the clergy; the "artigiano," or artisans, including craftsmen and small shopkeepers; the "contadini," or peasants, who owned or leased tiny plots of land; and the "giornalieri," or day laborers who looked each day for work on the estates, and who were rarely employed more than a third of the year. The vast majority of the people were either peasants or farm laborers, who lived in a chronic state of poverty and deprivation. The farm laborers were poorest, but in many communities the peasants controlled so little land that they were economically no better off, even though landownership did give them a somewhat higher status.[3]

Recent studies of Southern Italian communities have made it clear that relatively little change has occurred in the over-all economy and social structure, and that the conditions which existed at the turn of the century still hold today.[4] Consequently, it is possible to draw on studies made just before the immigration to America,[5] as well as on those conducted in contemporary communi-

3. For a convenient summary of Southern Italian life, see R. A. Schermerhorn, *These Our Children*, Boston: D. C. Heath, 1949, Chap. 11.

4. See, for example, Edward C. Banfield, *The Moral Basis of a Backward Society*, New York: The Free Press of Glencoe, 1958; and Donald Pitkin, "Land Tenure and Farm Organization in an Italian Village," unpublished Ph.D. Dissertation, Harvard University, 1954. For a detailed analysis of the poverty of Sicily, see Danilo Dolci, *Report from Palermo*, New York: Orion Press, 1959.

5. These are based largely on interviews with immigrants in America. Cf. Phyllis H. Williams, *Southern Italian Folkways in Europe and America*, New Haven: Yale University Press, 1938; or on interviews in America combined

ties.[6] Since most of the Southern Italians who went to America came from the ranks of the day laborers and peasants, information about the ancestors of the West Enders can be taken from data about these two strata in past and present studies.

These data suggest strongly that the society and culture of the West Enders are quite similar to those of the Southern Italians, past and present. In Italy, as in the West End, households consisted of nuclear or expanded families.[7] Husband-wife relationships were segregated, and family life was adult-centered.[8] Children were reared by reward and punishment,[9] and parents had little interest in them as individuals, except to show them off.[10] Because of the poverty, children were expected to work as soon as they were old enough. Moreover, since the available work was unskilled, they had learnt all of the adult skills between the ages of seven and ten.[11]

The two studies of present-day Southern Italy found no evidence of an extended family, noting that the land was too poor to justify several family members working on it jointly.[12] Covello reported that among the Sicilians whom he studied the extended family had existed around the turn of the century.[13] It then had provided mutual aid and companionship under the leadership of a family head, who was chosen informally from among the adult men, and who maintained the family honor, supervised disputes, and administered interhousehold aid.[14] Functioning as a social rather than an economic unit, it seems to have been only a more

with informal research in Italy, cf. Leonard Covello, "The Social Background of the Italo-American School Child," unpublished Ph.D. Dissertation, New York University, 1944; and Walter H. Sangree, "Mel Hyblaeum: A Study of the People of Middletown of Sicilian Extraction . . . ," unpublished M.A. Thesis, Wesleyan University, 1952. My account here rests heavily on the detailed description in Covello's study.

6. Most of my observations are drawn from Pitkin, *op. cit.*, and Banfield, *op. cit.*

7. Covello, *op. cit.*, p. 237; Pitkin, *op. cit.*, p. 114.

8. Covello, *op. cit.*, pp. 562–563.

9. Banfield, *op. cit.*, pp. 154 ff.

10. Pitkin, *op. cit.*, pp. 219–220.

11. Covello, *op. cit.*, pp. 364 ff.

12. Banfield, *op. cit.*, p. 10; Pitkin, *op. cit.*, pp. 114, 245.

13. Covello, *op. cit.*, pp. 238 ff.

14. *Ibid.*, pp. 236–241.

cohesive and slightly more structured form of the family circle which has been reported in all of the studies, past and present.

Social life was centered almost exclusively around the family circle of relatives, and people outside it were conceived to be strangers.[15] Friendship as we know it was rare, and people who did become friends were adopted into the family through god-parentship.[16] Only relatives were invited into the home.[17]

Although the available studies provide no data on the existence of peer groups among adults, Pitkin has noted that boys and girls did separate themselves into age-graded groups.[18] Moreover, there was little respect for old people,[19] and Covello reported that a family head was replaced quickly if he became too old, or was senile.[20] These data suggest that the relationship between the generations, as in the West End, was less important than that within the generations. Relatives of similar age associated with each other, and the men competed for the leadership of the family circle. Covello noted that this provided the primary opportunity for individualism in Southern Italian society.[21]

Southern Italians, like West Enders, were only marginally attached to the community. Although people were expected to attend church, there was little involvement in the church itself.[22] As the priests generally supported the landowners, a strong anticlericalism developed among the peasants and farm laborers, especially among the men.[23] The Southern Italian attitude was summarized, as follows, by one of Sangree's respondents: "Fatalism is our religion; the church just supplies the pageantry of life." [24] In addition, there was widespread belief in animistic superstitions such as the evil eye, a malevolent spirit that caused illness and other disasters.

The rejection of the outside world was more intense than in

15. *Ibid.*, pp. 271–275.
16. *Ibid.*, pp. 294 ff.
17. *Ibid.*, pp. 140, 290.
18. Pitkin, *op. cit.*, pp. 184–185.
19. *Ibid.*, p. 224.
20. Covello, *op. cit.*, pp. 245, 306.
21. *Ibid.*, p. 244.
22. *Ibid.*, pp. 208 ff.; Banfield, *op. cit.*, p. 17.
23. Covello, *op. cit.*, p. 223; Banfield, *op. cit.*, p. 17.
24. Sangree, *op. cit.*, p. 87.

the West End, and its boundaries began immediately outside the family circle. People from other communities, even nearby ones, were characterized as criminals.[25] The government and the police, run from Rome, were rejected with the traditional hostility felt toward Northern Italy. Within the community itself, the higher classes were treated as part of the outside world because they exploited the peasants and farm laborers, and denied them any opportunity to improve their lot.[26] Individual peasants or laborers who did manage to move to a higher social stratum were treated as renegades.[27]

Work patterns and attitudes in Southern Italy are not comparable to those of the West Enders because work was so desperately needed, so hard to find, and strenuously competed for when it was available. Children were put to work at an early age, for their help was needed to keep the family going.[28] Southern Italian parents saw little need for education once the child was old enough to work. They could neither have afforded to keep him in school, nor would the education he received have helped him to get a better job. Moreover, education was thought to remove the children from parental influence, and to question parental authority.[29] Indeed, in many towns, the schools were run largely for the children of the higher classes, and the children of peasants and laborers were neither expected nor encouraged to attend.[30]

Caretaking agencies were generally ignored, for they were thought to be for families who could not fall back on their families for help.[31] At the turn of the century, hospitals were run on a charity basis which the peasants and laborers were too proud to accept.[32] Furthermore, as most of the caretaking agencies were organized by people from Northern Italy, they were doubly suspect.[33]

25. Jerre Mangione, *Mount Allegro,* Boston: Houghton Mifflin, 1942, p. 6.
26. Pitkin, *op. cit.,* pp. 155 ff.; Banfield, *op. cit.* Chap. 4.
27. Covello, *op. cit.,* pp. 137 ff.
28. *Ibid.,* pp. 398 ff.; Banfield, *op. cit.,* pp. 20–23.
29. Covello, *op. cit.,* pp. 407 ff.
30. *Ibid.,* pp. 394, 404.
31. Williams, *op. cit.,* p. 75.
32. *Ibid.,* pp. 171–172.
33. *Ibid.;* Covello, *op. cit.,* p. 387.

Banfield's study, which dealt specifically with the lack of community organization and civic activity in a Southern Italian village, emphasized the total bifurcation between the immediate family and the rest of society:

> . . . the extreme poverty and backwardness . . . is to be explained largely but not entirely by the inability of the villagers to act together for their common good, or indeed for any end transcending the immediate material interest of the nuclear family. This inability . . . arises from an ethos . . . of *amoral familism,* which has been produced by three factors acting in combination: a high death rate, certain land tenure conditions, and the absence of the institution of the extended family. . . .[34]

> The hypothesis [of amoral familism] is that the [villagers] act as if they were following this rule: Maximize the material, short-run advantage of the nuclear family; assume that all others will do likewise.[35]

Banfield's description of the local patterns of political participation suggests that they are similar to those in the West End. He noted that, "In a society of amoral familism, only officials will concern themselves with public affairs, for only they are paid to do so. For a private citizen to take a serious interest in a public problem will be regarded as abnormal or even improper." [36] He found extreme suspicion of the politician, and indicated that, "Whether an office holder takes bribes or not, it will be assumed by the society of amoral familism that he does." [37] Likewise, "The claim of any person or institution to be inspired by zeal for public rather than private advantage will be regarded as a fraud." [38] He quotes a respondent: "If ever anyone wants to do anything, the question always is: what is he after?" [39]

Moreover, "In a society of amoral familists, there will be no

34. Banfield, *op. cit.,* p. 10.
35. *Ibid.,* p. 85.
36. *Ibid.,* p. 87.
37. *Ibid.,* p. 94.
38. *Ibid.,* p. 98.
39. *Ibid.,* p. 98.

leaders and no followers. No one will take the initiative in outlin-
ing a course of action and persuading others to embark on it—
except as it may be to his private advantage to do so—and if one
did offer leadership, the group would refuse it out of distrust." [40]
Even attitudes toward voting are similar:

> The voter will place little confidence in the promise of the
> parties. He will be apt to use his ballot to pay for favors al-
> ready received, rather than for favors which are merely prom-
> ised. Moreover . . . it will be assumed that whatever group is
> in power is self-serving and corrupt. Hardly will an election be
> over before the voters will conclude that the new officials are
> enriching themselves at their expense and that they will have
> no intention of keeping the promises they have made. [41]

From Immigrant to Second Generation

The Southern Italians who migrated to America came to better
themselves; many had intended to remain only long enough to
earn money so that they could purchase land in their home village, and become small landowners. Some were successful—especially among the early arrivals. But as the Italian immigration
increased in number, the large majority either were unable to save
enough to return home, or relinquished the original dream, and
brought their families to America. [42]

The studies of the immigrant generation would suggest that
the move to America resulted in little change in the pattern of
adult life. [43] The social structure which the immigrants brought

40. *Ibid.*, pp. 99–100.
41. *Ibid.*, p. 102. See also Sangree, *op. cit.*, pp. 78–79.
42. The most detailed description of this immigration is contained in
R. F. Foerster, *The Italian Emigration of Our Times*, Cambridge: Harvard
University Press, 1919. For brief summaries, see Paul J. Campisi, "Ethnic
Family Patterns: The Italian Family in the United States," *American Journal
of Sociology*, vol. 53 (1948), pp. 443–449; Francis Ianni, "The Italo-American
Teenager," *The Annals*, vol. 338 (November, 1961), pp. 70–78; and Nathan
Glazer, *Peoples of New York*, forthcoming.
43. My account of the immigrants and their children is based on Covello's
study in New York's East Harlem district. It is a detailed and sympathetic re-

with them from Italy served them in the new country as well. Those who moved to the cities, for example, settled in Italian neighborhoods, where relatives often lived side by side, and in the midst of people from the same Italian town. Under these conditions, the family circle was maintained much as it had existed in Southern Italy.

The outside world continued to be a source of deprivation and exploitation. The immigrants worked in factories and on construction gangs, but while work was more plentiful than in Italy, people had to strive as hard as ever to support their families. Situated on the lowest rung of the occupational hierarchy, they were exploited by their employers and by the "padrone," the agent who acted as a middleman between the immigrants and the labor market. Moreover, the churches in the immigrant neighborhoods were staffed largely by Irish priests, who practiced a strange and harsh form of Catholicism, and had little sympathy for the Madonna and the local saints that the Italians respected. The caretaking agencies and the political machines were run by Yankees and other ethnic groups. As a result of the surrounding strangeness, the immigrants tried to retain the self-sufficiency of the family circle as much as they could. They founded a number of community organizations that supported this circle, and kept away from the outside world whenever possible.

The major changes took place among the children, especially as a result of their contact with American schools. Since parochial schools were not yet in existence, the children were required to attend the public ones. Covello found that when the immigrants first arrived, there was considerable hostility toward the public school system. Not only did the schools take the children out of the job market and prevent them from contributing to the family income, but they also seemed to upset the Southern Italian conception of the child, and the child's own relation to the parents. The school's teaching—that the child has his own life, that he should study during school hours, and play afterwards—was foreign to the immigrants. They felt that by encouraging play, the

port, and although unpublished, the best source of information on the social structure and culture of the Italian immigrant in America. Covello, *op. cit.,* Parts II and III.

schools were preventing the children from growing up, and that by keeping boys in school when they could be working, the schools were impairing their masculinity. Covello quotes one of his informants as saying: "The schools made of our children persons of leisure—little gentlemen. They lost the dignity of good children to think first of their parents, to help them whether they need it or not." [44]

Gradually, however, the immigrants accepted the fact that there was no work for young children in America. They also discovered that there were laws which not only prevented them from working but which required them to go to school. Consequently, they sent the children to school, and, except in case of family need, permitted them to finish the elementary grades. Even so, there was considerable grumbling about the American laws. Covello quotes another immigrant respondent: "Someone decides not to allow the drinking of wine, so he makes a law without asking the people. Same with going to school. How can you respect such a law?" [45]

When the children were asked to go to high school, however, the immigrants rebelled. The family needed the extra income, and, since jobs were available for the boys, there was no reason for them to attend school. Thus, the immigrants had not really changed their attitude about education. They had merely adjusted it to fit American conditions.

The children themselves were caught between two cultures. While the school taught them to behave like American children, the parents demanded that they be useful and obedient family members. Covello has suggested that the outcome of the struggle between the two depended largely on the peer group. In neighborhoods where Italian children were a minority in the school population, they began to feel that the parental culture was inferior, and adopted the ways of the non-Italian majority. In predominantly Italian neighborhoods, however, the parents won out. The children of high-school age then decided that they should side with the family rather than remain in school. Since their peers supported this choice, the students took to widespread and frequent truancy —with the full support of their parents.

44. *Ibid.*, p. 467.
45. *Ibid.*, p. 603.

Consequently, the children who grew up in predominantly Italian neighborhoods were for the most part not weaned away from the Italian social structure. There are several reasons for this. First, the choice was clearly one between school and family, rather than between school and work, for even those children who could not obtain jobs stayed away from school. Also, whereas the school treated them as children, the parents considered them to be adults. Had the children been interested in learning, they might have rebelled against their parents, but it is clear that they were not interested. They had grown up with the belief that education was children's activity and that it was irrelevant to getting or holding a job. Since unskilled jobs were still available, what they were learning in school was of no use occupationally. The longer they stayed in school, the greater the gap that developed between them and their parents.

Covello indicates clearly that the second generation did reject many of the culture patterns which parents had brought with them from Italy—the superstitions, the old styles of dress, the recreational activities, and all other rural traditions which were irrelevant in America. At the same time, however, they did not reject the family-centered social structure. Covello quotes one man about his youth: "I loathed Italian customs with all my heart, but I would never let anything stand between me and our family." [46]

Another change, which may have begun in the first generation but which was really visible only in the second, was an increase in the freedom and family influence of the woman. In Southern Italy, women were subservient to, and almost completely dependent on, the men. They could not work as laborers, and no other jobs existed. While daughters could help around the house, their major contribution to the family was to retain their virginity until the parents could arrange a marriage that might be economically or socially beneficial to them. Thus, father and brothers guarded them closely to make sure that their hymens and their reputations both remained inviolate.

In America, many of these restrictions fell away. Even in Italy, the girls had chafed at their lack of freedom of movement and of choosing a spouse. Consequently, the American school that seemed

46. *Ibid.*, p. 537.

like a prison to the second-generation Italian boy was an avenue of escape for the girl. Also, as she was taught by women, she was able to adjust more comfortably to the dominant school culture, which was, after all, predominantly female. More important, the American economy did not discriminate sexually. Thus women were able to get jobs on their own, and could contribute to the family coffers. At the same time, the advantages of the arranged marriage evaporated. Now that a man could work to improve himself economically or socially, he no longer needed to depend on his daughter's marriage for such benefits. Moreover, the social and residential fluidity in the Italian neighborhood diminished in importance the union of two families through arranged marriage. It no longer meant what it had in the static small town of Southern Italy. Thus the girls were free to choose their own boyfriends and husbands. But they were still restricted in many other ways. Their virginity was guarded as closely as before, and they were expected to marry a man of Italian background, preferably of equal or higher status.

Once the girl was married, and the children came, she usually moved back quickly into the traditional role, for she could no longer work and was dependent once more on the man. Even so, her status in the family was not quite the same: jobs were available to her, and if the husband did lose his job, she could go to work temporarily. Moreover, even in childhood she had learned that much of American mass production was designed with her in mind, including the movies that put her on a pedestal. Thus, the American culture of school, church, and consumer goods invited her more readily than it did the man. Indeed, the male's corner hangout, the streets, and the stag environments in which he spent his spare-time as a young man were not respected by the American climate of opinion. Much of the energy of Yankee caretakers and reformers, in fact, was devoted to persuading him to accept female-dominated institutions.

American culture, however, could not penetrate the family circle. Thus, whereas the children who became the adults of the second generation retained little of the Italian culture, they did retain most of its social structure. In short, they live in the ways that I have described in the preceding chapters.

A comparison of the lives of the West Enders with those of the immigrants suggests a number of other changes. For the West Enders, life is much less of a struggle than it was for their parents. There are more jobs, more secure ones, and better paid as well. As economic conditions improve, the ethos which Banfield calls amoral familism has begun to recede in importance. Most West Enders, for example, no longer need to fear their neighbors and unrelated people as a threat to their own existence. These "others" are no longer competitors for a small number of scarce jobs, but people with whom one can associate. Consequently, social life and mutual aid are not entirely restricted to the family circle; West Enders can and do make friends more easily than their ancestors.[47]

Nor is the outside world as threatening as it was to immigrants. The second generation is not barred from it by language, and it can maneuver in the outside world if absolutely necessary. As a result, the attitude toward caretakers, the law, city government, and other phases of the outside world is no longer based on total incomprehension and fear.

The processes by which these generational changes came to be were of course not always painless. In too many cases, the family circle and other immigrant institutions could not cope with acculturation, poverty, and the other degradations forced on the newcomers and their children by the outside world. Some turned to delinquency, crime, and violence to resolve their difficulties; others were beset by individual and family breakdowns. Although these problems affected only a minority of the population, they too are a part of the transition from immigrant to second-generation status.

The Slowness of Change:
The Basis of the Peer Group Society

Some aspects of a group's way of life change more rapidly than others. Moreover, the observer's perception of change is affected by

47. A number of other changes between Italians and Italian-Americans are described as part of a larger study of drinking patterns in G. Lolli, E. Serianni, G. Golder, and P. Luzzatto-Fegiz, *Alcohol in Italian Culture,* New York: The Free Press of Glencoe and Yale Center of Alcohol Studies, 1958. This study notes, for example, that Italian-Americans go to church more than Italians

his own perspective, by the indices he uses, and by his own value judgments about the desirability of change per se.

These considerations affect any attempt to summarize the comparison of the West Enders to the generations that preceded them. Clearly, there has been considerable change in the standard of living, and in certain patterns of culture. At the same time, however, the many parallels between Southern Italian society and the West Enders suggest that many basic features of the way of life have not changed. The old social structure has remained intact.

What accounts for the stability of the social structure in the face of what would seem to be a rather drastic change in environment? The static, poverty-stricken, and highly stratified rural society of Southern Italy bears little resemblance to the frequently changing, more prosperous, and comparatively open society of urban-industrial Boston. *A brief review of the three generations may suggest the answer: the environment has not really changed as drastically as it appears.* This review will also make it possible to outline more clearly the basis of the peer group society as a response to the opportunities and deprivations in the environment.

The Italians who came to America were not farmers or peasants, but town-dwelling farm laborers who worked for absentee owners and managers. Although there was some evidence of the existence of a clanlike extended family, the occupational role of the farm laborer made it impossible for the extended family to function as a unit. The farm laborer, who was paid in wages that barely supported even his wife and children, could exist only in a nuclear family household.

Since people lived under conditions of extreme poverty, and in a static social system from which escape—other than by emigration—was impossible, the overriding goal was the survival of the nuclear family. Moreover, as marriages were contracted to advance —or at least not to retrogress—the economic and social position of the families involved, they had to be arranged. Consequently, husband and wife were usually not as close as in partnerships based on love. Since children had to go to work at the earliest op-

---

(p. 22); that they report drinking for social reasons, rather than for their health (pp. 68–69); that they get drunk more often (p. 85); and that unlike Italians they get drunk in the presence of the opposite sex (p. 88).

portunity, they were raised to adult status as quickly as possible, which was accomplished by treating them as small adults from an early age.

The nuclear family is neither entirely self-sufficient nor independent; nor can it satisfy all the needs of daily life. It is particularly handicapped in dealing with emergencies. Consequently, other institutions must be available. But when every family was involved in a struggle to survive—as was the case with the Southern Italian farm laborer—few people could be called on for aid, or trusted to give it when their own families were equally in need. Nor could they be treated as friends and companions, for they might take advantage of this relationship to help themselves in the fight for survival. Moreover, in order to attract friends, one had to be able to make a good impression. This required a dwelling unit to which people could be invited without shame, money to pay the costs of entertaining, and a considerable amount of trust over a long period of time. As one of Covello's respondents put it: "Friends are a luxury we cannot afford." Community agencies, were they churches, schools, or welfare agencies, could not be trusted because they were controlled by the employer. It made no difference when they had been founded for beneficial purposes; they were rejected by their intended clients as a matter of pride.

Under such conditions, relatives were the only source of group life and mutual aid. Being tied to each other by what were felt to be irrevocable ties of blood, they could face each other without putting on appearances, without feelings of shame, and without suspicion that the relationship would be exploited. In a society where no one could afford to trust anyone else, relatives had to trust each other. Moreover, when survival depended on the ability to work strenuously for long hours, older people were at a disadvantage. Possessing no special skills or traditional knowledge not also available to younger people, they had little influence in the group once they had become too old to support themselves. In addition, since relatives had to double as friends, people naturally gravitated to family members with whom they had the most in common. Consequently, they were drawn to peers.

The Southern Italian farm laborers lived not simply in poverty, but in poverty in the midst of a visibly higher standard of living enjoyed by the artisans, the middle class, and the gentry. In some areas they resorted to strikes and to class conflict; in others, to emigration.[48] But until these solutions were possible, most farm laborers lived in a state of extreme relative deprivation, a state made even more painful because of the close proximity of more fortunate people. In such circumstances, the restriction of aspirations was emotionally a most functional solution—at least in the short range—since it prevented the development of frustrations, which were frequently harder to endure than physical deprivation. Parental lack of interest in education, detachment from the larger community, and unwillingness to fight the exploiting powers— all were practical solutions in a society in which mobility was so restricted that there was no reason to expect benefits from schooling, and where the oversupply of labor made it possible to starve out rebellious individuals. While these solutions were harsh and denying, they also reduced stress, and made life as bearable as possible. Since the achievement of object-goals was certain to be frustrated, children were reared to reject them. The development of empathy was also discouraged; too great a sensitivity to the problems of other people would have been hard to endure.

Many of the conditions that gave rise to this way of life accompanied the Southern Italians in their move to America. In Italy, they had labored from sunrise to sunset on the farms of landowners; in America, they worked long hours as laborers for factory owners or contractors. Moreover, since they did not gravitate to the highly mechanized and rationalized assembly line jobs, the nature of their work did not change radically either. Many worked with the earth—pick and shovel in hand—in both countries, although in America, they brought forth construction projects rather than farm products. In Italy, they had lived in densely built-up and overcrowded small towns, barren of vegetation; in America, they moved into equally overcrowded and barren tenement neighborhoods. Indeed, their trip across the ocean took them only from rural towns to urban villages.

Most of these parallels continued into the adulthood of the sec-

48. John S. MacDonald and Lea D. MacDonald, "Migration Versus Non-Migration: A Typology of Responses to Poverty," paper read at the 1961 meetings of the American Sociological Society.

ond generation. Not until World War II, in fact, and the subsequent prosperity of the postwar era, did their economic position differ radically from that of their forebears. Even then, many West Enders have been dogged by unemployment, layoffs, and other forms of economic insecurity. Since they—as well as their parents—have often been employed in marginal industries, they also have felt themselves to be exploited occupationally. Moreover, like their ancestors, they have been beset by serious illness, premature death, infant mortality, and by other of the sudden and unpredictable tragedies that so frequently hit low-income people.

Many other parallels exist between Southern Italy and Boston. The immigrants who settled in Boston found a society stratified not only by class but also by ethnic background and religion. In fact, in Boston—more so perhaps than in other cities—they encountered a hereditary aristocracy that at the time of the Italian influx still held considerable social, economic, and political power. Since then, its place has been taken by the Irish and by other groups, all of them culturally different from the Southern Italians. In short, the world outside the home was and still is dominated by people different in class and culture, by outsiders to be suspected and rejected.

Thus, the environment that the immigrants and the West Enders have encountered in America has differed in degree rather than in kind; it is less hostile and depriving, of course, but it is otherwise still the same. There have been no radical changes in the position of the working class vis-à-vis other classes, or in the position of minority ethnic groups vis-à-vis the majority. As a result, there have been as yet no strong pressures or incentives among the West Enders for any radical change in the basic social structure with which they respond to the environment.

From Second to Third Generation: Signs of Change [49]

In addition to the changes that have already taken place between the past and present generations, other changes are only now

49. This section is speculative, since it deals with a generation only now reaching adulthood. It is based on observations of West Enders, a few ex-West

developing. Noticeable among a few West Enders today, they are likely to become more prevalent in the next generation. These changes are the result of processes in the larger society that are creating new opportunities for West Enders. They also will make it more difficult to maintain some of the traditional ways of life.

The major source of opportunities is occupational. A few West Enders are now beginning to move into white-collar technical jobs, actually the modern equivalents of skilled factory work. They are also beginning to enter service occupations, notably in sales, in which their ability for self-display and for competitive group activity is helpful.[50]

The third generation will be able to respond to the new occupational opportunities partly because their parents believe in the need for education as a means of obtaining job security. Parents also can now afford to keep children in school at least until high school graduation. Whether or not the third generation actually will take up these opportunities will depend, of course, on their willingness to stay in school, and to learn what is necessary to compete for stable and secure jobs. I assume that an increasing number of third-generation adolescents will remain in school.

New occupational and educational attainments are likely to have repercussions on the structure of the family, and on the peer group society generally. For one thing, they will create more social and cultural differences between people. This, in turn, will affect the family circle, for relatives who have responded to the widening opportunities may begin to find that they have less in common, and are no longer compatible in their interests. At the same time, since people have fewer children than in previous generations, the number of potential family circle members will be reduced. Consequently, the family circle may be somewhat harder to maintain than in the second generation.

Although someday these trends may even decimate the circle, other changes are likely to attract new recruits. I have already

Enders who had left before redevelopment, and on additional observations made among a handful of Italian families in a suburban community near Philadelphia which I studied after I concluded my field work in the West End.

50. Whether these opportunities will be available to the third generation in as plentiful amounts as I am suggesting depends on the consequences of automation on the labor market in the coming decades.

noted that as unrelated people cease to be competitors in the struggle for survival, they can become allies in the search for companionship. Indeed, the desire for companionship combined with the decreasing number of compatible kin can mean that friends and neighbors will begin to play a more important role in the social life of the peer group society.

Meanwhile, other changes are taking place in the nuclear family unit. The decimation of the family circle by differential mobility is one step in a larger social process that brings nuclear family members into a more intimate dependence on each other. For while friends can replace relatives in a number of functions, rarely do they help each other as fully or be as close as people bound by blood ties. Other changes are reinforcing the cohesion of the nuclear family. With the disappearance of arranged marriages, husband and wife are emotionally closer to each other than were their parents and grandparents. Moreover, the nature of the educational process—both in and out of the classroom—is such that husbands and wives now grow up with a more similar background than was true in previous generations. By and large, both sexes are exposed to the same subjects in school. In addition, they are taught by the school, and by American culture generally, that the man may participate in child-rearing and household duties and in spare-time activities with his wife with no reflection on his masculinity. Given the increasing influence of the wife, and the larger number of common bonds between the marriage partners, the segregation of roles now existing in the family is likely to decrease.

Moreover, as the economic functions of the child have disappeared completely, the child's need to become an adult as rapidly as possible has disappeared also. Indeed, as relatives become less close, parents are likely to discover that the child can help to draw husband and wife together. Thus will begin the shift from the adult-centered family to the child-centered one, and the eventual development of the kind of nuclear family structure now prevalent in America.

Also, relations between parents and children are likely to become closer. With fewer ethnic differences between the second and third generation than existed between the first and second, parents will feel more capable of advising their children. This could result in increased family conflict, if only because questions which were never raised before between parents and children will now be thought of as proper subjects of discussion. Family conflict also may be engendered by the fact that children will make greater demands on their parents, not only for goods but also for freedom to participate in children's and teenagers' activities.

Such a family is also likely to increase its participation in the outside world. Reduced suspicion and a decrease in cultural differences will make it less necessary for the next generation to reject the outside world as strongly as did the second. With more economic security, installment buying will seem less risky, and changing tastes will attract people to the consumer products and services that are now rejected. Already, the desire for modernity has made itself felt among some pioneering West Enders. And while the postwar suburbs have attracted only a few, they are likely to seem less frightening to the next generation. Indeed, it is probable that young mothers who look askance on the life of the street and wish closer supervision over their children's activities will find the attractions of suburban life most advantageous, even should their husbands not share this enthusiasm or their urgency about the children. Even now, the bright and sometimes garish pleasures of California and Florida are luring some West End vacationers, and will do so increasingly in the next generation. I remember how intensely a West End mother in her early twenties spoke of her plan to move to California, if only she could persuade her husband to give up his ties in Boston.

By virtue of the women's greater receptivity to education, and their premarital employment in the white-collar world, they are likely to take the lead in the process of change. The husbands may resist their pressure, and will probably be more reluctant to give up the old ways, especially since these were designed—intentionally or not—to maximize their freedoms and privileges. But because the wife remains subordinate to the husband in most families, because she is thoroughly indoctrinated in her home-maker role, and because she is hesitant about leaving the house to go to work, she may be unable to implement many of the changes of which she dreams. Her traditional role could act as a brake on her aspirations and perhaps as an accelerator on her frustrations.

Moreover, the social forms of the outside world will continue to be less attractive than its products, for the unwillingness and inability to concern oneself with object-oriented ways of behaving is likely to remain, among women as well as men. Churches and formal organizations, civic associations, government agencies, and politicians—all will probably be suspect even in the next generation, and participation in such activities is likely to be notably less among people of Italian background than among others.

Most of the people who will be making these changes are routine-seekers. As life becomes more secure, they no longer need— or want—to live for the gratifications of the moment. Not only is the search for adventurous episodes losing its urgency, but the drawbacks of action-seeking now loom larger than they did before. The lulls between episodes, the depression that sometimes accompanies the waiting, and the negative consequences of action-seeking now make it seem much less desirable. The availability of more predictable forms of gratification within the family and the peer group also takes something away from the pleasures of successful action-seeking. Its attractiveness as a way of life is thus being reduced, especially after adolescence. The parental desire to have children grow up respectably encourages this development, as does the increasing influence of women, who are the more earnest advocates of routine-seeking.

Yet parental desires are not always achieved, and, indeed, parental behavior may contradict them. Thus, some third-generation people will pursue action as fervently as did their ancestors. But increasingly, they will be those people who have grown up in idiosyncratic or pathological surroundings. Therefore the search for action will be a consequence of distinctive—and increasingly deviant—childhood experiences, rather than a prevalent way of life that stems from the economic and social insecurity of an entire group.

Obstacles to Change:
The Pattern of Social Mobility

The changes that I have just described make up an over-all pattern of social mobility on the part of West Enders and the coming generation. That is, they are not simply responses to pressure for change from the outside society, but also represent personal desires to take advantage of the opportunities which are offered by that society, even at the cost of giving up old behavior patterns.

Mobility—be it social, occupational, or geographical—can be classified in many ways. For understanding the changes just discussed, two types are of primary importance: one concerns the social unit that is undertaking to change itself, and distinguishes between *individual* and *group* mobility. The second concerns the destination of the mobility, and distinguishes between *internal* and *external* types.

Individual mobility is that undertaken by a single individual or family unit which acts apart from other individuals or families; it is idiosyncratic.[51] Group mobility takes place when a large number of individual members of a group move in the same direction, at the same time, and for the same reasons. Changes in the group's way of living exemplify the latter; the departure of an individual West Ender into an exclusive suburban neighborhood is an example of the former.

The second typology is related to the first. Internal mobility changes the behavior of the group, but neither breaks it up nor significantly alters its structure. External mobility, on the other hand, does break up or alter the group significantly. This typology can also be applied to individuals. For example, whereas the West Ender who becomes a lawyer but uses his skills to serve the group is internally mobile, the one who leaves the group to seek professional success in the outside world is externally mobile.

West Enders do not reject mobility or change, but they do take more readily to some types than to others. Most of the instances of mobility which I have discussed in the previous section are group moves, and they are internal. The changes that are made affect

51. The individual also may be acting in ways that later will be followed by the group; in that case he is a pioneer or forerunner, and his behavior is not idiosyncratic but a first stage in the process of group mobility. In order to distinguish between idiosyncratic and pioneering mobility, it is necessary to know the changes that have been taking place in the groups to which the individual belongs, as well as some idea of the direction in which the groups are moving. Of course, an individual may be a pioneer for a group without knowing that from a sociological perspective he is a "cog" in the long-range process.

life within the peer group society, and they alter the lives of group members. They do not, however, break up the peer group society. And while they do reduce the gap between it and the outside world, they do not cause it to disappear. Changes that involve a transformation of attitudes and relationships toward the outside world and participation in its activities are still discouraged. As a result, external mobility is almost nonexistent. When it does take place, it is done so by an individual who as a result must leave the group.

The rejection of external mobility is largely a rejection of middle-class elements in the outside world. The West Ender has little sympathy for what he believes to be the goals and behavioral requirements of this way of life. Moreover, he rejects the conscious pursuit of status and the acquisition of artifacts that would require him to detach himself from his peers, and to seek ways of living in which they cannot share. Similarly, the West Enders' low opinion of suburban life; of college attendance based on other than purely occupational goals; of the careerism of white-collar people; of caretakers and other professionals; and of the tastes, leisure preferences, and "cultural" interests of the people they call "high society"—this is nothing more than a rejection of middle-class society and culture.

There are a number of reasons for the negative attitude toward the middle class. One stems from the occupational position of the West Enders vis-à-vis this class. Some of them, working in industries and service occupations which cater to the middle class, are thereby involved in the preparation of the goods and services which constitute part of this differing life style. As they help to create the images that accompany middle-class living, they are thus placed in a behind-the-scenes relationship where they can see the artifice which goes into the creation of these images. The West Ender, working only to make a living, thus has little affection for the products he turns out. Consequently, it is easy for him to debunk these products and to feel superior toward the eventual users. For example, a West End contractor described the $40,000 houses he was helping to build as cold and cavernous, and expressed no interest in living in such structures. Likewise, a barber who worked in Cambridge thought the hair styles of his Harvard student customers "ridiculous," adding that, "They are all a bunch of fags up there." He thoroughly enjoyed the thought of helping to make them look foolish. Finally, a West Ender who worked in advertising described some of his work as that of preparing deceptive illustrations which would persuade—and deceive—middle-class people into buying the advertised products.

Of course, every group that provides a service or product to another can see the behind-the-scenes artifice in the production process, and is thus able to make fun of the clients who do not share its own taste. The people who create the mass media entertainment for audiences like the West Enders, for example, may feel much the same as the West Enders who build the houses or cut the hair of the middle class. Because the West Ender has less income, power, or status than his clients, his ability to scoff allows him to feel that he is as good as, if not better than, they. Aware that the middle-class people reject him in turn, their hostility allows him to maintain his pride, as well as his cultural differences.

The rejection of middle-class ways is also based on the West Ender's fears regarding the middle-class world, and on the recognition that he lacks the skills to participate in this world. As I have noted earlier, his inability to understand bureaucratic behavior or object-oriented groups, and the absence of the kind of empathy needed to interact with middle-class people all create discomfort or fear. So does his lack of education, which he feels to be an obstacle in communicating with them.

Most West Enders have little opportunity to interact with middle-class people. Of those who do, some reject this contact out of shyness, while others react more antagonistically. On the few occasions when I tried to bring West Enders into contact with middle-class acquaintances and friends, they either refused the invitation or participated only minimally. This reaction struck me most forcefully one evening when I had interviewed a local politician, a very mobile West Ender who was quite influential in Boston's political life. I had invited him to join me for a subsequent social engagement with two graduate students who were very much interested in the West End, but he excused himself with obvious embarrassment. Apparently, he could not face middle-class people in a relatively unstructured and obviously nonpolitical relationship.

The fear of contact with middle-class people is based on feelings of inferiority, and consciousness of some real—and some imagined —deficiencies. But as I noted in Chapter 4, such feelings should not be mistaken for envy. Certainly, most West Enders would like to have middle-class incomes, and the other advantages which this class enjoys. But they would use these opportunities to enhance peer group life, without embracing what they feel to be undesirable, unhealthy, and even immoral middle-class ways. The basic reason, then, for the rejection of the middle class is that West Enders are unwilling to make the changes in their own way of life that would thus be required of them.

West Enders not only keep their distance from the middle class, but they will reject other West Enders who stray too far from the peer group society and adopt middle-class ways. Relatives and friends whose tastes for furniture or clothes begin to move in a middle-class direction are criticized for having gone "high society," and people who have moved away from the group are described as renegades or deserters. Only those few who can achieve upward mobility in the occupational sphere without becoming "uppity" in their consumption patterns and their choice of friends are likely to be spared from scorn.[52]

The pressure on the individual to remain in the group and not to stray into middle-class territory was brought home to me in a situation involving some people who had moved out of the West End some years earlier. One of them who had broken her ties to the peer group society had moved into a non-Italian neighborhood, and maintained only superficial connections with her family circle in the West End. Her occasional visits were followed by much criticism of her "snobbish" ways and her "indecent" taste in clothes. One day, this woman invited a West End relative to work with her on a part-time basis in a job which required calling on suburban residents in a quasi-social, quasi-commercial role. The relative, a bright and lively woman, is quite modern in her own tastes, her

52. It should be borne in mind that my study was limited to West Enders and to ex-West Enders who maintained social contact with them. I could not discover how many West Enders had left the neighborhood for middle-class areas and life styles, since they would not—or could not—come back. My guess is that the number of upwardly mobile people who left the West End was small.

desire for travel, her rejection of the traditional shyness of Italian women, and her influential role in her own family. But while she would have liked to have taken the job, she could not bring herself to do so. Her husband was very much opposed to her being out of the house in the afternoons, ostensibly because she would not be able to take care of the household. His actual resistance, however, stemmed from the fact that he did not want her to continue her flirtation with strange ways. Already he had been criticized for having a wife who wore the pants in the family. In the resulting discussion, the wife asked other peer group members for advice—and some of them urged her to go ahead—but after some days of indecision, she turned down the job.

Because of the group rejection of middle-class ways, the individual who does wish to seek a career, to live in middle-class neighborhoods, and to adopt other patterns of middle-class culture must therefore be able to separate himself from the peer group society. In short, he must be able to live his life apart from the people with whom he has grown up, and take both their criticism and ostracism. For this reason, moving into the middle class requires considerable emotional strength, and the availability of group support to substitute for that previously obtained from the family circle and the peer group. Such a move thus implies individual and external mobility, but because of the difficulties that must be endured, and the obstacles that must be overcome, it is sought today by only a few people.[53]

In this respect, too, West Enders are following traditional ways, for departure from the group in the past was discouraged as much as it is today. Thus, Covello, writing about the class structure of the Southern Italian village at the turn of the century, reports:

> Even if a member of the peasant group succeeded in breaking through [to another occupation] the peasant community regarded him still as a member of the peasant class. A doctor or lawyer who returned to his old environment was strongly aware of jealousy, envy, and even resentment among his former associates.[54]

53. The conditions under which individual mobility takes place are discussed in Chapter 11.

54. Covello, *op. cit.*, p. 139.

Among the immigrants, a similar reaction obtained against men who went into the legal and medical professions. The family circle was willing to help finance a young man who wanted to go into business, since this was a group move, and would benefit the group as a whole. But those who sought careers which depended on individual skill and training were discouraged in no uncertain terms because it drew them away from the group.[55]

The resistance to change and the influence of tradition are also noticeable in the way in which West Enders talk about the past and the future. I suggested earlier that the West Enders have retained little allegiance to Italian culture, and show little respect for older people. At the same time, however, they do express considerable sympathy for the immigrant generation's way of life, and frequently talk about the good old days.

The major themes in the nostalgic talk about the past are family cohesion, individual spontaneity, and the lesser demands of the children. In the old days, West Enders say, the family was more of a unit, helped each other, disregarded differences among relatives, and maintained the segregation of sex roles.

> In the old days, there were no cars or luxuries, no one had anything . . . people were communal. No one cared what anyone else did, they tolerated differences more. . . . Men and women knew their place; it was better then. Whether it's right or not, I don't know, but there was more fun.

The spontaneous life of the family circle of the past is stressed, too. "Everyone lived better and did things on the spur of the moment.[56] There was always open house . . . all-night card parties . . . the old men made alcohol, and everyone stayed up till 3 A.M.[57] The landlords didn't care whether you made noise; they liked to live too."

55. *Ibid.*, p. 503.

56. The spontaneity and uninhibited behavior of the immigrant generation is also a favorite theme of Italian-American novelists. See, for example, Mangione, *op. cit.;* Joseph Caruso, *The Priest,* New York: Popular Library, 1958; and Armando Perretto, *Take a Number,* New York: Popular Library, 1958.

57. I might add a skeptical note about the accuracy of the belief that all-night partying has decreased. I remember many extremely lively weekday gatherings that continued long after midnight.

The major complaint now is the increasing wants of the children:

> The kids are getting too many things, it's making them confused. So many things, toys to choose from . . . he has two hundred crayons . . . and [such things have] increased their wants. In the old days, parents gave them as much as they could afford, but the kids were satisfied . . . life was happier, the children had more fun and wanted less.

Today, the children are less willing to respect the adult-centered family. "Aunts and grandparents spoil the kids, and the kids are more cocky now." West End men also talk about their childhood exploits, and stress that while their behavior had been sometimes illegal, it had never been threatening: "When we were kids, we used to sneak into the circus or take boat trips without paying, but we were never delinquents." "Living is too expensive now," said one mother, "I get mad when they blame juvenile delinquency on parents or on mothers when they go out to work, because mothers have to work if they want enough money to send their kids to school."

Most of these comments reflect the memories that adult West Enders have of their own childhood, and the perspective they had as children of the immigrants' way of life. They did not see many of the hardships of adult life—the poverty and the lack of opportunity that often set family against family and neighbor against neighbor. Moreover, as I noted in Chapter 3, childhood and adolescence are generally felt to be the best, and freest, stages of life. In effect, those who sentimentalize the past are principally comparing the responsibilities of adulthood with the freedom and spontaneity of their youth.

The frequency with which nostalgia appears in the conversation suggests that it is also a sign of the changes taking place among West Enders, and an indication of their resistance to these changes. As relatives are drawn out of the family circle, the cohesion of the circle is mourned. When the development of new aspirations by children threatens the adult-centered family, the traditional patriarchy is remembered fondly. And the comparison of today's delinquents with the past generation's mischief-makers notes and opposes the increasing power of the children in the family.

Much of the nostalgia which I have described comes from the more mobile West Enders, those who have moved furthest away from the past they are reifying. Although their own actual behavior is not guided by the standards they attribute to the past, these standards do exert some influence over them, and are made explicit when the pressures of change become too great.

The Future of the Peer Group Society

The previous two sections of this chapter have presented somewhat contradictory assertions about the West Enders. One has pointed to several indices of change; the other, to the various types of resistance to change. The resistance has emanated largely from the second generation, and the signs of future change have been associated with the third. Which of these two tendencies will dominate undoubtedly depends on whether the opportunities now being offered by the larger society will continue, and on whether the third generation will accept the opportunities and pressures that demand the surrender of traditional ways of life.

What is likely to happen to the peer group society under these conditions? For one thing, the social forces that are beginning to create incompatibilities in the family circle, to increase the role of friends in social life, and to bring husband, wife, and children closer together do not as yet seem powerful enough to alter the basic social structure in radical ways. Indeed, the social arrangements that produce person-orientation, the belief in traditional sex roles, and the gratifications of peer group social life are still strong. Conversely, the attractions of education as an end in itself, of the career, and of organizational participation are beginning only now to make themselves felt. But as these attractions are associated with middle-class life, and are thus rejected by the second generation, they are likely to be resisted for the same reasons by the third.

Moreover, as peers are an important source of companionship in practically all of American society, this is likely to help to support the retention of the peer group principle in Italian life. Yet

226 The Peer Group Society

the peer group probably will be less significant than it has been in the past, and it may no longer be the emotional center of life for its members, especially as other attractions make the routine on which it is based seem less desirable. But the emotional and social functions it performs and the difficulty of finding substitutes for them among the people and institutions outside the peer group will probably be enough to keep it intact for another generation.

Although third-generation peer groups will be likely to feel less hostility toward the outside world than do present ones, they still will probably not fully participate in it. Indeed the middle class will continue to seem to be different because it is different. Thus the majority of third-generation people will keep some distance between it and themselves. Even with augmented prosperity, then, the third generation will not be swept into the middle-class institutions and ways of life that have increasingly come to dominate the American scene.

At the same time, an ever expanding number of individuals will leave the peer group society for the middle class. Moreover, as the peer group society undergoes changes that make it more similar to the rest of society, it will resist these desertions less strenuously. Not only will it be unable to stop relatives and friends who seek more drastic changes, but the movement into the middle class will seem a less drastic step than it does to West Enders today. Consequently, for the restless individuals of the next generation, external mobility will be a less hazardous venture.

PART THREE The West
Enders and American
Society

CHAPTER 11 The Subcultures of the Working Class, Lower Class, and Middle Class

The Peer Group Society:
Class or Ethnic Phenomenon?

One of the initial purposes of this study was to compare a low-income population such as the West Enders to the middle class, and, if possible, to isolate some of the basic differences between them. The relative stability of the social structure across the generations from Southern Italy to the West End, which I described in the last chapter, would seem to suggest that there might be an Italian way of life. This idea in turn would support the hypothesis that the peer group society is an ethnic phenomenon and that the principal differences between the West Enders and the middle class are ethnic ones.

An alternative hypothesis, however—that the peer group society is a working-class phenomenon and that class differences separate the West Enders from the middle class—is more justified. The West Ender is a descendant of farm laborers who became blue-collar workers in urban America. As I have tried to show, the similarities in ways of life over the generations have resulted from the similar economic and social positions that the Southern Italian and the West Ender have occupied in the larger Italian and American societies respectively.

The hypothesis is further supported by studies of other working-class populations which have shown that these, too, exhibit many characteristics of the peer group society. The same is true of other ethnic groups whose members are of blue-collar status. Such characteristics, however, are not displayed by those of white-collar status. Consequently, the class hypothesis offers a better explanation than the ethnic one.

The characteristics that West Enders share with other working-class groups can be conceived as forming a working-class subculture, which differs considerably from both lower- and middle-class subcultures. A description of these subcultures and of the differences between them indicates why attempts to transform working-class people in the middle-class image have failed. It also points to some of the major problems of working- and lower-class subcultures, and suggests some proposals for how planners and caretakers should deal with these problems. These proposals will be presented in the next chapter.

A Survey of Working- and Lower-Class Studies [1]

A wealth of evidence from other studies indicates that the peer group society is a class, rather than an ethnic, phenomenon. My survey of these studies will be cursory. It will consider various social structural and cultural characteristics in the order in which I have described them among the West Enders.

Although the existence of a peer group society has not been reported in other working-class populations, Walter Miller's study of an Irish and Negro neighborhood did conclude that: "Lower class society may be pictured as comprising a set of age-graded one-sex peer groups which constitute the psychic focus and refer-

1. Most of the reported studies deal with the working class, some with the lower class, and others fail to distinguish between the two. Differences between the two classes will be discussed in the next section. In the survey, I shall use the term "working class" to describe both, unless the study cited refers specifically to lower-class people.

ence group for those over twelve and thirteen." [2] The distinction between the peer group society and the outside world is much like Hoggart's dichotomy of "us" and "them" in the British working-class.[3] He writes:

> . . . the world outside is strange and often unhelpful . . . it has most of the counters stacked on its side . . . to meet it on its own terms is difficult. One may call this, making use of a word commonly used by the working classes, the world of "Them." . . . The world of "Them" is the world of the bosses, whether those bosses are private individuals or . . . public officials. . . . "Them" includes the policemen and those civil servants . . . whom the working classes meet. . . . To the very poor, especially, they compose a shadowy but numerous and powerful group affecting their lives at almost every point. . . . "They" are "the people at the top" . . . who . . . "get yer in the end," "aren't really to be trusted," "are all in a clique together," "treat y'like muck." [4]

Similarly, a study of American working-class women notes their separation from "the outer world," and their fear of its " 'chaotic and catastrophic' qualities." [5] In some ways Redfield's conception of the relationship between the peasant and the elite is like that between the West Ender and the outside world.[6] Moreover, Lewis's description of the Mexican "culture of poverty" bears a number of resemblances to the way of life of the poorest West Enders.[7]

My description of routine- and action-seekers is paralleled in many ways by S. M. Miller and Frank Riessman's distinction between the "unskilled, irregular worker . . . [who] . . . lacks the

2. Walter B. Miller, "Lower Class Culture as a Generating Milieu of Gang Delinquency," *Journal of Social Issues*, vol. 14, No. 3 (1958) pp. 5–19, at p. 14.

3. Richard Hoggart, *The Uses of Literacy*, London: Chatto and Windus, 1957, Chap. 3.

4. *Ibid.*, p. 62.

5. L. Rainwater, R. Coleman, and G. Handel, *Workingman's Wife*, New York: Oceana Publications, 1959, pp. 44–45.

6. Robert Redfield, "Peasant Society and Culture," in *Little Community and Peasant Society and Culture*, Chicago: University of Chicago Press (Phoenix Books), 1960, pp. 36–39.

7. Oscar Lewis, *The Children of Sanchez*, New York: Random House, 1961, pp. xxiii–xxvii.

disciplined, structured and traditional approach of the stable worker and stresses the excitement theme." [8] Their analysis, based on a review of American working-class studies, reflects the general sociological distinction between working and lower class.[9] Walter Miller's study of lower-class culture describes in more systematic detail what I have called action-seeking. He notes its "focal concerns" with such qualities as toughness, daring, adroitness in repartee, excitement, and rejection of superordinate authority.[10] His discussion of excitement observes that:

> For many lower-class individuals the rhythm of life fluctuates between periods of relatively routine or repetitive activity and sought situations of great emotional stimulation. Many of the most characteristic features of lower-class life are related to the search for excitement or "thrill." [11]

The largest amount of data is available on family life. The segregation of family roles and the separate lives of husbands and wives have been reported in studies of the English working class,[12] among Puerto Ricans, both in Puerto Rico and in New York,[13] in a

8. S. M. Miller and Frank Riessman, "The Working Class Subculture: A New View," *Social Problems,* vol. 9 (1961), pp. 86–97, at p. 95.

9. See, for example, W. Lloyd Warner and Paul S. Lunt, *The Social Life of a Modern Community,* New Haven: Yale University Press, 1941, which distinguishes between and describes upper-lower and lower-lower classes; and the work of his associates, for example, August B. Hollingshead, *Elmtown's Youth,* New York: Wiley and Sons, 1949.

10. Walter B. Miller, *op. cit.,* summarized from Chart I, p. 7.

11. *Ibid.,* pp. 10–11. See also his "Implications of Urban Lower-Class Culture for Social Work," *Social Service Review,* vol. 33 (1959), pp. 219–236; and Warren Miller's novel of the episodic life in a lower-class Negro gang, *The Cool World,* Boston: Little, Brown, 1959.

12. See, for example, J. M. Mogey, *Family and Neighborhood,* London: Oxford University Press, 1956, p. 58; and Elizabeth Bott, *Family and Social Network,* London: Tavistock Publications, 1957, pp. 58 ff. Bott also cites a number of earlier studies with a similar finding, and notes that not all working-class families are segregated.

13. Helen Icken, "From Slum to Housing Project," unpublished study made for the Urban Renewal and Housing Administration, Commonwealth of Puerto Rico, 1960, mimeographed, p. 55; Elena Padilla, *Up from Puerto Rico,* New York: Columbia University Press, 1958, pp. 151–152.

Mexican family,[14] and in a national American working-class sample.[15] A study of Polish-Americans describes this segregation as follows:

> . . . the pairs are not "one" . . . the marriage relation is not intensive. There is not a ceaseless seeking out of the other's motivations, no rigid set of expectations to which the other must conform.[16]

The same study also notes the men's need to display and defend their masculinity.[17] Similar findings have been reported in most working-class populations regardless of ethnic origin.[18] The subordinate role of children in what I have called the adult-centered family has been observed among New York Puerto Ricans [19] and in a general survey of working-class culture.[20] Two American studies point out the lack of interest in children as individuals.[21] The pattern of permitting freedom to boys, and of keeping girls at home has also been found among Puerto Ricans.[22]

The central role of the peer group has been suggested, as previously noted, by Walter Miller's study of Irish and Negro lower-class adolescents.[23] Another American study found that:

14. Lewis, *op. cit.*, p. 335.

15. Lee Rainwater, *And the Poor Get Children*, Chicago: Quadrangle Books, 1960, p. 69; and Social Research, Inc., "Status of the Working Class in Changing American Society," Chicago: Social Research, Inc., February, 1961, mimeographed, p. 80.

16. Arnold W. Green, "The 'Cult of Personality' and Sexual Relations," in Norman W. Bell and Ezra F. Vogel, eds., *A Modern Introduction to the Family*, New York: The Free Press of Glencoe, 1960, pp. 608–615, at pp. 614–615.

17. *Ibid.*, p. 614.

18. Walter Miller, "Lower Class Culture as a Generating Milieu of Gang Delinquency," *op. cit.*, p. 9; Rainwater, *op. cit.*, pp. 84–85; Icken, *op. cit.* Lewis's study of a Mexican family gives innumerable examples of this phenomenon.

19. Padilla, *op. cit.*, pp. 179 ff.

20. Miller and Riessman, *op. cit.*, p. 92. They use the term "parent-centered."

21. L. Rainwater, R. Coleman, and G. Handel, *op. cit.*, p. 89; and Social Research, Inc., *op. cit.*, pp. 161, 163.

22. Icken, *op. cit.*, p. 57; Padilla, *op. cit.*, pp. 186 ff.

23. Miller, "Lower Class Culture as a Generating Milieu of Gang Delinquency," *op. cit.*, p. 14.

Husband and wife tend to have few, if any friends in common. Relationships with friends tend to be on a single-sex basis. . . . Often relatives are the only friends. If husband or wife do have friends who are not relatives, they have them as individuals and not as couples.[24]

Many studies have shown the existence of the family circle, notably in England,[25] and among New York Puerto Ricans.[26] The prevalence of spending one's social life with relatives more than with friends has been reported in England [27] and in a variety of American working-class groups.[28]

A number of findings on group life and personality have suggested that many of the elements I have summarized as person-orientation are found among working-class people generally, and one survey of American studies describes them as person-centered.[29] This article also notes the practice of personalizing bureaucracy and other outside world situations, as does an account of English working-class life.[30] A study of American working-class women describes their problems in regard to self-control, and shows how lack of self-control encourages their children in turn to express anger through violence.[31] It also suggests that working-class adolescents express themselves motorically, or physically, while middle-

24. Social Research, Inc., *op. cit.*, p. 82.

25. Mogey, *op. cit.*, p. 97; Bott, *op. cit.*, p. 112; Michael Young and Peter Willmott, *Family and Kinship In London,* London: Routledge and Kegan Paul, 1957, Chap. V.

26. Padilla, *op. cit.*, pp. 112 ff. She calls it "the great family group."

27. Madeline Kerr, *The People of Ship Street,* London: Routledge and Kegan Paul, 1958, pp. 106–108. Young and Willmott report the rejection of mobile relatives, *op. cit.*, pp. 143–144.

28. Floyd Dotson, "Patterns of Voluntary Association among Urban Working Class Families," *American Sociological Review,* vol. 16 (1951), pp. 687–693, at p. 691; Rainwater, Coleman, and Handel, *op. cit.*, p. 107; Bennett M. Berger, *Working-Class Suburb,* Berkeley: University of California Press, 1960, p. 68; and Social Research, Inc., pp. 63, 82. Rainwater, Coleman, and Handel also note the working-class woman's difficulty in making friends. *Op. cit.*, p. 108.

29. Miller and Riessman, *op. cit.*, pp. 93–94.

30. *Ibid.*, and Hoggart, *op. cit.*, p. 28.

31. Daniel R. Miller, Guy E. Swanson *et. al., Inner Conflict and Defense,* New York: Holt, Rinehart, and Winston, 1960, Chap. 14.

class adolescents use conceptual and symbolic modes.[32] Another study of American working-class women stresses the importance of group life, the fear of loneliness, and their concern with what others think of them.[33] An analysis of lower-class interview respondents has described in considerable detail their tendency to be concrete and particularistic, to think anecdotally, to personalize events, and to see phenomena only from their own perspective: [34] they do not "assume the role of another toward still others." [35] The limited repertoire of roles also has been described in a study of an English group,[36] and the inability or unwillingness of people to adopt other roles has been reported as lack of empathy in a previously mentioned study of Middle Eastern peasants.[37]

A number of American studies have shown the scarcity of working-class participation in what I have described as community life.[38] For example, the West Enders' pattern of being religious but not being identified with the church has been found among other American groups, both Protestant and Catholic,[39] and in England as well.[40]

Both American and English studies have reported the working-

32. *Op. cit.*, Chap. 15. A national survey reports that "respondents with less education tend to be less introspective about themselves, whether about strong points or shortcomings." G. Gurin, J. Veroff, and S. Feld, *Americans View Their Mental Health*, New York: Basic Books, 1960, p. 69.

33. Rainwater, Coleman, and Handel, *op. cit.*, pp. 64–66. See also Hoggart, *op. cit.*, p. 72.

34. Leonard Schatzman and Anselm Strauss, "Social Class and Modes of Communication," *American Journal of Sociology*, vol. 60 (1955), pp. 329–338; and Anselm Strauss and Leonard Schatzman, "Cross Class Interviewing: An Analysis of Interaction and Communicative Styles," in Richard N. Adams and Jack J. Preiss, ed., *Human Organization Research*, Homewood, Ill.: Dorsey Press, 1960, pp. 205–213.

35. Schatzman and Strauss, *op. cit.*, p. 331.

36. Kerr, *op. cit.*, Chap. 17.

37. Daniel Lerner, *The Passing of Traditional Society*, New York: The Free Press of Glencoe, 1958.

38. Dotson, *op. cit.*, p. 688; Berger, *op. cit.*, p. 59; Rainwater, Coleman, and Handel, *op. cit.*, pp. 114 ff. See also Morris Axelrod, "Urban Structure and Social Participation," *American Sociological Review*, vol. 21 (1956), pp. 13–18.

39. Berger, *op. cit.*, pp. 45 ff.; Rainwater, Coleman, and Handel, *op. cit.*, p. 123.

40. Hoggart, *op. cit.*, pp. 94–97; Kerr, *op. cit.*, pp. 135–136.

class' detachment from work,[41] the concern with job security,[42] and the negative evaluation of white-collar workers and bosses.[43] The West Enders' ambivalence about education is also widely shared. The conception that school should teach children to keep out of trouble has been described by an English study; [44] that education must contribute to the occupational success of the individual, by many studies, including an American [45] and a Puerto Rican one.[46] Two studies have indicated that working-class mothers want more education for their children than do the fathers.[47]

I have already reported the prevalence of the general conception that the outside world is not to be trusted. This extends also to a skepticism about caretakers,[48] a reluctance to visit settlement houses,[49] and a fear of doctors and hospitals that seems to be found in all countries.[50] Similarly, working-class people everywhere believe—or know—the police to be crooked, and politicians, corrupt. In America,[51] England,[52] and Mexico,[53] researchers have described

41. A concise review of studies of work patterns and attitudes of working-class and lower-class people is found in Joseph A. Kahl, *The American Class Structure*, New York: Holt, Rinehart and Winston, 1957, pp. 205–215.

42. Ephraim H. Mizruchi, "Social Structure, Success Values and Structured Strain in a Small City," paper read at the 1961 meetings of the American Sociological Association, mimeographed; Social Research, Inc., *op. cit.*, pp. 57–58.

43. Katherine Archibald, "Status Orientations among Shipyard Workers," in Reinhard Bendix and Seymour M. Lipset, eds., *Class, Status and Power*, New York: The Free Press of Glencoe, 1953, pp. 395–403; Young and Willmott, *op. cit.*, p. 14.

44. Hoggart, *op. cit.*, p. 98.

45. Social Research, Inc., pp. 51–53; see also Archibald, *op. cit.*, p. 399; and Mizruchi, *op. cit.*

46. Padilla, *op. cit.*, p. 198.

47. Herbert H. Hyman, "The Value System of Different Classes," in Bendix and Lipset, *op. cit.*, pp. 426–442, Tables III, IV; and Icken, *op. cit.*, p. 34.

48. Padilla, *op. cit.*, p. 264.

49. Albert Cohen, *Delinquent Boys: The Culture of the Gang*, New York: The Free Press of Glencoe, 1955, pp. 116–117.

50. Hoggart, *op. cit.*, p. 42; Kerr, *op. cit.*, p. 39; Lewis, *op. cit.*, p. xxviii.

51. Miller and Riessman, *op. cit.*, p. 91.

52. Hoggart, *op. cit.*, p. 87.

53. Lewis, *op. cit.*, pp. xxvii, 351, 389. On the personalization of government, see Miller and Riessman, *op. cit.*, p. 93; Padilla, *op. cit.*, p. 256; and Lewis, *op. cit.*, p. 332.

the working- and lower-class antagonism toward law, government, and politics.

Conversely, the mass media are accepted, often more enthusiastically than by other classes. A recently published study of American television viewers has made this finding, and noted the working-class audience's interest in and identification with performers.[54] Several studies have also suggested the preference for action dramas over other forms of media content, not only in America,[55] but all over the world.[56] In Green's study of a Polish group, the rejection of romantic films by young working-class adults was described as follows: "At the local movie house, when the hero pauses in pursuit of the villain to proffer the heroine a tender sentiment, whistling and footstamping greet his fall from grace." [57]

As I have not attempted to make a complete survey of the literature, I have mentioned here only some of the many similarities between the West Enders and other groups. Even so, it should be evident that, by and large, the peer group society is associated with working- and lower-class life. Moreover, the data show that many of its features are found among other ethnic groups who have come to America from Europe—notably the Irish and Polish—as well as among racially differentiated groups, such as the Negroes and the Puerto Ricans. Incidentally, the peer group society also cuts across religious lines, for many of its characteristics appear not only among Protestants in England and America, but among European and Latin Catholics as well.

Some differences—including a few ethnic ones—do exist between the West Enders and other working-class people. Yet many of these differences can be traced to class factors operating in past and present generations. Italian-Americans, for example, differ from the Irish-Americans in a number of ways. The Irish are more respectful of paternal authority, of the older generation, of the

54. Ira O. Glick and Sidney J. Levy, *Living with Television*, Chicago: Aldine Publishing Company, 1962, Chap. III, VII.

55. See, for example, Berger, *op. cit.*, pp. 74–75.

56. Herbert J. Gans, "American Films and Television Programs on British Screens: A Study of the Functions of American Popular Culture Abroad," Philadelphia: Institute for Urban Studies, 1959, mimeographed, Chap. 4.

57. Green, *op. cit.*, p. 613.

church, and of authority in general. Irish men are also much closer to their mothers than are Italian men, a fact that has a number of implications for family structure, family dynamics, and even for the ways in which mental illness is expressed.[58]

Many of these differences can be related to the fact that the Irish immigrants came from landowning, peasant families. In Ireland, the father was the sole owner of the family farm, and thus was free to choose as to which of his sons would inherit it. As a result, sons were in a subordinate position.[59] One study of the Irish peasantry notes, in fact, that sons were called boys until the day the father surrendered the farm to one of them, even if they themselves were middle-aged adults.[60] The conditions which the Irish immigrants found in America evidently did not encourage any major change in family structure. Certainly, one could argue that those Irish-Americans who turned to politics and the priesthood found that the relationship between the political boss and his underlings and between the Bishop and his priests was much the same as that between the farm owner and his sons. Needless to say, not all Irish-Italian differences can be explained purely by class factors, or by cultural differences which developed from economic conditions in Europe. They do seem, however, to be of primary importance.

West Enders also differ from other working-class, and especially lower-class, groups in the role that the mother plays in family life. Studies of the English working class, for example, have stressed the importance of the "Mum" and the dominance of the mother-daughter relationship over all others, even when the daughter is married and has children of her own.[61] Similarly, studies of the Negro, Puerto Rican, and Carribean lower classes have shown the

58. These differences between the Irish are reported in Ezra F. Vogel, *op. cit.*, and M. K. Opler and J. L. Singer, "Ethnic Differences in Behavior and Psychopathogy," *International Journal of Social Psychiatry*, vol. 2 (1956), pp. 11–22. See also Mark Zborowski, "Cultural Components in Responses to Pain," *Journal of Social Issues*, vol. 8 (1952), pp. 16–30; and Paul Barrabee and Otto van Mering, "Ethnic Variations in Mental Stress in Families with Psychotic Children," *Social Problems*, vol. 1 (1953), pp. 48–53.

59. Conrad M. Arensberg and Solon T. Kimball, *Family and Community in Ireland*, Cambridge: Harvard University Press, 1940, pp. 47 ff.

60. *Ibid.*, pp. 51, 56.

61. The previously cited studies by Young and Willmott, and by Kerr describe this relationship in great detail.

family to be what anthropologists call matrifocal.[62] The mother is the head of the household, and the basic family unit includes her, her children, and one or more of her female relatives, such as her mother or aunt. Often the man is a marginal and only intermittent participant in this female-based household.[63] American studies of the lower class have reported what Walter Miller calls "serial monogamy"—a pattern in which a woman lives and has children with a series of men who desert her or whom she asks to leave.[64]

The reason for this pattern among Negroes can be found in the fact that in past and present, they have lived under conditions in which the male's position in the society has been marginal and insecure. Under slavery, for example, the formation of a normal family was discouraged, although the female slave was allowed to raise her own children. Since the days of slavery, the Negro's economic position has been such as to maintain much of this pattern. The man who has difficulty in finding a steady job and is laid off frequently finds it difficult to perform the functions of a male breadwinner and household head. Moreover, when the woman is able to find steady employment or can subsist on welfare payments, she tends to treat the man with disdain and often with open hostility, especially if he complicates her life by making her pregnant. Under these conditions, there is no incentive for the man to remain in the family, and in times of stress he deserts. Moreover, when the male children grow up in a predominantly female household—in which the man is a powerless and scorned figure—their upbringing encourages ambivalence as to male functions and masculinity. Thus, the pattern is perpetuated into the next generation.[65]

The hypothesis that the female-based family can be traced to

62. See, for example, Raymond T. Smith, *The Negro Family in British Guiana*, London: Routledge and Kegan Paul, 1956; and for America, E. Franklin Frazier, *The Negro Family in the United States*, Chicago: University of Chicago Press, 1939.

63. Walter B. Miller, "Lower Class Culture as a Generating Milieu of Gang Delinquency," *op. cit.*, p. 14.

64. Walter B. Miller, "Implications of Urban Lower-Class Culture for Social Work," *op. cit.*, p. 225.

65. Walter B. Miller, "Lower Class Culture as a Generating Milieu of Gang Delinquency," *op. cit.*, p. 9.

class and, more specifically, to occupational factors is supported by studies describing this family type among peoples who have not been slaves.[66] It has been found, for example, among Puerto Ricans, both on the island and in New York. It seems, however, to be more prevalent among Puerto Ricans from sugar cane areas, which have a plantation economy much like that under which the Negro endured slavery.[67] The hypothesis is supported in another way by the fact that a somewhat similar family constellation prevails when the man's occupation separates him from his family for long periods. Thus, a study of sailors' families in Norway indicates that the woman takes over the dominant role in the family, and overprotects her children.[68] Although the girls show no negative consequences, the boys seem to develop what Tiller calls a defensive feminine identification, and compensatory masculine traits. When such boys become adults, they thus favor occupations that stress masculinity and minimize female contact and the family role.

The female-based family, however, is not found among West Enders, and the reasons perhaps can also be traced to occupational factors. Although the West Enders' ancestors suffered from unemployment, the totally agrarian economy of Southern Italian society and the extremely strenuous character of farm labor created no employment opportunities for women. Indeed, the family could best survive if the woman stayed home and bore a large number of children who could eventually add to the family's income. As a result, the woman did not take on an economic function, and the man maintained his position in the family even though he could not always support it adequately. This family constellation seems to have been strong enough to endure in America during those periods when the man was unemployed and the woman could find a job. Needless to say, some family instability and male marginality or desertion has occurred among the immigrants and the second

66. I have not been able to find any explanation of the dominant role of the "Mum" in the English working-class family. It should be noted, however, that this family is not female-based.

67. I owe this suggestion to Howard Stanton. In the sugar cane economy, there is work for only three to four months a year.

68. Per Olav Tiller, "Father Absence and Personality Development of Children in Sailor Families," Oslo: Institute for Social Research, 1957, mimeographed.

generation, but such cases have been considerably fewer than among newcomers with female-based families.

Finally, the West Enders may be contrasted to the Jews, an ethnic group which came to America at about the same time as the Italians, but with a different occupational history.[69] The Jews who emigrated from Poland and Russia around the turn of the century were neither farm laborers nor peasants, but peddlers, shopkeepers, and artisans with a more middle-class occupational tradition. They also differed from their fellow immigrants in their belief in education, partly for reasons related to this tradition. Although they worked initially as unskilled and semiskilled laborers in America, they reacted differently to their environment than did the ethnic groups from peasant and farm labor origins. Superficially, the Jewish family structure resembled the Italian one, with a nuclear household surrounded by a large family circle. Because of the high value placed on education, however, the immigrants did not restrain their children from contact with the outside world. As already noted, they encouraged the children to use the schools and settlement houses to prepare themselves for white-collar and professional occupations. Thus, the Jewish young people pursued careers that drew them apart from the parental generation at the same time that their Italian neighbors rejected such careers as "lonely ventures" that could only break up the cohesion of the family circle. Although the Jewish immigrants did bemoan the children's acculturation into styles of life congruent with their higher occupational level, they also took pride in the successful mobility of their offspring.[70]

I would not want to claim that the West Enders are like all

69. This account draws on Marshall Sklare, *Conservative Judaism,* New York: The Free Press of Glencoe, 1955; and Nathan Glazer, *American Judaism,* Chicago; University of Chicago Press, 1957.

70. For a detailed study of differences between American-born Italians and Jews, see Fred L. Strodtbeck, "Family Interaction, Values and Achievement," in D. C. McClelland, A. Baldwin, U. Bronfenbrenner, and F. Strodtbeck, *Talent and Society,* Princeton: D. Van Nostrand, 1958, pp. 135–194. He compares Jewish values, such as the belief in education, the desirability of individual achievement, and the striving for mobility and for rational mastery of the world to the Italians' familism and fatalism. Even so, he suggests that "differences between Italians and Jews are greatly attenuated when class level is held constant." *Op. cit.,* p. 154, based on an unpublished study by B. Tregoe.

other working-class and peasant ethnic groups, or that all differences between them and other populations can be explained by class factors. Indeed, many differences between the ethnic groups must be attributed to other factors in their cultural traditions and in their American experience.[71] Until comparative studies of these groups are made that hold class constant, however, we will not know exactly where these differences are located, nor how they can be explained.

A Description of Working-Class, Lower-Class, and Middle-Class Subcultures

The identification of the peer group society as a class phenomenon makes it possible to suggest some propositions about the working class that will distinguish it both from the lower and middle classes. These propositions rest on a specific definition of class.

Class can be defined in many ways, depending on the theoretical, methodological, and political orientation of the researcher.[72] Some sociologists have argued that class is a heuristic concept, nominalist in nature, which serves as a methodological device to summarize real differences between people in income, occupation, education, and related characteristics. Other sociologists have viewed classes as real aggregates of people who share some characteristics and group interests, who favor each other in social relationships, and who exhibit varying degrees of group consciousness. In the latter category, one school of sociologists has explained class mainly on the basis of occupational characteristics, on the assumption that work determines access to income, power, and status,

71. See here especially Zborowski, op. cit., and Opler and Singer, op. cit. Since the West End was a multi-ethnic neighborhood with relatively little variation in class, the studies now being conducted by the Center for Community Studies among the various ethnic groups may shed further light on these differences.

72. The comments that follow are a highly oversimplified description of the various points of view, and serve only to introduce the hypotheses about class that follow below. More sophisticated discussions of the major "schools" in the study of class are available in Bernard Barber, *Social Stratification*, New York: Harcourt, Brace and World, 1957; Milton M. Gordon, *Social Class in American Sociology*, Durham: Duke University Press, 1958; and Kahl, op. cit.

and that it has considerable influence on an individual's behavior patterns.

Others see classes as more than occupational aggregates, that is, as strata in the larger society, each of which consists of somewhat—but not entirely—distinctive social relationships, behavior patterns, and attitudes. The strata thus are composed of subcultures and sub-social structures. For the sake of brevity, however, I shall henceforth describe them only as subcultures. While occupation, education, income, and other such factors help to distinguish the subcultures, the exact role of these factors is thought to be an empirical question. The strata are defined as subcultures on the assumption that relationships, behavior patterns, and attitudes are related parts of a social and cultural system. The word "system" must be used carefully, however, for many similarities and overlaps exist between them. Moreover, these systems are quite open, and movement between them is possible, though—as I shall try to show—not always easy. Considerable variation also exists within each stratum, for social mobility and other processes create innumerable combinations of behavior patterns.[73]

The heuristic conception of class, not being very productive for social theory, need not concern us here. The two remaining ones each have some advantages and disadvantages. The occupational conception is most useful for understanding societies in the early stages of industrialization, when unemployment is great, and when an individual's job is both a determinant of and an index to his way of life. But in a highly industrialized society with considerable occupational variation and much freedom of choice in jobs—as well as in other ways of life—too great a concern with occupation, or any other single factor, is likely to lead the researcher astray. For instance, when a blue-collar worker earns more than a white-collar one, and can live by the values of the middle class, it would be a mistake to classify him as working class. Similarly, when a white-collar worker lives like a blue-collar one, even in a middle-class neighborhood, one should not consider him middle class.

73. Even so, studies of status inconsistency have shown that many of these combinations create marginality both in social position and cultural allegiances.

The great advantage of the subcultural conception is that it makes no a priori assumptions about the major differences between the strata or the determinants of these differences. It treats them rather as topics for empirical research. Unlike the other approaches in which class is defined in terms of easily researchable indices, the subcultural conception is harder to employ, however, for the characteristics and determinants of each class subculture must be carefully delineated.

The voluminous literature of class studies in America and elsewhere and the considerable similarity of the classes all over the industrialized world have made it possible to begin a delineation of the principal class subcultures. While I shall not attempt this task here, I do want to suggest what seem to me to be some of the major "focal concerns" [74] of four of the subcultures: working class, lower class, middle class, and professional upper-middle class. These brief outlines are based on observations made in the West End and elsewhere, and on the research literature. For the most part, they describe the subcultures in America and in one period of the life cycle: that of the family which is rearing children.

Perhaps the most important—or at least the most visible—difference between the classes is one of family structure. *The working-class subculture* is distinguished by the dominant role of the family circle. Its way of life is based on social relationships amidst relatives. The working class views the world from the family circle, and considers everything outside it as either a means to its maintenance or to its destruction. But while the outside world is to be used for the benefit of this circle, it is faced with detachment and even hostility in most other respects. Whenever feasible, then, work is sought within establishments connected to the family circle. When this is not possible—and it rarely is—work is primarily a means of obtaining income to maintain life amidst a considerable degree of poverty, and, thereafter, a means of maximizing the pleasures of life within the family circle. The work itself may be skilled

74. I borrow this term from Walter Miller, who uses it as a substitute for the anthropological concept of value in his study of lower-class culture. See "Lower Class Culture as a Generating Milieu of Gang Delinquency," *op. cit.*, p. 7. I use it to refer to behavior as much as to attitude, and to phenomena of social structure as well as culture.

or unskilled; it can take place in the factory or in the office—the type of collar is not important. What does matter is that identification with work, work success, and job advancement—while not absolutely rejected—are of secondary priority to the life that goes on within the family circle. The purpose of education is to learn techniques necessary to obtain the most lucrative type of work. Thus the central theme of American, and all Western, education— that the student is an individual who should use his schooling to detach himself from ascribed relationships like the family circle in order to maximize his personal development and achievement in work, play, and other spheres of life—is ignored or openly rejected.

The specific characteristics of the family circle may differ widely —from the collateral peer group form of the West Enders, to the hierarchical type of the Irish, or to the classic three-generation extended family. Friends may also be included in the circle, as in the West Enders' peer group society. What matters most—and distinguishes this subculture from others—is that there be a family circle which is wider than the nuclear family, and that all of the opportunities, temptations, and pressures of the larger society be evaluated in terms of how they affect the ongoing way of life that has been built around this circle.

The *lower-class subculture* is distinguished by the female-based family and the marginal male. Although a family circle may also exist, it includes only female relatives. The male, whether husband or lover, is physically present only part of the time, and is recognized neither as a stable nor dominant member of the household. He is a sexual partner, and he is asked to provide economic support. But he participates only minimally in the exchange of affection and emotional support, and has little to do with the rearing of children. Should he serve as a model for the male children, he does so largely in a negative sense. That is, the women use him as an example of what a man should not be.

The female-based family must be distinguished, however, from one in which the woman is dominant, for example, the English working-class family. Although this family may indeed revolve around the "Mum," she does not reject the husband. Not only is he a member of the family, but he is also a participant—and a positive model—in child-rearing.

In the lower class, the segregation of the sexes—only partial in the working class—is complete. The woman tries to develop a stable routine in the midst of poverty and deprivation; the action-seeking man upsets it. In order to have any male relationships, however, the woman must participate to some extent in his episodic life style. On rare occasions, she may even pursue it herself. Even then, however, she will try to encourage her children to seek a routine way of life. Thus the woman is much closer to working-class culture, at least in her aspirations, although she is not often successful in achieving them.

For lower-class men, life is almost totally unpredictable. If they have sought stability at all, it has slipped from their grasp so quickly, often, and consistently that they no longer pursue it. From childhood on, their only real gratifications come from action-seeking, but even these are few and short-lived. Relationships with women are of brief duration, and some men remain single all their lives. Work, like all other relationships with the outside world, is transitory. Indeed, there can be no identification with work at all. Usually, the lower-class individual gravitates from one job to another, with little hope or interest of keeping a job for any length of time. His hostility to the outside world therefore is quite intense, and its attempts to interfere with the episodic quality of his life are fought. Education is rejected by the male, for all of its aims are diametrically opposed to action-seeking.

The *middle-class subculture* is built around the nuclear family and its desire to make its way in the larger society. Although the family circle may exist, it plays only a secondary role in middle-class life. Contact with close relatives is maintained, but even they participate in a subordinate role. Individuals derive most of their social and emotional gratifications from the nuclear family itself. One of the most important of these is child-rearing. Consequently, the middle-class family is much more child-centered than the working-class one and spends more of its spare time together. Outside social life takes place with friends who share similar interests. The nuclear family depends on its friends—as well as on some caretaking institutions—for help and support. Relatives may also help, especially in emergencies.

The middle class does not make the distinction between the family and the outside world. In fact, it does not even see an outside world, but only a larger society, which it believes to support its aims, and in which the family participates. The nuclear family makes its way in the larger society mainly through the career of its breadwinner. Thus work is not merely a job that maximizes income, but a series of related jobs or job advances which provide the breadwinner with higher income, greater responsibility, and, if possible, greater job satisfaction. In turn his career enhances the way of life of the rest of the family, through increases in status and in the standard of living.

Education is viewed, and used, as an important method for achieving these goals. The purpose of education is to provide the skills needed for the man's career and for the woman's role as a mother. In and out of school, it is also used to develop the skills necessary to the maintenance and increase of status, the proper use of leisure time, and the occasional participation in community activities. Thus, much of the central theme of education is accepted. But the idea that education is an end in itself, and should be used to maximize individual development of the person, receives only lip service.

The subculture I have described here is a basic middle-class one; a more detailed analysis would distinguish between what is currently called the middle-middle class and the lower-middle class. The upper-middle-class subculture is also a variant of the basic middle-class culture. There are at least two such subcultures, the managerial and the professional. Since I shall be concerned with the latter in subsequent sections of this chapter and the next, it is of primary interest here.

The *professional upper-middle-class culture* is also organized around the nuclear family, but places greater emphasis on the independent functioning of its individual members. Whereas the middle-class family is a companionship unit in which individuals exist most intensely in their relationships with each other, the upper-middle-class family is a companionship unit in which individuals seeking to maximize their own development as persons come together on the basis of common interests. For this subculture, life is, to a considerable extent, a striving for individual development and self-expression, and these strivings pervade many of its relationships with the larger society.

Therefore, work is not simply a means for achieving the well-being of the nuclear family, but also an opportunity for individual achievement and social service. Although the career, income, status, and job responsibility are important, job satisfaction is even more important, although it is not always found. Indeed, professional work satisfaction is a focal concern not only for the breadwinner, but often for the woman as well. If she is not interested in a profession, she develops an alternative but equally intense interest in motherhood, or in community activity. Child-rearing, moreover, gives the woman an opportunity not only to maximize her own individual achievements as a mother, but to develop in her children the same striving for self-development. As a result, the professional upper-middle-class family is not child-centered, but adult-directed. As education is the primary tool for a life of individual achievement, the professional upper-middle-class person not only goes to school longer than anyone else in society, but he also accepts its central theme more fully than do the rest of the middle class.

This concern with individual achievement and education further enables and encourages the members of this subculture to be deliberate and self-conscious about their choices. They are a little more understanding of the actions of others than the members of less educated strata. Their ability to participate in the larger society, plus their high social and economic status, also gives them somewhat greater control over their fate than other people, and make the environment more predictable. This in turn facilitates the practice of self-consciousness, empathy, and abstraction or generalization.

The possession of these skills distinguishes the upper-middle class from the rest of the middle class, and even more so from the working and lower class. For the latter not only live in a less predictable environment, but they are also detached from the outside world, which increases their feeling that it, and, indeed, all of life, is unpredictable. In turn this feeling encourages a pervasive fatalism that pre-empts the optimism or pessimism of which the other classes are capable. The fatalism of the working and lower classes, as well as their lack of education and interest in personal development and object goals, minimizes introspection, self-consciousness, and empathy for the behavior of others.

Class: Opportunity and Response

The subcultures which I have described are *responses* that people make to the *opportunities* and the *deprivations* that they encounter. More specifically, each subculture is an organized set of related responses that has developed out of people's efforts to cope with the opportunities, incentives, and rewards, as well as the deprivations, prohibitions, and pressures which the natural environment and society—that complex of coexisting and competing subcultures—offer to them. The responses which make up a subculture are compounded out of what people have retained of parental, that is, traditional responses, the skills and attitudes they have learned as children, and the innovations they have developed for themselves in their own encounters with opportunity and deprivation.

These responses cannot develop in a vacuum. Over the long range, they can be seen as functions of the resources which a society has available, and of the opportunities which it can offer. In each of the subcultures life is thus geared to the availability of specific qualitative types and quantities of income, education, and occupational opportunities. Although I have used occupational labels to distinguish between the major subcultures,[75] a man's job does not necessarily determine in which of these he shall be placed. In the long run, however, the existence of a specific subculture is closely related to the availability of occupational opportunities. For example, the functioning of the family circle and the routine-seeking way of life in the working class depend on the availability of stable employment for the man. The lower-class female-based

75. It is relevant to note that the words I have used to label the class subcultures are somewhat misleading. For example, I describe the middle class not as a group in the middle of the economic and power structure, but as a subculture focally concerned with the nuclear family. Likewise, the working class obviously works no more or less than any other group. Only the lower-class label fits well, since this subculture is in so many ways a response to the deprivations to which it is exposed.

family is a response to, or a method of coping with, the lack of stable male employment. The goals of middle- and upper-middle-class culture depend on the availability of sufficient income to finance the education that is necessary for a career, and on the availability of job opportunities that will allow middle-class individuals to find the type of job satisfaction for which they are striving.

When these opportunity factors are lacking, the cultural responses made by people are frustrated. Should opportunities be deficient over a long enough period, downward mobility results. Should they disappear entirely, the subculture will be apt to disintegrate eventually. For example, working-class culture can function for a time in a period of unemployment, but if no substitute sources of stability are made available, people initially resort to protest. Eventually, the family circle begins to break up under the strain, and its members adopt many if not all of the responses identified with the lower-class subculture.

Similar reactions take place in the other subcultures, although the ways in which they are expressed may differ. If job opportunities are lacking so as to frustrate the career desires of the middle class, or the professional desires of the upper-middle class, one reaction is to transfer aspirations elsewhere, for example, into nonwork pursuits. Since upper-middle-class people are able and willing to act in the larger society, they may also develop social and political protest movements in order to create these opportunities, or to change society. Bourgeois socialist movements in America, taking their lead from the Marxist aim to "humanize" work so that it will provide quasi-professional job satisfaction to all people, are examples of such a reaction. Although downward mobility in the working class results in the adoption of lower-class responses, middle-class downward mobility does not bring about a working-class response. People may depend more on relatives as adversity strikes, but other differences between middle- and working-class subcultures remain in effect.

Downward mobility is also possible in the lower-class subculture. Since this culture is initially a response to instability, further instability can result only in family disintegration, total despair, and an increase in already high rates of mental illness, antisocial and self-destructive behavior, or group violence.

Conversely, when opportunity factors are increasingly available, people respond by more fully implementing their subcultural aspirations, and by improving their styles of life accordingly. For example, working-class people responded to the post-World War II prosperity by selecting from the available opportunities those elements useful for increasing the comfort and convenience of their way of life. They did not strive for middle-class styles. Nor did they reshape the family, adopt careers, or surrender their detachment from the outside world.

Periods of increased opportunity also encourage marginal members of each subculture to move into others to which they are aspiring. For example, lower-class women with working-class goals have been able to send their boys to school with the hope that they will be able to move into working-class culture. Whereas some of them have been able to make the move as adults, others have found that they could not summon the emotional and other skills necessary to succeed in school or job. In many cases, opportunities simply were not as freely available as expected, and sudden illness or other setbacks propelled them back into the lower-class culture.

Upward mobility that involves movement into another class subculture is relatively rare because of the considerable changes which people must make in their own lives, often against great odds. Thus the majority are content to improve the style of life within their own subcultures. They may, however, encourage their children to make the move in the next generation.

Although opportunities can increase or decrease rapidly and drastically over time, the subcultures I have described are relatively slow in changing their basic structure and content. In many ways contemporary working-class culture is a continuation of European peasant cultures, and some features of the middle- and upper-middle-class subcultures can be traced back to the post-Renaissance and to the beginnings of the urban-industrial revolution. Improvements and changes in the level of living take place all the time, as modern ideas, habits, and artifacts replace traditional ones. But the focal concerns of each subculture change more slowly.

Changes in the distribution and quality of opportunity factors do, of course, have significant effects. They influence the extent to which subcultural aspirations can be realized, and they help to determine the position of each subculture within the over-all class hierarchy. This in turn affects the political influence that each of them can exert on many matters in the national society, including the distribution of opportunities itself.

Moreover, new opportunities and the need for new skills can increase the number of people found in any one subculture, just as the demise of opportunities can reduce it. For example, whereas the reduction of temporary, unskilled labor is likely to shrink the lower-class subculture, the increased need for professionals has led to the enlargement of the middle and upper-middle class. In short, new opportunities bring higher incentives, which in turn encourage people to move into other subcultures, although a generation or two may pass before they adopt all of the primary focal concerns of their new way of life. At any one point in time, then, many people could be said to be living between subcultures. Radical changes in the society can even bring entirely new subcultures into being, although this has happened only infrequently in the course of history.

Class and Mobility among the West Enders

I have tried to show that the movement from one class to another is a cultural change that requires not only access to the prerequisite opportunities, but the willingness and ability to accept them. This is especially true of the move from working class to middle class, and may be illustrated by a description of the mobility process among the West Enders. This analysis will require some prior comments about class and ethnicity that will apply the definition of class proposed in the previous section to the West Enders and that will summarize the relationship between class and ethnic origin in the life of the peer group society.

So far, West Enders have had relatively few of the opportunities necessary for entry into the middle-class subculture, and even those few are of recent vintage. On the other hand they have not demanded access to these opportunities. For example, a number of college scholarships offered by one of the area settlement houses had frequently gone begging ever since the Jewish exodus from the West End. In short, it should be clear from the picture of the peer group society I have drawn in the preceding chapters that the West Enders are not yet eager to move into the middle class. While they now have many of the comforts and artifacts that once only the middle class could buy, they have not thereby become middle class.[76] Their culture is still that of the working class.

This applies not only to the routine-seekers, but even to some of the action-seekers as well. Aside from the never married, only the married action-seekers who have effectively detached themselves from their families, and made them female-based, can be considered lower class. The remaining action-seekers have at least one foot in the working-class culture, and participate sufficiently in the family to maintain a viable role. Thus their children are likely to grow up without the characteristics found in children from female-based families.

One of the distinguishing marks of a working-class group is its detachment from the larger society. This is found also among some ethnic groups, but it is not an ethnic phenomenon per se. While it is true, for example, that the West Enders' detachment from the larger society has been supported by ethnic differences between themselves and the outside world, it is also true that the detachment has not been caused by these differences. Indeed, the review of other working-class studies has indicated that this detachment from the outside world can be found among all working-class populations even when they are not ethnic minorities. Conversely, the high degree of Jewish mobility would suggest that ethnic status is no significant hindrance in entering either the larger society or the middle class.

Because working-class culture is different from middle-class culture, the move from one to the other is a difficult one, requiring behavior and attitude changes of considerable social and emotional magnitude. The most important changes are cutting the attachment

76. For a similar argument regarding a group of auto-workers and an English working-class population respectively, see Berger, *op. cit.*, Chap. 7; and Peter Willmott, "Class and Community at Dagenham," London: Institute for Community Studies, 1960, mimeographed.

to the family circle and the peer group society, and a concurrent shift from person- to object-orientation.

Thus, in order for a West Ender to begin the move into the middle class, he must first break—or have broken for him—his dependence on family and peers. His striving must shift moreover from peer group goals toward object-goals, such as a career, prestige, wealth, or individual development. And these goals must be pursued alone, or with people of like mind.

Since these goals conflict with family and peer group relationships, the peer group society naturally discourages such striving. The opposition to mobility which I described in the previous chapter is specifically directed against object-orientation. Indeed, what West Enders dislike most about the outside world and the middle-class culture is their stress on object-goals that interfere with person-oriented relationships. This is clearly illustrated by the West Enders' belief that suburbanites are lonely people and that the middle-class career requires inhuman exploitation of others. It is also exemplified by their complaints that adults today are striving for individual goals, and children for things, rather than for the emotional satisfactions of a cohesive family circle, as in the past. As I noted in Chapter 10, the peer group society's opposition to mobility is such that movement into the middle class must therefore be an individual venture.

This venture, a process which seems to begin in childhood or adolescence, requires that the young person be isolated from his family and peer group by a combination of pressures which push him out of these groups, and incentives which pull him into the outside world.[77] Many events can produce the requisite isolation, but among the most frequent are the possession of special talents, personal crises, and late arrival into the peer group.

Every population—even a low-income one—produces a number of young people with special gifts or talents, be these intellectual or artistic. Among the West Enders, however, young people with such talents are generally ostracized by their peers. And, unless their gifts are athletic or forensic and are useful to the group, these

77. Whyte's observations of how corner boys become college boys also suggested that this process starts at an early age, and results in isolation from the peer group. See his *Street Corner Society*, Chicago: University of Chicago Press, 1943, 2nd ed., 1955, pp. 106–107.

young people are often forced to choose between their talents and their peers. Parents are more tolerant of their talents, but since they are detached from the children's activities, they can offer little overt support. In fact, they may even discourage the child should his talent be identified with the opposite sex. On the other hand, representatives from the outside world, such as teachers and settlement house workers, do offer incentives. They encourage the young person to develop his talent, and provide opportunities for proper training. At the same time, these caretakers also make special efforts to draw gifted West Enders out of the peer group society. This in turn helps to isolate the youngster even further from his peers.

When the individual's talents are moderate, and his motivation to develop them weak, he is likely to suppress them in order to stay with the group. Should he be especially talented and strongly motivated, however, the peer group ostracism and the incentives from outside world representatives can combine to take him out of the peer group society, and into the training grounds of the middle class. Even so, he is likely to be ambivalent about this break. One West End youngster, for example, who wanted to be a singer of semiclassical music practiced on the sly, because his friends made fun of him. Another West Ender, an extremely creative adult, has never reconciled the conflict between his desire to use his talents and his wish to be a part of a peer group that shows little interest in and even some hostility toward them. Still ambivalent as to these gifts, he envies creative people who are encouraged by their families and friends. Needless to say, in a low-income group, hurdles are also placed in the way of the talented person by economic considerations and the immense social distance between the low-income person and the upper-middle- and upper-class world of the arts.

A second impetus to mobility seems to come from crises or traumatic experiences that are accompanied by unexpected isolation from the peer group society. This hypothesis is based on the experiences of two West Enders. One, a young man who had contracted tuberculosis in adolescence, developed a new set of goals while spending a year in a hospital bed. After recovery, he went to college and, later, into a profession. Another young man, who comes from a respected West End family, had been failing in school and participating in delinquent acts. Finally, when his life had reached an absolute nadir, he spent an entire night sitting up with his father, reviewing his past and his prospects for the future. He explained that as a result of these experiences, he developed a new set of goals. Subsequently, he too entered the professions. Such instances as these suggest that, for some, the move into middle-class culture requires a personal crisis, which is followed by a transformation that bears some resemblance to a religious conversion.

A third factor that encourages mobility is delayed entrance into the peer group society, which thus isolates the individual from the group during his formative years. This possibility was suggested by the fact that two of the most mobile individuals whom I encountered in the West End had both been born in Italy and had come to America just before their teens.[78] Only marginally attached to peer groups as adolescents, both have departed considerably, although not entirely, from the ways of the peer group society in adulthood.[79]

Another factor that acts on the individual is parental or familial encouragement to become upwardly mobile, but as I have suggested in earlier chapters, this is largely absent among the West Enders, although it seems to be important among Jews.

These factors function as pressures on the individual. In addition, almost all young West Enders are exposed to some pulls from the outside world—albeit in varying degrees of intensity—which offer them incentives for leaving the group. These come from the mass media, as well as from the schools and the other caretakers. But as only a few individuals respond to them, it must be assumed that the incentives themselves are not sufficient. Isolating pressures which push the individual out of the group are also necessary, and seemingly even more important.

This difficulty of breaking from the group and becoming mobile

78. I have also noticed that among other ethnic groups, many important leaders of second- and third-generation populations are immigrants who came to America as children.

79. I should note, however, that their parents migrated after the main Italian exodus, and were of higher status than other immigrants. This may also explain their mobility.

has also been observed by other researchers. Ellis' study of un-married career women, for example, concluded that:

> The evidence is consistent with the theory that upward social mobility is likely to be an outgrowth of basically neurotic drives resulting from unsatisfactory early primary group relations, and that mobility leads to a continuation of superficial, imperma-nent primary group relationships and other overt manifesta-tions of emotional maladjustment.[80]

Another study found vertical mobility "to be a factor in both schizophrenia and psychoneurosis. . . . This does not necessarily mean that mobility is the only or even the principal causative fac-tor." [81] At present, it is not known to what extent mobility is a result of difficulties experienced early in life, and to what extent it stems from parental desires for their children or from other in-centives, and is a cause of these difficulties.

In associating mobility with object-orientation, I have con-sidered only what might be called *total* mobility, that is, instances of people who make the move from working class to middle class in one jump of relatively short duration. There are other people whose mobility is more *segmental*. They enter occupations associ-ated with the middle class—including the professions—but rather than seeking object-goals, they only want to be among people of higher status. Lacking any strong identification with their profes-sion or with other middle-class values, they may not shift from person- to object-orientation at all. Instead, they merely apply person-oriented ways amid middle-class colleagues and friends, meanwhile retaining many of their other old behavior patterns and attitudes. Since such people are culturally between two classes, they are often described as "social climbers."

Finally, my discussion here has been limited to cases of success-

80. Evelyn Ellis, "Social Psychological Correlates of Upward Social Mobility among Unmarried Career Women," *American Sociological Review*, vol. 17 (1952), pp. 558–563, at p. 563. It should be noted that mobility is more difficult for women—other than through marriage—than for men.

81. A. Hollingshead, R. Ellis, and E. Kirby, "Social Mobility and Mental Illness," *American Sociological Review*, vol. 19 (1954), pp. 577–584, at p. 584.

ful mobility. Other individuals may break with the peer group society, but then fail to find a niche in the larger society. In this case,
such people are likely to suffer considerable pain and even mental
illness, especially if their unsuccessful break results eventually in
downward mobility. I did not encounter such individuals during
my stay in the West End, but, then, one would not expect them
to come back to the area once they had broken with the group.

Object-Orientation and Middle-Class Culture

I have suggested that one of the steps in becoming middle class
is the development of object-goals. But while it might follow that
the middle class is a subculture of the object-oriented, I do not
believe this to be the case. Indeed most middle-class people are not
noticeably more object-oriented than working-class ones. The striving for object-goals, therefore, seems to be a temporary phase that
is associated with the individual type of mobility. If and when the
sought object is achieved, many people "settle down" and become
more person-oriented again, only this time with a new group of
friends who share their characteristics and interests. Examples of
this settling-down process may be found among the ambitious young
corporate executives who later become "organization men," or
among intellectuals who give up creative work for faculty politics
and sociability once they have achieved their academic career
goals.[82] The pleasures of group life then become more important
than the socially isolating pursuit of object-goals.

Some people, of course, never stop striving for object-goals,[83]
and are likely to be socially marginal all their lives. The more successful become leaders. The less successful may become the isolates
on the block who ceaselessly compete for status, and try to keep up
with real or imagined Joneses.

Whereas such people may be quite visible to the superficial ob-

82. In many cases, they are worn down by this pursuit, especially if it involves rebellion against socially or politically powerful groups and values.

83. If object-orientation is an attribute of mobility, it should also manifest
itself in downward mobility. Object-oriented people whose striving is unsuccessful may transfer their aspirations to a new object, for example, to the
pursuit of a scapegoat who can be blamed for their failure, or to such other
"objects" as alcohol or narcotics.

server, they are numerically a minority in the total population.[84] Most middle-class people—whether they have come from the working class or not—are quite person-oriented. Their career moves and their choices of residential areas, organizational affiliations, cultural interests, and leisure-time activities usually depend more on the wishes of family and friends than on specific object-goals which they are pursuing. In this respect, they differ little from the West Enders. The major difference—and it is an important one— is that among the West Enders, person-orientation is based on a close association with the family circle and the peer group which the individual maintains all his life, and which is built into his personality structure. Middle-class people, on the other hand, choose from a wider range of people the individuals and groups with whom they spend their lives, remain somewhat more detached from them, and can even leave them for others without serious feelings of loss.[85]

This kind of middle-class person-orientation is perhaps similar to that which David Riesman and his associates have described as "other-direction," and which they have contrasted to a striving for object-goals that they call "inner-direction." [86] If my hypothesis is correct, however—that object-orientation is only a temporary phase for most people—the historical shift from inner- to other-direction which they describe could be interpreted differently.

Insofar as inner-direction is similar to what I have called object-orientation, it would appear to be an infrequent, but ever present, phenomenon, which accompanies individual mobility. Consequently, one might argue that it was neither as prevalent in nineteenth-century America, nor as likely to disappear in the twentieth

84. A lively genre of popular fiction—and biography—describes ambitious people who can never stop striving for object-goals, and who lead unhappy and friendless lives as a result. The critique of modern suburbia is another way of expressing this reaction against mobility.

85. In another context, I have described this relationship as quasi-primary, that is, not as close as in the peer group society, but not as distant as in secondary-group relationships. Herbert J. Gans, "Urbanism and Suburbanism as Ways of Life: A Re-evaluation of Definitions," in Arnold Rose, ed., *Human Behavior and Social Processes*, Boston: Houghton Mifflin Co., 1962, pp. 625–648, at p. 634.

86. D. Riesman, N. Glazer, and R. Denney, *The Lonely Crowd*, New Haven: Yale University Press, 1950, Chap. 1.

century, as the authors of *The Lonely Crowd* have suggested.[87] The historical evidence on this subject is scattered and poor, and, indeed, most of what we know about the past has come from people who made their mark in the world. They were highly visible to contemporary observers and historians precisely because they were pursuing some object-goal with fanatic determination. Such people continue to appear in American society today, although the increased size and complexity of the society make it more difficult for them to operate as individual entrepreneurs. Today, moreover, they are likely to be heading a corporate board or executive committee, where they are somewhat less visible. The people who carried out the day-to-day operations that enabled the nineteenth-century entrepreneurs to succeed—and the pioneers who were in the center of the convoys of covered wagons that opened up the frontier—were surely less inner-directed or object-oriented than those at the head. Indeed, they probably functioned as part of a family circle or other group much as do the majority of twentieth-century Americans.

Object-orientation is thus a minority pattern in any era, past or present. The professional upper-middle-class subculture, however, is particularly object-oriented, and does have a larger than average contingent of intensely mobile people. Moreover, it encompasses the intellectuals, who have a virtual monopoly on the public analysis and evaluation of society. Like all other subcultures, it tends to see the world from its own perspective. Therefore, it is particularly sensitive to the differences between itself and the rest of society, and much of the subculture's social analysis is concerned with examining these differences. For example, such distinctions as other-direction and inner-direction, local and cosmopolitan, person-orientation and object-orientation are in many ways dichotomies between "them" and "us." If they are not intended as such by their formulators, they are often interpreted in this way by the upper-middle-class subculture itself.

Moreover, much of its critique of the "mass society" proceeds from a value judgment that all people should live by the standards

<hr/>

87. It should be noted that Riesman and his associates wrote mainly about the upper—middle class, while my comments are based on observations among working-class and lower-middle-class populations.

of this subculture. This critique bears some similarity to the peer group society's rejection of the outside world. In both cases, "they" are criticized for lacking "our" attributes. Yet there are also many differences between the two critiques. For example, while the peer group society rejects those who differ, upper-middle-class professionals encourage them to give up their differences and to adopt the principal behavior patterns and values of the upper-middle-class subculture.

The programs that professionals have developed to achieve this aim are intended to make people object-oriented. As I suggested in Chapter 7, the missionary caretakers' stress on self-development, on cultural achievement, and on activity as an end in itself is based on the identification of object-orientation with middle-class culture. This object-orientation can be found not only in the goals of the settlement house and public library, which I described earlier, but also in those of public recreation, the community center movement, public education, adult education, the mental health movement, the good government movement, and a host of other public, semi-public, and philanthropic endeavors.

It now becomes possible to understand why so many of these movements have had relatively little success in converting clients, not only among the West Enders, and in other working- and lower-class neighborhoods, but in middle-class ones as well. They have attempted to make people object-oriented simply by attracting them to their facilities, and by hoping that their participation in agency programs and contact with agency staff might result in conversion through a kind of osmosis. They have failed, however, to provide the social and economic opportunities that encourage the object-oriented response, and they have vastly underestimated the difficulty of the change from person- to object-orientation. Most of the successful conversions have taken place among young people who have left home and family emotionally, and who have developed surrogate relationships with caretakers, be these settlement house workers, librarians, or youth group leaders. But if the number of people who are ready to leave their families is small, so is the number of trained workers who can function effectively as surrogate parents or siblings. The caretakers' success with the mobile Jewish youngsters earlier in the century must probably be attributed to qualities within the Jewish subculture which predisposed the children to object-orientation at home before they arrived at the caretaking institution. These predispositions, however, are not to be found among most of the children from other European ethnic groups or from Negro and Puerto Rican populations who have subsequently come into the schools and settlement houses.

CHAPTER 12 An Evaluation of the Class Subcultures and Implications for Planning and Caretaking

Basic Assumptions of the Evaluation

As I noted in the Preface, this study was partially motivated by my curiosity about the middle-class bias of city planners and care-taking agencies, and by my desire to discover whether or not this bias was justified. These are research aims that require an evaluation of the major subcultures. Such an evaluation, if properly done, would have to be based on a systematic comparative study of all the class subcultures. After investigating the individual and social consequences of the major behavior patterns of each, it then would have to reach conclusions as to their advantages and disadvantages for each one, and for the larger society as well.

My study had much humbler aims. It was not even primarily concerned with judging the West Enders, or the working-class sub-culture to which they "belong." Consequently, it is possible only to make some preliminary evaluations of this subculture and the lower-class one. These conclusions in turn lead to some proposals for the programs of the planning and caretaking professions who work with the two subcultures.

The evaluations and proposals stem from my personal value judgments, observations I made in the West End, and the findings of other research on working- and lower-class populations. I must first state a basic value judgment which supports many of the evaluations to follow: that what I have called the professional upper-middle-class subculture is more desirable than all the rest. If cultures can be compared in the abstract, without concern for the opportunities that encourage them, and the social conditions necessary for their existence, I believe that this culture provides a fuller, more diverse life, a greater range of choices of behavior in all major spheres of life, and the ability to deal more adequately with changing conditions and with problems than do any of the other subcultures. It is by no means perfect, but it is more desirable than the others. If society could be reconstructed from top to bottom, if man could alter his physical and social environment at will, if resources were unlimited, if opportunities could be created and distributed without restriction, and if people could choose their subculture freely, I believe that the professional upper-middle-class subculture would be the most deserving of choice.

Needless to say, these conditions do not exist, and it is doubtful whether any of them will come into existence in our lifetime. To say that they should exist preserves ideological purity, but does not help the planner or caretaker who is powerless to bring them into being. Thus, a more pragmatic evaluation is needed and must begin with the assumption that although the present distribution of opportunities is not satisfactory, it is unlikely to be altered radically in the near future. Therefore, a usable evaluation must, in turn, begin by identifying those changes in the opportunity structure that *have* to be made whatever the difficulties or the costs. Beyond this, the subcultures themselves must be evaluated on the extent to which they provide people with satisfying ways of responding to the opportunities they are likely to be able to obtain in the next decade or two.

The Evaluation of Working- and Lower-Class Subcultures

It should be evident from the description of the West Enders in the previous chapters that I believe the working-class subculture to be a generally satisfactory way of adapting to the opportunities which society has made available. Even so, it does have a number of negative features that constitute disadvantages both to working-class people and to the larger society.

One of these is the inability to participate in formal organizations and in general community activity. Although the lack of interest in voluntary associations is relatively unimportant, the inability to organize per se deprives working-class people of a method of political representation that is very important in a pluralistic society. Generally less well represented in the political arena than the economically more powerful, and socially more skillful groups, they are thus hampered in expressing their point of view, and in defending their interests. Consequently, they delegate the political representation function to others, yet only at some cost. Urban political machines and labor unions defend their interests, but the leadership of these organizations is not always fully representative. Moreover, when these agencies are not responsive, working-class people may turn to authoritarian and occasionally violent forms of protest—more out of desperation than choice. But such solutions are not always desirable or effective.

A related drawback is the general inability to understand bureaucratic behavior and object-orientation. This encourages the development of a conspiracy theory to explain the outside world, and breeds suspicions that are frequently inaccurate. As a result, the already existing gap between the working class and the larger society is widened.

Much of the time, the working class can protect itself from real or imagined injury by minimizing its dependence on the larger society. But this solution, which may work in prosperous times and in periods of social stability, is not always effective. In depressions, emergencies, and periods of rapid social change, however, the many indirect relationships to the larger society become apparent, mainly as they are being interrupted or altered. It is at these times that normal methods of class conflict over the distribution of opportunities go awry, and the gap between the working class and the larger society—notably the government—threatens to become harmful to both. The former is hurt by its inability to understand and deal with the changes that are taking place; the latter, by its inability to develop methods to solve the resulting problems even when it wants to do so. This state of affairs was illustrated only too well by the redevelopment of the West End. As I shall show in Chapters 13 and 14, the West Enders could not defend their interests, and the redevelopment agency was unable to understand their needs. Similarly, as automation and other technological changes alter the labor market, and reduce the need for semiskilled and unskilled workers, the working-class subculture's detachment from the larger society hampers the adjustment to changing conditions. Fortunately, the belief in education as a means to occupational success has allowed many working-class people to train themselves for the new job types that are now needed, and the problem is not as severe as it is in the lower class.

Another disadvantage of the working-class subculture is its rejection of certain types of caretakers, especially those whose services cannot be provided by the family circle. I am thinking here especially of the unwillingness to use medical specialists and psychotherapists. Although such caretakers may treat their clients as if they were middle class—which explains why they are so often rejected even when cost is no problem—the health goals which they further are sought by the working class as much as by any other. The family circle does provide a considerable amount of advice and emotional support to its members, but not always of the right kind. Indeed, some forms of care cannot be given by laymen, especially if the latter share the patient's mistaken beliefs. In dealing with mental illness, for example, the aid given by the family circle can even be harmful.

Finally, the emphasis on group life, the low value placed on privacy, and the general conservatism of the working-class culture all penalize those who deviate. For most people, this is no problem. Those who deviate by being mobile, for instance, are able to leave. But for people who are not mobile and who are different without wanting to be—such as those with neuroses that detach them from the group—the sanctions against deviance are harsh.

More intensive research of the dominant cultural patterns would undoubtedly indicate other patterns with deleterious consequences. For example, the impulsive child-rearing methods may have undesirable effects for some children who, for one reason or another, do not learn to cope with them. Only a highly detailed and longitudinal study of the subculture, however, will be able to unearth such patterns.

My limited observations suggest that, on the whole, the advantages of working-class subculture do outweigh the disadvantages. The latter are real, and ought to be removed, but they are not overwhelming. Thus, given our present knowledge, there is no justification for planning and caretaking programs which try to do away with the working-class subculture. John Seeley has suggested why it should not be done away with in his description of a Polish working-class group with whom he once lived:

> . . . no society I have lived in before or since seemed to me to present so many of its members . . . so many possibilities and actualities of fulfillment of a number at least of basic human demands: for an outlet for aggressiveness, for adventure, for a sense of effectiveness, for deep feelings of belonging without undue sacrifice of uniqueness or identity, for sex satisfaction, for strong if not fierce loyalties, for a sense of independence from the pervasive omnicompetent, omniscient authority-in-general which at that time still overwhelmed to a greater degree the middle-class child. . . . These things had their prices, of course—not all values can be simultaneously maximized. But few of the inhabitants whom I reciprocally took "slumming" into middle-class life understood it or, where they did, were at all envious of it. And, be it asserted, this was not a matter of "ignorance" or incapacity to "appreciate finer things," but an inability to see one moderately coherent and sense-making satisfaction-system which they didn't know as preferable to the quite coherent and sense-making satisfaction-system they did know.[1]

Although his evaluation puts the case a little more enthusiastically than I might, it says very well that working-class culture is a positive response to the opportunities and deprivations which it encounters.

This is not true, however, of the lower-class subculture. Like all other cultures, it too tries to cope with the existing opportunities

1. John R. Seeley, "The Slum: Its Nature, Use and Users," *Journal of the American Institute of Planners*, vol. 25 (1959), pp. 7–14, at p. 10.

and deprivations, and to make life as bearable as possible. That it fails to succeed is largely the result of the intense deprivations with which it is saddled. Moreover, the response to these deprivations has consequences which make it difficult for lower-class people to accept opportunities for improvement if and when they are available.

Although lower-class culture has innumerable problems, perhaps the basic one is occupational. It seems to produce people who can work only in unskilled jobs. These jobs, however, are becoming more and more scarce, and they may virtually disappear in the not so distant future—surely to no one's sorrow. But while lower-class women have developed working-class or quasi-working-class aspirations, the female-based family seems to raise men who find it difficult to develop the skills and the motivations that are necessary for obtaining and holding the jobs that will be available. In addition, these men are ambivalent about themselves and their role in society, and thus have considerable problems in achieving some sort of personal stability even when they want it, and even when they have gained some measure of economic stability. At present, then, lower-class culture breeds men who find it increasingly difficult to survive in modern society, and who, in a more automated future, will be unable to do so.

Lower-class women seem to be able to achieve some measure of stability—however problem-laden it may be—within and through the family. Even so, they are content neither with the subculture, nor with the female-based family, and try to see that their children escape it. This in itself suggests a major difference between the lower class and the other subcultures. The people within other subcultures are by and large satisfied with them and pass them on much more willingly to their children, at least to the extent that culture is ever transmitted deliberately. Lower-class women may not often succeed in raising their children to reject the culture they live in, but the mere fact that they try illustrates the absolute qualitative difference between the lower-class subculture and all the others.

There are more persuasive illustrations of this difference. Many lower-class children grow up in homes ravaged by alcoholism, drug addiction, and mental illness, and the subculture that they inherit is overlaid with pathology, for besides the comparatively more functional elements of lower-class subculture, there are many that are the result of pathological conditions, such as being raised by mentally ill parents. For example, many of the focal concerns of lower-class culture described by Walter Miller are useful methods of coping with the environment,[2] but there are some forms of action-seeking that reflect desperation more than adaptation. The episodes of riotous pleasure do not make up for the depression and self-destruction that accompany them. Significantly, the lower class not only has higher rates of mental illness than the others, but these rates are considerably higher than those of the working class.[3] Indeed, the difference in rates between these two classes is so great as to suggest that many elements of lower-class life are not merely culturally different from other ways of life, but that they are in fact pathological.

Implications for Planning and Caretaking

As already noted, planners and caretakers provide services based on middle-class values, although it would be more correct to say that, often, the values are those of the professional upper-middle class. In addition, these professions work with a distorted picture of the class structure, for they generally distinguish only between a middle and a lower class. Also, they recognize only one lower class, including within it both the working and the lower class I have described. Consequently, they attribute the pathology that exists in the lower class to the working class as well. More important, they assume that this combined lower class is basically a frustrated version of the middle class, and that it exists only because lower-class clients cannot gain access to the opportunities and services available to the middle class. If the clients could obtain these, so the thinking goes, they would quickly relinquish their present cultures. This conception of the class structure is

2. "Lower Class Culture as a Generating Milieu of Gang Delinquency," *Journal of Social Issues*, vol. 14, No. 3 (1958), pp. 5–19.

3. August B. Hollingshead and Fredrick C. Redlich, *Social Class and Mental Illness*, New York: Wiley, 1958, Chap. 7. The authors also note that male rates in the lower class (Class V) are higher than female ones, a disparity not prevalent in other classes. *Op. cit.*, p. 200.

well adapted to the belief systems of the planning and caretaking professions, since it assumes that cultural change can be induced by providing the improved residential conditions and adequate amounts of educational, recreational, health, and other facilities which they supply. All that is needed is the allocation of more resources to these professions, so that they can saturate non-middle-class neighborhoods with the facilities, programs, and skills they have developed.

While this theory may be useful for influencing decision-makers to increase budgetary allotments to the professions concerned, it is much less useful for developing sound planning and caretaking programs. Its inapplicability is indicated by the failure of planners and caretakers to win working-class people over to middle-class culture. This fact, as well as many others, should be sufficient to show that the working-class subculture cannot be changed simply by presenting it with middle-class services. The theory is even less appropriate for dealing with the lower-class population. Here, the deprivation is so intense and the needs so distinctive that the provision of more playgrounds, public health facilities, social workers, and even schools cannot even come close to solving the problems. Although these services are desirable, they can contribute little or nothing to the amelioration of a pathological way of life.

What, then, ought to be done? If planners and caretakers wanted to achieve their goal of inducing people to become upper middle class, they would first have to recognize that their present programs are insufficient. Alternative programs would have to begin with the assumption that this subculture, like all others, is based on prerequisite opportunities of income, education, and occupation. They would also have to realize that it is built on a family structure, as well as a set of skills and values that first motivate and then enable people to make the cultural move.

Consequently, planners and caretakers would need to call for large-scale social and economic change: the redistribution of income, the imparting of new occupational skills, the provision of other opportunities to increase the level of living of the people now lacking upper-middle-class advantages, and the elimination of racial, ethnic, and class discrimination in the institutions that support the upper-middle-class culture. They would also have to develop ways of helping people move out of old subcultures into the new one and find methods to reduce the strains that accompany this change.

This is a utopian proposal, for these professions presently lack the power to make—or even to propose—such radical social and political changes. Nor do they have the knowledge necessary to help people move from one culture to another. While this invalidates neither the goal nor the programs necessary to bring it about, it does suggest the need for a more modest approach—one that can be more immediately implemented.

What can planners and caretakers do *now?* First, they should maintain their present programs, which largely attract the predisposed, the working-class people who are already motivated to make the cultural move. Although such people are few in number, the caretaking agencies have been successful in helping them in the move. This is true also of some planning and renewal policies, notably in public housing. But the planners and caretakers have perhaps not done enough to make sure that opportunities are available for the mobile people to guarantee the eventual success of their move. Further efforts along this line are desirable.

But the most important needs are those of the nonmobile working class and of the lower class. Here, planners and caretakers have done relatively little. With respect to the former, their concentration on mobile people has prevented them from offering their skills and services and resources to the large majority of people who want to remain in the working-class subculture. In this area, much can still be done. For example, settlement houses should offer more activities designed to meet the needs and demands—many of them unspoken—of the nonmobile in working-class neighborhoods. Thus, settlement houses can step up their recreational programs for children, especially the younger ones, in order to provide a kind of day-care facility for mothers who have to work, or who have many children underfoot in a small apartment. They can offer "hanging out" places for adolescents and can program movies and social activities to reduce the drain on their pocketbooks. In communities where the school curriculum is solidly middle class, the settlements can provide informal educational aid to help the nonmobile working-class youngster get along in school and reconcile the conflicts that arise between the school's aspirations and his own. Another important function is that of counseling. Working-class adolescents do have problems that they cannot talk over with their parents and peers. Similarly, adults have problems that they cannot discuss with relatives, priests, or caseworkers.

Many settlement houses already program such activities, but they do it in such a way that only the mobile people use them. What is needed, then, is a revamping of the ethos—or social climate—of the house, so as to make it inviting to nonmobile clients. One solution is to staff it with some internal informal caretakers from the neighborhood. While these persons may lack professional certification, they are much more likely to be successful in communicating with their neighbors, and in attracting them to the settlement house in the first place.[4]

Planners and caretakers can also formulate programs that help to overcome some of the disadvantages of the working-class subculture described earlier, such as bridging the gap to the outside world, finding substitutes for community participation, and helping nonmobile deviants who cannot find a niche in the group.

The greatest need, however, exists in the lower class. Because of the deprivations that it must endure, and the pathological elements in its subculture, it should be given the highest priority in future planning and caretaking. Here also is the greatest challenge, for present approaches have been even less successful than those with working-class clients. The first step must be to give up the well-meaning but useless attempt to confront lower-class people with middle-class values and programs. Since the major aim of lower-class women is to move their children into the working class, this ought also to be the goal of planning and caretaking. Such a goal will make it necessary for planners and caretakers to understand the working-class subculture before they can offer much help to the

4. This was one of the suggestions made by Whyte in his study of the North End. For his formulation and the settlement house reaction to his proposals, see *Street Corner Society*, Chicago: University of Chicago Press, 1943, 2nd ed., 1955, pp. 98–108, 275–276, 354–356.

lower class. They must also become familiar with the lower-class subculture—especially its female-based family. Until research has unearthed the processes that produce pathology, as well as the ones that encourage mobility, efforts to work with lower-class clients will have to be based on *ad hoc* experimentation. Such experiments can be a fruitful source of knowledge, however, whether they succeed or fail.

In the development of planning and caretaking programs for lower-class clients, the increased provision of basic economic and social opportunities is of the first priority. Until these are available, few lower-class people will be motivated to change their lives to respond to them. Also, as so much of the lower class is nonwhite, the provision of these opportunities will require the concurrent alleviation of racial discrimination. It is here that changes in the opportunity structure must be made at all costs. This will require an influx of funds and other resources—and in large amounts—that planners, caretakers, and community decision-makers can allocate. It will also require, among other things, improvements in patterns of influence and political representation for the lower class that can no longer be postponed.

If opportunities can be increased in these ways, they will probably stimulate a lower-class response that draws on already existing working-class aspirations. Since this response develops only slowly —and more slowly in the lower class than in all others—the extension of opportunities must be accompanied by programs that will help lower-class people learn to take advantage of them. This means finding ways of developing motivations, of imparting new skills and new attitudes. It also means offering support during the long, slow climb out of the lower class, even in the face of frequent recidivism. Admittedly, such a program will be very difficult, for lower-class people are likely to be more hostile to planners and caretakers than less deprived populations. Living so close to the edge of despair, they have developed many ways of immunizing themselves against the outside world, and against false hope. Thus, methods must be found of helping people who reject help.

In order to achieve any success in aiding lower-class clients, planners and caretakers must be able to achieve rapport with them.

By rapport, I mean the establishment of a professional-client relationship that is based on respect for the client,[5] and that neither manipulates, patronizes, nor blames him for a condition for which he is not responsible. Peter Marris has recently warned:

> Any social reform directed at the shortcomings of people, rather than of society, is handicapped by the humiliating imputations of its policy. . . . Unless slum children qualify for skilled jobs, they will remain poor, but to claim that they can qualify only if they will take education more seriously is profoundly threatening. It suggests that they have only themselves to blame for their present poverty. . . .

> Of all reformers, the social worker who carefully avoids an authoritarian manner is at bottom the most hurtful to pride. Armed with his theories of group therapy, he invites his patients—for he understands them in terms of maladjustment— to accept him as an equal. He does not command or exhort, but manipulates. . . . This technique involves the fundamentally arrogant assumption that social deprivation is an inadequacy of personality which he has a right to cure, but without consulting the wishes of the victims. They react by manipulating him in return, and with a lifetime's experience of evading authority, often beat him at his own game.[6]

The planning and caretaking professions have developed out of nineteenth-century middle-class reform movements. Thus the middle-class value pattern is now well institutionalized, not only in programs, but in the recruitment and training of professionals, in the creation of a professional image and self-image, and, most important, in the structure of professional-client relationships. The development of a democratic form of rapport, and the elimina-

5. Thomas Gladwin, "Poverty—An Anthropologist's View," in National Conference on Social Welfare, *The Social Welfare Forum, 1961,* New York: Columbia University Press, 1961, pp. 73–86, at p. 76.

6. Peter Marris, "A Report on Urban Renewal," London: Institute for Community Development, 1962, mimeographed, pp. 17–18, and as published in Leonard J. Duhl, ed., *Environment of the Metropolis* (tentative title), New York: Basic Books, forthcoming.

tion of the relationships that Marris has described so well will consequently require changes in the entire institutional complex of the planning and caretaking professions. Programs as well as relationships with clients will have to take lower- and working-class values and needs into account, and encourage the lower-class client to participate in a meaningful and human way.[7]

These changes will necessitate first a thorough analysis of the entire range of activities of the planning and caretaking professions that affect clients. This analysis must distinguish between three types of activities: those which have no class connotations, or ones which are shared by professionals and clients of all classes; those which have middle-class elements that are, however, essential to the professional function; and those which have middle-class elements that are not essential to this function but that needlessly separate professional from client. The three types can be illustrated in the doctor-patient relationship. To begin with, presumably the doctor and the patient both seek the latter's well-being. But whereas some of the therapeutic methods used by the doctor are either accepted by all classes, or are so technical that they have no class connotations whatsoever, others definitely do have such connotations. Current methods of analytic psychiatry, for example, require the patient to use psychological skills and particular ways of facing himself that are found primarily among middle-class people. So far, at least, psychotherapy has had difficulty in "getting through" to working- and lower-class people.[8] Yet other methods of care stem from the doctor's own middle-class background, and his way of relating to the patient usually includes patterns that support his upper-middle-class professional image.[9]

If rapport with lower-class clients is to be achieved, changes will thus have to be made in activities with class connotations. Where middle-class elements are essential to the planning or caretaking function, this will be extremely difficult. Where such

7. This proposal has been made by many social scientists working in or with these professions.

8. See, for example, Hollingshead and Redlich, *op. cit.*, pp. 339–340.

9. See Chapter 6. For a detailed discussion of class and other conflicts in this relationship, see Eliot Freidson, "Dilemmas in the Doctor-Patient Relationship," in Arnold Rose, ed., *Human Behavior and Social Processes,* Boston: Houghton Mifflin, 1962, pp. 207–224.

elements are nonessential, they can be removed if the professions themselves are willing. For example, settlement houses and social workers do not have to describe all adolescent activities that violate middle-class values as delinquency; their functions can continue unimpaired with a culturally more tolerant concept. Likewise, planners must realize that poverty forces lower-class people to live in much less attractive surroundings than those of middle-class people, and should thus be able to refrain from labeling any low-income neighborhood that diverges from middle-class standards as a slum.[10] It is true that the boundaries between cultural differences among the classes and pathological conditions are often hard to determine. But surely the loose application of middle-class standards that refuses even to distinguish between them is a nonessential practice that can be eliminated without violating planning and caretaking functions.

I am not suggesting that these professions surrender their entire repertoire of methods and values to the goal of achieving lower-class rapport. Just as the doctors cannot use ineffective methods of treatment to maintain rapport with his patient, neither can the settlement house sponsor delinquency, nor the planner develop schemes that make lower-class housing worse than it is now.

Admittedly, the change in orientation that I have suggested will be immensely difficult to make, for it questions the basic beliefs of the professions concerned. It demands that dedicated and hard-working middle-class people give up methods and symbols internalized through years of training and practice, and exchange them for new approaches catering to a strange and hostile culture, and to suspicious, deprived people. A voluntary transformation would require saint-like qualities, and it is unrealistic to expect it from people who must gain personal gratification and social reward from their work.

Some changes can be made, however, by reducing the emphasis on middle-class values in professional training, and by acquainting the professions with the problems and cultural patterns of the lower class as these are unearthed by social science research. Already this is being undertaken, as social scientists are being invited

10. For a definition distinguishing between slum and low-rent neighborhoods, see Chapter 14.

to participate in the research and teaching programs of the planning and caretaking professions.

Even so, this is not likely to be sufficient. Since it is doubtful that middle-class professionals can soon develop the knowledge and empathy needed to communicate with lower-class clients, it may be necessary to dichotomize these professions—assigning professionals to develop the programs, and recruiting skilled nonprofessionals to adapt them to lower-class clients and carry them out.

These nonprofessionals should be people who have themselves come out of lower-class culture, and have successfully moved into a more stable way of life—either working- or middle-class—but have not rejected their past. Many mobile people tend to turn their back on the culture from which they have come, and become more hostile toward it than anyone else. Yet there are some people who, in making the change, have developed a considerable amount of empathy toward both old and new culture. Since they know the conditions and the culture that are to be changed, and the way of life that is being sought by and for lower-class clients, they should be more successful in achieving rapport with such clients than are middle-class professionals. But while these empathic people exist in large numbers, they are hard to find. Some have been drawn into settlement houses and into group work with adolescent gangs. Most of them, however, probably earn their living in factories and offices, without ever using their talent—for it is a talent—to mediate between the classes.[11] Although many obstacles stand in the way of such mediators, and although their recruitment into planning and caretaking functions alone would not solve the basic problem, their participation would at least make it easier for planners and caretakers to serve those clients who need them most.

This need is so great that one is hard put to think of programs which deserve higher priorities in the allocation of public resources. American society may be affluent, but the lower class has benefited

11. One such person is "Doc," the man who introduced Whyte into the street corner society of the North End. He was quite successful in bringing North Enders into the settlement house, but because he did not attend college, and lacked professional certification, he was rejected as a settlement house worker. After considerable difficulties in obtaining other employment, he eventually became a factory supervisor, where he has been successful because he can mediate between management and labor. Whyte, *op. cit.*, pp. 43–44, 342–343.

least from this affluence, and its way of life has improved very little in recent decades. Although there are an increasing number of knowledgeable planners and caretakers, public funds still are spent largely for protecting the larger society from the self-destructive and antisocial behavior of the lower class, rather than for the elimination of the causes that create this behavior. Deprivation and pathology are thus allowed to continue from generation to generation, perpetuating misery and destroying human beings who deserve a better fate. So far, society has not been able or willing to attack the problem at its roots. Moreover, the political and business leaders who are so influential in urban policy-making, and who guide the planning and caretaking agencies, have generally evaded the issue. The planners and caretakers themselves have acquiesced in this evasion by misplaced confidence in existing programs. Perhaps they cannot bring about the necessary changes alone, but they must take the initiative.[12]

12. In all fairness, it should be noted that thoughtful caretakers from a variety of professions are moving in this direction even now. Moreover, planners in a number of cities have recently begun to develop programs in "social planning" to aid the lower class, although in some cases, these programs have concentrated on the expansion and coordination of existing—and thus not always appropriate—caretaking services.

PART FOUR Epilogue

CHAPTER 13 Redevelopment of the West End

Introduction

When I began this study, the West End was facing destruction as a slum under the urban redevelopment program. For more than seven years, federal and local agencies had been preparing the plans, and getting the necessary approvals for tearing down the old structures and for building a new neighborhood—not for the West Enders, but for high-income tenants of luxury apartment buildings. One of the original reasons for making a study was to discover how the West Enders as individuals and as a community were reacting to the eventual—and then imminent—destruction of their neighborhood.

Had the West Enders exhibited the expected stress, the book might have dealt with these phenomena in much greater detail.[1] As it turned out, however—for reasons to be described below—most West Enders did not react in this fashion, and continued to follow their normal routines.[2] Because of this and because of my greater

1. When I use the term West Ender in this chapter and the next, I mean all of the people in the area, regardless of ethnic background. Even so, most of my observations about redevelopment were made among the Italian West Enders. Whenever I refer to someone of Italian background, however, this will be indicated.

2. At least they did so as long as I remained in the area. I left in May, 1958, shortly after the city had taken title to the land, but before people had begun to move. The chapter deals with events up to that time only. The full

interest in the workings of the peer group society, the discussion of redevelopment has been limited to this epilogue.

The epilogue is in two sections: a sociological analysis of the redevelopment process and its impact on the West End in the present chapter; and an evaluation of the redevelopment plan from a city planning and general social welfare perspective in the concluding one.[3]

A Chronology of the Redevelopment Process

The idea for redeveloping the West End dates back to the turn of the century, when the area was already known as a densely occupied low-income neighborhood. Although the concept of slum was in wide use at that time, programs of slum clearance were then undertaken only by private philanthropists, mainly for the purpose of erecting model tenements to encourage commercial builders to improve designs and building practices. Edward Ginn, a Boston publisher and civic leader, built such a model tenement in the West End in 1907. Called the Charlesbank, it was still occupied at the time of my study, and was torn down early in the clearance process.

In the late 1930's, Nathan Straus, one of the founders of the public housing movement in America, visited the West End and suggested that the entire area be cleared and replaced with public housing. Although his advice was not heeded, the creation of the federal slum clearance program after World War II did lead the Boston Planning Board to suggest that the West End, together with the North and South Ends, were ripe for clearance. In 1950, the Boston Housing Authority applied to the federal government for preliminary planning funds to study the West End, together with the South End and Roxbury. This study began in 1951, but work proceeded slowly, and it was not until April, 1953, that the decision to redevelop the West End was announced officially. At this time,

---

impact of the redevelopment will be described in considerable detail, of course, by the long-term study being conducted by the Center for Community Studies.

3. Since I was highly critical of the redevelopment process, my sociological analysis is affected by my point of view. The reader is therefore advised to look over the introduction to the concluding chapter for a brief statement of that point of view.

federal funds were requested for the final planning study that would determine both the actual clearance schedule and the redevelopment plan.

Five more years were to pass before plans became reality. The initial redevelopment plan had excluded some of the streets in the upper end that were not thought to be blighted enough to justify clearance. But the advice of mortgage bankers—that it would be difficult to sell the cleared land were it surrounded by aging if well-kept tenements—necessitated a revision in the plans. These revisions were made, and the necessary federal and local approval of the plan was secured in 1956.

At about that time, the first stirrings of protest were heard from the West End. A small group of young West Enders organized the Save the West End Committee, and with the help of a Beacon Hill resident, who had opposed other city modernization schemes in the past, they carried on several years of opposition to the project.

The Committee received little overt support from the rest of the West Enders, and its opposition did not significantly interrupt the city's planning. Soon after federal and local approval of the plan was obtained, the project was opened to bidders. One of the bidders was a three-man group, consisting of a local investor who owned and managed a number of downtown office and commercial buildings—and who was therefore personally concerned over the decline of the retail area—a New York financier and builder, and a politically influential young Boston lawyer. The latter had risen to fame some years earlier, when, as a Harvard student just arrived from New York, he almost single-handedly had organized the New Boston Committee, a reform movement that had elected the incumbent Mayor. After the election, he became the Mayor's confidential secretary and then opened his own law office.

This trio had offered the second highest bid for the land, but then the high bidder dropped out, and it received the contract—a change that created a minor political storm. Although rumors spread that the Mayor had engineered the switch as a political reward for the lawyer's role in his election, the lawyer and his associates claimed that the high bidder's own second thoughts about the profitability of the project had brought on his withdrawal.

The developer's plans for the new West End were for a 2400-

unit complex of elevator apartment buildings—and a handful of townhouses—to be rented for about $45 a room, a figure that placed the project firmly in the luxury housing category.[4] The plans were presented at a public hearing in April, 1957, and approved by the City Council and the Mayor three months later.

The state and federal government, however, were not entirely satisfied with the city's handling of the project, and demanded that it be transferred from the Housing Authority to a newly constituted Redevelopment Authority. Once this was done, the state approved the plans. In October, 1957, the new Redevelopment Authority commissioners held an informal hearing in the West End regarding the scheme they were taking over from the Housing Authority. Two hundred people from the West End attended this hearing, most of them strongly opposed to the redevelopment. According to one of the commissioners with whom I later spoke, his group was impressed with the protest. But after "a lot of soul-searching," the commissioners concluded that the process had gone too far to be reversed, and decided to go along with the plan. The Authority—which had taken over the old staff of the redevelopment section of the Housing Authority—then moved swiftly to obtain final federal approval. In January, 1958, the city and the federal government signed the contract that would require the latter to pay two-thirds and the former, one-third of the cost of purchasing the land, relocating the present residents, and clearing the site for the redeveloper.

Surveyors started to come into the West End at that time, and in February, 1958, a site office was set up to handle relocation surveys and other procedures for relocation and clearance. The city took official title to the land under the power of eminent domain during the last week in April, thus marking the beginning of actual redevelopment and relocation. This in turn enabled the Save the West End Committee to file suit against the project, charging that the West End had been declared a slum on the basis of false statistics.[5]

4. By 1961, these rents had been increased to $125 and up for one-room efficiency apartments, and $292 and up for three-bedroom units. The townhouses were considerably more expensive.

5. The Committee's claim will be discussed more fully in the concluding chapter.

The Committee was unable to obtain a temporary injunction, however, and by the time the case was heard and its appeal defeated,
the West End was almost totally cleared.

When schools closed for the year in June, 1958—some of them
never to reopen—West Enders began to move out in large numbers.
The exodus continued throughout 1958, and by November of that
year, 1200 of the 2700 households had departed. After a slowdown
during the winter, the moveouts resumed in spring of 1959; by the
summer of 1959, the West End was emptying rapidly. As the
Redevelopment Authority began to tear down buildings as soon as
they had become vacant, this encouraged the departure of people
in neighboring structures. Thus the relocation process, which had
been expected to take three to four years, was completed after little
more than eighteen months. By the summer of 1960, only rubble
remained where two years ago had lived more than 7000 people.[6]
Meanwhile, foundations were being laid for the first of the new
apartment buildings, and in January, 1962, the initial residents of
the new West End started to move in.

Redevelopment: The City's Reasons

There were many reasons for the city to redevelop the West
End. Boston is a poor city, and the departure of middle-class residents and industry for the suburbs has left it with an over-supply
of tax-exempt institutions and low income areas that yield little
for the municipal coffers. Through the federal redevelopment
program, the city fathers hoped to replace some of the low-yield
areas with high-rent buildings that would bring in additional
municipal income. Moreover, they believed that a shiny new redevelopment project would cleanse its aged, tenement-dominated
skyline, and increase the morale of private and public investors.
This in turn would supposedly lead to a spiral of further private
rebuilding in the city.

The West End was thought to be particularly suitable for redevelopment. Because of its central location adjacent to Beacon

6. For a more detailed chronology of the project's history, see Robert Hanron, "West End Project Could Be Spark to Revitalize Boston," *Boston Sunday
Globe*, December 20, 1959, p. 14A.

Hill and near the downtown shopping area, real estate men had long felt that the area was "ripe" for higher—and more profitable —uses. The long block fronting on the Charles River was considered attractive for luxury housing. Some businessmen believed that the decline of the downtown shopping district could be ended by housing "quality shoppers" on its fringes. Moreover, Massachusetts General Hospital was expanding rapidly, and its trustees had long been unhappy about being surrounded by low-income neighbors.

The process of buying and clearing land and relocating residents, however, is expensive. Indeed, no redevelopment project of any scale is likely to be approved unless there are definite assurances that the cleared land will be purchased by a builder. Moreover, Boston had already had an unfortunate experience with its first redevelopment scheme: the "New York streets" project, planned for industrial re-use, which had stood virtually empty for several years after it had been cleared. But because of the West End's favorable location, developers and investors displayed interest from the beginning in making the area a high-rent district.

Political considerations also had to be taken into account, for the project had to be approved by the City Council and the Mayor. Here, too, all the signs were promising. The business community and the city's newspapers were favorably inclined, as were the political leaders of the city outside the West End. And even the West End protest seemed muted. Some years earlier, when it had been proposed to clear the North End, the citizens and the political leaders of that area had raised such an outcry that the project was immediately shelved. But the local politicians in the West End were too few and too powerless for their protests to be heeded. Nor could the West Enders themselves make their voices heard. The Save the West Committee's protest was noted, but as the group's membership was small, and since the Beacon Hill civic leader who supported it was known for his sponsorship of unpopular—and strange—causes, the Committee, in effect, had no political influence. Moreover, the local settlement houses and other caretaking agencies all approved of the redevelopment, partly because their lay leaders were drawn from the Boston business community, and partly because the staffs of these agencies felt that the fortunes of the West Enders would be thereby improved. The Catholic Archdiocese, whose local church was to be saved for architectural reasons, also gave its blessing. Consequently, both the Mayor and the City Council voted for the project, the latter almost unanimously.

Finally, all of Boston was convinced that the West End was a slum which ought to be torn down not only for the sake of the city but also for the good of its own residents. This belief was supported by the general appearance of the area, by studies that had been made in the West End by public and private agencies, and by stories that appeared in the press. In 1957, for example, a popular Boston columnist could wildly exaggerate both past and present conditions in the area to claim that:

> The West End is today definitely a slum area. In fact it has always been. . . . It gradually degenerated into a rooming-house section and then went from bad to worse. . . . Around the turn of the century . . . every conceivable sort of vice that makes for a slum flourished. . . . That was nearly sixty years ago. Any change since has slowly slid towards the worse.[7]

After calling the area a cesspool, he urged his readers to "come back in ten years, and you won't know the reborn city." [8]

Once the relevant agencies had given their blessings, the redevelopment officials went into action, using the procedures they had established in the city's first redevelopment project, and the guides and requirements set up by the federal government. When the site office had been established, the Authority then carried out appraisals to determine the prices to be paid the owners of structures, and a relocation survey to aid in the resettlement of the tenants. After the Authority had taken over the land under eminent domain, it also became responsible for the supervision and maintenance of the buildings, and for the collection of rents. In accordance with federal law, it made plans to assure that every West Ender would be relocated into a "decent, safe, and sanitary" dwelling unit elsewhere; in public housing, should the family's income make it

7. Bill Cunningham, "Two Projects to Alter Boston," *Boston Herald*, November 17, 1957. Compare the brief history of the area in Chapter 1.
8. *Ibid.*

eligible; or in other apartments that West Enders could find either on their own, or with the help of the Authority were they not eligible for public housing. If tenants paid their rent while in the West End, they received a moving allowance of $25 per room of furniture once they had moved. Should the unit to which they moved fail to meet the triple criterion of standardness, the Authority promised to find them another place in which to live. In these activities and others, the Authority staff believed itself to be acting in the best interests of the city and of the West Enders as well.[9]

The West Enders' Perception
of the Redevelopment Process

To the West Enders, the many years between the announcement that the area would be redeveloped and the actual clearing of their neighborhood appeared quite differently than it did to the city and its officials. No one with whom I talked was quite sure when the West Enders had first heard about the plans for redeveloping their neighborhood. The Planning Board's recommendation in 1949 had been made public, of course, and the press had also carried stories of the preliminary planning studies that had begun in 1951. At that time, the residents were opposed to the redevelopment, but did not feel themselves sufficiently threatened to be alarmed.

The initial announcement, however, did have some more important consequences. During the postwar era, the West End—like most other inner city districts—had begun to lose some of its recently married couples to the suburbs. The announcement itself undoubtedly spurred additional moves, and it seems also to have discouraged other people from moving into the West End. Whatever the causes, the vacancy rate in the area began to climb, especially in buildings owned by absentee landlords, who then began to have a change of heart about the redevelopment. Eventually, in fact, they became its most fervent adherents, and in later years urged the city and federal government to hasten the process, since they were losing money on vacant apartments that they could no longer rent.

9. These activities are discussed in detail in the next chapter.

Tenants, and resident owners whose buildings were still occupied, were almost unanimously opposed to the redevelopment. Some of the tenants in the most dilapidated structures were hopeful that government action would provide them with better places to live. But the vast majority of West Enders had no desire to leave. As I have tried to show throughout the book, they were content to live in the West End, and were willing to overlook some of its physical defects in comparison with its many social advantages. Those who had been born there cited the traditional belief that "the place you're born is where you want to die." Even criticism of the area would sometimes be stilled by the remark, "never disparage a place in which you've grown up." Many of the people who had left the West End at marriage would come back occasionally—if only to shop—and one man whose family had left the area shortly after his birth twenty years earlier insisted that "you always come back to the place of your childhood."

Most people were not very explicit at that time about their feelings toward the area. Since the West End still existed, and since they had never known anything else, they could not estimate how its disappearance might affect them.[10] "What's so good about the West End? We're used to it," was one quite typical comment. Subsequently, however, I heard more anguished remarks that indicated how important the area and its people were to the speaker. In December, 1957, the day after the federal government gave the city the go-ahead, one young Italian man said:

> I wish the world would end tonight. . . . I wish they'd tear the whole damn town down, damn scab town. . . . I'm going to be lost without the West End. Where the hell can I go?

Another West Ender told me: "It isn't right to scatter the community to all four winds. It pulls the heart out of a guy to lose all his friends." Shortly before the taking, a barber in his early sixties

10. For a more detailed discussion of the West Enders' reactions, see Marc Fried and Peggy Gleicher, "Some Sources of Residential Satisfaction in an Urban 'Slum,'" *Journal of the American Institute of Planners*, vol. 27 (1961), pp. 305–315; and Marc Fried, "Grieving for a Lost Home," in Leonard J. Duhl, ed., *The Environment of the Metropolis* (tentative title), New York: Basic Books, forthcoming.

ended a discussion of death that was going on in the shop with
these comments:

> I'm not afraid to die, but I don't want to. But if they tear the
> West End down and we are all scattered from all the people I
> know and that know me, and they wouldn't know where I was,
> I wouldn't want to die and people not know it.[11]

Perhaps because most people were opposed to the redevelopment, they could not quite believe that it would happen. Over the
years, they began to realize that the redevelopment plans were in
earnest, but they were—and remained—skeptical that the plans
would ever be implemented. Even on the day of the taking, the
person just quoted told me: "I don't believe it; I won't believe it
till it happens. I'll wait till I get my notice. . . . You'll see, they'll
start at the lower end, and they'll never come up here."

There were several reasons for the West Enders' skepticism.
First, they had considerable difficulty in understanding the complicated parade of preliminary and final approvals, or the tortuous
process by which the plans moved back and forth between the Housing Authority, the City Council, the Mayor, the State Housing Board,
and the federal Housing and Home Finance Agency. Instead of
realizing that each approval was one step in a tested and finite
administrative precedure, the West Enders saw it as merely another
decision in a seemingly purposeless, erratic, and infinite series. Thus,
when the federal housing agency did give its final approval in
the winter of 1957, most West Enders did not understand that this
was the last step in the process. They recalled that the same agency
had approved it several times before, without any visible result.
Thus, they felt certain that there would be more meetings, and more
decisions, and that twenty-five years later, the West End would still
be there.

Their failure to understand the process can be traced back
partly to the poor information that they received from the press

11. I should note that I have selected the most demonstrative comments of
the many I heard about the destruction of the area. That they are not atypical
is supported by findings—and even more poignant statements—reported in
Fried, "Grieving for a Lost Home," *op. cit.*

and the city agencies. The latter, assuming that West Enders understood the nature of the process, did not attempt to describe it in sufficient detail. Moreover, city officials did not see that to West Enders, all government agencies were pretty much the same, and that notions of city-state-federal relationships were strange to them. The West Enders in turn paid little attention to the press releases, and were more receptive to distorted facts and the many rumors that they could hear from friends and neighbors.

Moreover, they noted that official announcements were vague about when things would begin to happen in the West End, and that if estimates were given, they were usually wrong. In January, 1956, for example, the Housing Authority's pamphlet pointed out that it was impossible to predict when the various agencies involved would give their approval, but that it might happen within eight months, and that relocation would begin in the winter of 1956–1957.[12] This estimate turned out to be false.

Nor could West Enders really conceive of the possibility that the area would be torn down. They had watched the demolition of parts of the North End for the Central Artery—the city's expressway system—and while they disapproved, they realized that a highway was of public benefit and could not be opposed. But the idea that the city could clear the West End, and then turn the land over to a private builder for luxury apartments seemed unbelievable.

Their skepticism turned to incredulity when the city awarded the redevelopment contract to the second highest bidder. The lawyer's ties with the Mayor convinced them that the redevelopment was a politically motivated plot to take the West End for private profit with government help. The idea that a private builder could build apartments then estimated to rent for $40 to $50 a room— more than they were paying for five- and six-room apartments— was hard to believe. And that the government could encourage this venture seemed incomprehensible except as a result of political corruption, the exchange of bribes, and the cutting in of politicians on future profits.[13] As one West Ender among many pointed out:

12. Boston Housing Authority, "West End Progress Report," Boston: The Authority, January, 1956, p. 1.

13. I heard from several disparate sources that one of the city councilors had asked for a sizable "campaign contribution" in exchange for a favorable

The whole thing is a steal, taking the area away from the people, and giving it to some guys who had paid off everyone else. . . . It is just someone making money at our expense. There are many areas lots worse than this one. Look at [the Mayor], a city clerk once, and now he's rich enough to buy up Boston itself. Yes, just a city clerk and look at him now.

Thereafter, all of the steps in the process were interpreted as attempts to scare the West Enders out of the area, so that the values of the buildings would be reduced and the private developers could buy them more cheaply. But even then, people were skeptical that this scheme would come to fruition, partially because it was so immoral. Many West Enders argued that only in Russia could the government deprive citizens of their property in such a dictatorial manner.

Also, West Enders found it hard to think far ahead. Even if they could admit to themselves that the area might eventually be "thrown down"—as they put it—it was still difficult to think about what might happen years hence, especially in the absence of incontrovertible evidence. As already noted, Housing Authority announcements were not considered reliable. Nor were announcements and newspaper stories generally accepted as evidence; people had to see more concrete examples of the city's plans before they would believe that the city was in earnest. For example, the registered letters, which the Redevelopment Authority sent to all West Enders indicating that it had taken over the area, were less persuasive than the announcement that as of May, 1958, rents were to be paid not to landlords but to the city's relocation office. Only when people saw their neighbors—and especially their landlords—going to that office to pay their rents did all of them realize that the end had come. Conversely, a few weeks earlier, when the announcement of the taking was imminent, West Enders were much cheered by the city's repaving of streets immediately outside the project area and by the gas company's installation of more modern gas meters in West End apartments. These were concrete actions that could be taken as evidence, especially since they seemed to

---

vote on the redevelopment. Since his vote was not needed, he did not get the money. Eventually, he voted for it anyway.

prove what West Enders wanted to believe—that nothing was going to happen—and were considered much more reliable than official announcements or news stories.[14] And finally, of course, West Enders simply denied the possibility of redevelopment because they did not want it to happen. They were content to live in the West End, and could not imagine living elsewhere, or going about the city looking for "rooms."

As a result, life in the West End went on as always, with relatively little overt concern about the redevelopment, and with even less public discussion of it. On the days following the announcement of another decision in the process, people would talk about it heatedly, but then it would be forgotten again until the next announcement. There had been so many announcements, and so many meetings, and nothing ever seemed to happen afterwards. Surely it would be safe—and easy—to assume that nothing would ever happen.

As a result of this attitude, the oncoming redevelopment had little impact on the lives of most West Enders until the very end. The daily routine continued as before, the evenings were given over to peer group life, and holidays were celebrated as always. Some gradual changes could be noticed by the more observant. For example, landlords had been advised early in the decade not to make extensive repairs, and this increased the friction between them and their tenants when something went wrong in the building. People also noticed that, over the years, vacant apartments did not fill up again, or that they were rented to people who had not been seen previously in the West End: Gypsies, newcomers to the city, and people from the South End—the city's most transient district. And the local parish began to cut down on its school operations—admitting new students only to the first grade.

14. These feelings even affected me. Although I knew enough about redevelopment procedures to realize that the process was moving toward its inevitable climax, I was opposed to the redevelopment, and hoped it would not take place. Since I was not in touch with city officials, occasionally I would begin to share the West Enders' beliefs that "our children will still be here when they break it up," and wondered whether the rumors that the project had collapsed might not be true. It is thus understandable that West Enders, who knew much less about the process, and could not call city officials to get the facts, would hold these beliefs more stubbornly.

But all this had no major impact on the long-term residents of the area. Community organizations, such as the Holy Name Society, continued to function as before.

Only the merchants and the caretakers were directly affected. As empty apartments were not rerented, storekeepers, whose total receipts were never large, began to find their incomes shrinking even further, and some of them closed down. Even so, I would estimate that only about 10 per cent ceased operations in the year before the onset of relocation. And there were always rumors that some would reopen soon.

The caretaking agencies knew, of course, that the area would be redeveloped, and were not in doubt over the outcome of the long process. This knowledge, the gradual reduction in the number of their clients, and the appearance of some of the lower-class new-comers, sapped their morale. For although most of the agencies and their staffs were in favor of the redevelopment, they were also sorry to see the neighborhood torn down, and its residents dispersed. They did not voice their feelings in public, but at the annual board meeting of one of the settlement houses, the staff put on a skit about the redevelopment which reflected its ambivalence toward the destruction of the West End. The caretakers also tried, with little success, to prepare the West Enders for what was about to happen.[15] Some of them urged the redevelopment agency to improve its relocation procedures, but by then it was too late.

The best illustration of the lack of impact of the redevelopment process on the West Enders was the failure of the Save the West End Committee to attract their overt support, and the absence of other forms of protest. As noted earlier, the Committee came into being in 1956, when a handful of West Enders met with a local civic and political leader who had long been interested in the West End. An upper-class Bostonian whose family and forebears had been active in caretaking projects in the area since the turn of the century, he helped to build the park, pool, and boating area along the banks of the Charles River and had participated in other improvement projects since the 1930's.[16] He felt that the West End

15. For some examples, see Chapter 7.
16. His father had been a founder of the public playground movement in America; and his relatives, who included all of the famous names of Boston's

was not a slum and also argued that the city had no right to take private property—especially that of poor people—for luxury apartment buildings. He promised to support the group politically and financially, and, with his help, the Committee rented a vacant store in the area. Over the years, it held a number of meetings, spoke at public hearings, published pamphlets and leaflets, went to Washington to try to overturn the decision, and eventually took its case to the courts. The Committee sought of course to enroll the neighborhood in its work, but attracted only a small—although loyal—group of members, who kept up a steady barrage of protest over the years. Not until the very end, however, did they gain a wider audience.

One of the major obstacles to the Committee's effectiveness in its own neighborhood was its outside leadership. Although many West Enders had heard of the civic leader who helped to guide the Committee, they knew also that he lived outside the area, and that however strong his sympathy, he was in class, ethnic background, and culture not one of their own. Nor was he at ease among the West Enders. While he identified with the neighborhood, he often seemed to feel more strongly about the facilities on the River bank —which were of little interest to the West Enders—than about the tenement streets and their occupants.

Moreover, the other active members—and the people who originally asked for his guidance—were neither typical West Enders, nor the kinds of people who could enroll them. Among the most active were an Italian writer and an artist, a young Jewish professional, a single Polish woman, and a number of elderly ladies who lived in the Charlesbank Homes. While some of them did have leadership ability, almost all of them were in one way or another marginal to their own ethnic groups in the West End. Thus, they could not attract these groups to their cause.

This inability had nothing to do with the Committee's point of view, for that was based on the beliefs shared widely by a majority of the West Enders: That the redevelopment was motivated by political chicanery and individual greed; that government actions

aristocracy, had helped to build the West End settlement houses. They also supported the charities and social welfare agencies that served the area and the larger community.

to scare the West Enders into leaving stemmed from sympathy or collusion with the builders; and that until definite proof was available, there was no reason to believe the West End would actually be torn down.

The Committee, however, did not develop a program that would require West Enders as a whole to take action. Its pamphlets and speeches expressed the same indignation and incredulity felt by all, but it did not ask them to act, other than to come to meetings, help the Committee in its mailings, and stay in the West End.

Yet all of these considerations for the Committee's lack of success in gaining active neighborhood support paled before the most important one: the inability of the West Enders to organize in their own behalf. Indeed, other causes were only effects of that basic inability. Had the West Enders flocked to meetings in larger numbers, the leadership would probably have gone to someone whom the residents would have followed. As it was, they watched the activities of the Committee with passive sympathy. Some were suspicious: they argued that the Committee consisted of people who had been left out when the graft was distributed; that the leadership was Communist; and that a Jewish officer of the Committee was related to one of the developers. The majority, however, did agree with all that the Committee claimed, and shared its anger. But even then they could not break out of the peer group society, and organize in common cause. It was impossible to fight city hall; this was a function of the local politician. If he failed, what else was there to do? Action-seeking West Enders would have relished a march on City Hall to do violence to the officials principally associated with the redevelopment, but the act of joining with neighbors to work together for halting the redevelopment was inconceivable. At the meetings at which West Enders spoke, they spoke as individuals, about their own individual cases. The local politicians who appeared at these meetings spoke *to* the West Enders rather than *for* them; they convinced the audience of their own opposition to the redevelopment, and tried to display themselves as loyal representatives of the West End. But they too were unable —and perhaps unwilling—to organize an effective protest movement.

Even the resident leaders of the Committee—notably those of

Italian background—were ill-at-ease about guiding a protest group which called for citizen participation. They realized that their Beacon Hill supporter could not attract the West Enders, but they were also skeptical as to their own ability to rally them. In addition, they were ambivalent about their personal involvement. They were able to make speeches, and to share their anger with an audience, but other activities came less easily. Being a leader without any proof of results, spending time away from family and friends, or from second jobs and other individual pursuits was difficult. When Committee members were asked to carry out the routine tasks of organization, and failed to come through—as was often the case—the leaders who gave the orders resented having to carry out these tasks themselves. They were hurt that they should give up their own free time, and extend themselves for the group if no one else did, and if there was no reward for such self-deprivation. Thus, the Committee itself was constantly split by bickering, by people withdrawing from activity when no support was forthcoming, and by individuals offering new solutions and making speeches to each other when more prosaic activity was called for.

The leaders were also hampered by lack of information. The politicians claimed—with some justification—that since they were opposed to the project, they had not been kept properly informed by redevelopment officials. Also, they and the leaders of the Committee were unable to deal properly with what information was available. Like most other West Enders, they believed that the project's fate was in the hand of one individual, the Mayor, and that it could be overturned simply by persuading him of its immorality. As unable as the rest of the West Enders to follow the series of steps that led to the final taking of the land, some of them believed until the last moment that the redevelopment would never take place. They accepted the rumors that swept the area like everyone else, and could not detach themselves sufficiently from their neighbors to look objectively at the doings of the outside world. Thus, none of the prerequisites or minutiae of organizational activity came easily to the Committee leaders. Much of the time, only their anger at the outrage they felt was being perpetrated against themselves and their neighbors kept them going.

The truth was, that for a group unaccustomed to organizational activity, saving the West End was an overwhelming, and perhaps impossible, task. Indeed, there was relatively little the Committee could do. The decision to redevelop the West End had been made early in the decade, and it had received the blessings of the city's decisive business leaders and politicians. The West End's local politicians all opposed the redevelopment, but were powerless against the unanimity of those who favored it. As noted in Chapter 8, the election of city councilors at large rather than by wards since 1951 had reduced the influence of individual districts. Smaller areas, with few voters, were especially hard hit; and the West End, which was losing population at this time, was virtually disenfranchised. Nor did the West End have other attributes of power such as those displayed by the neighboring North End, which had successfully repulsed efforts toward its own redevelopment. This area had a larger population and a much larger business community—some of it politically influential. Most important, the North End was the center—and symbol—of Italian life in Boston. Its destruction thus would have been a threat—or at least an insult— to every Italian voter in Boston, and the city's politicians simply could not afford to alienate this increasingly influential vote. Conversely, although the Italians were also the largest group in the West End, they were not in the majority. And since they had attained a plurality only comparatively recently, the area had never really been considered an Italian neighborhood. Thus, it is doubtful whether even a unanimous turnout in opposition by the West Enders would have been sufficient to set in motion the difficult process of reversing years of work by local and federal agencies, and giving up the large federal grant that financed the clearance of the area.

The Coming of Redevelopment:
The Last Days of the West End

With every decision, the more knowing West Enders began to realize that the days of the area were numbered. When the state gave its approval in October, 1957, and the federal government signed the final contracts in January, 1958, the die was cast. Even then, many West Enders were still not sure that these steps would lead to action. Conflicting signs appeared to confuse those who were looking for concrete evidence. Surveyors were sent by the city to map the area, but as noted before, the repaving of streets leading into the project area gave some people hope that another decision would soon be forthcoming which would spare the neighborhood. Other surveyors came to interview the residents, to find out where they wished to be relocated, and how much rent they could afford. Some people refused to answer; a few threw out the interviewers; but the majority answered, and then discounted the significance of the questionnaire.

Thus, in the spring of 1958, life went on pretty much as before. There were fewer businesses than had started the winter, and others were threatening to shut. A barber, who had closed his shop at the age of eighty-four, died shortly afterwards, and many people felt his death had been caused by the redevelopment "scare." But otherwise, the routine prevailed. Housewives prepared for Passover or Easter, and gave their apartments the traditional spring cleaning.

On April 22, 1958, stories began to appear in the city papers that letters would be sent to the West Enders any day, announcing the taking of the land and the beginning of redevelopment. Only the week before, one of my neighbors had insisted, "They're still arguing about something; it might be five years yet." Another was thinking that nothing at all might happen, and that he would find a first-floor apartment in the area, and fix it up properly. Even the newspaper stories had relatively little impact. Many people did not read the papers regularly, and heard about it from neighbors. "It's just another attempt to scare us," said one; "I'm not frightened by the article, we'll wait till we see something." One of the local politicians was among those not yet convinced.

On April 25, all West Enders received registered letters from the Redevelopment Authority announcing the taking, explaining that rent was to be paid to the city from now on, and pointing out the procedures involved in relocation. But as the letters were written in the traditionally formal language of official agencies, I doubt seriously that many West Enders read them through to the end. There could be no doubt now, however, that the West End was coming down. Even so, the real impact of the decision did not come until about a week later, when the May rent payments were due

at the relocation office. The idea of no longer paying rent to the
landlord and of taking it to a city office was the concrete evidence
West Enders needed to accept the redevelopment of their neighborhood.

The first reaction was a feeling of relief that the suspense was
over, and that hopes would no longer be raised or lowered by contradictory evidence. For some people, the news was a real shock.
But most West Enders were not overly excited. They now accepted
what they had known or suspected all along, and what they should
have realized earlier. For many years, they had considered the
possibility of the neighborhood's destruction, and even if they had
rejected the idea each time, the periodic reappearance of the threat
had left a residue of belief. What they had denied so fervently
before they could now accept more easily.

The shock was softened by other conditions. One was the in-
evitability of the event. "Underneath we are all upset, but what
can we do?" asked one West Ender. Another mitigating factor was
the traditional resignation toward the behavior of the outside
world. As West Enders had always expected the worst from this
world, the redevelopment was just another in a long series of
deprivations and outrages. Also, the inability to look ahead helped
to hide some of the hard times West Enders would soon be facing.
Indeed, they neither thought much about moving, nor where they
would go. Since the city had estimated that relocation would take
three years, some felt they could remain in the West End for a
considerable time yet.

Finally, there were many who still did not accept the facts, and
looked for even more concrete evidence. As one lady put it, "We
won't believe it until we see something; we'll find out when something happens." Others found solace in the belief that the taking
was illegal, since the city could not charge rent under eminent
domain, and since they had not paid the landlords for their property when they took it.[17] One of my neighbors argued that there
had been no taking: "They didn't even give the landlords a dollar.

17. This belief was based on facts. Under state law, the city could not
charge rents in areas taken by eminent domain. Since federal regulations required that cities collect rents, however, the city had to find a way of accom-
modating itself to conflicting directives. It did so by requiring West Enders
to pay for "use and occupancy."

I won't believe it until I see something come down." Another neighbor pointed out that the only people who had started to move were nurses and transient middle-class residents in the area; the real West Enders were staying put.

The notices also drew people closer together, and offered them some opportunity for feelings of revenge against the landlords. A Holy Name picnic, which took place as scheduled two days after the notices came, attracted an overflow crowd. A few days later, one of my neighbors remarked, "Everyone is more friendly, like old times: why couldn't it be like that before?" Tenants who felt that they had been mistreated by their landlords were glad that the latter would now be paying rent like everyone else. Some landlords raised the rents that relatives were paying, at the last moment, in the hope of increasing the value of their buildings, and other tenants were pleased at the discomfort this caused. There was some feeling of relief that one no longer needed to be polite to landlords. As one neighbor said, "Now we can have some parties; we don't have to worry about the landlord anymore." But tenants also felt sorry for the "good" landlords and the resident owners, whose properties had been taken by the city without immediate payment.

Since the city had now become the landlord, and promised to keep the buildings in good condition, some West Enders thus made demands on the city to make those repairs which landlords had neglected. The demands were motivated partly by revenge, and partially by the belief that if the area was indeed a slum, the city ought to do something about it. The people who were angriest sought more direct forms of revenge, and found it by withholding rent payments. After the first week in May, only half the people had paid their rent to the city. At the end of the year, however, the relocation office reported that only about 150 households had actually withheld rent monies for any length of time.

In the weeks immediately following the taking, the area's anger caused the Save the West End Committee to experience an energetic but short-lived renaissance. Right after the announcement, the Committee scheduled a mother's march on City Hall, a form of protest which had worked well for the West End some decades earlier, when the neighborhood had still been predominantly

Jewish. But as no one except the leaders of the march appeared at the appointed time, it had to be cancelled. One of the Italian men explained that they would not allow their women to take part in such forms of public display.

Then, in the week after the taking, the Committee underwent a change of leadership. A young Jewish student, who had been an inactive member of the group, suddenly became interested following the announcement—spurred on considerably by the anger of his family which had now lost its store and livelihood. Since the Committee's original area leaders had lost hope, he was asked if he wanted to take over. Thereupon, he formulated an eleven-point program which included an appeal not to pay rent, and not to move out; a march on City Hall to see the Mayor; and a scheme for rehabilitating the area with the monies being paid to the city as rents. A public meeting was called for May 5, about ten days after the taking, and over two hundred people—the largest crowd ever to attend a Committee meeting—showed up. They listened enthusiastically to an area politician urge the people not to move, and somewhat less so to the student's eleven-point program. But for some, the meeting restored the hope that the area might still be spared.

This hope—fantastic as it seemed—was based on the previously mentioned assumption that the redevelopment had been planned and executed by the Mayor, and that if he could be persuaded to change his mind, the West End might be saved. Immediately after the meeting, however, plans for implementing the program foundered over the question of how to persuade the Mayor. The philosophy student, a pacifist, and a follower of Gandhi's principles of civil disobedience, urged people to be kind and loving to their enemies, and to persuade the Mayor through nonviolent methods. Even at the public meeting, this proposal had been received with grumbling. At a long strategy session afterwards, the old leaders of the Committee, and some other West Enders who had stayed behind—all Italians—disagreed strongly. "The Mayor is a thief," they said, "and how can you trust a thief or respect him?" Some suggested a one-hundred-car caravan to City Hall that would threaten the Mayor with violence if he did not call off the redevelopment.

Since the student would not agree to demonstrations of violence, and since the others refused to follow his approach, the Committee was virtually stymied. Nevertheless, another meeting was called for the following week, and notices were posted in the West End proclaiming that there was still hope:

> For five years, and once in every three months, they have been announcing, in big headlines, that the West End would fall and that we would be cast forth from our homes before the dawn of another season. These were lies, for we're still here, and we're not moving. . . .

Again the meeting drew over two hundred people, but the local politician who had been the main speaker the week before did not come as he had promised, and the West Enders felt that they had been deserted. Again, they did not respond to the student's appeal for a Gandhian approach, and by now it was evident that he would not be accepted as a leader. Moreover, the laws about incitement to riot made it impossible for any of the speakers to urge non-payment of rent, leaving West Enders no other way of expressing their anger. At one point in the meeting, the teenagers, who made up about 15 per cent of the crowd, heckled the speakers both for not resorting to violence, and for trying to fight city hall. They were soon quieted by some of their elders, but it was clear that the situation was hopeless. Although another meeting was held the subsequent week, the audience was smaller, and by the end of the month, people began to think about moving.

As buildings began to empty, the remaining tenants were loath to remain in them, and even those who had planned to stay to the bitter end began to leave. People were afraid of being alone, of being the last in the house and thus isolated from the group. Then, unknown teenagers began to roam through semi-deserted buildings, using them for nocturnal parties, setting fires, and vandalizing wherever they could.[18] The families still remaining in these build-

18. Some of the adolescent vandalism pleased the West Enders. The night after the wrecking equipment first arrived in the area, it was seriously damaged by angry teenagers—or at least they were said to be responsible—and thereafter the equipment had to be guarded around the clock.

ings became fearful and moved more quickly than they had intended. The empty structures were torn down as soon as the last tenant left, and the resulting noise and dirt encouraged people in adjacent buildings to move also. Consequently, the West End was emptied in little more than eighteen months after the official taking of the land.

Although federal regulations require that relocated tenants be helped in finding apartments, most of the people moved themselves without calling on the agency's help. In November, 1958, a redevelopment agency official estimated that of the first 1200 households, probably no more than 150 to 200 had been relocated by the agency.[19] The people who had thought for years about buying a house did so, and the rest turned to relatives and friends in other districts for help in finding a place. As a result, many of the Italians went to other Italian neighborhoods, in Somerville, Everett, East Cambridge, and Medford, which were located just outside Boston's city limits. There they moved into old areas similar to the West End—some slated for eventual redevelopment at that time—and one frequently heard that one or another neighborhood was just like the West End, although people would add quickly that it was not really so.

I was told that before the West End was totally cleared—and even afterwards—West Enders would come back on weekends to walk through the old neighborhood and the rubble-strewn streets. The last time I saw the area, it had been completely leveled except for the buildings that had been marked for preservation. A museum of Yankee artifacts and the library—now closed—remained at one corner, the Hospital at another. The Catholic church—where services were still being held for parishioners living on the Back of Beacon Hill—stood in lonely isolation in the center of the cleared area. The Hospital had graded some of the adjacent property for temporary parking, and at a far corner, fronting on the river, the first of the new buildings were going up. The cleared area looked very tiny, and it was hard to imagine that more than 20,000 people had once lived there.

19. A similar reluctance to call on the official agency for help has been observed in many other redevelopment projects elsewhere.

CHAPTER 14 An Evaluation of the Redevelopment Plan and Process

Introduction

This chapter is an evaluation from a planning and more general social welfare perspective of the process described in the previous chapter. When I first began my research, I had not intended to evaluate the fate of the West End from these perspectives. In fact, my point of view developed as a result of the field work. Consequently, it is relevant to preface the evaluation by describing briefly how I reached my conclusions.

At the start of the study, I had not thought systematically about the pros and cons of redevelopment, or taken a position on any of its policies.[1] As my field work in the West End progressed, however, I began to develop that identification with the people, and sympathy for their problems which is experienced by many participant-observers.[2] Contact with planners in the Boston area ac-

1. Some years before, I had worked in a renewal agency, but my functions were such that I did not give much thought to the over-all program. The conclusions which I eventually reached about the West End, however, were influenced by many conversations about planning and redevelopment in earlier years with two old friends and colleagues, planners both: John Dyckman and Martin Meyerson.

2. For a further discussion of this process, see the Appendix.

quainted me with the problems of the city, and encouraged me to look at the West End from a planning perspective. Inevitably, then, I began to feel not only that the redevelopment decision itself was not entirely justifiable, but also that the planning being done for the West End did not take into account the needs of the residents who, among others, were supposed to benefit from slum clearance. My thinking on the issue was stimulated further by discussions among the research staff of the Center for Community Studies. Several of my colleagues believed the area to be a slum in need of redevelopment; some—especially those of us doing field work in the West End itself—took the opposite position, and I defended this point of view in a number of staff meetings.

My feelings regarding the redevelopment came to a head about three months after the beginning of field work. One day, I had attended, as an observer, a monthly meeting of West End settlement house staff members and other caretakers at which redevelopment agency officials explained the redevelopment process and the planning that had taken place for it. Appalled by the lack of planning for the West Enders, I felt, more than ever, that something ought to be done about it. Since the research project had been originally designed also to include service functions in the area of mental health, I thus circulated a memorandum on the topic. In it, I took the position that were the West Enders' mental health to be served, the project's service function might best be accomplished by action to correct the redevelopment planning. My proposal was not feasible, however, since the Center staff was too small to undertake any kind of service activity.

In the weeks that followed, I found it difficult to keep my ideas to myself, and, in the course of my field work, talked about them to West Enders.[3] I had come to know the leaders of the Save the

3. Under some conditions, such talk might bias the results of participant-observation research. Since almost all West Enders were opposed to the renewal project long before I came on the scene, the research results were not affected. Indeed, once I had made my position clear, a number of people who previously refused to talk to me changed their minds, and made my research task easier. I should explain that at the start of the Center for Community Studies' work, the Center was regarded by some as a front for the Housing Authority. For a while, the research project thus served as a scapegoat for the redevelopment, and a substitute target for the West Enders' hostility to it. As a participant-

West End Committee, and they urged me to publish a critique of the redevelopment process. For a month or so, I was torn between my research role and my desire to correct what I felt to be a prime example of social injustice as well as poor planning. At one point, I even considered resigning from the research project, and joining the Committee. Eventually, I decided to forego any attempt at individual action, feeling that since I was not myself a West Ender, I really had no right to take what would probably have been a leading position in the fight. More important, I believed that it was too late to halt the redevelopment process in the West End, and that my activities might endanger the Center's research project. For while the results of this study could not help the West Enders, they could later contribute more to correcting the abuses of redevelopment on a nation-wide scale than would my desire to act have helped the West Enders. Consequently, I stuck to my research role until the end of my field work, when, through the help of a Harvard colleague, I obtained an interview with one of the Redevelopment Authority commissioners. He listened to my critique of the redevelopment process, and then asked that I write a memorandum detailing my proposals for changing it. This I wrote at once, drawing on the earlier paper I had circulated among the Center staff, but disassociating it from my opinions. The paper listed a number of policies which could still be instituted to improve the relocation process and to reduce the injustice which would soon be meted out to the West Enders. The proposals contradicted much of the then existing program, but they were feasible. They could have been implemented, however, only by someone passionately concerned with the West Enders, and ready to spend a considerable amount of time, energy, and political influence to change the scheduled procedures.

The memorandum was never acknowledged. Later that summer—after I had returned to the University of Pennsylvania—I was urged to publish it. The rest of this chapter is an expanded revision of this publication.[4]

---

observer, I was spared from this scapegoating, and the practice subsided before the Center began its interviewing program.

4. It appeared as "The Human Implications of Current Redevelopment and Relocation Planning," *Journal of the American Institute of Planners*, vol. 25

The planning analysis considers three questions: whether or not the West End was in fact a slum; the benefits and costs of the redevelopment for the individuals and institutions affected by it; and the quality of the redevelopment and relocation planning. Some recommendations for urban renewal generally are appended.

The West End: Slum or Low-Rent District

The term "slum" is an evaluative, not an analytic, concept. Consequently, any definition of the term must be related, explicitly or implicitly, to the standards of the age, and more important, to the renewal policy in which it is used. Current definitions of the term include two criteria—the social image of the area, and its physical condition. Federal standards for determining whether an area is eligible for renewal funds are based almost entirely on the latter. It is the local agency, however, that selects the area to be proposed for action; and, in most communities, the area's physical condition is a necessary but not sufficient criterion. What seems to happen is that neighborhoods come to be described as slums if they are inhabited by residents who, for a variety of reasons, indulge in overt and visible behavior considered undesirable by the majority of the community. The community image of the area then gives rise to feelings that something should be done, and subsequently the area is proposed for renewal. Consequently, the planning reports that are written to justify renewal dwell as much on social as on physical criteria, and are filled with data intended to show the prevalence of antisocial or pathological behavior in the area. The implication is that the area itself causes such behavior, and should therefore be redeveloped.

Usually, the physical condition of the area is such that it is eligible for renewal. Conversely, there are areas, such as Boston's North End, which meet physical criteria, but which are socially and politically strong enough to discourage any official or politician

---

(1959), pp. 15–25. Since it was written, a number of the more advanced cities have stressed rehabilitation rather than clearance in their urban renewal programs, Boston included. At this writing (January, 1962), the new emphasis is still to be tested in practice, but I have taken account of it in the revision of my earlier article.

from suggesting them for clearance or large-scale rehabilitation.

The federal and local housing standards which are applied to slum areas reflect the value pattern of upper-middle-class professionals. These professionals, like the rest of the middle class, allot a higher value to housing (as measured by percentage of income to be spent for shelter), and place greater emphasis on the status functions of housing than does the working class. Also, the signs of housing status used by the two classes differ. In addition, the professionals' evaluation of the behavior of slum residents is based on class-based standards that often confuse behavior which is only culturally different with pathological or antisocial acts.

Generally speaking, these standards are desirable bases for public policy, despite their class bias; and many of them should be applied to the poorer areas of the city—*were they followed by a program which provided the residents of these areas with better housing*. Presently, however, these standards are used to tear down poor neighborhoods, while better housing for the residents is not made available.

Consequently, unless urban renewal policy is drastically altered, other definitions of the slum should be developed. Existing physical standards so far have failed to make a distinction between *low-rent* and *slum* housing, or low-rent and slum districts, community facilities, street patterns, and the like. This distinction, however, is an important one. Residential structures—and districts—should be defined as slums only if they have been proven to be physically, socially, or emotionally *harmful* to their residents or to the larger community. Low-rent structures and districts may be distinguished from slums by the fact that they provide shelter that may be *inconvenient* but that is not harmful. Slums should be eliminated, but low-rent structures must be maintained—at least in the absence of better housing—for people who want, or for economic reasons must maintain, low rental payments and who are willing to accept high density, lack of modernity, and other inconveniences as alternative costs.

Buildings that are structurally unsound, for example, are clearly harmful to their residents. So are dwelling units infested by rats. Five-story tenements, however, cannot be considered harmful—except for old people who cannot climb stairs. Nevertheless, such structures are usually described as obsolescent by planners and housing officials, and obsolescence in turn is a major criterion for defining a building as a slum. But obsolescence per se is not harmful; the judgment is merely a reflection of middle-class standards—and middle-class incomes. Indeed, there is no talk of obsolescence when alley dwellings of an earlier vintage than tenement buildings are rehabilitated for high rentals, as in Washington's Georgetown district.

A set of parallel social standards is even more difficult to define, because most of the social problems found in slums cannot be traced to the area itself. Undoubtedly, some people live in slums because they have problems or unacceptable behavior patterns. But economic and social conditions, rather than the slum itself, have caused these. While the neighborhood environment may "infect" a few people previously without problems, this happens much less frequently than is commonly believed.[5] For purposes of definition, then, it is necessary to distinguish between undesirable behavior patterns which are related causally to the neighborhood and those which are not. Thus, for renewal purposes, a slum may also be defined as an area that, because of the nature of its social environment, can be proved to create problems and pathologies, either for the residents or for the larger community.

Should children be drawn into illegal activities, for example, and it can be *proved* that the neighborhood, rather than conditions of lower-class life, is responsible, that neighborhood might be called a slum. The same would apply if residential overcrowding inhibited privacy and led to intra- or interfamilial conflict. Overcrowding, however, is caused by socio-economic deprivations that force people to live under such conditions, rather than by the neighborhood or the dwellings themselves. Urban renewal policies that require such people to move without giving them the wherewithal or the housing to live under less crowded conditions thus do not solve the problem. It should be clear that absolute standards for determining whether a building or an area is harmful to its residents cannot be easily formulated. Some conditions are harmful to some types

5. Irving Rosow, "The Social Effects of the Physical Environment," *Journal of the American Institute of Planners,* vol. 27 (1961), pp. 127–133.

of occupants and not to others. Consequently, each area must be studied and evaluated individually. More important, while some conditions that are harmful can be eliminated by urban renewal, others cannot.

This critique of the conventional definition of slum can be applied to the West End. The planning study used to certify that the area was a slum concluded that:

> . . . the West End is in dire need of redevelopment because (1) the land is overcrowded with buildings served by narrow streets where housing is mixed in with marginal commercial uses; (2) the majority of the dwellings in the area are dilapidated and substandard: (3) the steadily declining population of the area suffers from high rates of such indices of bad environment as juvenile delinquency and tuberculosis; (4) the standard of school, community services, and play spaces is far below a desirable level.[6]

Each of these criteria deserves brief comment. There is no doubt that the area was overcrowded with buildings, and that some, though not all, of the streets were narrow. According to the report, buildings covered 72 per cent of the land. Overcrowding of buildings on the land must be distinguished, however, from overcrowding of people within buildings or apartments. Whereas the latter is harmful, the former is not, except that it may deprive some people of inadequate supplies of air and sunlight, and prevent fire engines and sanitation equipment from proper access. Although the first and second floors of many of the West End buildings did receive less air and sunlight than is desirable, there is as yet no proof that this was harmful to West Enders, for they spent much time outside. These apartments may have been harmful, however, to older people who could not get outside. I do not defend them as desirable, but I can understand why low-income West Enders preferred them at rentals of $30 or less to lighter and airier apartments elsewhere that would have cost $75 or more. While the

6. Boston Housing Authority, "The West End Project Report," Boston: The Authority, 1953, p. 1.

area's high land coverage was inconvenient for parking, it could not be considered harmful, except on those streets too narrow for fire engines and sanitation trucks.[7]

Partially because of the high land coverage, the West End had little playground space. Even so, the children made little use of a playground located in the center of the area, and preferred to play on the streets—where the excitement and action they valued was available—or on the paved yards surrounding one of the schools. Additional open space for baseball and one or two modern playgrounds would have been desirable, but these could have been supplied without tearing down the entire neighborhood.

Nor can the fact that housing was mixed with marginal commercial uses be considered harmful. As far as I could ascertain, none of the industrial firms created undesirable noise or smoke. More important from the West Enders' standpoint, they did provide employment to people in the area. Many of the small stores were economically marginal when compared to modern chain stores, but they served the West Enders, and were able to compete with a supermarket located on the edge of the neighborhood.

While the report is correct in noting that the population of the area had been declining steadily, this is no indication that the neighborhood was harmful to its residents. Much of the decline can be attributed to reduction in family size, which in turn increased the amount of space available for each family. Five- and six-room apartments that once had housed families with eight or ten children now provided comfortable living quarters for families with three or four children. Moreover, until the announcement that the area would be redeveloped, there were few vacant apartments. The decline in population and family size did leave the area with more school facilities than it needed, but this problem could have been solved by tearing down the oldest school buildings and creating play space instead.

The Authority's statement that the area was saddled with high rates of tuberculosis and juvenile delinquency has been questioned

7. For a more detailed—and even more favorable—defense of these and other characteristics of neighborhoods like the West End, see Jane Jacobs, *The Death and Life of Great American Cities*, New York: Random House, 1961, especially Part I, and Chap. 15.

by a study conducted by the Save the West End Committee. This study showed that of the twenty-one existing cases of tuberculosis in the district in 1955, all but three were located in the skid row area adjoining the West End, rather than in the area proposed for clearance.[8] A similar critique was made of the delinquency statistics provided by the Authority.[9] Although I did not make an independent study of these statistics, my observations did not suggest any undue incidence of either of these pathologies.

The Authority's report also indicated that the West End had a high rate of payments for Aid to Dependent Children and old-age assistance; that West Enders had a median income 23 per cent below the city median and a low level of education.[10] These facts, however, prove only that the area was inhabited by poor people, many of them old or in need of help; they do not prove one way or the other that the area was a slum.

The Authority's main argument for describing the area as a slum rested on the fact that 63.5 per cent of the dwelling units were judged substandard in 1953 by an appraisal based on criteria developed by the American Public Health Association.[11] The APHA appraisal, which has been used widely in urban renewal, consists of thirty differentially weighted items for judging buildings and individual dwelling units. Although the appraisal items are generally sound, the weighting does reflect middle-class values, and the items themselves do not distinguish sufficiently between harmful conditions, such as rodent infestation, and inconvenient ones, such as rooms lacking closets.[12] Further, the Authority's survey of the West End reported only total appraisal scores, but did not indicate to what extent these scores measured harmful, as compared to inconvenient, conditions. Nor did it distinguish between items requiring demolition and those that could be taken care of by rehabilitation or minor repairs.[13]

8. Save the West End Committee, "A Plea against Smashing the Houses of the West End . . . ," Boston: no date indicated, mimeographed, pp. 12–15.
9. *Op. cit.*, pp. 15–17.
10. Boston Housing Authority, *op. cit.*, p. 19.
11. *Ibid.*, p. 14.
12. American Public Health Association, "An Appraisal Method for Measuring the Quality of Housing," New York: The Association, 1946, Part II, Chap. 2.
13. Boston Housing Authority, *op. cit.*, p. 14.

The findings of this survey were questioned by other evaluations. On the basis of my own observations, I wrote in 1958:

> I would estimate that at the time of the land taking, probably from 25 to 35 per cent of the buildings in the project area were structurally unsound, uninhabitable because they had been vacant for some time, or located on alleys too narrow for proper sanitation and fire prevention.[14]

This judgment has since been supported by the more systematic study conducted by the Center for Community Studies. Its interviewers found that of the *buildings,* 23 per cent were excellent or good, 41 per cent fair, and 36 per cent poor or very bad. Hartman, who analyzed these judgments, also found that of the *dwelling units,* 40 per cent were in excellent or good condition, 34 per cent were fair, and only 25 per cent were in poor or very bad condition.[15] He noted that these characterizations "implicitly refer to the context of West End standards—an excellent West End apartment is not likely to be of the same quality as an excellent apartment on Beacon Hill." [16]

These figures also include an increase in dilapidation between 1953 and 1958, some of which can be attributed to the fact that when the plans for redevelopment were announced in 1951, landlords were advised not to make extensive repairs on their properties. Many West Enders claimed—with some justification—that parts of the area deteriorated rapidly as a result, especially where apartments or entire buildings became and remained vacant in the years that followed. The worst buildings were those owned by absentee landlords; many of the resident owners maintained their buildings more adequately.

14. Gans, "The Human Implications of Current Redevelopment and Relocation Planning," *op. cit.,* p. 17.

15. Chester Hartman, "Housing in the West End," Boston: Center for Community Studies Research Memorandum C 1, October, 1961, mimeographed, p. 2. These figures are based on observations made while interviewing women age twenty to sixty-five, and thus exclude rooming houses and units occupied by older males, and all unoccupied buildings. There were, however, fewer vacant units in 1953 than at the time of the interviewing in 1958.

16. Hartman, *op. cit.,* p. 2.

I do not mean to claim that the West End was free of slum buildings prior to 1951. Such structures did exist. They were most numerous in the lower end of the area, and, ironically, in the blocks just outside the area slated for redevelopment. Even so, the 1950 United States Census—the sole source of information about West End housing conditions prior to the announcement of redevelopment—showed that only about 20 per cent of all dwelling units were dilapidated, or lacked a private bath.[17] Since most West End apartments had private baths, this figure represents an index of dilapidation.

It would be fair to conclude that the majority of the structures in the West End provided low-rent rather than slum housing. Moreover, tenants kept their apartments in good order, and during the postwar prosperity, many West Enders had been able to modernize the interiors. As Hartman's figures document, poor buildings frequently contained well-kept apartments. Indeed, visitors to the area were often surprised at the discrepancy between the outside of the buildings and the apartments themselves, and had some difficulty maintaining their belief that the West End was a slum.

As noted in Chapter 1, rents were extremely low—a fact that enabled the many people in the area who never escaped the threat of job loss and layoff to keep their fixed housing costs low enough to survive. Low rents also made it possible for the many elderly people in the area to maintain independent households even while remaining near married children.

The West Enders themselves took the poor maintenance of the building exteriors, halls, and cellars in stride, and paid little attention to them. The low rents more than made up for these deficiencies, and for the generally rundown appearance of the area. Moreover, they did not consider these conditions a reflection on their status. Having no interest in the opinions of the outside world, they were not overly concerned about the image which the West End had in the eyes of outsiders. They did not like to be called slum dwellers, of course, and resented the exaggerated descriptions of West End deterioration that appeared regularly in the Boston press. Nor were they happy about the rooming houses that bordered the

17. Hartman, *op. cit.*, p. 2n. Census figures are based on the judgment of hastily trained enumerators, and are thus less reliable than other appraisals.

West End, or the skid row occupants who sometimes wandered into it. Unlike the middle class, however, they did not care about "the address." Consequently, the cultural differences between working- and middle-class residential choice suggest that the prevailing professional housing standards—which reflect only the latter— could not be rigidly applied to the West End.[18]

Nor did the West End satisfy the social criteria that would have made it a slum. Residents with social and emotional problems, with behavior difficulties, and with criminal records could be found in the area, partially because of the spillover from the adjacent skid row, and because of the low rents. This was especially true after 1950, when increasing vacancies attracted single transi- ents, Gypsies, and "multiproblem" families. Such people obtained apartments in the West End because landlords could no longer af- ford to reject what they defined as "undesirable" tenants. The presence of such tenants helped to convince the community at large that the West End was a slum. Yet all this time the West End was also a major area of first settlement for newcomers with- out problems or criminal records: especially immigrants from Italy, from Displaced Persons camps in Europe, from rural New England, and from French Canada. Thus, the area had an important but un- recognized function in the city. Even so, the majority of West Enders were people who had lived there since before 1950. Many of them also had problems, especially those associated with low income and acculturation. But the problems of old residents and newcomers alike had not been created by the neighborhood. If anything, the stability of a large part of the population created a more desirable social climate for newcomers than existed in the other major area of first settlement in Boston, the South End.

In summary, the West End was a low-rent district—both physi- cally and socially—rather than a slum. Total clearance might have been justified if the end result had been better living conditions for the West Enders, that is, if the area could have been rebuilt for them with modern structures and in such a way that the exist-

18. See also Chapter 2. For a more detailed analysis of these differences, see Marc Fried and Peggy Gleicher, "Some Source of Residential Satisfaction in an Urban 'Slum,'" *Journal of the American Institute of Planners*, vol. 27 (1961), pp. 305–315, and Hartman, *op. cit.*

ing social structure could have been preserved there for the people who wanted to remain in it. But none of this would have been possible under the urban renewal policies of the 1950's, which required the relocation of site residents and rebuilding for a new set of occupants by private enterprise.[19] This scheme was no solution for the West Enders, however, for it did not improve their living conditions and relocation only added new problems.

A wiser scheme would have been to rehabilitate drastically the harmful structures and tear down those that were structurally unsound or otherwise beyond salvage. The majority of buildings could have been given less intensive treatment or left alone. Spot clearance could have created additional open space for small parks, playgrounds, and parking areas. This solution would have maximized the benefits of renewal for the West Enders. But renewal is supposed to consider the public interest as well. Therefore, it is necessary to discuss the benefits and costs of redevelopment for the larger community.

The Benefits and Costs of Redevelopment

The certification of the West End for redevelopment was not entirely the result of its alleged or actual status as a slum. Because of its central location, realtors and civic leaders had long felt that the area should be devoted to economically more profitable uses. The Charles River frontage, for example, was thought to be desirable for high-rent apartments. As noted earlier, the desire of the Massachusetts General Hospital for higher income neighbors and the belief that the shrinkage of the central retail area could and should be halted by settling "quality shoppers" nearby contributed to the clear-

19. It should be noted that the Housing Authority study which described the area as a slum did not propose total clearance. About 12 per cent of the existing dwelling units were to be retained or rehabilitated. Moreover, in the re-use plan, only 58 per cent of the residential acreage was alotted to high-rent housing; 27 per cent was devoted to public or middle-income private housing, and 15 per cent to retained and rehabilitated structures. Boston Housing Authority, op. cit., p. 32. Even so, such a plan would not have allowed more than a handful of West Enders to remain in the area. As noted earlier, fears that investment capital would not be attracted by this plan caused it to be changed to one totally devoted to high-rent housing.

ance decision. So did the city's desperate need for a higher tax base, and its equally urgent search for some signs of economic revival. Throughout the 1950's, politicians, business leaders, and the press described the West End redevelopment scheme as a major factor in —and symbol of—the city's emergence from its economic doldrums.

Even so, the plans were implemented only because developers were interested in buying the cleared land for high-income housing. Meanwhile, other Boston neighborhoods in which the housing was more deteriorated and even dangerous received a much lower priority for renewal,[20] because they were not attractive for high-rent housing, or because of area political opposition.[21]

The rebuilding of the West End should be profitable for the builders. They are obtaining the cleared land in sections and can cease building—with only the loss of a $100,000 bond—if the demand for luxury apartments is satiated before all the sections are developed.[22] No one knows as yet whether there will be enough tenants for 2400 high-rent units. The ongoing redevelopment of the Scollay Square area for an office building complex, however, probably will aid the West End project. A successful West End project should also add to Boston's declining tax base, and could give a psychological lift to the business community. Several questions can be raised, however, as to its over-all benefit to the larger community:

20. In 1960, the city reorganized its redevelopment agency, and brought in a new director. He is embarking on a city-wide renewal program based on different criteria, and stressing rehabilitation more than clearance.

21. As noted earlier, this was especially true of the North End, where apartments were in poorer condition than in the West End. According to the 1950 Census, 78 per cent of its dwelling units were either dilapidated or lacked a private bath. Hartman, *op. cit.*, p. 3.

22. A number of questions could also be raised about the developer; the fact that the corporation was formed only a few days before the contract was awarded it, that it had only $1000 in equity at that time, that it was only the second highest bidder for the land, and that it may have received the contract through political influence. I could not make an independent study to answer these questions. For a detailed description of these charges, see Robert Hanron, "West End Project Could Be Spark to Revitalize Boston," *Boston Sunday Globe*, December 20, 1959. Conversely, it should be noted that the developer chose an architect-planner of national repute to design the new West End, and has attempted to make it an attractive—albeit very expensive—place to live.

1. The project has been planned on the assumption that high-income residents benefit the city, while low-income ones are only a burden and a source of public expense. This assumption ignores the vital economic and social functions played in the city economy by low-income people. Indeed, the reduction of the city's low-rent housing supply by close to 3000 units will undoubtedly make it more difficult for the present and future industrial force of a low-wage city to find centrally located and suitably priced housing.

2. The tax and other economic benefits of the redevelopment may be counteracted by the loss of property values and tax yields in the areas from which tenants will be drawn. Although no one can predict who will rent the new West End apartments, the majority will come most likely from older high-rent areas of the city, rather than from the suburbs or from newcomers to the metropolitan area.

3. The central business district may benefit less than expected: the new tenants probably already do much of their shopping downtown, and many of the West Enders who did all but their food buying downtown have left the city.

Moreover, the benefits that will accrue to the city must be weighed against the economic and social costs paid by the West Enders in being forced out of their neighborhood with nothing more than a moving allowance of $75 to $100. Tenants had to bear the financial burdens of higher rentals for new apartments—not necessarily better in quality than the old ones. For many West Enders, this required drastic budgetary changes with consequent cutbacks in other sectors. Because of the shortage of suitable apartments, a number of them had to buy suburban houses at prices which were beyond their ability to pay.

Most of the small businessmen in the area lost their stores, and thus their source of livelihood. Although federal relocation regulations did allot $2500 for moving expenses to those who re-established their businesses elsewhere, few were able to do so since the city is already oversupplied with small stores. Ironically, the businessmen who were prosperous enough to relocate, and who therefore needed less help, were given funds for moving. But those who lost their stores, and were most in need of aid, were given nothing.

Many resident owners of tenement buildings who were able to live modestly from rentals also lost their source of livelihood, for they did not receive enough for their buildings to allow them to purchase others. Conversely, the absentee landlords, who had not maintained their buildings, and who had been losing money from vacancies during the years preceding redevelopment, were benefited by the clearance.[23]

For tenants, owners, and businessmen alike, the destruction of the neighborhood exacted social and psychological losses. The clearance destroyed not only buildings, but also a functioning social system. The scattering of family units and friends was especially harmful to the many older people. Whereas the younger West Enders felt that they could adjust to a new neighborhood, the older ones will probably be less adept at making the change. Even while I was still in the West End, a number of deaths were attributed to the impact of the redevelopment decision.[24] People with serious social, economic, and emotional problems were faced with yet further problems by the need to move from a familiar and inexpensive neighborhood. Also, since the redevelopment had publicly identified West Enders as slum dwellers, some were met by discrimination and rejection in their new neighborhoods.

Some West Enders did benefit from the redevelopment, especially those among the most poorly housed who were able to find better apartments. Others gained by being given a push toward a move to middle-class neighborhoods and the suburbs which they had wanted to make but had delayed because of inertia.[25] Some will be benefited by new experiences and unexpected opportunities resulting from the move.

More detailed analyses—some of them over a long period of years—will be necessary to determine the final benefits and costs of the redevelopment for the larger community, as well as for

23. At the time of my study, it was commonly thought that since they had the funds for legal fees, and the political know-how for choosing the right lawyers, they would be able to go to court, and obtain higher prices for their buildings than would the resident owners.

24. I was not able to discover whether these attributions were at all justified.

25. Actually, many of the families in this position had already left the West End between 1950 and 1958.

the builders, the central district, and the West Enders themselves.[26] Even so, the variety of costs which West Enders have already paid are heavy. They represent hidden subsidies to the redevelopment program. In effect, a low-income population has subsidized the clearance of its neighborhood and the apartments of its high-income successors both by its own losses and by its share of the federal and local tax monies used to clear the site. It is doubtful whether the moving allowance that West Enders received can even begin to balance these costs.

The Relocation Plan and Process [27]

The city's planning for redevelopment concerned itself primarily with the land of the West End once it had been cleared. It paid little attention to the West Enders and their needs before or after clearance. To make matters worse, very little planning was done for the relocation of the 2700 households in the area—and that was done poorly. The process by which redevelopment and relocation actually proceeded also ignored the West Enders' needs, thus placing yet further burdens on their shoulders.

The city's relocation plan assumed that 60 per cent of the people were eligible for public housing, that all of them would move into such units, and that the private housing market would provide enough apartments and houses for the remainder. Although

26. My statements about the economic, social, and emotional costs of clearance and relocation are hypotheses based on my observations at the time the area was facing clearance, and on subsequent observations of a handful of relocated families. These costs will be described in more detail by the Center for Community Studies' ongoing research program among relocated West Enders. Corroboration of my hypotheses has already appeared, however, in the Center's initial findings. Thus, Fried reports that 54 per cent of the women and 46 per cent of the men interviewed expressed severely depressed or disturbed reactions to the tearing down of the buildings in which they lived. This rose to 64 per cent among the women who had lived in the West End for a very long time, and to 73 per cent among those who had felt very positive about the area before they had to move. Marc Fried, "Grieving for a Lost Home," in Leonard J. Duhl, ed., *The Environment of the Metropolis* (tentative title), New York: Basic Books, forthcoming.

27. The comments made in the previous footnote apply to this section also.

the plan was approved by federal officials, none of these assumptions were preceded by adequate study, and all of them were open to serious question at the time of the land taking in 1958.

Many eligible West Enders, for example, were unwilling to go into public housing. They rejected this alternative partly because they accepted the negative image given public housing by the Boston press; because they knew they would be unable to live with relatives, friends, and neighbors of their own ethnic group; because they considered public housing tenants to be inferior in status; and because they did not wish to be subjected to administrative restrictions on their activities, especially those limiting family income.

As a result, anyone even slightly familiar with the West Enders could have predicted that the vast majority would have to find housing in the private market. The Authority's relocation plan, however, did not consider this possibility. Even the assumption that enough private housing would be available for the 40 per cent ineligible for public housing was based on inadequate study. The Authority made an analysis of apartments listed in the classified sections of the newspapers, without any attempt to discover whether these units would satisfy the federal requirements that they be "decent, safe, and sanitary," or whether they would meet the needs of the West Enders. Many of these advertised vacancies, in fact, were of such low quality that they could not be rented to anyone. Landlords listed them with the West End relocation office because they knew that the West Enders had little choice in the housing market.

As it turned out, only about 10 per cent of the West Enders moved into public housing.[28] The rest obtained housing in the private market and did so by their own efforts. That they were successful was probably due in large part to the aid of relatives and friends in other parts of the metropolitan area who looked for vacancies in their own neighborhoods. What proportion of the West Enders did find satisfactory and suitably priced housing and how many have adjusted to new neighborhoods and new neighbors is not yet known. My own limited observations suggest that many moved into

28. This figure is based on the number of West Enders in the Center for Community Studies interview sample who moved into public housing. I am indebted to Chester Hartman for this tabulation.

old, low-rent neighborhoods in the cities surrounding Boston, some of which were already being considered for future urban renewal. Moreover, the arrival of the West Enders—publicly branded as slum dwellers—seems to have fortified the conviction of some of these cities that these areas too should be renewed. Thus it is possible that some West Enders will have to go through the entire process all over again.[29]

The failure of the official relocation procedures to help the West Enders can be traced to several deficiencies. First, these procedures were developed by middle-class professionals, who thus assumed that the West Enders' housing requirements and preferences were similar to their own. Although the West Enders were asked into which neighborhoods they wished to move, the relocation procedures gave first priority to the requirement that the new unit be decent, safe, and sanitary. This in turn was usually interpreted to mean fitting middle-class standards.[30] West Enders, however, were equally if not more concerned about social considerations. They wanted to move into neighborhoods in which they could find relatives, friends, and neighbors of their own ethnic group. They also wanted physically satisfactory housing; but, as already indicated, their own criteria for such housing differ from middle-class ones. The relocation staff's lack of interest in social criteria of housing choice was based partly on a desire—implicit in much of planning and housing ideology—to break up ethnic ghettoes, in the belief that this would encourage people like the West Enders to adopt middle-class standards and behavior patterns. Moreover, the middle-class values embedded in the relocation procedures assumed that nuclear families were self-sufficient and independent. Consequently relocation officials failed to see the ties that existed between such families. They did not know of the existence of family circles, and could not comprehend the desire of West Enders to be near relatives.

29. Thus, a Boston reporter wrote in 1960 that "certain cities are 'squawking to the skies' about the influx of West Enders," and noted also that "it is appalling the number of moves some people have had to make because . . . Boston failed to know the relocation plans of Cambridge." Virginia Bright, "Officials Have Learned a Lesson from West End," *Boston Sunday Globe*, May 15, 1960.

30. I have no quarrel with the requirement, which is written into federal housing law, but only with narrow interpretations of it.

Finally, while relocation was geared to move households, it failed to consider the need for moving institutions and social systems in which people live.[31] Admittedly, no one knows at this point how such institutions and social systems can be moved, but the procedures used in the West End precluded any experimentation in "social relocation."

The processes by which relocation and clearance were implemented were as negligent of residents' needs as had been the prior planning. During the five years in which the Housing Authority and its successor were obtaining the proper local and federal approvals, communication from the two Authorities to the West End kept the people in a state of constant uncertainty. True, the agencies did follow the letter of the law—and of bureaucratic procedure—but they failed to consider the West Enders' attitudes. For example, during the period when the plan was awaiting approval by the various participating agencies, the local Authority was extremely careful to give out no information about which it was not absolutely certain, or which was not required by the rule books. The informational vacuum thus created in the West End was filled with rumors. Moreover, the officials assumed that the West Enders were as expert as they in understanding the complex administrative processes of redevelopment, and that they could thus interpret properly the cryptic news releases which were issued periodically.

The officials neither attempted to discover the effects of their announcements, nor the way in which these were actually interpreted. Thus, the long years of delay between the announcement of redevelopment and the final taking were generally assumed by the West Enders to stem from the city's desire to confuse them, scare them out of the West End, and thus reduce the acquisition costs of property and the scope of the relocation problem. Since the West Enders did not organize in middle-class ways to protest the redevelopment, the officials failed to realize either the amount of hostility toward the project, or the reasons for this hostility. This

31. Peabody House's move to Somerville was dictated in part by the assumption that many West Enders would move into this community, and by the House's desire to help them adjust to their new neighborhoods. As I have shown in Chapter 7, however, settlement houses played only a minor role in the West Enders' social system.

in turn helped to stifle any incentive to plan for the West Enders' needs.

The pattern of poor communication on the part of the redevelopment officials and the negative interpretation of their plans and procedures by the West Enders continued after the Authority had set up a project area relocation office and had announced the taking of the properties by eminent domain. The agency continued to be vague on those topics of most importance to the residents, for example, on the relocation and clearance schedules. As a result, some West Enders understood admonitions to move as soon as possible to mean that the relocation office had been set up to scare people out of the area. Suggestions as to the availability of vacant housing in areas of lower socio-economic status than the West End were interpreted to mean that the city wanted to push West Enders into the worst slums of Boston. Moreover, the redevelopment agency's official notification to the landlords that their structures had been purchased for $1 under eminent domain procedures—plus its failure to include this token payment or to explain why it was not included—convinced many people that the city was not keeping its promises to treat them fairly and was going to cheat them out of their payments.

Likewise, the way in which the redevelopment agency took the land caused considerable hurt among the older immigrants. They could not understand how the buildings they had worked so hard to own could suddenly be taken away from them, with no assurance as to when or what they would be paid. Moreover, they were told at the same time to pay rents for their own apartments in these buildings or face eviction. Thus, many of the landlords who earned their livelihoods from rents were simultaneously deprived of both a source of income and the funds with which to pay the rent demanded from them.

Although the residents and redevelopment officials attributed the communication failure to each other's negative motivations, the actual difficulties originated elsewhere. The redevelopment agency was concerned mainly with following local and federal regulations governing relocation. These regulations said nothing about understanding the consequences to the residents of its official acts. Thus, the agency had no real opportunity for learning how the West End received its letters and announcements, or interpreted its actions.

Indeed, it is questionable that such an opportunity would have been exploited. The officials concerned were not policy-makers; they were hired to carry out their prescribed duties. They did feel sorry for some of the West Enders, especially those with serious problems, and these they tried to help in various ways not required by their job. But since they believed that relocation would improve the living conditions for most of the residents and that the redevelopment was for the good of the city, they could not really understand why the West Enders were hostile and often unwilling to cooperate. As a result, when redevelopment officials took action affecting project area residents, they were not likely to deliberate either on the residents' attitudes or on their predicament.

Finally, the scheduling of relocation and of clearance did not take into consideration the fact that the developer was acquiring the land in sections, or the possibility that he might not find enough tenants to justify his purchase of the remaining sections. Indeed, should it turn out that those portions of the West End farthest away from the Charles River and from Beacon Hill cannot be rebuilt for high-income tenants, other plans will have to be made for the vacant land. Meanwhile, people may have been relocated and buildings demolished needlessly.

Some Causes of the Defects in Urban Renewal

In summary, redevelopment proceeded from beginning to end on the assumption that the needs of the site residents were of far less importance than the clearing and rebuilding of the site itself. Great pains were taken with planning for buildings, but planning for the West Enders was done on an *ad hoc* basis, almost as an afterthought. To give just one example, although the local and federal agencies had detailed maps of the West End's sewer system, they did not seem to know the simple fact that a number of owners living in the area depended on the rents they collected for their income.

Perhaps the clearest indication of the relatively low priority of the West Enders in the redevelopment process is the fact that the funds allocated to relocation were less than 5 per cent of the total cost of taking and clearing the land. This represented only about

1 per cent of the cost of clearance and rebuilding. The real cost of relocation, however, was very much higher, and was paid in various ways by the people who had to move. In short, the redevelopment of the West End was economically feasible only because of the hidden subsidies which the residents provided—involuntarily, of course.

This critique is directed neither at renewal nor relocation per se, but at the specific policies which use public funds to subsidize the erection of high-rent housing, and which penalize the low-income population, without any proof that these inequities are in the public interest.[32] Moreover, the specific criticisms made of Boston procedures are not intended to blame any individuals within the local or federal agencies. It is important to emphasize that what happened cannot be attributed to evil motives. No laws were broken, and many officials acted with only the best intentions toward the West Enders. Needless to say, more empathy and research on the part of the officials involved, and more criticism of the program by planners, and those who make Boston's public policy, might have ameliorated the process to some extent. Even so, the officials who carried out the program in Boston were no better or worse than their colleagues in other cities.

Good intentions, empathy, and criticism are of little help, however, if the basic procedures are at fault. Thus, the responsibility for what happened in the West End rests to a considerable extent on the system of procedures that has emerged from years of legislative and administrative decision-making beginning with the 1949 Housing Act. It also rests on the unintended or unrecognized consequences of these procedures when they are actually implemented. This system, however, is intrinsically related to the country's economic and political structure, especially to the long-standing public policy of giving private enterprise a free hand in the profitable sectors of the housing market. This policy then, and the powerful realtor, builder, and banker lobbies which have insisted on its inclusion in all urban renewal legislation, must also be implicated in the process that took place in the West End. For ex-

32. In addition, the critique applies to the redevelopment agency as it was constituted in 1958. The reorganization of this agency, noted earlier, should result in an improvement of the renewal process. Many of its less desirable features are built into the federal regulations, however, and these had not been altered significantly by the Kennedy Administration as of January 1962.

ample, since the Boston redevelopment agency, like all others the country over, had to provide sufficient incentives to attract a private redeveloper, its decisions—beginning with the selection of the West End as a renewal site—were shaped by the demands or the anticipated demands of the developer and the sources of investment capital.

Once more it must be stressed that the observations presented here about the effects of relocation were made before the advent of relocation. The study now being conducted by the Center for Community Studies is measuring the effects of clearance and relocation in a systematic manner, and will provide scientifically validated data on many of the observations reported here. The Center's study will thus answer the most important question raised: to what extent are the effects of relocation beneficial or detrimental for those who have to move? The answer should supply renewal and planning agencies with the kind of information they need, to decide whether the benefits of rebuilding the city are worth the costs that renewal area residents must bear under present policies. Whatever the conclusions of the Center's studies, however, my thesis —that current renewal policies benefit the developer most, the area residents least, and the public interest in as yet unmeasured quantity—will remain valid. For even if all of the effects of relocation were positive, the unequal and unjust distribution of costs and benefits built into current procedures still would not be justified.

Some Recommendations for Urban Renewal

Urban renewal and the rehousing of slum dwellers are necessary and desirable objectives. The means of achieving them, however, ought to be chosen in relation to these objectives, rather than to such extraneous ones as attracting middle- and upper-income citizens back from the suburbs, contributing potential shoppers to a declining downtown business district, creating symbols of "community revival," or providing more statusful surroundings for powerful community institutions. Redevelopment should be pursued primarily for the benefit of the community as a whole and of the people who live in the slum area; not for the redeveloper or his eventual tenants. The recommendations that follow are based largely on this principle:

1. Renewal projects should be located first in those areas which are slums as defined above, that is, in which it can be proven that the housing and facilities present social and physical dangers to the residents and to the larger community. The availability of a redeveloper ought to be a consideration, but one of lesser priority.

2. Before areas for renewal are finally chosen, independent studies should be made which not only provide proof that the area is a slum, but which also take into account the values and living patterns of the residents. These studies should be made by persons who have no connection either with the project area or the redevelopment agency.

3. Renewal proposals that call for the relocation of an entire neighborhood should be studied closely to determine whether the existing social system satisfies more positive than negative functions for the residents. Should this be the case, planners must decide whether the destruction of this social system is justified by the benefits to be derived from renewal.

4. Projects that require large-scale relocation—especially any project that requires the rehousing of more people than is possible, given the existing low-rent housing supply in the community—should be studied in a similar manner. Such projects should not be initiated until the community has built sufficient relocation units to assure the proper rehousing of the residents. *Proper* should be defined by the standards of these residents as well as by those of housing and planning officials. If private enterprise is unable to provide these units, city, state, and federal funds will have to be used. Moreover, if relocation housing is built prior to the renewal project, and in sufficient quantity, and if it is attractive, it is likely to draw enough people out of the slum areas to reduce the market value of slum structures. Consequently, some of the costs of providing such relocation housing will be offset by lower acquisition costs at the time of renewal.

5. Should a community be unwilling or unable to provide the required relocation housing, it should not be permitted to engage in renewal operations.

6. Urban policy makers ought to recognize the functions performed in the city by the low-income population. Moreover, they should make sure that sufficient housing is available for them and in the proper locations (including some near the central business

district) for their needs. The federal government should encourage the supply of such housing by increasing its subsidies when the renewal plan calls for the rehabilitation or construction of low-income dwellings.

7. Greater emphasis should be placed on the rehabilitation of low-rent housing, and less on its clearance. Such rehabilitation should be based on standards that provide decent, safe, and sanitary—but economically priced—dwelling units. In order to make this possible, existing standards should be restudied, to distinguish between those requirements which bring housing up to a standard but low-rent level from those which are "fringe benefits" and cause rehabilitated units to be priced out of the low-rent market. Frequently, current rehabilitation takes low-rent apartments and transforms them into dwelling units that fit the demands, tastes, and pocketbooks of middle- and upper-class people, rather than those of their present residents.

8. Experiments should be made with:
   a. Flexible subsidies, so that federal contributions are increased if the re-use is low- or middle-income housing; and reduced if it is luxury housing.
   b. Requirements that the redeveloper construct or finance some relocation housing, especially if he proposes to redevelop the site with housing out of the price range of the present site residents.

If the purpose of urban renewal is to improve the living conditions of the present slum dwellers, relocation thus should become one of the most important, if not the most important, phases of the renewal process. This principle suggests a number of proposals for procedural change:

9. As a general policy, relocation should be minimized unless adequate relocation housing is available in the proper locations, and unless the relocation procedures can be shown to improve the living conditions of the people who are moved. When the plan calls for rehabilitation, it should be implemented without relocation as much as possible.

10. The relocation plan should take priority over the renewal phases of the total plan, and no renewal plan should be approved

by federal or local agencies until a proper relocation scheme has been developed.

11. This relocation plan should be based on a thorough knowledge of the project area residents, so that the plan fits their demands and needs and so that officials will have some understanding of the consequences of their actions before they put the plan into effect. The federal agency ought to re-evaluate its relation to the local agencies, raising its requirements for approval of the local relocation plan and relaxing its requirements for such phases as rent collection. This would make it possible for the local agency to be more sensitive to the needs of the project area residents, and more flexible in ways of dealing with them.

12. Local and federal agencies should provide interest-free or low-interest loans to relocatees who wish to buy new homes.

13. These agencies should provide similar loans to project area landlords whose present buildings provide decent, safe, and sanitary housing; thus allowing them either to purchase new buildings in other areas, or to rehabilitate old buildings and make them available to project area residents.

14. Landlords with units eligible for relocation housing anywhere in the community should be encouraged to rent to relocatees through such incentives as rehabilitation loans, subsidies for redecorating, and the like.

15. When project area rents have been low, so that residents' housing costs are raised sharply as a result of relocation, the federal and local agencies should set up a rent moratorium to allow relocatees to save for future rentals before moving. The length of this moratorium should be based on the gap between project area and relocation area rentals.

16. Liquidation funds in lieu of moving allowances should be provided to small store owners and other businessmen who will not be able to reopen their firms elsewhere. Other federal and local programs should be made available to provide occupational retraining and similar vocational aids to those who want them.

17. Communication between the redevelopment agency and the residents, and other agency-resident relationships should assure that:

a. The amount of information given to site residents is maximized, and the development of rumors due to information vacuums is prevented.

    b. Officials are trained to understand the inevitably deprivatory nature of relocation for the residents, so that they have more insight into what relocation means to the residents, and can develop a more tolerant attitude toward their reactions of shock and protest.

18. The relocation staff should be strengthened by the addition of:

    a. Social workers who can provide aid to residents faced with additional problems resulting from relocation, and who can make referrals to other city agencies that deal with such problems.[33] The relocation staff should also call on resource persons in those areas to which site residents are moving, and employ them to facilitate the adjustment of the relocatees in their new neighborhoods.

    b. Real estate technicians who can develop a thorough inventory of the city's housing supply, and who can also weed out unscrupulous landlords who are likely to exploit the relocatees.

19. In relocation projects that involve the destruction of a positive social system, experiments should be conducted to:

    a. Find ways of relocating together extended families living in separate but adjacent households—provided they want to be moved en masse.

    b. Make it possible for important project area institutions and organizations to re-establish themselves in those neighborhoods which have received the majority of relocatees, or in central locations where they are accessible to scattered relocatees.

    c. Develop group relocation methods to allow members of an ethnic group who want to stay together to move into an area as a group. This is especially important in neighborhoods with available relocation housing in which there are presently no members of that ethnic—or racial—group.

20. The experience in most renewal projects indicates that the

---

33. The West End relocation office has done some pioneering work in this respect, partially as a result of the efforts of area caretakers.

large majority of people relocate themselves, and that only a small proportion are relocated by the agency. In the future, procedures should be revised with this in mind. Then, the major functions of the relocation agency should be:

a. To make sure that the supply of relocation housing is sufficient to give relocatees a maximal choice of decent, safe, and sanitary dwelling units at rents they are willing to pay and in neighborhoods in which they want to live.

b. To provide information and other aids that will enable relocatees to evaluate these dwelling units, and to make the best housing choice in relation to their needs and wants.

c. To offer relocation service to the minority that chooses to be moved by the agency.

Many of the proposals will increase the cost of relocation, which in turn will raise the cost of renewal.[34] This is only equitable. Project area residents should not be required to subsidize the process, as they do presently. In time, the higher cost of renewal will become the accepted rate. Moreover, since redevelopers often stand to make considerable profit from their renewal operation, they should eventually be asked to bear part of this increased cost. The redeveloper, for example, could be asked to include some propor-

34. In commenting on these proposals, Martin Meyerson has suggested the possibility of substituting instead a sizable "relocation bonus" to tenants, landlords, and businessmen, to compensate them for the discomforts and other costs of relocation. Such a bonus, which might be $2500 or more, would relieve the renewal agency of all further obligations and thus simplify its operations. Moreover, since the size of the bonus would be such as to provide a real incentive for relocation, slum dwellers would welcome renewal rather than resent it. The size of the bonus would decrease the likelihood of their being identified as slum dwellers. The cost of the premium would probably be no higher than that of the measures I have proposed, while at the same time reducing the possibility of undesirable forms of government interference. Moreover, the recipients would be free to spend the money on alternatives that are more important to them than housing. There is, of course, always the danger that lower-class recipients would spend their bonus unwisely or lose it to unscrupulous entrepreneurs. This could be counteracted, at least in part, by raising the bonus if the money is spent on housing and by postponing payment until the relocatee has moved to nonslum housing. Such a qualification would also encourage relocatees to spend at least part of their premium on housing.

tion of relocation expenses in his costs and pass them on to his tenants as their share of the renewal charges. Alternatively, the city could bear the initial relocation costs, and require the redeveloper to repay part of them should his project show more than an agreed upon reasonable profit. In either case, the higher the rentals of the new housing, the higher should be the share of relocation costs to be paid by the redeveloper.

Current renewal and relocation procedures have been discussed mainly in terms of the inequities being born by the project area residents. These procedures, however, can also be shown to have undesirable consequences for renewal itself. For example, projects based on inadequate relocation plans simply push site residents into the next adjacent low-income area, and create overcrowding that leads to the formation of new slums. Thus, the city is saddled with additional problems and new costs, which eventually overwhelm the apparent short-run benefits of the renewal project. Moreover, poorly handled relocation frequently results in political repercussions which can endanger the community's long-range renewal plans. Consequently, my proposals have beneficial implications not only for the site residents, but for the future of urban renewal itself.

The conclusions and recommendations presented here are based on observations in a single redevelopment project. Even so, most of them are applicable to renewal projects in other cities. Similar ones, in fact, have been developed in studies of the process in such cities.[35]

In a number of ways, however, the West End project was atypical. First, the plan called for total clearance, a method that has been

35. Among the best of these studies are: Community Surveys, Inc., "Redevelopment: Some Human Gains and Losses," Indianapolis: Community Surveys, Inc., 1956 (by John R. Seeley and associates); and Philadelphia Housing Association, "Relocation in Philadelphia," Philadelphia: The Association, 1958. For a study of the impact on urban renewal on small businesses, see William N. Kinnard, Jr., and Zenon S. Malinowski, "The Impact of Dislocation from Urban Renewal Areas on Small Business," Storrs: University of Connecticut, July, 1960. For an excellent analysis and evaluation of renewal in a number of American cities by a British sociologist, see Peter Marris, "A Report on Urban Renewal," London: Institute of Community Studies, 1962, mimeographed, and in Duhl, *op. cit.*

proposed less frequently of late. Many of the projects currently being planned emphasize rehabilitation. This method is as yet untested, however, and frequently requires almost as much relocation as a clearance project.

Second, the West End differed from most other urban renewal projects in that it was a neighborhood of European ethnic groups. Whereas over 95 per cent of its population was white, most other renewal projects have been in predominantly nonwhite areas: 80 per cent of them according to one estimate.[36] In such areas, the housing is usually of a poorer quality. Moreover, there is probably less community life, fewer long-standing relationships between residents, and less attachment to the neighborhood than in the West End. Therefore, my argument against clearance would often be less justified in these areas.

Conversely, nonwhite slum dwellers have far lower incomes, poorer jobs, less job security, as well as more social and emotional problems than do West Enders. Also, they have considerably more difficulty in finding other housing. Consequently, the negative effects of relocation are probably much greater, and the lack of proper planning for redevelopment and relocation much more serious than it was in the West End. The recommendations proposed above are therefore more urgent for typical renewal areas than for those resembling the West End.

36. Charles E. Silberman, "The City and the Negro," *Fortune*, vol. 65 (March, 1962), pp. 89–91, 139–140, 144–146, 152–154, at p. 90.

APPENDIX On the Methods Used in This Study

The Purposes and Methods of the Study

The findings of any study are intrinsically related to the methods used to develop them. Although this study may be described generally as based on participant-observation, a more detailed description of the methods is necessary to indicate the over-all perspective of the research, and some shortcomings of the findings.

Findings are also affected by research purposes. As I indicated in the Preface, I had two major reasons for making this study: a desire to understand neighborhoods known as slums, and the people who live in them; and a desire to learn firsthand what differentiates working- and lower-class people from middle-class ones. These questions were based partly on my concern about middle-class bias in the planning and caretaking professions. The extent to which this concern has influenced my study should be evident from the book, and especially from the evaluations made in Chapters 12 and 14.

Having been trained in sociology at the University of Chicago during the era when Everett C. Hughes and the late Louis Wirth —to name only two—were dominant influences in the Department of Sociology, I believed strongly in the value of participant-observation as a method of social research. As a result, I felt that I could best achieve my study purposes by living in a slum myself.

Although I had wanted to do the study for several years, other projects had prevented my searching for a suitable area. Consequently, I was very pleased when I was offered the opportunity of making a study in the West End—a particularly suitable neighborhood. Not only was it known as a slum, but it also was a white area, and thus somewhat easier for a white participant-observer to enter. For while the method is difficult enough to use when it requires a trip across class barriers, it is much more so when racial barriers also exist. Much as I would have liked to do the study in a Negro slum, I doubted at the time whether many Negroes would have accepted a white participant-observer in their midst. The West End was also attractive because it was adjacent to the North End, the district described in William F. Whyte's classic *Street Corner Society*. Not only were my purposes based on some of the same values that guided his study, but my belief in the desirability and feasibility of the project had also been much encouraged by his book, as well as by the detailed description of the way in which he went about his study.[1]

My actual field work employed six major approaches:

1. *Use of the West End's facilities.* I lived in the area, and used its stores, services, institutions, and other facilities as much as possible. This enabled me to observe my own and other people's behavior as residents of the area.

2. *Attendance at meetings, gatherings, and public places.* I attended as many public meetings and gatherings as I could find, mostly as an observant spectator. I also visited area shops and taverns in this role.

3. *Informal visiting with neighbors and friends.* My wife and I became friendly with our neighbors and other West Enders, spending much time with them in social activities and conversations that provided valuable data.

4. *Formal and informal interviewing of community functionaries.* I interviewed at least one person in all of the area's agencies and institutions—talking with directors, staff members, officers, and active people in settlement houses, church groups, and other volun-

1. "On the Evolution of Street Corner Society," in William F. Whyte Jr., *Street Corner Society*. Chicago: University of Chicago Press, 2nd ed., 1955, pp. 279–358.

tary organizations. I also talked with principals, ministers, social workers, political leaders, government officials—especially those concerned with redevelopment—and store owners.

5. *Use of informants*. Some of the people I interviewed became informants, who kept me up to date on those phases of West End life with which they were familiar.[2]

6. *Observation*. I kept my eyes and ears open at all times, trying to learn something about as many phases of West End life as possible, and also looking for unexpected leads and ideas on subjects in which I was especially interested.

The data which evolved from the use of these methods were written down in field notes, and placed in a diary. They were subsequently analyzed for this report.

The Types and Problems of Participant-Observation

The first three of the methods I used are usually described under the rubric of participant-observation—a generic and not entirely accurate term for a variety of observational methods in which the researcher develops more than a purely research relationship with the people he is studying. The actual types of participant-observation which I used, and the problems which I encountered, therefore deserve more detailed consideration.

Variations in the participant-observation method can be described in different ways. One principle of classification is the extent to which the researcher's participation is known to the people he is studying: that is, whether it is kept secret, revealed partially, or revealed totally.[3] I have found it more useful to classify the approaches in terms of differences in the actual behavior of the researcher. This produces three types:

1. *Researcher acts as observer*. In this approach, the researcher

2. Anthropologists use informants to get basic information about the culture they are studying; I used them mainly to get data about specific institutions in which they were functioning, and to check observations or impressions gathered in my field work.

3. This principle has been used by Raymond L. Gold, "Roles in Sociological Field Observations," *Social Forces*, vol. 36 (1958), pp. 217–223; and by Buford H. Junker, *Field Work*, Chicago: University of Chicago Press, 1960, Chap. 3.

is physically present at the event which he observes, but does not really participate in it. Indeed, his main function is to observe, and to abstain from participation so as not to affect the phenomenon being studied—or at least, to affect it no more than is absolutely unavoidable. Much of my participation was of this type, when I was using the area's facilities, attending meetings, or watching the goings-on at area stores and taverns.

2. *Researcher participates, but as researcher.* In this case, the researcher does become an actual participant in an event or gathering, but his participation is determined by his research interests, rather than by the roles required in the situation he is studying.[4] For example, in social gatherings, the researcher may try to steer the conversation to topics in which he is especially interested. In such instances, he might be described as a "research-participant."

3. *Researcher participates.*[5] In this approach, the researcher temporarily abdicates his study role and becomes a "real" participant. After the event, his role reverts back to that of an observer—and in this case, an analyst of his own actions while being a real participant. For example, he may go to a social gathering as an invited guest and participate fully and freely in the conversation without trying to direct it to his own research interests. Afterwards, however, he must take notes on all that has happened, his own activities included. Needless to say, even during the most spontaneously real participation he can never shed the observer role entirely, if only because he knows he will write it all down later.

In attending meetings and other public gatherings, I acted as observer. In using the West End's facilities, I was usually a real participant, sometimes a research-participant or observer. The informal visiting with friends and neighbors employed a mixture of real and research participation. Given the short time I had for field work, the research participation role turned out to be most

4. He must, of course, follow the rules that guide participation in the event, or he will be ejected. For example, he cannot tell people to stop talking about a topic that does not interest him.

5. These three types cut across what Morris and Charlotte Schwartz have described as passive and active participation. See their "Problems in Participant-Observation," *American Journal of Sociology,* vol. 60 (1955), pp. 343–353, at pp. 348–350.

productive. The real participation was most enjoyable, but it turned out to be a time-consuming approach. Also, while it is most useful when the object of study is a single group or institution, it is less so in a general community study. Although being a real participant allows the researcher to understand the functioning of a group like no other method can, it also cuts him off from other parts of the society which are closed to its members. For example, it would be impossible for a participant studying one political party to study the opposition party as well.

In using these three types of participant-observation, I encountered several problems which deserve some consideration: the difficulty of entry into the community; the identification with the people being studied; and doubts as to the ethics of the approach.

The problem of entry into West End society was particularly vexing. As the West Enders were a low-income group, they had neither been interviewed by market researchers nor been exposed to the popular sociology of the slick magazines. Consequently, they were unfamiliar with the methods and goals of sociology. Also, they were suspicious of middle-class outsiders, especially so because of the redevelopment threat. As a result, I was somewhat fearful at the beginning whether I would be able to function as a participant-observer once I had told people that I was a researcher.

The Center for Community Studies on whose staff I served had already made contact with one of the settlement houses, and the workers, being middle-class, were willing to be interviewed and to help out in the study. They also referred me to some of their loyal clients, but these, I soon found out, were in several ways unlike the large majority of West Enders. Nor did any of them resemble "Doc," the man whom William F. Whyte had met at the start of his study and who had offered to guide Whyte into the society of the North End.[6] Although the early weeks of the study were indeed anxious ones, I did not waste them, using the time to interview the staff members of West End institutions and the officers of its organizations. Eventually, however, the problem almost resolved itself, this time by the same sort of lucky accident that had befallen Whyte. My wife and I were welcomed by one of our neighbors and became friends with them. As a result, they invited

6. Whyte, op. cit., p. 291.

us to many of their evening gatherings and introduced us to other neighbors, relatives, and friends. These contacts provided not only pleasant companionship, but a considerable amount of data about the workings of the peer group society.

As time went on, I became friendly in much the same way with other West Enders whom I had encountered at meetings or during informal interviews. They too introduced me to relatives and friends, although most of the social gatherings at which I participated were those of our first contact, and their circle.

After I had been in the area for about three months, I became a familiar face, and was able to carry on longer conversations with storeowners and other West Enders. Finally, the entry problem disappeared entirely. Indeed, I was now faced with a new one: having more data than I could ever hope to analyze.

Even my most notable failure in gaining entry produced useful information. Feeling that I should not limit myself entirely to being with people who spent their evenings at home, I decided to do some research in the area taverns. After making the rounds of the West End bars and finding most of them a haven for older men and Polish or Irish West Enders, I finally chanced on one which served as a hangout for a group of young Italian adults of the type that Whyte called "corner boys." From then on, I visited there only. But as much as I tried to participate in the conversation, I could not do so. The bar, though open to the general public, was actually almost a private club: the same dozen or so men came there every night, and—since some of them were unemployed or not working during daylight hours—during the day as well. Moreover, I suspect that some of them were engaged in shady enterprises. In any case, they were extremely loath to talk to strangers, especially one like myself who came unintroduced, alone, and then only irregularly about once a week. Also, much as I tried, I could not really talk about the subjects they covered or use the same abundance of four-letter profanity. After several unsuccessful attempts, I gave up trying to intrude and sat quietly by, from then on, as an observer. As it turned out, however, I learned a lot from listening to their conversations and to their comments about the television programs that they watched intermittently.

One of the factors that complicated the entry problem was my initial desire to be only an observer and a real participant, that is, to gather data simply by living in the West End and to learn from the contacts and conversations that came my way just by being there. I soon found that this was impossible. There were simply too many questions that I could not ask in my role as an ordinary—and newly arrived—resident. Given the short time I had in which to do the research, I could not wait for these questions to come up spontaneously in the conversation. Consequently, I told people that I was doing a study of the neighborhood, especially of its institutions and organizations. I also sensed quickly that they were familiar with historical "studies," and thereafter described my research as being a recent history of the area. The revelation of my research role ended a few relationships, but on the whole, it helped my study, and made it easier for me to approach people with unusual questions.

In addition, I wanted initially to refrain from interviewing as much as possible, except among people such as agency staff members and organizational leaders who were used to it. I made this decision partly on epistemological grounds—doubting whether I would get trustworthy data—and partly because I was not sure that I could be both interviewer and participant-observer in the same neighborhood. When I found that I was not gathering enough data, I changed my mind and, subsequently, I did interview a number of West Enders. But this was always done quite informally and without a questionnaire, except one lodged firmly in my memory. I did no door-to-door-interviewing, however, partly because I did not like to do it, and because I found it difficult to assume the detached role of the interviewer who comes as a stranger, never to be seen again. Although I never considered myself to be a West Ender, I did think myself to be enough of a participant in the life of the area to feel uncomfortable about also being an interviewer.[7]

A second problem of participant-observation is that of identification with the people one studies. Every participant-observer becomes emotionally involved not only in his study, but also with the people, since it is through their willingness to talk that he is

7. I did, however, help to pretest the interview schedule being used by the larger study, and interviewed, without discomfort, an ex-West Ender who had left the area some years earlier.

able to do his research. And this involvement does have some advantages: it allows the observer to understand the people with whom he is living, and to look at the world through their eyes. At the same time, it can also blind him to some of their behavior patterns, and thus distort the study.[8]

The identification is probably more intense if the people being studied are suffering from deprivation, and if they are a low-status group whose point of view is not being taken notice of in the world outside. In such a situation, the researcher feels a need to do something about the deprivation, and to correct false stereotypes about the people. This reaction also befell me. As I noted in Chapter 13, I quickly became convinced that the redevelopment of the area was unjustified, and that the planning was being poorly handled. Since no one seemed to be interested in the West Enders' point of view, I thus took it upon myself to state it in the ways I have described in Chapter 14.[9] Indeed, this identification can be socially useful—at least from the liberal perspective—for the sociologist then becomes an informal spokesman for groups who themselves lack the power to voice their demands in the larger society.

Although identification can detract from the objectivity of the research, it need not do so—especially if the researcher knows what is happening to him. Moreover, the identification, likely to be strong at the beginning, decreases in intensity as the research proceeds.[10] It is reduced even further in the time which elapses between the end of field work, the data analysis, and the writing of the report. Instances of overidentification in the field work can therefore be dealt with in later stages of the research. In my case, the dangers of identification were somewhat reduced by their being channeled largely into the redevelopment issue, a topic peripheral to the main purposes of my study. Thus, I expressed my identification with the West Enders through my critique of the redevelopment process,

8. Morris and Charlotte Schwartz call this affective participation, and indicate how it can be dealt with. *Op. cit.*, pp. 350–352.

9. Løchen has described how he defended patient perspectives and patient rights against the staff in his participant-observation study of a mental hospital. Yngvar Løchen, "Some Experiences in Participant-Observation from a Norwegian Mental Hospital Study," Bethesda: National Institute of Mental Health, no date, mimeographed.

10. Løchen, *op. cit.*

and was able to remain more detached about the social structure and culture of the West Enders.

The dangers of overidentification are also reduced by the many differences between the researcher and the people he is studying. Since the researcher is an observer more often than he is a real participant, he is always conscious of value clashes when they occur during the field work. Thus, while the participant-observer cannot argue with his informants and respondents as fully as he would like—because it might endanger his rapport—he is continually made aware of his own points of view on the subjects that come up in conversation. This not only produces insights useful to his research, but also keeps him detached from the people he is studying. He realizes that he cannot be like them, or that he should not even try to be.[11] At the same time, he becomes ever more sensitive to the fact that values arise out of the social position of those who hold them. Thus, when the researcher becomes a spokesman for the people he is studying, he is really arguing with those who fail to see this basic sociological fact. This accounts for the intensity of my reaction about the narrow-mindedness of the world at large. Thus, the chapters on the caretakers and on the redevelopment process—especially Chapters 7, 12, and 14—reflect dismay at the middle-class professional who expects people to share his own values even though they lack the opportunities and cultural background that have shaped his own views.

The third problem of the participant-observation approach concerns its ethical validity. Although I did tell people that I was in the West End to make a study, I described my research mainly as a survey of organizations, institutions, and the redevelopment process. I mentioned but did not stress my interest in studying the everyday life of West Enders, and did not mention at all that I attended social gatherings in the dual role of guest and observer.

11. I did not wear the middle-class uniform of suit, white shirt, and tie, however, in order to minimize my connection with the Hospital. Its support of the redevelopment program had antagonized many West Enders. I did not try to look like a West Ender but one day, while wandering through the area, some college students who were taking pictures there treated me—literally —as if I were a native. Their tone of well-meaning condescension made me see more clearly than ever why West Enders harbor uncomplimentary feelings toward the middle class.

At the time I felt sure that this admission would either have ended the relationships, or have made life so uncomfortable for them and for me that I could not have been either guest or observer. With some hindsight and additional participant-observation experience in another community, I feel now that I could have been more open about my role. Most people are too busy living to take much notice of a participant-observer once he has proven to them that he means no harm.

The fact that I was using friendly relationships for the collection of data, coupled with my feeling that I was thus exploiting these relationships, did create some guilt. My feelings of anxiety were somewhat alleviated, however, by the fact that my study was based neither on harmful or malicious ends. Needless to say, I had intended from the start to maintain the privacy of my informants. Thus, I have used no names in the report, and have frequently distorted facts that would make it possible for West Enders to recognize their erstwhile neighbors. In attributing quotes, I have freely used the term "neighbor" as a synonym for West Ender, and some of the people I have quoted were not really neighbors at all.

Although these explanations and safeguards do not solve the ethical problem of whether the ends of the study justified the means used in making it, I can see no easy solution to this problem. The social scientist attempts to describe the world as it is, and he must therefore observe people in their normal, everyday ways. Should he hide his purpose, either by not telling them of his participant-observation role, or by asking interview questions which get at more than they seem to on the surface, he does so because he has no other alternative. If he bares all his research purposes, he may be denied access to the very society he wants to study. If he forswears participant-observation and gathers his data solely by interviewing, he can get only reports of behavior, but not behavior itself. If he is completely open about his participant-observation or interview questions, his respondents are likely to hide information from him —not necessarily by intention—by giving him access not to behavior but to appearances; not to what people do, but how they would like their doings to appear publicly.

If research methods do involve some evasion, the social scientist is saddled with a great responsibility to the people he has studied.

The researcher must try to prevent any harm from coming to the people he has studied, either from his research or its publication. There is one exception: if the people studied are participants in what appears to the researcher as a gross miscarriage of justice, he has the right to publish his conclusion, even if the correction of the injustice might hurt them. Because these requirements force the researcher to set himself up as a judge over other human beings, he must take personal responsibility for these decisions and for the hurts his study could cause. Beyond that, he must be as objective as is humanly possible, not by renouncing value judgments, but by refraining from hasty and oversimplified ones, and by showing why people behave as they do, especially when this behavior violates prevalent norms.

All these precautions, of course, cannot do away with the fact that research, like all other human activities, is political; that it supports one point of view and vested interest at the expense of others.[12] The researcher must therefore take a political stand on some issues, and he should make it clear where his sympathies lie. This I have tried to do in Chapters 12 and 14.

The Analysis of the Data and Some of Their Limitations

The actual analysis of the data was quite simple. I recorded my observations and interviews as soon as possible after they had been completed, together with the generalizations they stimulated, and placed them in a field diary. When I came to write the study, I read and reread my diary several times, and then put the generalizations and some supporting observations on index cards. Eventually, I had more than 2000 of these. I then sorted and classified them by a variety of subject headings. The classification was determined in part by my initial research purposes, in part by topics in which I had become interested during the field work, and in part

12. For a clear statement of this fact, see John R. Seeley, "We Hidden Persuaders: Social Thought and Politics," An Address to the National Federation of Canadian University Students, McMaster University, 1961, mimeographed. My conclusions about the ethics of participant-observation have benefited from discussions with him and with Fred Davis.

by the observations made spontaneously while in the field. The content of the cards was then further digested into pages of notes listing the major generalizations and other ideas. An initial report was written from these notes in 1959.[13] Before I wrote this book, I reread the diary and took further notes on it. Subsequently, I expanded and rewrote the chapters of the original report, and added new concluding chapters and the epilogue on the redevelopment.

The study is based on quite simple—if not primitive—research methods, and its findings are hypotheses. Moreover, what evidence I have offered for them is illustrative rather than documentary. This is not accidental; from the start I had decided to give lower priority to methodological sophistication than to the search for hypotheses. I tried, of course, to be a careful observer, and a careful analyst of what I had observed, but I did not attempt to seek evidence for my hypotheses on a systematized basis. As a result, the findings have several limitations.

Many of the generalizations of the study fall into the category of what Merton has called "post factum sociological interpretation" in that they have been developed after the observations. Concerning this, Merton has warned:

A disarming characteristic of the procedure is that the explanations are indeed consistent with the given set of observations. This is scarcely surprising, inasmuch as only those post factum hypotheses are selected which do accord with these observations. . . . Post factum explanations remain at the level of plausibility [low evidential value] rather than leading to "compelling evidence" [a high degree of confirmation]. Plausibility . . . is found when an interpretation is consistent with one set of data. . . . It also implies that alternative interpretations equally consistent with these data have not been systematically explored, and that inferences drawn from the interpretation have not been tested by new observations.[14]

13. "The Urban Villagers: A Study of the Second Generation Italians in the West End of Boston," Boston: Center for Community Studies, November, 1959, mimeographed.
14. Robert K. Merton, *Social Theory and Social Structure,* New York: The Free Press of Glencoe, 2nd ed., 1957, pp. 93–94.

Merton's criticism can be applied to my own findings. I did try, however, to guard against overly facile interpretation by analyzing my data immediately after collecting them, and by putting both data and analysis into the field notes. Thus, I developed interpretations at once, rather than at the end of the study. This gave me an opportunity to test these notions in subsequent data collection, and to develop alternative ones if they did not fit later observations. Since I did not begin the study with a set of explicit notions that I wanted to prove at all costs, it was not difficult to surrender poor interpretations for better ones. Most of the generalizations reported in this book were thus developed during the field work.

Participant-observation also has another major drawback—the size and quality of the sample on which observations are based. Although my study sought to report on a population of close to 3000, I probably met and talked with no more than 100 to 150 West Enders.[15] Moreover, my most intensive contact was with about twenty West Enders, and most of my hypotheses about the peer group society are based on my observations of their ways. Because of the size of my sample, I did not attempt any statistical analyses. Nevertheless, I have used freely such quasi-statistical terms as "many," "most," "some," or "the majority of." Obviously, my use of these concepts is based on impressionistic evidence.[16]

Also, I could not determine to what extent any reported behavior pattern or attitude was distributed throughout the popula-

15. I include in this number neither the middle-class caretakers, nor other people working in the West End or with West Enders; they were not West Enders.

16. Howard S. Becker and Blanche Geer have developed new methods of participant-observation and data analysis which remove some of the dangers of post-factum interpretation, and make it possible to quantify data gathered by this method. Their methodological innovations are reported in Howard S. Becker, "Problems of Inference and Proof in Participant-Observation," *American Sociological Review*, vol. 23 (1958), pp. 652–660; and in Howard S. Becker and Blanche Geer, "The Analysis of Qualitative Field Data" in Richard N. Adams and Jack J. Preiss, eds., *Human Organization Research*, Homewood, Ill.: Dorsey Press, 1960, pp. 267–289. The field study in which these methods are applied is reported in H. Becker, B. Geer, E. Hughes, and A. Strauss, *Boys in White: Student Culture in Medical School*, Chicago: University of Chicago Press, 1961.

tion, nor could I inquire into subgroupings and subcultures among the West Enders, other than the most obvious ones of class and age. Even then, I did not apply the distinction between action-seeking and routine-seeking West Enders as fully as I might have. Thus, while the report may state that the West Enders act in a certain way, or hold a given attitude, only more extensive research will be able to indicate whether my generalization applies to all of the second-generation Italians in the West End, or only to certain subgroups among them.

The West Enders with whom I had the most intensive and most frequent contact were drawn more from working-class routine-seekers and mobile people than from the lower-class action-seeking population. Although I did have many opportunities to observe the latter, and to hear their actions discussed, they were harder to reach directly and therefore were reached less often in the time I had for field work. Moreover, some of the people I encountered were marginal to the peer group society, and for this reason were most cooperative with me. Conscious of the bias in my sample, and knowledgeable enough about the West End to evaluate the information I received from the marginal people, I was able to take these considerations into account when I analyzed my data. This does not, however, entirely eliminate the distortion due to lack of contact with the West Enders who are lowest on the educational and socio-economic level. Consequently, the book should be read with the reminder that I did not report as fully about the people for whom life was hardest, and for whom the outside world was most threatening.

Finally, more of my data were gathered from and about men than women. As I noted in my description of the peer group society, communication between the sexes is much more difficult than in middle-class society. Even though my wife participated in the field work and told me about the female social gatherings, my report does tend to place greater emphasis on the male portions of the peer group society.

This, then, is not a scientific study, for it does not provide what Merton has called compelling evidence for a series of hypotheses. It is, rather, an attempt by a trained social scientist to describe and explain the behavior of a large number of people—using his

methodological and theoretical training to sift the observations—
and to report only those generalizations which are justified by the
data. The validity of my findings thus rests ultimately on my judgment about the data, and, of course, on my theoretical and personal
biases in deciding what to study, what to see, what to ignore, and
how to analyze the products. Properly speaking, the study is a
reconnaissance—an initial exploration of a community to provide
an overview—guided by the canons of sociological theory and
method but not attempting to offer documentation for all the findings. In making this statement, I do not mean to cast doubt on the
conclusions I reached—I stand behind them all—or on the methods
I used. Participant-observation is the only method I know that
enables the researcher to get close to the realities of social life. Its
deficiencies in producing quantitative data are more than made up
for by its ability to minimize the distance between the researcher
and his subject of study.

Many of the hypotheses reported here can eventually be tested
against the results of more systematic social science research. Indeed,
the long-term study being conducted by the Center for Community
Studies is collecting data on many topics about which I have written here. The Center's findings not only will permit interpretations
based on more compelling evidence, but they will also provide an
opportunity to check on my study—and thereby on the usefulness
of my methods. Its report, based on a carefully analyzed sample
survey and on a number of other methods, will indicate how ac-
curately I have described the West Enders.

BIBLIOGRAPHY

American Public Health Association, "An Appraisal Method for Measuring the Quality of Housing," New York: The Association, 1946.

Angoff, Charles, *In the Morning Light*, New York: Beechhurst Press, 1952.

Archibald, Katherine, "Status Orientations among Shipyard Workers," in Reinhard Bendix and Seymour M. Lipset, eds., *Class, Status and Power*, New York: The Free Press of Glencoe, 1953, pp. 395–403.

Arensberg, Conrad M., and Solon T. Kimball, *Family and Community in Ireland*, Cambridge: Harvard University Press, 1940.

Axelrod, Morris, "Urban Structure and Social Participation," *American Sociological Review*, vol. 21 (1956), pp. 13–18.

Banfield, Edward C., *The Moral Basis of a Backward Society*, New York: The Free Press of Glencoe, 1958.

Barber, Bernard, *Social Stratification*, New York: Harcourt, Brace and World, 1957.

Barrabee, Paul, and Otto Van Mering, "Ethnic Variations in Mental Stress in Families with Psychotic Children," *Social Problems*, vol. 1 (1953), pp. 48–53.

Becker, Howard S., "Problems of Inference and Proof in Participant-Observation," *American Sociological Review*, vol. 23 (1958), pp. 652–660.

——— and Blanche Geer, "The Analysis of Qualitative Field Data," in Richard N. Adams and Jack J. Preiss, eds., *Human Organization Research*, Homewood, Ill.: Dorsey Press, 1960, pp. 267–289.

———, B. Geer, E. Hughes, and A. Strauss, *Boys in White: Student Culture in Medical School*, Chicago: University of Chicago Press, 1961.

Berger, Bennett M., "On the Youthfulness of Youth Cultures," Urbana: University of Illinois, 1961, mimeographed.

352 The Urban Villagers

Berger, Bennett M., *Working-Class Suburb*, Berkeley: University of California Press, 1960.

Bloch, Herbert, and Arthur Neiderhoffer, *The Gang*, New York: Philosophical Library, 1958.

Boston Housing Authority, "West End Progress Report," Boston: The Authority, January, 1956.

———, "The West End Project Report," Boston: The Authority, 1953.

Bott, Elizabeth, *Family and Social Network*, London: Tavistock Publications, 1957.

Bright, Virginia, "Officials Have Learned a Lesson from West End," *Boston Sunday Globe*, May 15, 1960.

Campisi, Paul J., "Ethnic Family Patterns: The Italian Family in the United States," *American Journal of Sociology*, vol. 53 (1948), pp. 443–449.

Caruso, Joseph, *The Priest*, New York: Popular Library, 1958.

Child, Irvin L., *Italian or American? The Second Generation in Conflict*, New Haven: Yale University Press, 1943.

Cloward, Richard A., and Lloyd E. Ohlin, *Delinquency and Opportunity*, New York: The Free Press of Glencoe, 1960.

Cohen, Albert, *Delinquent Boys: The Culture of the Gang*, New York: The Free Press of Glencoe, 1955.

Community Surveys, Inc., "Redevelopment: Some Human Gains and Losses," Indianapolis: Community Surveys, Inc. (by John R. Seeley and associates), 1956.

Covello, Leonard, "The Social Background of the Italo-American School Child," unpublished Ph.D. dissertation, New York University, 1944.

Cunningham, Bill, "Two Projects to Alter Boston," *Boston Herald*, November 17, 1957.

Dolci, Danilo, *Report from Palermo*, New York: Orion Press, 1959.

Dotson, Floyd, "Patterns of Voluntary Association among Urban Working Class Families," *American Sociological Review*, vol. 16 (1951), pp. 687–693.

Elizabeth Peabody House, "Annual Report, 1958," Boston: The House, 1959.

Ellis, Evelyn, "Social Psychological Correlates of Upward Social Mobility among Unmarried Career Women," *American Sociological Review*, vol. 17 (1952), pp. 558–563.

Farber, Bernard, "Types of Family Organization: Child-Oriented, Home-Oriented and Parent-Oriented," in Arnold Rose, ed., *Human Behavior and Social Processes*, Boston: Houghton Mifflin, 1962, pp. 285–306.

Firey, Walter, *Land Use in Central Boston,* Cambridge: Harvard University Press, 1947.

Foerster, R. F., *The Italian Emigration of Our Times,* Cambridge: Harvard University Press, 1919.

Foote, Nelson N., "Concept and Method in the Study of Human Development," in Muzafer Sherif and M. O. Wilson, eds., *Emergent Problems in Social Psychology,* Norman: University of Oklahoma Press, 1957, pp. 29–53.

Frazier, Franklin E., *The Negro Family in the United States,* Chicago: University of Chicago Press, 1939.

Freidson, Eliot, "Dilemmas in the Doctor-Patient Relationship," in Arnold Rose, ed., *Human Behavior and Social Processes,* Boston: Houghton Mifflin, 1962, pp. 207–224.

Fried, Marc, "Developments in the West End Research," Boston: Center for Community Studies Research Memorandum A 3, October, 1960, mimeographed.

———, "Grieving for a Lost Home," in Leonard J. Duhl, ed., *The Environment of the Metropolis* (tentative title), New York: Basic Books, forthcoming.

———, "A Social Science Approach to Health and Welfare Problems," paper delivered at the Harvard Medical Society, January, 1962, mimeographed.

——— and Peggy Gleicher, "Some Sources of Residential Satisfaction in an Urban 'Slum,'" *Journal of the American Institute of Planners,* vol. 27 (1961), pp. 305–315.

Friedenberg, Edgar, *The Vanishing Adolescent,* New York: Beacon Press, 1959.

Gans, Herbert J., "American Films and Television Programs on British Screens: A Study of the Functions of American Popular Culture Abroad," Philadelphia: Institute for Urban Studies, 1959, mimeographed.

———, "Diversity Is Not Dead," *New Republic,* vol. 144 (April 3, 1961), pp. 11–15.

———, "Hollywood Films on British Screens," *Social Problems,* vol. 9 (1962), pp. 324–328.

———, "The Human Implications of Current Redevelopment and Relocation Planning," *Journal of the American Institute of Planners,* vol. 25 (1959), pp. 15–25.

———, "Planning and Social Life," *Journal of the American Institute of Planners,* vol. 27 (1961), pp. 134–140.

———, "Urbanism and Suburbanism as Ways of Life: A Re-evaluation of

Definitions," in Arnold Rose, ed., *Human Behavior and Social Processes,* Boston: Houghton Mifflin, 1962, pp. 625–648.

Gans, Herbert J., "The Urban Villagers: A Study of the Second Generation Italians in the West End of Boston," Boston: Center for Community Studies, November, 1959, mimeographed.

Garigue, Philip, and Raymond Firth, "Kinship Organization of Italianates in London," in Raymond Firth, *Two Studies of Kinship in London,* London: Athlone Press, 1956.

Gehman, Richard, *Sinatra and His Ratpack,* New York: Belmont Books, 1961.

Gladwin, Thomas, "Poverty: An Anthropologist's View," National Conference on Social Welfare, *The Social Welfare Forum, 1961,* New York: Columbia University Press, 1961, pp. 73–86.

Glazer, Nathan, *American Judaism,* Chicago: University of Chicago Press, 1957.

———, *The Peoples of New York* (tentative title), forthcoming.

Glick, Ira O., and Sidney J. Levy, *Living with Television,* Chicago: Aldine Publishing Co., 1962.

Gold, Raymond L., "Roles in Sociological Field Observations," *Social Forces,* vol. 36 (1958), pp. 217–223.

Goodman, Paul, *Growing Up Absurd,* New York: Random House, 1960.

Gordon, Milton M., *Social Class in American Sociology,* Durham: Duke University Press, 1958.

Green, Arnold W., "The 'Cult of Personality' and Sexual Relations," in Norman W. Bell and Ezra F. Vogel, eds., *A Modern Introduction to the Family,* New York: The Free Press of Glencoe, 1960, pp. 608–615.

Gurin, G., J. Veroff, and S. Feld, *Americans View Their Mental Health,* New York: Basic Books, 1960.

Hanron, Robert, "West End Project Could Be Spark to Revitalize Boston," *Boston Sunday Globe,* December 20, 1959.

Hartman, Chester, "Housing in the West End," Boston: Center for Community Studies Research Memorandum C 1, October, 1961, mimeographed.

Hoggart, Richard, *The Uses of Literacy,* London: Chatto and Windus, 1957.

Hollingshead, August B., *Elmtown's Youth,* New York: Wiley and Sons, 1949.

——— and Frederick C. Redlich, *Social Class and Mental Illness,* New York: Wiley and Sons, 1958.

———, R. Ellis, and E. Kirby, "Social Mobility and Mental Illness," *American Sociological Review,* vol. 19 (1954), pp. 577–584.

Horton, Donald, and R. Richard Wohl, "Mass Communication and Parasocial Interaction," *Psychiatry*, vol. 19 (1955), pp. 215–229.

Hyman, Herbert H., "The Value System of Different Classes," in Reinhard Bendix and Seymour M. Lipset, eds., *Class, Status and Power*, New York: The Free Press of Glencoe, 1953, pp. 426–442.

Ianni, Francis A. J., "The Italo-American Teenager," *The Annals*, vol. 338 (November, 1961), pp. 70–78.

Icken, Helen, "From Slum to Housing Project," unpublished study made for the Urban Renewal and Housing Administration, Commonwealth of Puerto Rico, 1960, privately mimeographed.

Jacobs, Jane, *The Death and Life of Great American Cities*, New York: Random House, 1961.

Junker, Buford H., *Field Work*, Chicago: University of Chicago Press, 1960.

Kahl, Joseph A., *The American Class Structure*, New York: Holt, Rinehart and Winston, 1957.

Kerr, Madeline, *The People of Ship Street*, London: Routledge and Kegan Paul, 1958.

Kinnard, William N., and Zenon S. Malinowski, "The Impact of Dislocation from Urban Renewal Areas on Small Business," Storrs: University of Connecticut, 1960.

Kuper, Leo, "Blueprint for Living Together," in Leo Kuper, ed., *Living in Towns*, London: Cresset Press, 1953, pp. 1–202.

Lerner, Daniel, *The Passing of Traditional Society*, New York: The Free Press of Glencoe, 1958.

Lewis, Oscar, *The Children of Sanchez*, New York: Random House, 1961.

Løchen, Yngvar, "Some Experiences in Participant-Observation from a Norwegian Mental Hospital Study," Bethesda: National Institute of Mental Health, no date, mimeographed.

Lolli, G., E. Serianni, G. Golder, and P. Luzzatto-Fegiz, *Alcohol in Italian Culture*, New York: The Free Press of Glencoe and Yale Center of Alcohol Studies, 1958.

Lynch, Kevin, *The Image of the City*, Cambridge: Technology Press and Harvard University Press, 1960.

MacDonald, John S., and Lea D. MacDonald, "Migration versus Non-Migration: A Typology of Responses to Poverty," paper read at the 1961 meetings of the American Sociological Association, mimeographed.

Mangione, Jerre, *Mount Allegro*, Boston: Houghton Mifflin, 1942.

Marris, Peter, "A Report on Urban Renewal," London: Institute of Community Studies, 1962, mimeographed, and in Leonard J. Duhl, ed., *Environment of the Metropolis* (tentative title), New York: Basic Books, forthcoming.

356 The Urban Villagers

Matza, David, and Gresham Sykes, "Juvenile Delinquency and Subterranean Values," *American Sociological Review,* vol. 26 (1961), pp. 712–719.

Merton, Robert K., *Social Theory and Social Structure,* New York: The Free Press of Glencoe, 2nd ed., 1957.

Miller, Daniel B., and Guy E. Swanson, *The Changing American Parent,* New York: Wiley and Sons, 1958.

———, Guy E. Swanson, *et al., Inner Conflict and Defense,* New York: Holt, Rinehart and Winston, 1960.

Miller, S. M., and Frank Riessman, "The Working Class Subculture: A New View," *Social Problems,* vol. 9 (1961), pp. 86–97.

Miller, Walter B., "Implications of Urban Lower-Class Culture for Social Work," *Social Service Review,* vol. 33 (1959), pp. 219–236.

———, "Lower Class Culture as a Generating Milieu of Gang Delinquency," *Journal of Social Issues,* vol. 14, No. 3 (1958), pp. 5–19.

Miller, Warren, *The Cool World,* Boston: Little, Brown, 1959.

Mizruchi, Ephraim H., "Social Structure, Success Values and Structured Strain in a Small City," paper read at the 1961 meetings of the American Sociological Association, mimeographed.

Mogey, J. M., *Family and Neighborhood,* London: Oxford University Press, 1956.

Opler, M. K., and J. L. Singer, "Ethnic Differences in Behavior and Psychopathology," *International Journal of Social Psychiatry,* vol. 2 (1956), pp. 11–22.

Padilla, Elena, *Up from Puerto Rico,* New York: Columbia University Press, 1958.

Parsons, Talcott, *The Social System,* New York: The Free Press of Glencoe, 1951.

Perretto, Armando, *Take a Number,* New York: Popular Library, 1958.

Philadelphia Housing Association, "Relocation in Philadelphia," Philadelphia: The Association, 1958.

Pitkin, Donald, "Land Tenure and Farm Organization in an Italian Village," unpublished Ph.D. dissertation, Harvard University, 1954.

Rainwater, Lee, *And the Poor Get Children,* Chicago: Quadrangle Books, 1960.

———, R. Coleman, and G. Handel, *Workingman's Wife,* New York: Oceana Publications, 1959.

Redfield, Robert, "Peasant Society and Culture," in *The Little Community and Peasant Society and Culture,* Chicago: University of Chicago (Phoenix Books), 1960.

Riesman, D., N. Glazer, and R. Denney, *The Lonely Crowd,* New Haven: Yale University Press, 1950.

Rosow, Irving, "The Social Effects of the Physical Environment," *Journal of the American Institute of Planners,* vol. 27 (1961), pp. 127–133.

Ross, H. Laurence, "The Local Community and the Metropolis," unpublished Ph.D. dissertation, Harvard University, 1959.

Sangree, Walter H., "Mel Hyblaeum: A Study of the People of Middletown of Sicilian Extraction . . . ," unpublished M.A. thesis, Wesleyan University, 1952.

Save the West End Committee, "A Plea against Smashing the Houses of the West End . . . ," Boston: The Committee, no date, mimeographed.

Schatzman, Leonard, and Anselm Strauss, "Social Class and Modes of Communication," *American Journal of Sociology,* vol. 60 (1955), pp. 329–338.

Schermerhorn, R. A., *These Our Children,* Boston: D. C. Heath, 1949.

Schwartz, Morris S., and Charlotte G. Schwartz, "Problems in Participant-Observation," *American Journal of Sociology,* vol. 60 (1955), pp. 343–353.

Seeley, John R., "The Slum: Its Nature, Use, and Users," *Journal of the American Institute of Planners,* vol. 25 (1959), pp. 7–14.

———, "We Hidden Persuaders: Social Thought and Politics," an address to the National Federation of Canadian University Students, McMaster University, Toronto: York University, 1961, mimeographed.

———, R. Sim, and E. Loosley, *Crestwood Heights,* New York: Basic Books, 1956.

Silberman, Charles E., "The City and the Negro," *Fortune,* vol. 65, March 1962, pp. 89–91, 139–140, 144–146, 152–154.

Sklare, Marshall, *Conservative Judaism,* New York: The Free Press of Glencoe, 1955.

Smith, Raymond T., *The Negro Family in British Guiana,* London: Routledge and Kegan Paul, 1956.

Social Research, Inc., "Status of the Working Class in Changing American Society," Chicago: Social Research, Inc., February, 1961, mimeographed.

Steffens, Lincoln, *The Autobiography of Lincoln Steffens,* New York: Harcourt, Brace and World, 1931.

Strauss, Anselm, ed., *The Social Psychology of George Herbert Mead,* Chicago: University of Chicago Press (Phoenix Books), 1956.

——— and Leonard Schatzman, "Cross Class Interviewing: An Analysis of Interaction and Communicative Styles," in Richard N. Adams and Jack J. Preiss, eds., *Human Organization Research,* Homewood, Ill.: Dorsey Press, 1960, pp. 205–213.

Strodtbeck, Fred L., "Family Interaction, Values and Achievement," in D. C. McClelland, A. Baldwin, U. Bronfenbrenner, and F. Strodtbeck,

Talent and Society, Princeton: D. Van Nostrand, 1958, pp. 135–194.

Tiller, Per Olav, "Father Absence and Personality Development of Children in Sailor Families," Oslo: Institute for Social Research, 1957, mimeographed.

Vogel, Ezra F., "The Marital Relationships of Parents of Emotionally Disturbed Children," unpublished Ph.D. dissertation, Harvard University, 1958.

Warner, W. Lloyd, and Paul S. Lunt, *The Social Life of a Modern Community,* New Haven: Yale University Press, 1941.

Whyte, William F., Jr., *Street Corner Society,* Chicago: University of Chicago Press, 1943, 2nd ed., 1955.

Williams, Phyllis H., *Southern Italian Folkways in Europe and America,* New Haven: Yale University Press, 1938.

Willmott, Peter, "Class and Community at Dagenham," London: Institute for Community Studies, 1960, mimeographed.

Woods, Robert A., ed., *Americans in Process,* Boston: Houghton Mifflin, 1902.

Young, Michael, and Peter Willmott, *Family and Kinship in East London,* London: Routledge and Kegan Paul, 1957.

Zborowski, Mark, "Cultural Components in Responses to Pain," *Journal of Social Issues,* vol. 8 (1952), pp. 16–30.

NAME INDEX

Adams, Richard N., 235n, 348n, 351, 357
Angoff, Charles, 7n, 351
Archibald, Katherine, 236n, 351
Arensberg, Conrad M., 238n, 351
Axelrod, Morris, 235n, 351

Baldwin, A., 241n, 357
Banfield, Edward C., 199n, 200n, 203, 203n, 209, 351
Barber, Bernard, 242, 351
Barrabee, Paul, 238n, 351
Becker, Howard S., 348n, 351
Bell, Norman W., 233n, 354
Bendix, Reinhard, 236n, 351, 355
Berger, Bennett M., 71, 71n, 234n, 235n, 237n, 253n, 351, 352
Bloch, Herbert, 66, 66n, 352
Bogart, Humphrey, 191
Bott, Elizabeth, 50, 50n, 232n, 234n, 352
Bright, Virginia, 323n, 352
Bronfenbrenner, U., 241n, 357

Campisi, Paul J., 18n, 204n, 352
Caruso, Joseph, 89n, 114n, 223n, 352
Child, Irvin L., 18n, 19n, 34n, 122n, 352
Cloward, Richard A., 66, 66n, 68, 352
Cohen, Albert, 66, 66n, 236n, 352
Coleman, R., 231n, 233n, 234n, 235n, 356
Covello, Leonard, 57n, 64n, 199n, 200, 200n, 201, 201n, 202n, 204n, 205,

205n, 206, 206n, 207, 207n, 211, 222, 222n, 352
Cunningham, Bill, 287n, 352
Curley, Mayor James, 165

Davis, Fred, 346n
Denney, R., 259n, 356
Dolci, Danilo, 199n, 352
Dotson, Floyd, 234n, 235n, 352
Duhl, Leonard J., 274n, 289n, 321n, 334n, 353, 355
Durkheim, Émile, 66n
Dyckman, John, 305n

Eisenhower, Dwight D., 163
Ellis, Evelyn, 257, 257n, 352
Ellis, R., 257n, 354

Farber, Bernard, 55n, 352
Feld, S., 235n, 354
Firey, Walter, 6n, 353
Firth, Raymond, 46n, 354
Foerster, R. F., 204n, 353
Foote, Nelson N., 20n, 353
Freidson, Eliot, 275n, 353
Fried, Marc, 8n, 9n, 105n, 154n, 289n, 290n, 316n, 321n, 353
Friedenberg, Edgar, 69n, 353

Gans, Herbert J., 12n, 16n, 76n, 189n, 237n, 259n, 314n, 347n, 353, 354
Garigue, Philip, 46n, 354
Geer, Blanche, 348n, 351
Gehman, Richard, 193n, 354

359

SUBJECT INDEX

Negroes: compared with Italian-Americans, 62–63, 238–240, 262; and redevelopment, 335
North End, 6–7, 35–36, 174, 286, 298, 337
Nostalgia, 35, 71, 223–225

Object goals, 90, 92, 94, 258; *see also* Object-orientation, Person-orientation
Object-orientation: and bureaucracy, 164; and caretakers, 261; and child-rearing, 102–103; defined, 89–90; described, 89–92; and government, 165; and intellectuals, 260; and middle-class subculture, 258; and mobility, 96–97, 254, 257; and other concepts, 91n, 259–260; and person-orientation, 89–92; and professionalism, 123–124; and schools, 129; and self, 97–103; and social structure, 92, 102; and West Enders, 95–96; *see also* Person-orientation
Organizations, 113–114, 116–117
Outside world: and action-seekers, 121; attitude to, summarized, 120–121; and caretakers, 144, 153; and child-rearing, 60–61; and community compared, 106; and consumer behavior, 181, 183, 186; defined, 36, 106, 120–121; and government, 163, 169; hostility to, 60–61, 97, 121, 123, 167, 169, 186, 193–196; and mass media, 181, 183, 193–196; and medical care, 136–137, 141; and mobility, 256–257; and object-goals, 94; in other working-class groups, 231, 235–236; and person-orientation, 94–97; and politicians, 170–173, 176; and routine-seekers, 121; in Southern Italian society, 201–202, 213; structure of, 120–212; and work, 122, 127–128; as working-class phenomenon, 253

Participant-observation: ethics of, 344–346; limitations of, 348–349; problems in use of, 340–346; types of, 338–340; and value judgments, 344, 346
Peer groups: and adolescents, 65–66, 69–70; adult, 38–39, 74–82; in American society, 41; and child-rearing,

57–58; class differences in, 81; and community participation, 79, 106–108; and family circle, 74–75; and illness, 88; and individualism, 81–99; and internal caretakers, 159–160; isolation from, 254–256; lack of cooperative activity in, 89; and leadership, 108–109; over life cycle, 37–39; and marriage, 70–71; and mass media performers, 192–193; in middle class, 41; and object-orientation vs. person-orientation, 90–103; and school performance, 133–134; social relations in, summarized, 88–89; *see also* Peer group society
Peer group society: class or ethnic phenomenon, 229–230; and community, 106–110; defined, 36–37; and family circle, 38–39; generational change in, summarized, 197; and government, 164–166; and individual, 39–41; psychological implications of, 40–41, 80–81; in Southern Italian society, 201–202; stability of, 210–213; summary description of, 37–41; in third generation, 225–226; as working-class phenomenon, 230–231; *see also* Peer groups
Personalization of government, 164–165
Person-orientation: and attitude to government, 95–96, 164–167; defined, 89–92; described among West Enders, 92–97, 99–103; in middle-class subculture, 259; in other working-class groups, 234–235; and outside world, 94–97; and peer groups, 93–94; and politicians, 180; and religious morality, 96; and restriction of aspirations, 96–97; and role restriction, 100–101; and self, 97–103; source of in Southern Italian society, 212; *see also* Object-orientation
Planning and caretaking: implications of class evaluation for, 269–278; institutional changes in, required, 274–277; and lower-class subculture, 272–278; middle-class bias of, 269, 274–277; policy proposals for, 270–278; and working-class subculture, 271–272; *see also* Caretakers
Policy proposals: for lower-class subculture, 272–278; for planning and